#6 50

MODERN STUDIES IN PHILOSOPHY

LOCKE AND BERKELEY
A Collection of Critical Essays

Modern Studies in Philosophy is a series of anthologies presenting contemporary interpretations and evaluations of the works of major philosophers. The editors have selected articles designed to show the systematic structure of the thought of these philosophers, and to reveal the relevance of their views to the problems of current interest. These volumes are intended to be contributions to contemporary debates as well as to the history of philosophy; they not only trace the origins of many problems important to modern philosophy, but also introduce major philosophers as interlocutors in current discussions.

Modern Studies in Philosophy is prepared under the general editorship of Amelie Rorty, Associate Professor of Philosophy at Douglas College, Rutgers University.

DAVID M. ARMSTRONG is Professor of Philosophy at the University of Sydney, New South Wales, Australia, and has taught on the campuses of Yale and Stanford Universities. He is the author of *Berkeley's Theory of Vision, Perception and the Physical World, Bodily Sensations,* and *A Materialist Theory of the Mind.*

C. B. MARTIN is also Professor of Philosophy at the University of Sydney. He has held visiting appointments at Harvard and Columbia Universities and Brooklyn College, and is the author of *Religious Belief.*

MODERN STUDIES IN PHILOSOPHY

LOCKE AND BERKELEY

A Collection of Critical Essays

EDITED BY
C. B. MARTIN
AND D. M. ARMSTRONG

UNIVERSITY OF NOTRE DAME PRESS
NOTRE DAME   LONDON

First Hardbound Edition: 1968

University of Notre Dame Press

Notre Dame, Indiana 46556

Printed by special arrangement with Doubleday & Company, Inc.

Anchor Books Edition: 1968
Doubleday & Company, Inc.
Garden City, New York

Copyright © 1968 by D. M. Armstrong and C. B. Martin
All Rights Reserved

Manufactured in the United States of America

This does especial harm by nourishing the assumption that the study of philosophers like Locke and Berkeley is only a marginally useful activity which may be adequately conducted with the mind in neutral. In fact, it can be one of the most rewarding and demanding of philosophical exercises.

JONATHAN BENNETT

CONTENTS

Introduction, C. B. MARTIN and D. M. ARMSTRONG	1
John Locke on the Human Understanding, GILBERT RYLE	14
Locke's Concept of Experience, JOHN W. YOLTON	40
Locke's Distinction between Primary and Secondary Qualities, REGINALD JACKSON	53
Did Berkeley Misunderstand Locke? WINSTON H. F. BARNES	78
Substance, Reality, and Primary Qualities, JONATHAN BENNETT	86
Locke's Version of the Doctrine of Representative Perception, REGINALD JACKSON	125
Locke and the Problem of Personal Identity, ANTONY FLEW	155
Locke's Political Theory and Its Interpreters, CHARLES H. MONSON, JR.	179
The Social Bearing of Locke's Political Theory, C. B. MACPHERSON	199
Locke and the Dictatorship of the Bourgeoisie, ALAN RYAN	231
Berkeley's Denial of Material Substance, C. D. BROAD	255
Berkeley's Existence in the Mind, A. A. LUCE	284
The Mind and Its Ideas: Some Problems in the Interpretation of Berkeley, S. A. GRAVE	296
Berkeley's Sensationalism and the *Esse est percipi*-Principle, KONRAD MARC-WOGAU	314
The Argument from Illusion and Berkeley's Idealism, KONRAD MARC-WOGAU	340
Berkeley's Likeness Principle, PHILLIP D. CUMMINS	353
The Place of God in Berkeley's Philosophy, J. D. MABBOTT	364

Berkeley and God, JONATHAN BENNETT	380
Berkeley and the Tree in the Quad, E. J. FURLONG	400
Berkeley on "Abstract Ideas," MONROE C. BEARDSLEY	409
G. J. Warnock's *Berkeley*, J. F. THOMSON	426
A Note on Berkeley as Precursor of Mach and Einstein, KARL POPPER	436
Bibliography	450
Index	457

LOCKE AND BERKELEY
A Collection of Critical Essays

INTRODUCTION

Articles on Locke and Berkeley have been combined in this one volume partly because there did not seem to be enough papers of high quality to make two separate volumes and partly because in discussing either philosopher it is profitable and almost inevitable to oppose him to the other.

LOCKE
(C. B. MARTIN)

The serious study of Locke is not in fashion. Until recently, unabridged versions of Locke's *Essay* had been out of print for many years. Generations of students were taught from Pringle-Pattison's abridged edition. This was good enough to give them target-practice. However, too many crucial arguments and distinctions were omitted, and as a result the student was unable to know what Locke *said*, let alone what he meant.

Locke is inconsistent, obscure and repetitious. If it were not for the abundance of first-rate and still suggestive argument in his work, we could safely forget him as the object of serious study, and leave him to be the occasional sport of the young.

The purpose of this section of the introduction is to point out several commonly made mistakes and oversights in the interpretation of Locke. Though each of those to be mentioned can be found in recently published work, the sources will not be identified. The selection has been limited to instances that allow quick and decisive rectification.

Some Common Sins of Omission and Commission in the Interpretation of Locke.

1. *Locke assumes without question that all words are names of ideas.*
False.

In Book III, Chapter vii, of the *Essay,* "Of Particles" (omitted from the Pringle-Pattison abridged edition), Locke deals with words that "are not truly by themselves the names of ideas," such as "is," "is not," and "but."

2. *Locke thinks that words cannot occur significantly unless the relevant ideas are in the mind at the time of the utterance.*
False.

Justice is a word in every man's mouth, but most commonly with a very undetermined loose signification; which will always be so unless a man has in his mind a distinct comprehension of the component parts that complex *idea* consists of; and if it be decompounded, must be able to resolve it still on, till he at last comes to the simple *ideas* that make it up; and unless this be done, a man makes an ill use of the word, let it be *justice,* for example, or any other. *I do not say a man need stand to recollect and make this analysis at large every time the word justice comes in his way; but this at least is necessary, that he have so examined the signification of that name, and settled the idea of all its parts in his mind, that he can do it when he pleases.*   [III, xi, 9; editors' italics]

(All quotations are taken from the two-volume Everyman edition edited by John W. Yolton.)

Though the examining and judging of ideas by themselves, their names being quite laid aside, be the best and surest way to clear and distinct knowledge; yet, through the prevailing custom of using sounds for ideas, I think it is very seldom practiced. Every one may observe how common it is for names to be made use of, instead of the ideas themselves, even when men think and reason within their own breasts; especially if the ideas be very complex, and made up of a great collection of simple ones.

[IV, vi, 1]

Introduction 3

These quotations are omitted from Pringle-Pattison. Compare also IV, v, 4.

3. *Locke thinks that our experience must at first take the form of single unanalyzable elements which are the simple ideas and that our experience later comes to have a complex structure, complex ideas, by our activity of adding or combining the simple experiential atoms.*

False.

Apart from the usual difficulty created by his self-acknowledged tendency to use the term "idea" sometimes to apply to what is "within the mind" and sometimes to qualities of what is "external to the mind," Locke uses the phrase "complex idea" in three ways.

a. To mean "abstract complex idea." This use is not relevant to the present issue.

b. To mean something like "combinations or mixtures of simple ideas or simple aspects of experience." It seems that he is willing to allow that some ideas *cannot* exist uncombined with other ideas. For example, "It is true, solidity cannot exist without extension, neither can scarlet colour exist without extension; but this hinders not, but that they are distinct *ideas*. Many *ideas* require others as necessary to their existence or conception, which yet are very distinct *ideas*" (II, xiii, 11).

c. To mean something like "combinations or mixtures of simple ideas or simple aspects of experience that are *considered* as united together as one idea."

With these distinctions in mind, the following quotations should constitute a corrective.

> In this also, I suppose, *brutes* come far short of men. For though they take in and retain together several combinations of simple *ideas*, as possibly the shape, smell, and voice of his master make up the complex *idea* [sense (b)—Ed.] a dog has of him, or rather are so many distinct marks whereby he knows him: yet I *do not* think they do of themselves ever compound them and *make complex* ideas [sense (c) —Ed.] [II, xi, 7]

> As simple *ideas* are observed to exist in several combinations united together, so the mind has a power to

consider several of them united together as one *idea,* and that not only as they are united in external objects, but as itself has joined them.   [II, xii, 1]

4. *Locke thinks that ideas are mental "things."*
False.

Perhaps this misunderstanding springs from Locke's definition of "idea" as "whatsoever is the object of the understanding when a man thinks" (I, i, 8). But seventeenth-century usage allowed such an "object" to be a mode or property or a relation.

Locke uses the term "substance" ambiguously. Sometimes it means "the substratum" and sometimes it means "entity" or "thing." In terms of the former use, he lists just *three* kinds of substance—infinite immaterial, finite immaterial, and material. In Book II, Chapter xxiii, "Of Our Complex Ideas of Substances," he is largely concerned with the latter use, so that souls, teapots, rocks, and trees would all be kinds of substances. There is no mention of ideas as substances. When he does speak of the ideas of sensation and pain and pleasure, he speaks of them as "modes." In Section 17 of *Remarks Upon Some of Mr. Norris's Books,* he says, "Ideas may be real beings, though not substances; as motion is a real being though not a substance." Locke would never have thought that ideas or experiences could be the parts of Hume's "bundles."

5. *A notable sin of omission is the very common failure to point out that Locke had considered and rejected what he thought were the only alternative theories of meaning to his doctrine of abstract ideas.*

a. Locke was aware that the meaning of a term was not its extension.

(1) He knew that a term could have a meaning and lack an extension.

For were there now no circle existing anywhere in the world (as, perhaps, that figure exists not anywhere exactly marked out), yet the *idea* annexed to that name would not cease to be what it is, nor cease to be as a pattern to determine which of the particular figures we meet with have or have not a right to the name *circle,* and so to show which of them, by having that essence, was of that *species*. And though there neither were nor had been in nature such a beast as a *unicorn* nor such a fish as a *mermaid*, yet, supposing those names to stand for complex abstract *ideas* that contained no inconsistency in them, the *essence* of a *mermaid* is as intelligible as that of a *man*; and the *idea* of a *unicorn* as certain, steady, and permanent as that of a horse. [III, III, 19]

Who can doubt but the *ideas* of *sacrilege* or *adultery* might be framed in the minds of men, and have names given them, and so these species of mixed modes be constituted, before either of them was ever committed; and might be as well discoursed of and reasoned about, and as certain truths discovered of them, whilst yet they had no being but in the understanding, as well as now that they have but too frequently a real existence? [III, v, 5]

(2) He knew that a term can differ in its extension without differing in its meaning.

All things that exist, besides their Author, are all liable to change, especially those things we are acquainted with, and have ranked into bands under distinct names or ensigns. Thus, that which was grass to-day is to-morrow the flesh of a sheep, and, within a few days after, becomes the part of a man: in all which and the like changes, it is evident, their real *essence*, i.e. that constitution whereon the properties of these several things depended, is destroyed and perishes with them. But *essences* being taken for *ideas* established in the mind, with names annexed to them, they are supposed to remain steadily the same, whatever mutations the particular substances are liable to. For, whatever becomes of *Alexander* and *Bucephalus*, the *ideas* to which *man* and *horse* are annexed are supposed, nevertheless, to remain in the same; and so the *essences* of those species are preserved whole and undestroyed, whatever changes happen to any or all of the individuals of those *species*.
[III, III, 19]

(3) He knew that a term can differ in its meaning without differing in its extension.

> ... for, men, though they propose to themselves the very same subject to consider, yet frame very different *ideas* about it; and so the name they use for it unavoidably comes to have, in several men, very different significations. ... For, though in the substance *gold* one satisfies himself with colour and weight, yet another thinks solubility in *aqua regia* as necessary to be joined with that colour in his *idea* of gold as anyone does its fusibility: solubility in *aqua regia* being a quality as constantly joined with its colour and weight, as fusibility or any others; others put in its ductility or fixedness, etc., as they have been taught by tradition or experience.
>
> [III, ix, 13; omitted from Pringle-Pattison]

b. Locke was aware that the meaning of a term was not its use with other terms. That is, significant utterance is not the playing of a word-game.

> ... he that hath words of any language without distinct *ideas* in his mind, to which he applies them, does, so far as he uses them in discourse, only make a noise without any sense or signification; and how learned soever he may seem by the use of hard words or learned terms, is not much more advanced thereby in knowledge than he would be in learning, who had nothing in his study but the bare titles of books, without possessing the contents of them. For all such words, however put into discourse according to the right construction of grammatical rules or the harmony of well-turned periods, do yet amount to nothing but bare sounds, and nothing else.
>
> [III, x, 26; omitted from Pringle-Pattison]

Locke therefore thought that since the nature of significant utterance could not be explained in terms of the relations between words or the relations between words and their extension, it can only be explained in terms of the relations between words and the mind of the utterer. The mind may seem an old-fashioned place to look to settle questions about significance. But the place is under-

Introduction

going renovation. Very soon we will be ready to allow Locke's stress on the relevance of the utterer's thoughts, purposes, and forms of experience to the significance of his utterance.

There is a deplorable shortage of good articles on Locke's *Essay*, and, as a result, important topics have had to be passed over in this volume. Gilbert Ryle's article is useful as an introduction to the *Essay* as a whole. Three of the other articles form a natural grouping, dealing with the currently much-discussed topic of the primary and secondary qualities. Locke's important and influential treatment of the topic is expounded in Reginald Jackson's paper. He argues that Berkeley misunderstood Locke on this matter, a view which is opposed by W. H. F. Barnes in his note "Did Berkeley Misunderstand Locke?" Jonathan Bennett carries on the philosophical discussion of the problem of primary and secondary qualities in his "Substance, Reality and the Primary Qualities," and also criticizes Berkeley for running together a number of different Lockean doctrines in the course of attacking Locke's account of physical reality.

Charles H. Monson's article "Locke's Political Theory and Its Interpreters" serves as an introduction to Locke's *political* philosophy. Locke has been widely accused of being the least disinterested of all political philosophers. We have therefore included C. B. Macpherson's "The Social Bearing of Locke's Political Theory," which presents what may be called a Marxist interpretation of Locke's political thought, while Alan Ryan in "Locke and the Dictatorship of the Bourgeoisie" defends Locke against Macpherson's interpretation.

BERKELEY
(D. M. ARMSTRONG)

The relative simplicity, clarity and brevity of Berkeley's writings mean that commentator and student have an easier task in arriving at Berkeley's meaning than they do in the case of Locke. (To say that the task is easier is not to imply that it is easy. Berkeleian scholarship is no exception to the rule that nothing is easy in philosophy.) So here, instead of correcting misapprehensions about Berkeley's views and arguments, it may be more valuable to warn the student about a feature of Berkeley's philosophical system that is not always noticed, or if noticed is not always emphasized: its lack of unity.

Berkeley's views are almost always interesting (although, in the present writer's view, almost always false); his arguings are often both brilliant and of the first importance; but his views do not form the closely connected system that he himself seems to have thought they formed, or, at any rate, been willing to allow his readers to think they formed.

Here are four central Berkeleian theses: (i) the immediate objects of sight are two-dimensional in nature, and are, in consequence, distinct from the objects of touch; (ii) Locke's Abstract Ideas do not exist; (iii) (Berkeley's central doctrine) physical objects are nothing but collections of "ideas" (sensations) whose being consists in being perceived; (iv) these "ideas" are directly given to us finite spirits by the Infinite Spirit: God. Now Berkeley thinks that it follows from (i) that the immediate objects of sight are nothing but "ideas." In fact this does not follow. Berkeley thinks, or at any rate seems prepared to let the reader think, that from (ii)—the rejection of Abstract Ideas—it follows that the being of physical objects consists in being perceived. In fact this does not follow. Berkeley also thinks that the existence of a God follows pretty directly from his doctrine of the nature of physical objects. But the extra premisses necessary to validate this step are very implausible. Once we see—and it is not at all hard to see—that (i) does not give even partial support to (iii), that (ii) does not give any support to (iii), and that the step from (iii) to (iv) depends on implausible premisses, the back of Berkeley's system is broken.

Let us spell this out.

The objects of sight. Berkeley's first published work, the *New Theory of Vision*, concerns the objects of sight

Introduction

and touch. He argues, in the first place (not originally), that since visible distance is a line turned endwise to the eye, and so projecting only one point in the eye whatever the distance be, it cannot be directly perceived by sight. The discriminations that vision makes immediately possible are two-dimensional only. He goes on to conclude that the immediate objects of sight must be distinct from the objects immediately seen. We need not examine this line of argument here. But Berkeley *also* argues, as a curtain-raiser to his *Principles of Human Knowledge*, that it follows that the immediate objects of sight cannot exist independently of the mind that perceives them. But why should we accept this step in the argument? Berkeley gives us no reason that is remotely satisfactory. Instead there is an incredible passage in Section 41 of the *New Theory* where he says:

> From what hath been premised, it is a manifest consequence, that a man born blind, being made to see, would at first have no idea of distance by sight: the sun and stars, the remotest objects as well as the nearer, would all seem to be in his eye, or rather in his mind. The objects intromitted by sight would seem to him (as in truth they are) no other than a new set of thoughts or sensations, . . .

Here Berkeley manages to slide smoothly from the view that distance is not immediately perceived by sight to the fantasy that the objects of sight are within the eye (despite the "rather" that follows this assertion it is an essential step in giving the "argument" a superficial appearance of validity to Berkeley and his readers), to the view that the objects of sight are "in the mind," to the view that they are "thoughts ['ideas'] or sensations." Nor does it seem possible to do better on Berkeley's behalf.

Abstract Ideas. In Section 10 of the Introduction to the *Principles*, Berkeley denies that it is possible to: ". . . abstract from one another, or conceive separately, those qualities which it is impossible should exist so separated." For instance, if it is impossible that color should exist without extension, as philosophers generally hold, then, according to Berkeley, it is impossible to *conceive* of color without conceiving it to be extended (although he allows in the addition made to Section 16 in the second edition that we can *consider* an object as having one property without *attending* to its necessary concomitant).

We need not concern ourselves here with the rights or wrongs of Berkeley's critique of Abstract Ideas. For example, we need not consider the question whether Berkeley's argument depends upon equating conceiving with imaging. All we need take notice of is another admission made by Berkeley earlier in Section 10:

> . . . I own myself able to abstract in one sense, as when I consider some particular parts or qualities separated from others, with which, though they are united in some object, yet it is possible they may really exist without them.

He gives as examples imagining a man with two heads, or the upper parts of a man joined to the body of a horse. To sum the point up: Berkeley allows that there are virtuous as well as vicious abstractions.

Now when, in the body of the *Principles*, Berkeley comes to put forward his view that the being of physical things lies in being perceived, he writes as if we have only to reject vicious abstraction to see the truth of his doctrine. He says in Section 4:

> It is indeed an opinion strangely prevailing among men, that houses, mountains, rivers, and in a word all sensible objects, have an existence, natural or real, distinct from their being perceived by the understanding.

And in Section 5 he goes on to say:

> If we thoroughly examined this tenet it will, perhaps, be found at bottom to depend on the doctrine of *abstract ideas*. For can there be a nicer strain of abstraction than to distinguish the existence of sensible objects from their being perceived, so as to conceive them existing unperceived?

But, of course, the whole question is whether this particular abstraction is, or is not, vicious. Can we, or can we not, conceive of unperceived physical things? No reference to abstraction casts any light on the matter. It is true that in these sections Berkeley does offer a ground for saying that the abstraction is vicious in this case. He does this by arguing that physical things are things perceived by sense, and that all we perceive by sense are our own ideas or sensations. And it is true that if this argument is correct it does seem to be a vicious abstraction to try to conceive physical things existing independently of perception. But then the argument shifts from Abstract Ideas to the question whether these extremely controversial contentions of Berkeley's about physical objects are, or are not, true.

Berkeley and God. So Berkeley's theory of vision and his rejection of Abstract Ideas really does nothing to support his doctrine that the being of physical objects lies in being perceived. His proofs of the existence of God, which take this doctrine as premiss, are not simply *non-sequiturs* as in the two cases just dealt with, but depend on extra premisses that almost no philosopher since Berkeley has been willing to grant.

Consider first what Jonathan Bennett in the paper "Berkeley and God" in this collection calls "the passivity argument." Physical objects have been resolved by Berkeley into ideas or sensations. Ideas or sensations, Berkeley argues further, have no power or activity in them: they cannot do or cause anything. In ordinary talk we *speak* of the fire making (causing) the kettle to boil, but since such a sequence is really only a sequence of sensations—kettle-being-put-on-the-fire sensations followed by kettle-boiling sensations—this way of speaking must be incorrect. Yet our sensations must *have* a cause. This cause can only be the will of a spirit, for only a will can *make* anything happen. We are not the cause of that great orderly train of experiences that constitute our sensations. So there must be some other very powerful spirit who is their cause. In this way Berkeley argues from the world to God.

This is the sort of argument that does not inspire any trust at all. Almost every step can be successfully challenged. It will only be noted here, what is seldom remarked upon, that the argument leaves Berkeley with a most serious inconsistency. Berkeley says that God sends us sensations in regular, as opposed to irregular, trains, so that we will be able to anticipate the course of experience. So God uses ideas as an instrument to act on our minds. And on any view of the world our sense-experiences are a guide to what we will experience next. But, if this is so, ideas, in causing us to have certain anticipations, have an effect upon our minds—even if only as instruments of God. So ideas are causes after all. Berkeley can make *ad hoc* adjustments to the premisses of his argument to allow for this, but only at the cost of making the premisses look still more implausible.

Bennett calls the second argument, on which Berkeley puts less weight, "the continuity argument." The being of physical objects depends on being perceived. But there are physical objects unperceived by any finite perceiver. These objects require an Infinite perceiver for their existence.

The trouble with this argument (apart from the havoc the *conclusion* creates in Berkeley's system when he has to work out just what it means in Berkeleian terms) is the complete unavailability to Berkeley of the second premiss. How on earth can *Berkeley*, who has accepted the first premiss, know that there are physical objects unperceived by any finite mind? Common-sense thought about the world takes it to be most probable—the opinion "strangely prevails"—but Berkeley is not entitled to the aid of common sense here.

Berkeley is rightly thought of as the founding father of Phenomenalism, which gives an account of physical things purely in terms of sensations or sense-data. It is no accident, as the Marxists say, that his philosophical descendants have accepted his view of the physical world, but have rejected the theological conclusions that he went on to draw.

So Berkeley's theory of vision, his critique of Abstract Ideas, his Phenomenalism and his theological views, although presented as systematically interconnected, in fact fall apart. This is not to denigrate Berkeley's philosophical achievement. If we understand by "the history of philosophy" those past philosophers who still speak to us today, Berkeley's position in the history of philosophy is secure. Such contributions as his criticism of Locke's doctrine of the unknowable substratum, his arguments against the separation of the primary and the secondary qualities and his criticism of the Representative theory of perception remain of permanent value (regardless of whether they are finally valid). But it is no service to Berkeley's greatness to pretend that his achievement is something different from what it really is.

It is easier to find articles of a good standard on Berkeley than it is on Locke. The papers by C. D. Broad, A. A. Luce, S. A. Grave and the first paper by Konrad Marc-Wogau take up the central theme of Berkeley's philosophy: his contention that the being of physical objects consists in being perceived. Grave's paper may be read as a reply to Luce. Marc-Wogau's second paper "The Argument from Illusion and Berkeley's Idealism" and Phillip D. Cummins' "Berkeley's Likeness Principle" consider two important *arguments* that Berkeley uses in the course of trying to establish his central view.

The role of God in Berkeley's system has been given a good deal of attention in recent years. The articles by J. D. Mabbot, Jonathan Bennett and E. J. Furlong take up this topic. Furlong's paper is a reply to Bennett's.

Berkeley's philosophy of science has also attracted recent interest. Sir Karl Popper's "A Note on Berkeley as Precursor of Mach" is in fact a brilliant survey of this aspect of Berkeley's thought.

JOHN LOCKE ON THE HUMAN UNDERSTANDING
GILBERT RYLE

My purpose in this address is not to discuss or even to mention a great number of the views which Locke puts forward in the *Essay*, but solely to try to state what in my view is the important contribution to philosophy which he made and for which he deserves to be ranked among the great philosophers. I shall, in consequence, squander no time in appraising him as an historical influence or as the founder or offspring of this or that philosophical school. For I shall, I think, be doing him a greater honour if I can point out how he threw new light where darkness was before.

The minds of thinking men in the late seventeenth century were woefully harassed by the numbers of disparate bodies of propositions which demanded their acceptance. Even within the field of theology—interest in the cruces of which was then more widespread among educated men than is even now interest in the cruces of the natural sciences—traditional revelation, personal illumination, authority, and faith were all severally acclaimed as sure grounds for the truth of most important propositions about God and human destiny. And besides theology, the newly developed mathematical disciplines were hardly distinguished, even by the masters of them, from the physical and metaphysical speculations which they thought demonstrable by simple extension of the methods of mathematics, with the result that general propositions based on

From *Tercentenary Addresses on John Locke*, edited by J. L. Stocks, Oxford University Press, 1933. Reprinted by permission of the author and Oxford University Press.

experimental evidence, no less than the hypothetical constructions of dogmatic ontologies, pretended to the same sort of logical necessity as that which, whatever it is, holds between the successive steps of a mathematical deduction.

Worse still, the atomic hypothesis of the physicists had already been translated by Hobbes into a materialist metaphysic with paradoxical and alarming corollaries in his political, moral, and epistemological theories. Nor did his first and chief philosophical opponents, the Cambridge Platonists, make any lower claims to logical impregnability for their idealistic than he had done for his materialist conclusions.

Small wonder then that Locke discovered that before 'coming any nearer a resolution of those doubts which perplexed us'[1] 'it was necessary to examine our own abilities and see what objects our understandings were or were not fitted to deal with'. His object was 'to inquire into the original, certainty and extent of human knowledge, together with the grounds and degrees of belief, opinion and assent',[2] and for this end it was necessary to give a general classification of the main sorts of subject-matters about which we think and formulate propositions, the main sorts of propositions that we make about them, the main sorts of evidence upon which our propositions can be based, and the main sorts of conditions of mind in which we accept these propositions. And if, as turns out to be the case, there are found differences of kind in all these respects between the propositions of mathematics, those of the inductive sciences, those of history, those of theology, those of common-sense experience, those of moral philosophy, and those of dogmatic metaphysics, there will be an end to a great part of the disputes which arise when the credentials of one method of discovery are purloined to bolster up the conclusions of another.

Two convictions underlie his method of inquiry. The first is, to parody the title of Toland's heterodox book, his supposition of 'The Human Understanding not Mysterious', by which I mean that he consistently refused to ac-

[1] Epistle to the Reader.   [2] Bk. I, chap. 1, § 2.

cept any account of the ways or workings of the human mind which relied on the miraculous, the magical, or the transcendent. This shows itself both in his sustained criticism of the doctrine of Innate Ideas, which was in his own day the chief weapon of the Cambridge Platonists against the Hobbists, and also in his unsentimental exposure of the claims made in theology for traditional revelation and for the direct illumination appealed to by 'enthusiasts'. It shows itself too in the treatment he accords to the Scholastic doctrines of Substantial Forms, Essences, and the like.

The second underlying conviction is that the philosophical inquiry into such subjects as the human understanding should not embody 'the physical consideration of the mind', i.e. the attempt to discover by experiment or hypothesis causal laws governing the occurrence of mental states and happenings. The analysis of the concepts of knowledge, probable judgement, belief, guesswork, faith, sensation, perception, discernment, comparison, abstraction, and the rest, is not laboratory work—though what the nature of the process is he does not directly elucidate.

The pity is, as we shall see, that the one doctrine which above all others we tend to regard as Locke's central and official teaching, namely 'the new way of ideas', is partly and disastrously the product of just the sort of causal hypothesis which he abjures.

THE NEW WAY OF IDEAS

That human knowing and thinking are to be described as consisting in or, at any rate, containing 'ideas', is something which it never occurs to Locke to question. It was, after all, common ground to the Cartesians and the Cambridge Platonists, and it was natural, though most regrettable, that Locke should have deemed it his task merely to elaborate the theory and not to reconsider it. For, as I shall try to show, while the term 'idea' is used by Locke in a number of completely different senses, some of which embody no philosophical nuisance save brachylogy, there is one sense in which he uses the term, and one which is

John Locke on the Human Understanding

cardinal, for what are, in my view, the most damaging errors in the theories of knowledge of Locke and his successors, in which it must be categorically denied that there are such things as 'ideas' at all. And had this been the only sense in which Locke used the term, then his whole *Essay* would have been, what it is not, a laboured anatomy of utter nonentities.

Let us consider some of the main uses to which he puts this Pandora's box of a word.

(*a*) In his account of sense-perception Locke gives the usual treatment to the data of the five senses, and treats the sensible 'qualities', such as softness, hardness, coldness, warmth, white, red, sweet, stinking, and the rest as affections or states of the perceiving mind (on all fours with pains) caused by some physical impulse from the minute constituents of the external body upon the minute constituents of the appropriate organs of the percipient's body. He does not observe that the arguments which prove that these sensible qualities are relative to the percipient prove only that they are relative to the physical situation and condition of the percipient's body, and so he lightly assumes it for certain that they are dependent on the percipient in the special sense of being modifications of his *mental* condition. However, as pain, for example, or fear presumably are mental states, and can without too much peril be described therefore as being 'in the mind' as distinct from 'in physical objects', it makes sense (even if it is false) to say that colours, tastes, noises, smells, and 'feels' are in the same way 'in the mind', namely as being special conditions in which a mind may be on an occasion of perception.

Therefore, when Locke calls sense-data or sensible qualities 'ideas', while his theory may be false, there is no special objection to his using the term 'idea' as a special term of art to denote states of mind of this sort, namely feelings or sensations.

(*b*) Sometimes, though relatively rarely, Locke uses the term 'ideas' to denote 'images' or pictures in the mind's eye. This is, of course, the normal use of the word by Berkeley and Hume. Of images it is at least plausible to say that they are somehow mental, though it is hard to describe the precise way in which they are in the mind. They are, however, at least not directly the effects of external impact and so are not homogeneous with sense-data as Locke describes these.

(c) Sometimes, by 'idea' he simply denotes an act of thinking about something. For example, in his chapter 'Of the Association of Ideas'[3] he refers to many cases, which all of us could multiply indefinitely, where we are set thinking of one topic by the thought of another, even though neither has any real relevance to the other. This sense remains in use in ordinary speech to-day. We say 'the idea of so-and-so has just occurred to me', meaning no more than that something or other has just caused or occasioned us to think of the thing in question. In this use the term 'idea' denotes just acts of attention or consideration, and these are certainly acts of mind, but they have nothing special to do with sensations or with images, both of which we have already seen to be referred to by the term 'ideas'.

(d) Next, Locke explicitly uses the term 'ideas' as his paraphrase for the more academic 'notions', 'species', 'conceptions', and 'terms'; and he continually describes 'ideas' as what words are the signs of, or what words stand for or are the names of, or what e.g. are expressed by the words 'whiteness, hardness, sweetness, thinking, motion, man, elephant, crazy, drunkenness'.

In this use he is clearly referring to what we technically call 'concepts'. Now a 'concept' is nothing more or less than an apprehended attribute, property, quality, or character, and conception is the apprehension of an attribute, property, quality, or character.

This use divides into two. (1) In one sense 'having an idea' is simply knowing or thinking something to be of a certain character. When I know or think that something is moving, or that something is an elephant, I can go on, if I like, for the purposes of such inquiries as logic, to consider in abstraction the character which I have been con-

---

[3] Bk. II, chap. xxxiii.

sidering the object to have, namely being in motion, or being an elephant.

Now *usually* when Locke uses the term 'ideas' (except where his special representative theory of ideas is under consideration, which it pretty seldom is), he is simply referring to the mental acts of considering something to be of a certain character. And the acts of considering are certainly 'in the mind', in the sense of being acts performed by the mind. But the characters are not mental acts or states. No one in his wits could think that being an elephant is an occurrence in a person's mental life.

(2) And in the other sense not infrequently[4] when Locke speaks of 'ideas', he is referring not to the apprehending of a character but to the character or attribute itself. And this is clearly his meaning in the lengthy analyses that he offers of space, time, number, infinity, power, substance, activity, identity, personality. He is inquiring what it is to be in space, to be infinitely extensible, to be a substance, to be a person, &c., and not what it is to think of things as being one or other of these. And, as we shall see later, his famous definition of knowledge as the perception of the connexion and agreement or disagreement and repugnancy of any of our ideas is translatable simply into the assertion that knowing consists in seeing that a given character implies or excludes (i.e. implies the absence of) another character. He is not saying that knowing consists in a species of introspection.

So far we have no special objection to any one of the five given uses that Locke gives to the term 'idea'. They are all quite different from one another, so to call them all by one title is ruinously ambiguous; and each by itself is complex enough to make the term 'idea' a dangerous condensation. But none of these five uses conceals any special hypotheses or presuppositions.

(e) But there remains the last and most notorious use of the term—and the one with which Locke's name is peculiarly closely associated. The term 'ideas' is used to denote certain supposed entities which exist or occur 'in the

---

[4] Bk. II, chap. VIII, § 8; Bk. II, chap. XXVIII, § 1; Bk. IV, chap. I, § 6; Bk. IV, chap. VI, § 5, &c.

mind'. But they are 'in the mind' not, apparently as states or operations of the mind, nor yet are they merely 'in the mind' in the way in which the battle of the Marne is 'in my mind' when I am thinking about it. For they are clearly supposed to be dependent on minds for their existence. Later exponents of the theory speak of them as 'contents', as if the mind was a container in some (non-spatial) sense analogous to physical objects which spatially contain other physical objects. But this metaphor—which Locke does not employ—sheds only a deeper darkness.

However, the theory supposes that in some sense minds do support these 'ideas', and further that these ideas are objects for them, i.e. that minds attend to ideas and think about them. It also supposes that minds cannot immediately attend to or think about any other things save 'ideas'. So whenever we think of or are awake to anything, it is to these supposed mind-dependent entities to which we are attending and never directly to any real existence outside of (which I suppose means independent of) our minds. An idea is 'whatsoever is the object of the understanding when a man thinks . . . or whatever it is which the mind can be employed about in thinking . . .'[5]

There is supposed to be some relation between some of our ideas and real existences, for ideas of sensation are said to be produced in us by bodies; and 'ideas of primary qualities of bodies are resemblances of them, and their patterns do really exist in the bodies themselves'.[6] Ideas of secondary qualities are unlike but are the effects of powers in bodies.

Moreover, ideas are distinguished into 'real' and 'fantastical', of which the former are 'such as have a foundation in nature; such as have a conformity with the real being and existence of things or with their archetypes'. 'Our complex ideas of substances, being made all of them in reference to things existing without us and intended to be representations of substances as they really are, are no farther real than as they are such combinations of simple ideas as are really united, and coexist in things without

[5] Bk. I, chap. i, § 8.   [6] Bk. II, chap. viii, § 15.

John Locke on the Human Understanding

us.'[7] Again he speaks of 'simple ideas which are ἔκτυπα, or "copies"', and 'the complex ideas of substances are *ectypes* or "copies", too; but not perfect ones, not adequate'.[8] And in his chapter 'Of True and False Ideas'[9] he says: 'Thus the two ideas of a man and a centaur, supposed to be the ideas of real substances, are the one true and the other false; the one having a conformity to what has really existed, the other not.' He states the first and most obvious difficulty in the theory in his chapter 'Of the Reality of Human Knowledge':

> 'It is evident the mind knows not things immediately but only by the intervention of the ideas it has of them. Our knowledge therefore is real only so far as there is a conformity between our ideas and the reality of things. But what shall be here the criterion? How shall the mind, when it perceives nothing but its own ideas, know that they agree with things themselves? This, though it seems not to want difficulty, yet I think there be two sorts of ideas that we may be assured agree with things.'[10]

This relation between ideas and real things he describes elsewhere thus:[11] 'For since the things the mind contemplates are none of them, besides itself, present to the understanding, it is necessary that something else, as a sign or representation of the thing it considers, should be present to it; and these are ideas.'

The theory is then this: that the world contains a number of real things or substances. Some of these are minds. A mind cannot directly know other substances, but in lieu of this it has dependent on itself certain objects called 'ideas'. These are not, apparently, states in which the mind is (with the exception of sense-data which are) nor are they acts of thinking performed by the mind, but something else, the status of which is not (and could not be) specified. These, or some of them, are present proxies or 'ghosts' of absent substances or of absent qualities, mean-

---

[7] Bk. II, chap. xxx, § 5.   [8] Bk. II, chap. xxxi, §§ 12, 13.
[9] Bk. II, chap. xxxii, § 5.   [10] Bk. IV, chap. iv, § 3.
[11] Bk. IV, chap. xxi, § 4.

ing by 'present' 'capable of direct inspection' and by 'absent' 'incapable of direct inspection'. By means of these vicarious objects we can and without them we cannot think some thoughts and even get some knowledge about other substances. Finally, sense-data, images, acts of attention, the apprehensions of characters, and characters themselves (all of which were severally called 'ideas' in completely different senses of this word) are now classified as species of 'ideas' in this special sense of mind-dependent objects, functioning, sometimes, as *locum tenentes* for independent realities.

But it needs now no prolonged argument to show (1) that there is no evidence for the existence of these supposed mental proxies for independent realities, (2) that the assumption of them throws no light on the problem (if it is one) how we can think about or know things, but only multiplies gratuitously the number of things to be thought about or known; and (3) that it embodies a theory, unplausible in itself, which, if true, would make knowledge or even probable opinion about independent realities quite impossible.

1. If they existed or occurred, there should be empirical evidence of their existence or occurrence. But in fact introspection does not reveal them, and (I put it dogmatically) there is no causal inference to them. The argument on which Locke seems chiefly to rely, namely that the words which express our thoughts have meanings, proves nothing. For the word 'square', e.g., means a shape which physical objects do or do not have and not a mental something.

2. The assumption of 'ideas' does not explain how we think about or have knowledge of objects; for they are themselves described as objects about which we think and of which and the relations between which we have knowledge. If there is no difficulty in seeing how we can think about or have knowledge of ideas, then there is none in seeing how we can do so with respect to other objects like the moon or Julius Caesar. There is a prejudice that minds can only attend to what is part of or attached to their own being, but it seems to be due either to the futile super-

stition that minds are a species of container or to the popular mistake in logic of supposing that relations are not genuine in the way in which qualities and states are genuine characters of things.

3. Even if there did exist such things as 'ideas' were supposed to be, it is almost impossible so to describe them as to make sense of the assertion that some of them 'resemble' or 'represent' realities, and quite impossible to explain how we could ever know or even opine with probability that they do so, unless it is granted that we can have the same direct knowledge of realities as of the ideas of them. And if this is granted, there is no need to assume the existence of the mental 'ectypes'. Not a few philosophers have tried to evade representationism by denying the existence of the supposed archetypes of the ideas, and thus populating the world with nothing but minds and their ideas. And others have tried to accord to ideas truth of a non-representationist type by such dodges as internal coherence, systematic connectedness, and the like. But the problem which they try thus to solve is a sham one, since the alleged 'contents' for the objective validity of which they proffer such devious defences have no existence and so no properties or relations. They belong where 'phlogiston' belongs and where 'substantial forms' belong, namely to the folk-lore of philosophy.

The theory did, however, secure for Locke one important positive advantage in enabling him to draw what we shall see is a really crucial distinction between certain generically different types of propositions and consequently between certain generically different types of inquiry. For, as I have said, it was a part of Locke's purpose in writing the *Essay* to expose the nerves of the differences between the pure mathematical sciences, the natural or experimental sciences, moral and political philosophy, and theology. And for this purpose it was quite necessary not only to distinguish the sorts of evidence upon which are based the conclusions of these several types of inquiry, but much more to discover and find some way of formulating the differences between the sorts of subject-matters about which these propositions are. And this his theory of ideas partially enables him to do. For he is now in a position to say that the subjects of the propositions in arithmetic and geometry, for instance, are merely the species of ideas which he calls simple modes and are therefore not real existences or substances. Numbers, ratios, square-roots, pentagons, circumferences, and tangents are in fact being negatively described as not things in nature when Locke describes them in the seemingly positive term of 'ideas'. It is not, of course, a finally adequate analysis of mathematical propositions to say that they are only about 'ideas', for not only are they plainly not psychological propositions, but 'ideas' themselves are only psychological fictions. But as a provisional step, it does mark an important step away from the insidious indulgence of the Schoolmen of hypostasizing the terms of propositions of all sorts and thus, by multiplying entities without limit, of obscuring the distinction between propositions about matters of fact and propositions of quite other sorts.

> 'All the discourses of the mathematicians about the squaring of a circle, conic sections, or any other part of mathematics, concern not the existence of any of those figures; but their demonstrations, which depend on their ideas, are the same whether there be any square or circle, existing in the world, or no. In the same manner, the truth and certainty of moral discourses abstracts from the lives of men, and the existence of those virtues in the world whereof they treat . . .'[12]

We could, it may be hoped, find some other and less question-begging way of stating how it is that such propositions as those of mathematics and philosophy are about something, and yet are not about things in nature, than by saying that they are about ideas in our minds. But if we take Locke's account sympathetically, as a purely negative one, elucidating merely what such abstract propositions are *not* about, we shall find that a great part of Locke's treatment of the nature and relations of the several sorts of human inquiry only requires a little purely verbal trans-

[12] Bk. IV, chap. iv, § 8.

John Locke on the Human Understanding

lation to be seen as a successful, even revolutionary recharting of the fields of human knowledge and opinion.

Similarly the consideration of those propositions containing terms which seem to denote fictitious objects, such as propositions about centaurs, unicorns, and sea-serpents, has tempted logicians to suppose that, as these nouns are not meaningless, reality must in some unexplained fashion contain centaurs, sea-serpents, and unicorns. And to this extent it is a healthy if incomplete manipulation by Locke of Occam's razor when he denies the real existence of such supposed objects by his device of describing them as 'fantastical ideas' or as 'ideas' simply. Positively, of course, it is false that a sea-serpent is a mental state or operation; for sea-serpents have (or rather would have) scales and swim (or rather would swim) in the sea—attributes which could not possibly characterize 'ideas'. But negatively taken it is half-way to the true account of such propositions seemingly about fictitious objects, to say that they are about ideas. For it is true that they are *not* about things in nature. But this line of interpretation must be expanded later.

THE ORIGIN OF IDEAS

The historians of philosophy, abetted, it must be confessed, by those who set examination papers in philosophy to students, love to allocate philosophers to 'schools of thought', and Locke has suffered more than most from this facile pigeon-holing. He is generally written off not merely as an Empiricist but as the founder of the School of English Empiricism.

It is not quite clear what an Empiricist is, but it is quite clear that most of the doctrines which an Empiricist (as ordinarily defined) should hold are strenuously denied by Locke. That the evidence of particular perceptions can never be a foundation for true knowledge, that true knowledge is both completely general and completely certain and is of the type of pure mathematics, that inductive generalizations from collected observations can never yield better than probable generalizations giving us opinion but not knowledge, are doctrines which Locke's whole *Essay* is intended to establish. He even goes so far with the rationalist metaphysicians as to hold that the existence of God is demonstrable, and he is at one with the Cambridge Platonists in arguing that the principles of morality are demonstrable by the same methods and with the same certainty as any of the propositions of geometry.

But he shows the cloven hoof, it is alleged, in his assertion that 'the materials of all our knowledge, are suggested and furnished to the mind only by those two ways . . . viz. sensation and reflection'[13] (i.e. introspection); and 'Our observation, employed either about external sensible objects, or about the internal operations of our minds, perceived and reflected on by ourselves, is that which supplies our understandings with all the materials of thinking'.[14] He makes, of course, a sharp distinction between the materials of thinking and the constructions, combinations, comparisons, and abstractions which we make out of those materials. But it is ordinarily supposed that Locke's delimitation of the sources of the 'materials of thinking' should have forced him to the conclusion that there can be nothing more in thinking or knowing than the bare serial reception of these materials. But we must not vault to the conclusions which Locke did draw or should have drawn from this premiss until we have discovered what this premiss really is. To clear possible interpretations out of the way: by 'materials of thinking' and 'source of our ideas' (1) he *might* have meant (but in fact did not) the data, i.e. evidence, on which all the conclusions of our inferences are founded. Such a view would imply that all inference is inductive and, eventually, that no conclusions of inferences are certain. But it is clear that in fact he means something much more innocuous than that. (2) Or again he *might* have meant that images never occur unless we have previously experienced directly in sensation or introspection data of which they are reproductions; i.e. that images can only echo sense-data. This was certainly

[13] Bk. II, chap. II, § 2.   [14] Bk. II, chap. I, § 2.

Hume's way of taking Locke's principle that the materials of our knowledge originate in sensation or reflection. But I find no evidence that Locke meant this. All that he seems to mean is this: (a) that we can never think of anything as being of a given character, unless we have met with an instance of this character, where the character is a simple unanalysable one. Where it is a composite character, we must at least have met with instances of the simple characters, of which the composite character is compounded; and (b) that the only ways in which human beings can be directly acquainted with instances of characters are by sense-perception and introspection. The former proposition is plausible if not true; and is anyhow only an Aristotelian orthodoxy. The latter is also plausible and (if the former proposition be accepted) can only be rejected by any one who can show that there is at least one other species of perception. (It could be debated whether introspection really is a species of perception, but I cannot discuss this question here.) And if the former proposition (a) is rejected, there seems no alternative but to accept some sort of doctrine of innate ideas.

Of course Locke was handicapped by his physiological theory of sense-perception from giving any plausible account of how in particular perceptions we can come to know that *relations* of any sort hold between the objects which we perceive; for he had to hold that perceiving is barely acquaintanceship with our internal affections, with which such relational characters as 'intenser than', 'between', 'after', &c., could plainly not be classified. Nor, for the same reason, could he explain how particular perceptions introduce us to such principles of form as the substance-attribute form, the term-relation form and, perhaps, the principle of cause and effect. But these serious defects have no tendency to prove either that Locke was wrong in maintaining that we can only learn that there is such a thing as being of a given character from first meeting in perception with instances of it (where the character is a simple one), or that his acceptance of this view logically committed him to what I take to be the full empiricist position that all reasoning is induction.

Perhaps I should just allude here to another rather hollow objection which is popularly levelled against Locke's account of the source of our ideas. He says that in sensation the mind is passive, though active in the operations of combination, comparison, abstraction, &c., which it performs upon the data of sensation. And it is held to be highly wicked for a philosopher to say that the mind is passive. I do not myself think that the disjunction activity-passivity is of great importance—or even of much luminousness. However, Locke does seem to be confusing two quite different senses in which the mind is said to be passive in sensation which are worth distinguishing.

That I cannot choose but see what I see or hear what I hear or, for example, that it is not by an act of my will that onions smell as they do is true and obvious. And sometimes[15] by the distinction between passive and active Locke seems to be doing no more than referring to the distinction between those states of affairs which I bring about voluntarily and those which come about involuntarily. So 'passive' just means 'willy-nilly'. But generally Locke presupposes in his use of the term 'passive' his special causal theory of perception, by which the smell that I smell or the sound which I hear is a state of me caused by the impact upon me of something outside my skin. 'Passive' then means 'inflicted'. This causal theory may be false, but its refutation cannot be grounded upon a supposed *a priori* inappropriateness of the term 'passive' to states of mind. Before we can accept the supposed alternative doctrine that the mind is *active* in sense-perception, we should need to know whether 'active' means 'creating' or 'making a new combination of' or 'causing a change in', or whether it merely means 'tending to engender fatigue'.

I need not say much about Locke's treatment of the formation of derivative ideas, that is to say, of the operation of mind by which we come to apprehend compound characters, and to consider attributes in abstraction from the particular objects which we have found to exemplify them. For in the main his treatment of these topics is an

[15] Cf. Bk. II, chap. xxx, § 3.

unsatisfactory mixture of an attempt to give a logical classification of the types of general terms which occur in the propositions of the mathematical and natural sciences with a half-hearted attempt to button these subjects up into the strait jacket of his representationist theory of ideas. However, in his classification of space as a 'mode' as opposed to a substance, and especially in his not unimportant analyses of the concepts of extension, distance and place or relative position, and in his defence, against the Cartesians, of the distinction between space and body, he does not merely introduce us into the very heart of the controversy between the Cartesians and the Newtonians, but is half-way to supplying a satisfactory account of the differences between pure geometry and physics as well as of the way in which geometry enters into physics. He seems even to be inclined to the relational theory of space, but the authority of Newton seems to have been a stronger influence in the contrary direction. And in his treatment of infinity in which he distinguishes the infinity of space, time, and number from the notion of *an* infinite space, of *an* infinite time, or of *an* infinite number, it may be that there do lie the seeds of the final solution of the perplexities upon these matters which have so long occupied men's minds.

We shall have to return to consider Locke's treatment of what sort of truth it is which is contained in geometrical and arithmetical propositions; but the rest of the topics which Locke deals with in this book must be passed over as not being indispensable for the understanding of Locke's main objects and main achievements.

KNOWLEDGE

The propositions in which we formulate what we know or think or guess are divided, in quite the traditional way, into particular and general or universal. Particular propositions profess to state particular matters of fact and to be about particular existences. General propositions fall first into two main types, those which are certain, being either self-evident or demonstrable by self-evident steps from self-evident premisses, and those which are not certain but at best probable. The latter rest on the foundation of particular observations of particular existences. The former are either trifling, i.e. identical or analytic, or else instructive or 'synthetic' (to use Kant's term).

Now 'scientifical knowledge' must, he takes it, be of general truths; and to be 'certain' its truths must be either self-evident or rigorously demonstrable. Hence it follows that its propositions cannot be about particular existences nor founded on the evidence of propositions which are so. The propositions, therefore, of 'scientifical knowledge'[16] can only be about the relations of 'abstract ideas' in the way of agreement or disagreement. As he has in mind here such propositions as that the internal angles of a triangle are equal to two right angles, it is clear that the mysterious sounding phrase 'the agreement and disagreement of our ideas' refers simply to the propositions which assert that the having one general character implies (or implies the absence of) another character.

Locke was not enough of a logician to analyse very closely these notions of agreement and disagreement, i.e. implication and exclusion. But one point he makes quite clear. By the universal and certain propositions of science he does not mean either such propositions as 'what is green is green' *or* such propositions as 'what is green is coloured', *or* such propositions as 'a triangle is a plane figure bounded by three straight lines'. For a definition he regards as a proposition about the employment of a word; and what we call analytic propositions are for him only fragments of definitions. And these are, for him, 'trifling' propositions in the sense that nothing is learned, no new knowledge is got, when we see one of them to be true. It follows that the 'agreement' of which he speaks is not the 'is' of identity, nor yet is it the entailment of a generic character by a specific one, but something different. He thinks, namely, that there are some general propositions which we can know to be true which assert that the having

[16] Bk. IV, chap. III, § 26.

# John Locke on the Human Understanding

one attribute implies the having of another, when these are not only different attributes but further when neither is entailed in the other as generic in specific. And he thinks that the propositions of arithmetic and geometry as well as those of moral philosophy are of this sort; and indeed that 'scientifical knowledge' consists in the knowing of such implications.

So when he gives his notorious statement 'knowledge then seems to me nothing but the perception of the connexion and agreement, or disagreement and repugnancy, of any of our ideas. In this alone it consists. Where this perception is, there is knowledge; and where it is not, there, though we may fancy, guess, or believe, yet we always come short of knowledge,'[17] he is attempting not to give a definition of knowing as opposed say to guessing and believing, but to describe what it is that we know when we know something scientifically—namely, that it is never anything else but what we would call an implication (or exclusion) of one attribute by another. 'Ideas' here is just a synonym for 'quality' or 'attribute', and connotes, unless I am wrong, nothing at all of his 'proxy' theory of ideas. He does, however, reintroduce this in a ruinous fashion,[18] where he says 'Every man's reasoning and knowledge is only about the ideas existing in his own mind, which are truly, every one of them, particular existences; and our knowledge and reasoning about other things is only as they correspond with those our particular ideas.'

Locke is now in a position to show that the truth of the abstract general propositions of pure mathematics as well as of moral philosophy (which he is surely wrong in thinking homogeneous with mathematics) does not in the least depend upon whether there exist any objects having the properties the implications between which those propositions state. He is within an inch of saying that these propositions which express 'scientifical knowledge' are hypothetical. *They do not directly describe real existences.* They say what properties *would* follow, if something had certain other properties, and not that anything has them.

[17] Bk. IV, chap. I, § 2.   [18] Bk. IV, chap. XVII, § 8.

Now this seemingly unexciting discovery is of the greatest importance. For it proves that geometry does not (as the Cartesians thought) directly describe the world; and it proves that anyhow many philosophical statements have no ontological bearing—they do not describe transcendent entities, but merely say what *would* follow about any ordinary object if it was of such and such a character.

This is where Locke is an anti-Rationalist—not that he disputes our power to reach new certain and universal truths by pure reasoning (on the contrary it is in this process that, for him, science proper consists), but that he maintains, in effect, that all these truths are general and hypothetical and do not therefore give any description of what exists. Even the existence of God, demonstrable with mathematical certainty in Locke's opinion, must have for one of its premises the existence of the person making the demonstration, and *his* existence is perceived and not proved.

Knowledge of the highest type consists, then, for Locke in knowledge of what have since been called synthetic *a priori* truths, but these do not constitute either an ontology or natural science. But he makes no attempt to show wherein consist these rather mysterious relations of agreement and disagreement (or implication and exclusion) nor to prove that mathematical propositions are really synthetic.

KNOWLEDGE OF EXISTENCE

Besides the knowledge formulable in general or hypothetical propositions, in which field alone formal deduction or demonstration is possible, there is the field of matters-of-fact within which some little knowledge of an inferior sort and much probable opinion is possible. This divides into knowledge (*a*) of particular existences and of particular co-existences of qualities in particular substances on the one hand, and on the other (*b*) the judgement (it does not amount to knowledge) based on the evidence of particular instances that certain properties always accompany certain others.

(a) Locke offers no analysis of existential propositions, and so never even considers whether knowing that I, for example, exist is really a case of perceiving a relation between two qualities. He argues that this I can know in the full sense of the verb, namely that I exist. It needs no proof. 'We have an intuitive knowledge of our own existence and an internal infallible perception that we are.'[19] Whether this involves knowing who or what I am (ignorance or doubt about which would leave small significance to the existential proposition 'I exist'), Locke leaves it to Hume to discuss.

Next, we can prove the existence of God from our own existence, since 'what had a beginning must be produced by something else'. And lastly, though we can neither have intuitive nor demonstrative knowledge that anything else exists, yet we can have 'an assurance that deserves the name of knowledge'.[20] For, while quite ignorant *how* our data of sense are caused to arise in our minds, *that* they are caused by agencies outside us is so highly probable that we have the right to feel certain that an object exists at the time we are experiencing a sensation. But of course we can have no such assurance of the past or continued existence of external objects, or indeed of any moment of their existence except at the instant when the sensation is occurring. It will be seen thus that all our knowledge or assurance of the existence of other things, both God and bodies, presuppose our knowing that 'what had a beginning must be produced by something else'. Perhaps it was an interest in this special question of our knowledge of other existences that caused Hume to fix his criticism on the one (alleged) synthetic *a priori* proposition that every event must have a cause.

What exists is particular or, better put, the subject terms of existential propositions are not general or abstract terms but singular and concrete ones. It follows, therefore, that there can be no question of our knowing synthetic *a priori* truths which are also existential.

[19] Bk. IV, chap. IX, § 3.   [20] Bk. IV, chap. VI, § 3.

No collocation of propositions of the form 'x-ness implies y-ness' or 'whatever is x is y' can lead to a conclusion of the form 'Cicero exists' or 'Westminster Abbey has such and such mass'. Pure reason cannot inform us of a single particular matter of fact. So all the knowledge or assurance we can have about what exists or occurs in nature must either be or be based on the evidence of particular observations. If this is Empiricism then Locke is an Empiricist and, I would add, Empiricism is the truth.

THE NATURAL SCIENCES

But Boyle and Sydenham and 'such masters as the great Huygenius and the incomparable Mr. Newton' do not merely list particular observations. The discoveries of the natural sciences are or are intended to be laws, i.e. general propositions holding good not only of all observed but also of all unobserved, all possible as well as all actual instances of the type of phenomenon under examination. How do these differ from the general propositions of geometry and arithmetic?

Locke takes up this question by considering first of all how we come to classify things in nature into sorts. For the general propositions of the natural scientist will all be of the form that every object of such and such a sort has such and such properties. A living creature is classified as a lion or a body as a piece of gold because it is found to possess a certain set of qualities and is similar to many other objects which also have just the same or almost the same set of qualities.

But, unlike our procedure with abstractions which we can *define* to have such and such properties and no others, in respect of natural kinds we cannot arbitrarily coin our definitions of the properties essential to the kinds that nature provides. Even if, as Locke seems to think, things in nature are really members of real kinds, in such a way that in their inward constitution their properties are necessarily connected, yet we have no way of perceiving the necessity of the coexistence of the qualities which we observe to co-exist. When we come to distinguish lions from bears and tigers, we do not yet know why tawny fur goes with such and such a shape of head in the way in which we do know why in a right-angled triangle the square on the hypotenuse is equal to the sum of the squares on the other two sides.

We find several objects having in common a large set of qualities (though we can usually give no precise catalogue of these common characteristics), and so come to treat and name all the objects which have anyhow a large fraction of this set of qualities as members of the same sort. Moreover, we *suppose* that there is some principle, although we do not know it, necessitating that whatever has certain of these characteristics shall also have the rest.

'Our faculties carry us no farther towards the knowledge and distinction of substances than a collection of those sensible ideas which we observe in them; which, however made with the greatest diligence and exactness we are capable of, yet is more remote from the true internal constitution from which those qualities flow than, as I said, a countryman's idea is from the inward contrivance of that famous clock at Strasburg, whereof he only sees the outward figure and motions.'[21]

So the definitions which we give of the natural kinds which we establish do no more than list the properties which we constantly find to be concomitant. Thus our definitions are only of 'nominal essences', that is, of the bunches of properties which we have chosen to unify under one name. But how many such properties ought to be treated as necessarily concomitant we cannot know. 'We can never know what are the precise numbers of properties depending on the real essence of gold; any one of which failing, the real essence of gold, and consequently gold, would not be there, unless we knew the real essence of gold itself, and by that determined the species.'[22] Often Locke speaks as if the difficulty is merely a consequence of his causal theory of sense-perception or, what comes to

[21] Bk. III, chap. vi, § 9.   [22] Bk. III, chap. vi, § 19.

the same thing, of his theory that the secondary qualities of things are in the mind and not in things, namely that as all we can know of things is the sensations which they cause to occur in us, therefore the real internal constitution of things necessarily eludes our apprehension.

But in Book IV especially he puts his finger on the real nerve of the difficulty, which is, of course, the nerve of the whole problem of induction. The concomitance of what we take to be the 'sortal' properties of lions, say, or gold is generically different both from the relation of specific to generic quality ('entailment') and from the relations of agreement or disagreement (implication or exclusion) which we can know to hold between certain of our abstract ideas. So it is not merely that we do not yet see how to demonstrate by rigorous deduction that whatever has the other properties of gold must be soluble in *aqua regia*, but we can already see that there is no such logical implication. It is not an analytic proposition; it is not a self-evident synthetic one; and it is not one that can be demonstrated in a chain of propositions each self-evidently consequent from its predecessor.

> 'Thus though we see the yellow colour, and upon trial find the weight, malleableness, fusibility, and fixedness that are united in a piece of gold; yet because no one of these ideas has any evident dependence or necessary connexion with the other, we cannot certainly know that where any four of these are the fifth will be there also, how highly probable soever it may be; because the highest probability amounts not to certainty; without which there can be no true knowledge. For this coexistence can be no farther known than it is perceived; and it cannot be perceived but either in particular subjects by the observation of our senses, or in general by the necessary connexion of the ideas themselves.'[23]

This gives Locke the generic difference which he requires between the pure deductive or *a priori* sciences and the experimental sciences. The general propositions of the physical and other inductive sciences rest on the evidence

[23] Bk. IV, chap. III, § 14.

of regularly observed concomitances of properties; and these concomitances are not self-evident or necessary. So the conclusions of these sciences never can reach the certainty of mathematics, and in Locke's rigorous use of the term science, they cannot constitute scientific knowledge. They cannot rise higher than probability. 'We are not capable of a philosophical knowledge of the bodies that are about us, and make a part of us; concerning their secondary qualities, powers and operations, we can have no universal certainty.'[24]

THEOLOGY

It is likely that in Locke's mind and in the minds of his contemporaries, no more important or urgent question was discussed in the whole *Essay* than the question of the nature and certainty of the propositions of theology. Whether historical tradition can enable us to *know* that such and such things were revealed to certain of our forefathers, whether immediate revelation or inspiration yields a certainty of the same sort as our certainty of mathematical axioms, whether religious truths are above reason or according to reason or whether, although contrary to reason, they still demand unquestioning assent, these were questions of deep importance for Locke and for his age.

It seems not unlikely that it was from an inquiry into problems such as these that the *Essay* took its beginning. But, for us, Locke's treatment of these problems has by itself removed them from their pride of place in the forefront of philosophical interest. For we have no doubt now that historical testimony can yield nothing higher than probabilities; that whatever may be the authority of immediate inspiration, if and when it occurs, the claim that it has really occurred and not merely seemed to occur can never fully certify itself. Belief is belief and not knowledge; and no matter how transcendent its object or how elevated its effects may be, it can rise no higher than wholehearted assurance. And we are sometimes whole-heartedly

[24] Bk. IV, chap. III, § 29.

assured of what is not true. So the doctrines of theology rest on the fallible testimony of historians or the fallible testimony of the human heart, and may achieve indeed a degree of probability more than high enough for the confident and wise conduct of life; but they cannot emulate the demonstrability of mathematics nor even the broad statistical foundations of experimental science. From which follows the corollary, to which we are now well acclimatized, that it is in principle erroneous to seek to base or corroborate the premisses of mathematics, philosophy, or the natural sciences upon the conclusions of theology or the tenets of religious faith. These have their place in life, but they enjoy no precedence in rational inquiry.

What, then, was Locke's achievement? If I am not mistaken, it was something much greater than is usually allowed him. He was not merely the plain-spoken mouthpiece of the age or the readable epitome of its development; nor was it his task merely to anglicize and popularize the philosophical and scientific concepts and theories of his day. His title does not rest upon his rather frail claim to be the founder of psychology, nor yet upon his two-edged claim to be the founder of modern theories of knowledge. And to my mind there is no unkinder or unfairer testimonial to his philosophical writings than to say, what is often said, that in them the common-sense views of ordinary man find their best expression. Nor yet, in my view, is it a part of Locke's greatness as a philosopher that he expounded and popularized the theory (which he did not invent) of representative ideas. For I hold that the theory is not only an error, but the wrong sort of error, being in the main fruitful of nothing of positive value to the theory of knowledge.

Instead I claim for Locke that he did achieve a part of his ambition 'to be an under-labourer, in clearing ground a little, and removing some of the rubbish that lies in the way to knowledge' in that he taught the whole educated world the lesson (which might with profit be conned over in some quarters in our own day) that there are differences in kind, and roughly what these differences are, between mathematics, philosophy, natural science, theology, inspiration, history, and common-sense acquaintanceship with the world around us. In a word, his achievement is that he gave us not a theory of knowledge but a theory of the sciences. So that for which we should render him thanks is no exciting speculation or visionary promise of another world, no disclosure of startling secrets of earth or heaven or of human nature, but something else which, though it does not glitter, still is gold, namely a permanent emancipation from a besetting confusion. He taught us to distinguish the types of our inquiries, and thus made us begin to understand the questions that we ask.

LOCKE'S CONCEPT OF EXPERIENCE
JOHN W. YOLTON

The empiricist programme has been designed to show that all conscious experience "comes from" unconscious encounters with the environment, and that all intellectual contents (concepts, ideas) derive from some conscious experiential component. Some empiricists, but not all, have also argued that experience reports about the world. A strict empiricism might have to reject this latter claim; even to consider the possibility of knowledge being related to an external world is to operate on a reflective level, to seek to make sense of experience. The distinction between an *account* of the nature of experience (its structure, relations and contents) and *explanations* of experience is an important one. The phrase "the concept of experience" refers to the use made of some account of experience. The concept of experience need not be restricted to the experiential contents. Thus, Locke sought to show how experience is of the world, Hume tried to show how experience restricts our valid conceptual contents to certain sorts of ideas, eliminating others. Any account of experience will already be a conceptualization of experience: it must be made from the reflective level. But the account need be no more than a careful record of how the organism comes to the conscious level. Of course, such an account cannot be a straightforward description, since we cannot directly observe all of the processes operating in the production of awareness. The psychology of awareness must

This essay is a portion of an article from the *Journal of the History of Philosophy*, Vol. I (1963) under the title "The Concept of Experience in Locke and Hume." Some changes and additions have been made for this reprinting. Reprinted by permission of the author and the *Journal of the History of Philosophy*.

use the tools of extrapolation and conjecture. Nevertheless, we can still distinguish the psychological or descriptive account of experience from the metaphysical use made of that account.

Locke claimed that all mental contents come from two sources, sensory experience of the world and introspective awareness of our mental processes. The programme of Book II of his *Essay* was to exemplify, by reference to a number of different ideas and concepts, this derivation of our mental contents. The counter claim for Locke was innatism, the view held by many of his contemporaries and refuted in the first book of his *Essay*. In order to appreciate what Locke's alternative to innatism was, we must try to discover what the programme of derivation of ideas amounts to in his epistemology and what precisely he understood by the term "experience."

We must first note that he offers the programme of derivation in conjunction with a complex theory of mental operations. H. H. Price has remarked that it is "historically false that the Empiricists thought the human mind passive. It would be more just to criticize them for making it more active than it can possibly be."[1] Mental processes play a most active and decisive role in the genesis of all ideas in Locke's account. In the case of simple ideas of sense even, the mind must be attentive to what the senses report, else that report will go unrecorded, or be recorded only at the neural level (II, 1, §§ 6, 8, and II, IX, § 3).[2] Locke frequently draws the distinction between mental contents or processes and physical processes. In the "Epistle to the Reader," where he defines "determined idea," he is careful to distinguish idea from the sound we use as a sign of it (p. xxxix). In I, 1, § 2 he draws a distinction between the "physical consideration of the mind" and the non-physical consideration, although he does not have a name for the latter. He also speaks there of "sensations by our organs" and "ideas in our understanding."

---

[1] *Thinking and Experience*, p. 199, n. 1.
[2] References to Locke's *Essay* are to the Everyman Edition, edited by John W. Yolton (§ 332 and § 984), 1961 (revised in 1965).

Locke disclaimed any intention of going into the physical account of sensation. He simply accepted the current corpuscular theory. But although he is not always as precise as we would be about the physical and physiological levels of encounter, in distinction from the mental levels, he does hold to this division. In II, 1, § 3, for instance, he speaks of the senses conveying *"into the mind"* several "distinct *perceptions* of things." He explains that "convey" means that the senses carry into the mind "what produces there those *perceptions*." Presumably what he means is that the stimulus gets to the mind via the sensory equipment of the organism. He ends II, 1, § 25 by speaking of the sensory impressions having ideas annexed to them, but he remarks that it is the ideas which are *perceived*, although the mind is said to *receive* the impressions. The function of attention in this process is to notice the sensory impressions.

The problem of how one attends to the physical reports of the senses was not one that bothered Locke. It is difficult to determine just what role—and how important a one—attention plays in our becoming aware of the sensory reports. In II, 1, § 23 Locke tends to underplay that role. Sensation is defined as "an impression or motion made in some part of the body" and this motion "produces some perception in the understanding." Locke says that the mind employs itself about these impressions, but if the impressions are physiological, it could only employ itself about the perceptions produced by these impressions. The transition from nerve impulse to conscious content occurs, but Locke does not have much to say about how it is accomplished. One point is clear: the awareness of ideas is accomplished through the co-operative interaction of objects, neurophysiological processes, and awareness.

"Perception" was Locke's term for awareness. It is the first faculty and the first act of the mind exercised about its ideas. "Idea," of course, is a conscious mental content. Despite his remark in II, x, § 2 that ideas are nothing "but actual perceptions in the mind," his more careful statements keep act and content distinct. Without the act there can be no content, and, conversely, without a content there can be no act. Being conscious and having ideas are simultaneous conditions. Nevertheless, the act of being aware should not be identified with that of which we are aware. Quite apart from the question whether that of which we are aware is objects in the environment or only ideas in our minds, Locke saw the importance, for a theory of thinking, of stressing the first elementary act of recognition. To be aware is to be aware of some content of the mind; the simplest form of such awareness is what Locke describes as perceiving "each *idea* to agree with itself and to be what it is, and all distinct *ideas* to disagree, i.e. the one not to be the other" (IV, 1, § 4). Locke even makes the point, stressed recently by Price, that this level of recognition is infallible.

There are many other operations of the mind besides simple awareness, operations which play their role in the generation of more complex ideas. But we must not understress the part played by simple awareness; appreciation of this point will help to overcome that mistake of saying the mind for Locke is wholly passive. Locke said that it was wholly passive, but he could not have meant it in the sense in which it has been taken, i.e. that the stimulus is inscribed upon the mind without any help at all from the mind. The mind is "fitted to receive the impressions made on it" (II, 1, § 24), but no impressions will occur unless we attend to the stimulus.[3] The case is somewhat different in our awareness of our mental processes, since there is no sensory process involved. There are neural *processes* accompanying our various acts of thinking, although Locke did not know this; but what we are aware of in acquiring the ideas of thinking, perceiving, believing,

[3] The image of the "white paper void of all characters" (II, 1, § 2) is also misleading if taken to mean the mind starts from scratch. The white paper image was a counter to innatism which would have the mind filled with ideas and truths at birth. Locke went out of his way in Book I to say he was not denying "natural tendencies imprinted on the minds of men," e.g. tendencies to seek happiness and avoid misery (I, III, § 3). The various mental faculties to which Locke appeals are the most important supplement to the white paper; it is by their action that characters become inscribed.

reasoning, et cetera, are mental, not physical, processes. Some of the differences between awareness in reflection and awareness in sensation may disappear, if I am correct in suggesting that, strictly, Locke did not want to say we are aware of the sensory stimulus, but only of what it produces. Then awareness would be directed to mental contents and acts in both cases.[4] The difference would still remain, that in the one case neurophysiological processes play a causal role in the generation of mental contents, while in the other, although we know now that there are neural correlates for thought, it still seems incorrect to say these neural correlates cause us to have the ideas of thinking, willing, et cetera.

External sensible objects and internal operations of the mind are the things and processes upon which the attentive faculty of the mind is directed and from which ideas are derived in some way. Knowledge is both *founded in* and *derived from* these sources, in the sense that the material for knowledge, ideas, is generated by sensation and reflection, those two fountainheads of experience. The nature of this programme of derivation for complex ideas reflects some awareness that the way some ideas arise from experience differs rather markedly from the way other ideas arise. We have already noticed this difference between sensory and reflective ideas. The simple-complex terminology is first introduced as a way of talking about "the nature, manner, and extent of our knowledge" (II, 11, § 1). Simple ideas arise in or—a most revealing phrase—are "suggested to" but not made by the mind. To understand Locke's programme for the derivation of ideas, and to see what concept of experience he was working with, we need to take some specific examples of derivation and analyze them carefully.

[4] From this fact about awareness it does not follow that we cannot know things themselves. Ideas may "represent" things but representative ideas are compatible with knowledge of things. While the account of the knowledge of bodies is complex in Locke's *Essay*, his insistence upon a careful observation of objects as the way to such knowledge makes it clear that Locke did not view ideas as a screen between observers and objects.

Locke's Concept of Experience

The idea of solidity we have from touch and resistance sensations. Locke calls attention to the fact that in all our postures we are aware of a support to our body. Solidity becomes the "idea most intimately connected with and essential to body" (II, IV, § 1). The idea of pure space arises in conjunction with body and solidity as follows: a man conceives two bodies at a distance such that they could move towards one another and touch edges. This thought gives us the idea of space without solidity by a kind of intellectual operation or experiment. If we then think of one body moving without its place being immediately filled, we have the idea of pure space. Sensation and reflection have been used in the genesis of these two ideas, and sensation and reflection are what Locke means by experience. Thus, has he not given an experience-derivation for these ideas?

It is most important to notice that this sort of derivation of an idea like pure space by reflection differs radically from the derivation of the reflective ideas. That is, I reflect upon my own mental operations and in that way obtain the ideas of thinking, willing, doubting, et cetera. I employ the mental operation of reflection in order to obtain these reflective ideas. But I also employ reflection, and many other mental faculties, in obtaining many of the ideas of sense. Pure space is an example, the ideas of existence and of unity are two more. Locke says that these two latter ideas are suggested to the mind "by every object without, and every *idea* within" (II, VII, § 7). The idea of "one" is another example of an idea not derived directly and immediately from sense. Locke says "every *idea* in our understandings, every thought of our minds, brings this *idea* along with it" (II, XVI, § 1). This is a tandem idea, joined with other ideas. No distinct neurophysiological process stands behind the idea of one. The acquisition of any idea by sensation brings another along with it. Another such tandem idea is that of finite: "The obvious portions of extension that affect our senses carry with them into the mind the *idea* of finite" (II, XVII, § 2). The idea of substance as something over and above the sensible qualities is the most notorious tandem idea in Locke's account: he speaks of the mind being forced to think of a subject as a unifying entity for the qualities.

Suggestion is surely not the straightforward derivation from sensation which Locke seems to have in mind when he first states his programme. If we take some external object and say that it suggests to the understanding existence and unity, we do not mean there is some physiological process whereby this idea is generated. What is involved here is a kind of tandem process: along with some of our sensory ideas we find there come, when we are suitably advanced in thought, further ideas. We "consider things as there," which is the idea of existence, but this "considering" is a rather sophisticated mental operation. Locke makes frequent appeals to these mental operations of "considering," "taking notice," "reflecting." The idea of power is a paradigm case of the genesis of an idea with the help of these particular mental operations.

> The mind—being every day informed by the senses of the alteration of those simple *ideas* it observes in things without; and taking notice how one comes to an end, and ceases to be, and another begins to exist which was not before; reflecting also on what passes within itself, and observing a constant change of its *ideas*, sometimes by the impression of outward objects on the senses, and sometimes by the determination of its own choice; and concluding from what it has so constantly observed to have been, that the like changes will for the future be made in the same things, by like agents, and by the ways—considers in one thing the possibility of having any of its simple *ideas* changed, and in another the possibility of making that change; and so comes by that *idea* which we call *power*. [II, xxi, § 1]

For these acts of considering, the mind is not tied down to sensation or to a straightforward act of introspection: these mental faculties work independently of those two fountainheads of experience, generating a host of ideas far removed from experience. The whole of geometry, for instance, is generated by repeating or shortening the idea of length or degree (II, xiii, § 6). Section 13 of this same

chapter speaks of "dividing mentally"; a process of dividing and adding mentally gives us the idea of infinite duration (II, xiv, § 31; II, xv, §§ 2, 3).
When Locke comes to the derivation of our ideas of mixed modes, he clearly is dealing with that sort of derivation in which the mind constructs ideas itself. That Locke was aware of a sharp transition here is evidenced by section 73 of chapter xxi, where he drew a strong conclusion about derivation: we have now given, he there says, "a view of our *original ideas* from whence all the rest are derived, and of which they are made up." Now he takes us into a domain of ideas rather far removed from what he calls "nature" or "real being." Moral ideas are the best example of mixed modes: they are framed by the mind without reference to what exists really, either outside or within the mind. But the transition to such a derivation of ideas has been made, I would suggest, in Locke's frequent appeals to the "considering," "reflecting," "concluding" operations of the mind even on the level of those ideas supposed to be more closely related to the world. The way in which relational ideas are formed does not differ greatly from the way those ideas of unity, existence, infinity are formed. "The understanding, in the consideration of anything, is not confined to that precise object: it can carry any *idea* as it were, beyond itself or, at least, look beyond it to see how it stands in conformity to any other" (II, xxv, § 1). Just what is involved in "carrying" ideas or in "looking beyond" them is not made clear. But Locke ends this chapter by reaffirming the thesis that all ideas of relations "terminate in and are about simple ideas of sense." He proceeds to show how our ideas of cause and effect are derived from sensation or sensory ideas. We observe in sensation that some things bring other things into being, e.g. heat is the cause of the fluidity of the wax. A cause is "that which makes any other thing, either simple *idea*, substance, or mode, begin to be" (II, xxvi, § 2). Thus, Locke has shown how the relational idea of cause and effect arises from and terminates in sense. "For to have the *idea* of *cause* and *effect*, it suffices to consider any simple

idea or substance as beginning to exist . . ." (*Ibid.*). It is this "considering" which assists the process. The idea which arises is in effect an explanatory one: it makes sense of the experiences we have had; it has no sensed correlate in sensation.

What, then, does Locke's programme for the derivation of ideas amount to and what is the concept of experience he had in mind? Does the notion of derivation mean anything more to him than that the mind must first be aware of sensible ideas before it can have any other sorts of ideas? He summarizes his programme in II, xi:, § 8 as follows: "so that those even large *and abstract* ideas *are derived from sensation or reflection,* being no other than what the mind, by the ordinary use of its own faculties, employed about *ideas* received from objects of sense or from the operations it observes in itself about them, may and does attain unto." Having as the antithesis to his programme of derivation only the doctrine of innate inscription, Locke has shown how all ideas arise *after* experience, that is, after the organism has encountered the environment and been stimulated into neurophysiological and mental activity. Locke has addressed himself to the question of the genesis of specific ideas and has supplied us with accounts of that genesis. What he has failed to do in any systematic way is to distinguish the different sorts of processes which help to generate different ideas. There is not *one* sort of process nor *one* sort of idea. We might draw up a list of these differences.

1. *Sensory ideas* arise as a direct result of sensory stimulation and mental recognition. There is a neurophysiological process involved here, but the idea is a conscious mental content. Just how recognition takes place is a point not discussed by Locke.

2. *Reductive ideas* arise through the mind's adding together certain sensory ideas to obtain what we might call a class concept. These ideas can be reduced to sensory ideas. For example, an army is just a collection of individuals, and our idea of an army is a collective idea of a class of individuals.

3. *Introspective ideas* arise through the awareness of our own mental processes. No neurophysiological process seems involved here in the causal genesis although such processes are present. The ideas arise not through the intermediary of such processes but solely through our ability to be aware of our own mental, emotional, and internal bodily states.

4. *Non-sensory ideas* arise through the activity of the mind directing its attention to some feature of our sensory or introspective experience. It considers, reflects upon, concludes, et cetera, that such and such is the case, and a new idea is formed. These ideas are rather like explanations.

Thus in no case has Locke claimed that ideas arise in the organism in the absence of mental operations, although the first sort of ideas require relatively few and simple mental operations. The formation of types 1, 2, and 3 conform to his announced programme. Once we grant the term experience to cover both sensation and introspection, these first three sorts of ideas can be said to be derived from experience. But these by no means exhaust the sorts of ideas we have. By far the greater number of ideas discussed by Locke himself belong to type 4. The central ambiguity in his programme is the nature of reflection and its role in the derivation of ideas. We have seen that it is given a twofold role: it gives us introspective contents, but it also comprises a host of mental operations other than introspection.[5] When we allow the experience programme to cover both types of reflection, what is offered by Locke is a programme for which the only falsification would be proof of the innate claim. The concept of experience in this extended sense—any state or condition after awareness has arisen—would be of use to an empiricist only when the counter claim is that of innatism. Con-

[5] To appreciate the number and extent of mental operations in Locke's derivation programme, one need only begin to make a list of the mental terms used and referred to by Locke in Book II. A student of mine, Mr. P. J. White, has undertaken to compile such a list. He has discovered an intricate theory of thinking at work in that derivation programme with references to hundreds of mental processes and operations. *Vide* his unpublished M.A. thesis at the University of Toronto.

sciousness for Locke arises out of unconscious encounters with the environment, but not all mental contents are traceable to some experiential component.

Type 4 mental contents are clearly explanatory concepts, ideas which help each individual to make sense of his sensory experience. The ideas of unity, existence, substance, infinity, power, and cause are explanatory concepts constructed by the mind when confronted with specific sorts of experiences. They might also be termed the categories which structure awareness. But "derived from" and "constructed for the sake of" refer to different processes. The one gives us an account of the origin of awareness and of certain mental contents; the other presents us with an account of those explanatory concepts employed in understanding the experiential contents. In the absence of any experiential contents there can be no explanatory ones. Both types of mental contents make up "experience," in the sense of the world organized and structured by the conscious organism. Type 4 ideas in Locke's account are not full-blown metaphysical accounts of experience nor metaphysically deduced categories. Such accounts arise as an attempt by the philosopher to explain or unify the other sorts of ideas. But the mental contents derived from the mind's considering certain features of the world and experience are nonetheless metaphysical. In strictness, then, no idea *comes from experience* on Locke's programme since it is ideas of all sorts which *make up* or constitute experience. Ideas come from the activity of organism and environment, some processes stimulating the neurophysiological functions which are related to mental operations, others working entirely within the scope of thought and reflection. If Locke restricts experience to sensation and introspection, then he has not shown how all ideas are derived from experience. But if we allow the extension of this concept of experience to cover any act of the mind, then clearly any mental content will be experiential.

Explanatory concepts enable Locke to suggest how experience comes to be structured in terms of cause, unity, identity, substance, power, existence, etc. Locke does not

Locke's Concept of Experience

try to argue that experience *must be* structured in these terms; there is no transcendental deduction of universal and necessary categories. Nor does Locke wish to say these categorial ideas are logically or cognitively primitive.[6] We can characterize the difference between Locke and Kant by remarking that Locke dealt with the categorial ideas in the same genetic fashion as he did with more straightforward sensory ideas. But his account of their genesis is more complex than that of sensory ideas; it involves different and more sophisticated mental operations, and categorial ideas lack particular sensory correlations in experience.

The account of the origin of sensory ideas ties in closely with another aspect of the concept of experience I have not discussed in this paper, experience as the source of our knowledge of things. Opposing the method of relying upon maxims and *a priori* principles for a knowledge of nature, Locke insisted that *"Experience here must teach me* what reason cannot" (IV, XII, § 9). What Locke called "arguments from the nature of things themselves" (IV, XVI, § 6) leads to the science of nature. Those arguments involve the general consent of all men in all ages concurring "with a man's constant and never-failing experience, in like cases." Propositions like "fire warms a man," "fire makes lead fluid and changes the colour of consistency in wood or charcoal," "iron sinks in water but swims in quicksilver" are propositions about particular facts which agree to our constant experience and hence may be taken as near certainties (*Ibid.*).

> In the knowledge of bodies, we must be content to glean what we can from particular experiments, since we cannot from a discovery of their real essences grasp at a time whole sheaves, and in bundles comprehend the nature and properties of whole species together. Where our inquiry is concerning co-existence or repugnancy to co-exist, which by contem-

[6] Locke does give a list of eight *"original ideas* from whence all the rest are derived," in II, XXI, § 73. Moreover, existence and power are on that list. The precise role this list was meant to play by Locke is not, however, very clear. The passage is interesting and worth further study.

plation of our *ideas* we cannot discover, there experience, observation, and natural history must give us by our senses and by detail an insight into corporeal substances." [IV, xii, § 12]

In his admiration for Boyle, Newton, and Sydenham, Locke was praising these men for this method of carefully observing and recording the observed co-existence of qualities.

To see how experience as the source for our scientific knowledge of nature is related to experience as the set of ideas we acquire in interaction with the world requires us to work out the details of Locke's science of nature and his doctrine of signs. The derivation programme outlined in this paper is a prerequisite for these larger tasks.

LOCKE'S DISTINCTION BETWEEN PRIMARY AND SECONDARY QUALITIES
REGINALD JACKSON

Among the merits of Locke's *Essay on the Human Understanding* not even the friendliest critic would number consistency. Locke, indeed, himself acknowledges his inconsistency with disarming candour when, after distinguishing "qualities," as belonging to bodies, from "ideas," as mind-dependent objects of perception produced by qualities, he immediately proclaims that, if he sometimes speaks of these ideas as in the "things" (bodies) themselves, he would be understood to mean those qualities in "objects" (bodies) which produce them in us.[1] In the spirit of this announcement Locke makes one term serve such a variety of needs, that an attempt to show what he "really means" by a term is exposed to the objection that he means different things in different passages and that all the different meanings are equally "real". Yet, if the *Essay* is to be interpreted at all, it is necessary to search, among the conflicting usages of any term, for one which may be most conveniently selected as the normal usage, and by reference to which other usages may be classified as departures. Something of the sort is in any case bound to happen. The only question which is left to the critic to decide is whether his selection is to be made in accordance with a principle. Now, in spite of the passage cited above, in which Locke deliberately notifies his intention of sometimes using a term to mean what he has just defined it as not meaning, there seems something to be said for select-

From *Mind*, Vol. XXXVIII (1929). Reprinted by permission of *Mind*.
[1] *Essay*, II, viii, § 8.

ing where possible, as the normal meaning of a term, what Locke says he means by it. Where this is not possible—as when a definition is self-contradictory or in any way defeats its own purpose—the critic should still take account of the definition and state his reasons for modifying or rejecting it.

The aim of this article is to determine the nature of Locke's distinction between Primary and Secondary Qualities. This distinction has been represented, both by Locke's immediate successors and by a number of modern critics, in a way which is not only opposed to Locke's definitions of these terms, but which is also most awkwardly related to his distinction between "Qualities" and "Ideas". The *onus probandi* in a case of this kind rests on those who challenge the definitions. They should show that Locke habitually uses the terms in such a way as to preclude the meanings to which he pledges himself, or that the distinction in the terms in which he draws it is not only untenable (which is pretty certainly true both of Locke's distinction and of the distinction usually accredited to him) but also inconsistent with the purpose for which it is designed. In fact, however, so far from having been vindicated in the face of Locke's definitions, the supposed meanings seem to have been adopted without even a recognition of the discrepancy, and some writers use the terms now with the supposed meanings and now with those given in Locke's definitions without betraying any suspicion that they are not the same. The current distinction between Primary and Secondary Qualities is perhaps too well established to be shaken by objections based on the origin of the terms. But it is desirable in the interests of scholarship that the current distinction should be recognised to be different from Locke's distinction if it is different.

The distinction which Locke was supposed by Berkeley and Reid to have drawn, is between qualities of bodies (these qualities being supposed to be perceptible) and ideas, sensations, or, in current terminology, sensibilia (supposed not to exist independently of the perception of them and to be the effects of the action of bodies on minds). Modern writers who have followed Berkeley and Reid have in consequence supposed that Locke inherited the distinction between Primary and Secondary Qualities immediately from the Cartesians and ultimately from Democritus; and that, together with Boyle, he uses the terms Primary and Secondary Qualities to designate roughly the same things as he elsewhere calls Qualities and Ideas. According to the view of these modern writers, the distinction between Primary and Secondary Qualities is only a way of stating the Representative Theory of Perception. Secondary Qualities also have been identified, though much less commonly, with what Locke calls "the primary qualities of the insensible parts" of bodies. The source of both confusions is to be found in Locke himself and even in Boyle, who was really the author not only of the terms but also of the distinction itself.

In what follows it will be contended that Locke means by "primary qualities of bodies" simply *qualities of bodies*, that he calls them "primary" to distinguish them, not from other qualities as a kind of qualities, but from what are on his view only wrongly thought to be qualities, and that just because primary qualities are qualities they are, in accordance with the Representative Theory of Perception, necessarily imperceptible; and that by "secondary qualities" he means, neither qualities nor ideas, but a third set of entities, which he calls "powers of bodies to produce ideas by means of (primary) qualities". First Boyle's use of the distinction will be examined, when it will be found that the elusive "power" is liable to be identified, even by Boyle, now with the quality on which it depends and now with the idea or sensation which the body produces by means of the quality. Next, the purpose which the distinction serves in Locke's view of our knowledge of the external world, will be discussed, and it will be contended that, so far from having been inherited from the Cartesians, the distinction is required by just that doctrine which both Locke and Boyle held in opposition to the Cartesians. Locke's definitions will then be considered in detail, and will be found to be embarrassed by two main difficulties: (A) by the connection between the distinction between primary and secondary qualities and a number of other distinctions such as those between (*a*) qualities and ideas, (*b*) macroscopic and microscopic qualities, (*c*) determinate and indeterminate qualities; (B) by Locke's omission to distinguish between the meanings of the terms "individual" and "particular," and in consequence between two views of our knowledge of the external world. An attempt will then be made to deal with Locke's statements about the resemblance of "ideas of primary qualities" to primary qualities and the non-resemblance of "ideas of secondary qualities" to secondary qualities. In conclusion, the view against which this article protests will be traced in Berkeley and Reid and in a number of modern writers.

Boyle's tract called "The Origin of Forms and Qualities according to the Corpuscular Philosophy"[2] aims at vindicating against both Scholastics and Cartesians what is called the Mechanical Philosophy, and especially the view that the only characteristics which it is necessary to recognise as inhering in bodies are impenetrability, which is common to all bodies, and various determinations of the spatial qualities, shape, size, and "motion-and-rest". The objection against the Scholastics is that they attribute all "natural effects," which Boyle thinks otherwise and more parsimoniously explicable, to "real qualities" supposed "distinct from the modification of matter they belong to and in some cases separate from all matter whatsoever".[3] The objection against the Cartesians is that their refusal to recognise impenetrability as a quality, common to all bodies and distinguishing them from the space they occupy, makes it impossible to talk in any straightforward sense of bodies at all.[4] It is in their determinate shape, size, and motion-and-rest, Boyle holds, that bodies differ from one another, and it is by means of these qualities that bodies act on our senses and on other bodies.[5] The power of a body to act on the senses in a given way by means of its qualities is called a "secondary" or "sensible quality,"[6] and it is distinguished both from the qualities on which it depends and from the effect on the percipient. Boyle's

[2] *Works* (ed. 1772), IV.
[3] P. 11.   [4] P. 35.   [5] P. 36.   [6] Pp. 23–24.

own illustration, in his "Excursion about the relative nature of Physical Qualities",[7] both makes this clear and shows why a secondary quality is easily mistaken for either a quality or a sensation. Of a key which fits a lock, we say it has the power to turn the lock, and of the lock we say it has the power to be turned. Yet "by these new attributes there was not added any real or physical entity either to the lock or to the key."[8] The power to turn the lock does not belong to the key in itself: a change in the lock might deprive the key of its power without any change in the key. On the other hand, the power to turn the lock is different from both the act of turning the lock and the condition of the lock when turned, and is in no sense a quality of the lock. Emphasis of either of these negative truths easily leads to neglect of the other. The same danger attends the term "secondary quality". "Though by virtue of a certain congruity . . . to our sensories, the portions of matter they [sensible qualities] modify are enabled to produce various effects . . . yet they are not in the bodies that are endowed with them any real or distinct entities or differing from the matter itself furnished with such a determinate bigness, shape, or other such modifications."[9] Even in this passage, where Boyle is concerned only with the use of the term "secondary quality," the last clause comes very near to identifying the secondary quality with the qualities by means of which the body has it. It is, therefore, not surprising that he makes such statements, as that the heat of the sun is "but the brisk and confused local motion of the minute parts of a body,"[10] while strictly, on his view, it is the power of the sun to produce certain effects on other bodies and on percipients by means of this local motion. On the other hand, in summing up, Boyle runs into the other confusion, and identifies the sensible qualities with "the perceptions of these impressions" and "the effects or consequents of the . . . primary affections of matter."[11] The latter confusion is made the more likely by the use of the term "sensible quality", an inheritance from a point of view to which the doctrine of Rep-

[7] P. 18 et seq.   [8] P. 18.   [9] P. 18.   [10] P. 21.
[11] P. 63.

resentative Perception is opposed. Its use by both Boyle and Locke to indicate what according to them is neither sensible nor a quality is singularly unhappy and seems to be among the difficulties which misled Berkeley in his criticism of Locke.

Postponing the examination of some serious difficulties in Locke's definitions of Primary and Secondary Qualities, we shall try to show the part which a distinction between qualities and powers would play in his theory of the nature of the external world. The need for such a distinction is occasioned by that feature of Locke's view in which he fundamentally disagrees with Descartes. While agreeing with Descartes in recognising two kinds of substance, the Conscious and the Extended, and further in recognising a plurality of conscious substances, he disagrees in recognising a plurality also of material substances. In Dr. Broad's terminology, both Descartes and Locke are Differentiating-Attribute Dualists, but, while both are Specific-Property Pluralists with reference to Mind, Descartes is a Specific-Property Monist and Locke a Specific-Property Pluralist with reference to Matter.[12] In other words, Locke, as a protagonist of the Corpuscular Philosophy of Boyle, holds not only that the external world exists in itself and can be known through itself, but also that its parts exist in themselves and can be known through themselves.[13] Now it is certain that bodies are at least related to one another and probable that they are also related to minds. Locke at any rate doubts neither proposition. In order, therefore, to distinguish knowledge of an individual body through itself from knowledge of its relations to other things, he is anxious to preserve an absolute distinction between qualities and relations. According to this distinction, knowledge of the relations in which a given body stands is, indeed, knowledge about this body, and may even be a clue to knowledge of what this body is in itself. But it is no more than a clue. Knowledge of what a given body is in itself is knowledge, not of the relations in which it stands, but

---

[12] *The Mind and its Place in Nature*, p. 20 *et seq.*
[13] That Boyle uses the term "Substance" strictly seems clear from *The Origin of Forms and Qualities*, p. 42.

of the qualities which it has. Now many apparent qualities turn out on investigation to be relations, and it is not always easy to decide whether an apparent quality is really a quality or not. But it is not difficult to illustrate the meaning of the distinction as Locke understands it. The shape of a given table is, *prima facie* at least, a quality of this table; but its being in this room is a relation because it involves something other than this table. A change in a relation would not logically, though it might causally, involve a change in the table, or would not itself *be*, though it—or what caused it—might *cause*, a change in the table. But a change in its shape would be *eo ipso* a change in the table.

It is, accordingly, an important part of Locke's programme to smell out pseudo-qualities. Now there is one kind of relation which he thinks especially likely to be mistaken for a quality, the kind of relation which, according to his wider use of the term, he calls a "power". The power of a body either to produce new qualities in another body or to produce an idea in the mind of a percipient is in ordinary discourse spoken of as a quality. The source of the mistake is, Locke thinks, our ignorance of the quality or qualities "by means of which" the body has the power. But according to Locke a body can have a power only by means of a quality, and as long as we know only the power we are ignorant of what the body is in itself; while, if we know the quality, we do not need to mention the power in a statement of what the body is in itself. To say of a body that it has the power to produce a certain effect affirms no more than that the realisation of this effect is causally dependent on a number of conditions, of which only the possession of an unknown quality by the body is known to be actual. To this it may be objected that we can never be sure that the body has a certain power without knowing also the quality on which the power depends. And this may be true. But we do sometimes have at least a strong reason for supposing that a body has a certain power, even when we have no suspicion of the nature of the quality or when the nature of the quality is conjectured in order to account for the power supposed already known. Thus, if we observe what happens when a number of bodies, which are not known to differ in relevant qualities, are successively introduced into an otherwise unchanging environment, we treat the differences in what happens as evidence of different powers of the bodies. Now Locke thinks that when we believe that a body has certain powers, but are ignorant of the qualities on which these powers depend, we should supplement a statement of what the body *is*, which will consist of a list of its known qualities, by a statement of what it *does* under certain conditions, so far as what it does under these conditions is not already accounted for in our statement of what it is. But, when in our ignorance of qualities we thus have recourse to powers, we should, he thinks, treat the powers not as themselves qualities, but as signs of unknown qualities. So taken, they will indicate not our knowledge of what a given body is in itself, but our knowledge of our partial ignorance of what this body is in itself, an ignorance which Locke sometimes hopes may be made good by the progress of Physical Science.

The distinction between Primary and Secondary qualities is a special case of the distinction between Qualities and Powers, secondary qualities and powers proper being species of powers. But Locke's definitions are complicated and embarrassed by an attempt to take account of distinctions other than that between qualities and powers: and, in accordance with the principle that definitions should be accepted where possible, it will be necessary to adduce arguments to show that Locke's language in the definitions is not altogether the language he would have used had he been fully aware of its implications.

There is a most formidable difficulty in Locke's definition of primary qualities. If we have interpreted him correctly, Locke means by primary qualities, not a kind of qualities, but all qualities, and he calls them primary to distinguish them, not from other qualities, but from powers, which are in his view not qualities at all but only wrongly supposed to be qualities. "Primary" is thus equivalent to "in the strict sense". Moreover it is a knowledge of qualities that is to constitute a knowledge of what an

Locke's Primary and Secondary Qualities 61

individual body is in itself. Now it is clear that the qualities of a body may cease to qualify it and be succeeded by others, and it may even be true that at every moment some of the qualities of a body are perishing. In any case, since the powers of a body depend on its qualities, its qualities are not more stable than its powers, though they are perhaps more stable than its actual behaviour. To the claim, then, that a knowledge of the qualities of an individual body is a knowledge of what the body is in itself, it may be objected, that, if by an individual body is meant something that persists through perishing states, a knowledge of its qualities is only a knowledge of what the individual body becomes, or is at a given moment. What is so known is not the persistent individual but its perishing states, which just because they are states of it are other than it. Now such criticism if pressed perhaps compels the abandonment of the attempt to know the persistent individual. It is probably because he feels uneasy about this danger that Locke tries to meet it by defining primary qualities in such a way as to enable them to qualify an individual body throughout its different states. Unfortunately for his purpose, he can do this only by taking qualities abstractly and by abstracting from just those determinations of qualities which on his view distinguish one body from another. The determinations, which, if taken as always qualifying the individual, are fatal to its persistence, are indispensable to its distinguishability from other individuals. Thus, because a piece of wax, which is spherical and at rest at one moment, may be cubical and in motion at another moment, Locke is unwilling to include its determinate shape and its determinate motion-and-rest among its primary qualities. But at every moment it has shape and motion-and-rest, if we abstract from the determinate form in which alone these qualities can exist. These, therefore, are primary qualities. But every other body also has shape and motion-and-rest. And Locke is not unaware of this consequence, which is admitted in his definition, primary qualities being defined as "such as are utterly inseparable from the body, in what state soever it be; and such as in all the alterations and changes it suffers, all the force can be used upon it, it constantly keeps; and such as sense constantly finds in every particle of matter which has bulk enough to be perceived; and the mind finds inseparable from every particle of matter, though less than to make itself singly perceived by our senses".[14]

In order to support the view that, while Locke had in mind in this definition the dangers we have just considered, he could not have defined primary qualities in this way without losing sight of the work for which he designed them, we shall first enquire into the consequences of his definition if strictly followed, and shall then adduce habitual and central doctrines which are incompatible with it.

First we must attempt a distinction, which Locke does not draw, between the terms "individual" and "particular," which Locke uses indiscriminately.[15] It does not matter for our present purpose whether these two terms are usually used indiscriminately, nor whether the meanings we shall assign to them are backed by customary usage. It does not matter even if the distinction is one that cannot be maintained without qualification when critically examined. It is at least a distinction between two conceptions which will serve to distinguish two different theses between which Locke does not seem to have finally chosen. By an individual, we shall mean something that persists through passing states and is able to retain its identity amid change only because the perishing qualities are not essential to it because not part of what is meant by it. By a particular, we shall mean something to which every quality, that belongs to it at all, is essential, and which, consequently, if even one quality gives place to another, ceases to exist and gives up its place to a new particular. A particular can have duration, therefore, only if, and for as long as, all its qualities endure. Now there are two roads open to Locke. Either he may try to show that the material world consists of a number of individual substances, each existing in itself and knowable through itself: or he

[14] II, viii, 9.   [15] III, iii, 1, 2, 6.

may, giving up the view that the individual substances are knowable through themselves, contend only that they are knowable through their particular perishing states. If the latter alternative is chosen it would be accurate to say, not that individual substances are known through their perishing states, but that only the particular perishing states are known, which is to confess that the substantial reference of the term "state" will be a serious difficulty.

It is the former alternative that attracts Locke when he is not attacking the problem in detail. For, whatever the difficulty of vindicating it, Locke throughout takes the view that there are persistent individual material substances, and that somehow we know this. And it is the former alternative which his definition both requires and excludes; requires, because invariability is part of what he means by a quality; yet excludes, because, inevitably, the invariable qualities he enumerates do not serve to distinguish one body from another. Now, if we ask what on this view is meant by the identity of an individual with itself at different times, the only possible answer would seem to be that which Locke gives in his chapter on Identity and Diversity.[16] The identity of an atom, we are there told, an atom being "a continued body under one immutable superficies", is determined by its relation to the time and the place in which it began to exist. The identity of a mass is determined by the identity of its constituent atoms, "let the parts be ever so differently jumbled". As the identity of the mass cannot be determined independently of the identity of the atoms, only the identity of the atom need engage our attention. And here we find that Locke's account of the identity of an individual substance is open to a fatal criticism. For its identity rests not on invariable qualities nor on any sort of qualities but on a relation, one, too, to something which is itself relative, since Locke admits "place" to be a relative term.[17] Thus the attempt to pursue this alternative results in an account of the would-be substance in terms not of qualities but of relations, and by abandoning the Specific-

[16] II, xxvii, 2, 4.   [17] II, xiii, 7–10.

Property Pluralism defeats the purpose of the distinction between primary and secondary qualities.

But it is the latter alternative which, despite the definition, dominates Locke's treatment. To mark a distinction to which reference has already been made, we shall use the terms "determinate qualities" and "indeterminate qualities". An example of the former is "equilateral triangularity", of the latter, "shape". It will be seen that determinateness admits of degrees. Thus "triangularity" is a quality of a degree of determinateness intermediate between those of the examples just given. We shall reckon among determinate qualities all qualities not common to all bodies. With this distinction we shall adduce the habitual and central doctrines which seem incompatible with Locke's definition of primary qualities.

Both the secondary qualities and the powers proper of a body depend on the primary qualities of its insensible parts.[18] But the secondary qualities and the powers proper of a given body are peculiar to it. Therefore, the primary qualities on which they depend must also be peculiar to it. These are, therefore, not common to all bodies and are determinate qualities. Secondly, we are ignorant of the primary qualities of the insensible parts of bodies, and it is just because of this ignorance that in trying to describe a given body we have recourse to its secondary qualities and powers proper. But we are acquainted with the primary qualities of the sensible parts. The primary qualities of the sensible parts are, therefore, different from those of the insensible parts and must be determinate qualities. Thirdly, it is possible "to alter . . . the bulk, figure, texture, and motion"[19] of a body. This is possible only if the qualities are determinate. Fourthly, abstract ideas are formed by "leaving out" of complex ideas "what is peculiar to each".[20] Now ideas of primary qualities are one of two kinds of original ideas of sensation. They are, therefore, not abstract ideas. But they are like the qualities of which they are ideas, and these qualities must accordingly be determinate. This last argument, however, should not be

[18] II, VIII, 10, 14, 23.   [19] II, VII, 23.   [20] III, III, 7.

pressed, as Locke's doctrine about the origin of ideas is not set forth until the third book; and there are also great difficulties in the way of interpreting the statement that primary qualities are like the ideas they produce.[21]

In one section[22] it looks almost as if Locke were attempting to distinguish determinate qualities under the name "real qualities", which he applies to "the *particular* bulk, number, figure, and motion of the parts of fire or snow," which "are really in them". But almost immediately[23] the terms "real qualities" and "primary qualities" are used as synonyms. So that this is only another argument in support of the view that in practice Locke does not regard determinateness as excluded by his definition of primary qualities.

In view, then, of the difficulties which the alternative involves and of the passages just cited, we seem right in concluding that despite his definition Locke does recognise determinate primary qualities and does not consider their fluctuating character to be an impediment. Though variable, their variations, unlike those of relations, are *eo ipso* variations of what they qualify. They are what the individual substance is at a given moment at least, as contrasted with what it does or may do, and in general as contrasted with the relations in which it stands. It is with determinate qualities, thus understood, that the secondary qualities should be contrasted, if the distinction between primary and secondary qualities is to be kept free from the perplexities of other issues.

In examining Locke's definition of secondary qualities it is necessary to take account of a distinction which he draws between two kinds of powers, "powers to produce various sensations in us" and "powers to alter the bulk, figure, texture, and motion of another body".[24] Only the former are called "Secondary Qualities" while only the latter, "which are allowed to be barely powers," are thereafter called "Powers". But it remains true that Locke does hold that secondary qualities are powers in the non-technical meaning of the word, and are not qualities. We

[21] *Infra*, p. 68. [22] II, VIII, 17. [23] II, VIII, 22.
[24] II, VIII, 10, 23, 24; XXIII, 7, 8.

have maintained that by primary qualities Locke means not a kind of qualities but qualities in the strict sense. Conformably with this he means by secondary qualities not a kind of qualities but entities that are wrongly supposed to be qualities and are really relations. The force of the qualification "secondary" is negative. Such a term as quasi-qualities would render Locke's meaning with less likelihood of misunderstanding. He himself insists on the contention that the secondary qualities are not qualities any more than are those powers which are "allowed to be barely powers"; and he uses the term secondary qualities only "to comply with the common way of speaking".[25]

There is a further restriction in the definitions of both secondary qualities and powers proper. They are said to depend not on all the primary qualities of a body but only on the primary qualities of the insensible parts.[26] Locke follows Boyle in his doctrine that the conditions of the various sensations are to be sought in various arrangements of minute particles of bodies. The terms "sensible" and "insensible parts" are open to the objection that they imply, what Locke denies, that if they are of a sufficient size bodies are perceptible. Instead, therefore, of the phrases "primary qualities of the sensible parts" and "primary qualities of the insensible parts" it will be convenient to use the modern terms "macroscopic" and "microscopic qualities". It may be thought that the restriction of the term "secondary qualities" to powers depending on microscopic qualities is not important, on the ground that all powers depend on microscopic qualities, including the powers to produce ideas of primary qualities. But unless situation is included among the primary qualities, it is impossible to ignore macroscopic qualities in an attempt to discover the conditions determining such ideas of sensation as apparent size and shape. And Locke does not include situation, because he admits "place" to be relative.[27] It is clear, too, that the qualities referred to in the heading, "How primary qualities produce their ideas,"[28] are macroscopic qualities. Locke holds, therefore, that some

[25] II, viii, 10.   [26] II, viii, 10, 23.   [27] II, xiii, 7–10.
[28] II, viii, 11.

powers to produce ideas depend on macroscopic qualities. And the failure to classify these powers is not confined to the definition. Locke never uses the term "secondary qualities" to indicate these powers. The only explanation seems to be that he does not think it important to refer to them, because he thinks that we already know the qualities on which they depend. But for this restriction, it would be true that all ideas are produced by secondary qualities. It is in any case true that all ideas are produced by primary qualities. Indeed, but for the restriction just noted, we should be doing only justice to Locke's view of power as something distinct from both idea and quality, by saying that all ideas are produced by secondary qualities by means of primary qualities. But the restriction of secondary qualities to powers depending on the microscopic qualities is important and is probably the key to the problem which has now to be considered.

At least one important test of an interpretation of Locke's distinction between primary and secondary qualities is its success in dealing with the puzzling doctrine that primary qualities are like the ideas they produce in us, while secondary qualities are unlike the ideas they produce in us, and with the even more puzzling terminology according to which the ideas said to be produced by the primary qualities are called ideas of primary qualities, while those said to be produced by the secondary qualities are called ideas of secondary qualities.[29] On the view that primary qualities are themselves perceived, or that secondary qualities are mind-dependent ideas, it is hard to see what could be made of either the doctrine or the terminology. It remains to attempt to deal with these difficulties on the view that primary qualities are qualities and secondary qualities are powers. On this view one and the same idea may be said to be produced by either a primary or a secondary quality, in much the same way as one and the same law may be said to be produced by either the nature or the power of a legislature. But we have seen that Locke uses the term "secondary quality" only of powers

[29] II, VIII, 13, 15.

dependent on what he calls "the primary qualities of the insensible parts". The ideas of the secondary qualities are, therefore, probably held to be produced by microscopic qualities, while the ideas of the primary qualities are probably held to be produced by macroscopic qualities. Locke's doctrine then will be that macroscopic qualities produce resembling ideas, while microscopic qualities produce non-resembling ideas. But what the ideas produced by the microscopic qualities fail to resemble is not the secondary qualities, but the microscopic qualities themselves. There would be no sense in saying that an idea does not resemble a power to produce it. And in fact Locke is inclined to vary the statement that secondary qualities produce ideas that do not resemble them by such statements as that there is nothing like our ideas existing in the bodies themselves,[30] and that "what is sweet, blue, or warm in idea, is but the certain bulk, figure, and motion of the insensible parts, in the bodies themselves, which we call so".[31] This is a point worth making. It was, and still is, widely, if vaguely, believed, that bodies have colour, heat, etc., without its being noticed that if these are qualities of bodies they can neither be nor resemble sensibilia. It is clear, too, that on the Representative Theory of Perception, nothing is to be gained by supposing that microscopic qualities do resemble sensibilia.

But how can the macroscopic qualities, any more than the microscopic qualities, resemble the ideas they produce? At least one reason for maintaining the Representative Theory of Perception, with its distinction between qualities and ideas, is the recognition of the ubiquitous permeation of the objects of perception by illusory characteristics. It is in fact just because all ideas are unlike any qualities that, we might suppose, Locke holds that no ideas are qualities. He must know, then, that the statement, that "a circle or square are the same, whether in idea or existence, in the mind or in the manna",[32] is not true, if it means that a surface of a certain shape produces a percept of the same shape. There would be more to be

[30] II, viii, 15.   [31] II, viii, 15.   [32] II, viii, 18.

said for the statement that the perceived shape resembles the shape of the surface that produces it, to the extent to which a figure resembles its projection on a surface that distorts it. Locke might also say that we are able to allow for the distortion by an inference, or by a process which simulates inference, and so to arrive at an idea which completely resembles the shape of the surface and even perhaps of the whole body. But, if nothing short of complete resemblance is claimed, and that between the original idea of sensation and the quality that produces it, this can be allowed only if the quality is taken to be indeterminate, and the idea (impossible since it is an original idea) to be an abstract idea.

So much for the doctrine. But what is meant by calling these two sets of ideas, ideas of primary and secondary qualities respectively? The phrase "idea of" is readily taken to mean "apprehension of". But Locke does not think that either primary or secondary qualities (or the microscopic qualities on which secondary qualities depend) are perceived, and perception is the only kind of apprehension that is here in question. Moreover he defines "idea" as an object apprehended.[33] Lastly, it must be an object if the statement that it is like or unlike a quality is to be significant. Again, "idea of" might mean "idea, namely," the phrase being parallel to such phrases as "City of Troy"; and this is one possible interpretation of such phrases as "idea of blue", if "blue" is supposed to be a sensible and not either a group of microscopic qualities or a secondary quality. But again, Locke cannot be supposed to identify the idea and that which it is said to be "of" in the phrases we are examining, least of all when the idea is said to be unlike the quality, and not without extreme impropriety when it is said to be like the quality. Possibly "of" is equivalent to "representing" or "doing duty for". The idea of a primary quality (or rather a macroscopic quality) represents the quality in our complex idea of the body. This seems to be sanctioned by general usage. My "idea of a horse" is used to mean an object which I apprehend and

[33] *Intro.* 8, II, VIII, 8.

which represents and resembles, more or less according to my knowledge, a horse. But the idea of a secondary quality represents and fails to resemble, not a secondary quality, but the quality on which the secondary quality depends. Here, as often, Locke seems to confuse the secondary quality with the quality on which it depends. The accurate statement of his doctrine would seem to be, "Ideas which are produced by microscopic qualities are unlike those qualities, but they represent them in our naïve complex ideas of bodies".

Before passing to those writers who have represented primary qualities as perceptible qualities of bodies and secondary qualities as mind-dependent sensibilia, we shall cite a few passages in the *Essay* which countenance this interpretation. The passages we have just examined illustrate the tendency to identify secondary qualities with the qualities on which they depend. It is only by supposing that Locke does this that we have been able to attach any meaning to the phrase "idea of a secondary quality" and to the statement that secondary qualities are unlike the ideas they produce in us. And the statement that "what is sweet, blue, or warm in idea, is but the certain bulk, figure, and motion of the insensible parts, in the bodies themselves" involves the same inaccuracy as Boyle's identification of the heat of the sun with the motion of its parts. But Locke more frequently identifies secondary qualities with the sensations they produce. Thus he draws a distinction between secondary qualities immediately and mediately *perceivable*.[34] He also compares them to pain and says: "Take away the sensation of them; let not the eyes see light or colours, nor the ears hear sound; let the palate not taste, nor the nose smell; and all colours, tastes, odours, and sounds, as they are such particular ideas, vanish and cease, and are reduced to their causes".[35] The qualification "as they are such particular ideas" should really read "or rather the ideas which these powers produce". Locke also, like Boyle, uses the term "sensible qualities" as a term equivalent to "secondary qualities",[36] which

[34] II, viii, 26; xxiii, 7.   [35] II, viii, 17.   [36] II, viii, 23.

Locke's Primary and Secondary Qualities 71

leads to confusion in Berkeley. The difficulty is largely due to the fact that, whether secondary qualities are to mean powers as with Locke, or unknown qualities as with Reid, we have as a rule only one word to indicate both the secondary quality and what Locke calls the idea of it. Lastly, there are many passages in which bodies and their qualities are said or implied to be perceptible. The terms "sensible" and "insensible parts", strictly read, have this implication, and it is explicit in such statements as, "We perceive these original qualities"[37] and the "[primary qualities of bodies] are really in them—whether anyone's senses perceive them or no".[38] Such irregularities have encouraged the supposition that the primary qualities themselves become ideas by being perceived, which is inconsistent with the whole doctrine of Representative Perception, as embodied in Locke's distinction between Qualities and Ideas. It may be noted, before leaving the passages opposed to the view we have taken, that "Quality" is defined as "the power to produce any idea in our mind".[39] But it seems clear from the paragraph which precedes that in which this definition occurs that Locke really means qualities to indicate "modifications of matter", in which case this is no more than another instance of his inaccuracy.

It remains to trace what seems an erroneous interpretation of Locke's distinction in the writings of Berkeley and Reid and of some modern critics.

Berkeley in *The Principles of Human Knowledge* understands Locke to mean by primary and secondary qualities not imperceptible qualities and powers but perceptible qualities and mind-dependent ideas. Thus "those who assert that figure, motion, and the rest of the primary or original qualities, do exist without the mind" acknowledge that "secondary qualities do not, which they tell us are sensations existing in the mind alone, that depend on and are occasioned by the different size, texture, and motion of the minute particles of matter".[40] Again, those "who make a distinction between primary and secondary quali-

[37] II, VIII, 12.   [38] II, VIII, 17.   [39] II, VIII, 8.   [40] X.

ties" are said to mean extension, etc., by primary qualities, and by secondary qualities "all other sensible qualities".[41] This implies that both primary and secondary qualities are sensible qualities and Berkeley has already defined sensible qualities as "the ideas perceived by sense".[42] The awkwardness of this interpretation appears in the argument that what has been proved of "certain sensible qualities", namely, that they "have no existence in matter, or without the mind" "may be likewise proved of all other sensible qualities whatsoever".[43] The awkwardness arises from the fact that Locke's distinction between primary and secondary qualities is grounded on the Representative Theory of Perception, which Berkeley's version of the distinction ignores and precludes. The result is that Berkeley, in order to argue that the variability of our ideas, which Locke found incompatible with the view that the ideas of the secondary qualities resemble qualities of bodies, is equally incompatible with the view that the ideas of the primary qualities do so, has to take "the existence in matter or without the mind" of "sensible qualities" to mean their resemblance to qualities of matter, and by implication to represent Locke as having maintained that primary qualities resemble qualities but that secondary qualities do not. In fact the distinction between qualities and ideas of qualities, on which Locke's whole doctrine of our knowledge of the external world is based, becomes meaningless when qualities are taken to be themselves ideas, some mind-dependent, and some independent. The argument that the primary qualities "are inseparably united with the other sensible qualities",[44] an argument which has been often renewed, notably in the first chapter of Bradley's *Appearance and Reality*[45] (where, however, Bradley does not claim to be discussing Locke's distinction), is valid only if secondary qualities are taken to mean mind-dependent ideas. If the terms are used in accordance with Locke's definitions, there is no difficulty whatever in conceiving primary qualities without secondary qualities, the difficulty being rather to conceive them with secondary

[41] IX.   [42] VII.   [43] XIV.   [44] X.   [45] Pp. 16–17.

Locke's Primary and Secondary Qualities 73

qualities; and there is further no reason on Locke's view why primary qualities should be able to be conceived without secondary qualities, for Locke never asserts that they exist without secondary qualities, but only that often the secondary qualities fail to produce ideas.

Reid in his *Inquiry into the Human Mind* habitually takes Locke to mean by secondary qualities what Reid calls sensations or ideas,[46] and accordingly traces back the distinction between Primary and Secondary Qualities to Democritus.[47] He himself means by secondary qualities the unknown qualities of bodies which produce sensations in us,[48] the qualities by means of which bodies have secondary qualities according to Locke. Reid claims that his usage is in accordance with common sense.[49] He admits, however, that nothing could be more shocking to the plain man than that colour should be alleged to be in that which he conceives to be invisible.[50] Yet he himself means by colour the unknown cause of a known effect,[51] and it is only by making perception cover the whole process of apprehension of both sign and significate that he can say on his view that colour is a quality of something visible. In fact the plain man has to be shocked one way or another. Either we may try to save such statements as "This body is blue", by taking blue to mean, either, with Reid, an unknown quality of the body which causes the presentation of a sensibile, or, with Locke, the power to produce a sensibile by means of the unknown quality; or we may try to save such statements as "this colour is brighter than that", by taking colour to mean what Reid calls a sensation and what Locke calls "an idea of a secondary quality".

Reid's criticism of Locke[52] provides a good illustration of the elusive nature of what Locke meant by power. It is because he recognises no third entity, but takes the only possible alternatives to be the view that secondary qualities are unknown qualities and the view that they are ideas, that Reid, seeing that Locke did not accept the former,

[46] *Inq.*, V, 4, 8; VI, 6.   [47] V, 4.
[48] II, 8; IV, 1; VI, 4, 5.   [49] VI, 5.   [50] VI, 5.
[51] VI, 4.   [52] VI, 6.

supposes that he must have accepted the latter, and chooses the former for himself. His difficulty appears clearly in the following passage: "We see then, that Locke, having found that the ideas of secondary qualities are no resemblances, was compelled, by a hypothesis common to all philosophers to deny that they[53] are real qualities of body. It is more difficult to assign a reason why, after this, he should call them secondary qualities; for this name, if I mistake not, was of his invention. Surely he did not mean that they were secondary qualities of the mind; and I do not see with what propriety, or even by what tolerable licence, he could call them secondary qualities of body, after finding that they were no qualities of body at all."[54] This quite misses Locke's view that it is because they are relations of a body to something else that the secondary qualities should not be regarded as qualities, and yet, though they do not belong to a body in itself, that they do belong to it in some sense, while they belong to the mind in no sense.

As there are many statements which may be made about either sensibilia or powers to produce sensibilia, it is not always possible to ascertain which of these two meanings a writer assigns to the term "secondary quality". But the identification of secondary qualities with sensibilia, which is usually accompanied by the supposition that primary qualities are perceptible, seems to be common to a number of modern critics.

Thus Prof. Campbell Fraser, both in his article in the *Encyclopædia Britannica*[55] and in his edition of the *Essay*, both identifies secondary qualities with ideas of secondary qualities and takes primary qualities to be perceptible. In the article, commenting on Bk. II, c. 8 of the *Essay*, he declares the distinction between primary and secondary qualities to be a distinction between two kinds

---

[53] Reid does not seem to distinguish between Locke's "secondary qualities" and Locke's "ideas of secondary qualities". It is hard to see what this distinction could be if secondary qualities are taken to mean ideas. *Cf.* Berkeley's difficulty in his argument for the reduction of primary qualities to the status of secondary qualities (*supra*).
[54] VI, 6.   [55] Art., "John Locke."

of "sense-data", the primary qualities being "revelations of external things in their mathematical relations" and the secondary qualities being "sensations". In the introduction to his edition of the *Essay*, he says that Locke refers all secondary or imputed qualities of outward things to the mind[56] and cites with approval Berkeley's argument that it is impossible to have ideas of solid atoms without imputing some secondary qualities.[57]

Prof. Gibson in his *Locke's Theory of Knowledge* is less definite. But he seems, like Reid, to miss the alternative which Locke chose, when he says, "As powers in the things, the secondary qualities can be nothing but primary qualities".[58] He seems also to take secondary qualities to be sensibilia when he says that "any apparent characteristics of a thing which it possesses at one time but not at another are merely *indications of* relations in which it stands to other things and to our minds and are secondary qualities".[59] It is not surprising, therefore, that he should hold that "the doctrine covered by these terms originated among the Greek Atomists and was revived by Galileo and Descartes".[60]

Prof. Kemp Smith in his *Prolegomena to an Idealist Theory of Knowledge*, in discussing the passage in *Il Saggiatore*, where Galileo is supposed to have anticipated Locke's distinction between primary and secondary qualities, but in which Galileo really draws a distinction between qualities and what Locke calls ideas,[61] in a footnote[62] credits Locke only with the terms, and treats the distinction as one among sensibilia. And in the *Studies in the Cartesian Philosophy*, in the chapter on Cartesian Principles in Locke, he takes the same view: "We do not

[56] CXXVIII.
[57] CXXIX. *Cf.* also footnotes, p. 168, n. 4, p. 173, n. 2 (which gives a strange interpretation of Locke's doctrine of "Resemblance"). P. 158, n. 1 (which identifies primary qualities with visual and tactual sense-data). P. 170, n. 4 (which identifies secondary qualities with sensations). *Cf.* also *Selections from Berkeley*, 5th ed., p. 38, n. 3, p. 42, n. 3.
[58] Pp. 102–103.
[59] P. 101. (Italics mine.)   [60] P. 101.
[61] *Il Sag.*, sec. 48.   [62] P. 22.

know that constitution of the minute parts on which all the other qualities depend ... even if we did, we would not be able to perceive any connexion between it and the sensation which the body produces in us. Primary and secondary qualities are not related as substance to its properties but as cause to effect."[63] Again, "If that is a true interpretation of the movement of Locke's mind, he would thereby be brought to hold that what is true of the unbridgeable qualitative differences between the secondary qualities must be true of all sensations regarded as mental states".[64]

Dr. Whitehead, in *The Concept of Nature*, interprets Locke in the same way. "Locke met this difficulty by a theory of primary and secondary qualities. Namely, there are some attributes of matter which we do perceive. These are the primary qualities, and there are other things which we perceive, such as colours, which are not attributes of matter, but are perceived by us as if they were such attributes. These are the secondary qualities of matter."[65]

Dr. G. A. Johnston takes the same view in his *Development of Berkeley's Philosophy*, where he identifies secondary qualities with ideas of secondary qualities.[66] So, too, Dr. Höffding in his *History of Modern Philosophy* assigns the authorship of the distinction between primary and secondary qualities to Galileo and treats it as a distinction common to all exponents of the Representative Theory of Perception.[67]

The current use of the terms "primary" and "secondary qualities" hardly needs illustration. Bradley's use of the terms in *Appearance and Reality* has already been noticed. They are similarly used by Dr. Alexander in *Space, Time and Deity*.[68] And they have been recently defined in this sense with great precision by Dr. Broad. "A Primary Quality is a determinate characteristic which, we have reason to believe, inheres literally and dyadically in some physical object in some determinate form or other." "A Secondary Quality is a determinate characteristic which certainly inheres or seems to inhere literally and dyadically

[63] P. 211.   [64] P. 184.   [65] P. 27.   [66] Pp. 40–41.
[67] Vol. I, pp. 183, 384.   [68] Vol. II, pp. 55–56, 138.

in the objective constituents of some perceptual situations in some determinate form or other, but which there is no reason to believe inheres literally and dyadically in any physical object." "A Primary Quality, may, but need not, inhere literally and dyadically in some objective constituent."[69] As examples of secondary qualities he cites colour and temperature, as examples of primary qualities which inhere in both physical objects and objective constituents, shape, size and position, and as examples of primary qualities which inhere only in physical objects, electric charge and magnetic properties. With the convenience or otherwise of this use of these terms for the purposes of current speculation this article is not concerned. But, if the interpretation of Locke's distinction which this article attempts is the true one, the current usage needs to be distinguished from it.

[69] *Mind and its Place in Nature*, p. 206.

DID BERKELEY MISUNDERSTAND LOCKE?

WINSTON H. F. BARNES

In a paper published some years ago (reprinted in this volume, pp. 53–77 above) Mr. Reginald Jackson argued that Locke's doctrine of Primary and Secondary Qualities had been persistently misinterpreted by subsequent philosophers. The real doctrine which Locke expounds is, as the author shows, the doctrine that primary qualities are genuinely qualities of bodies, whereas secondary qualities are 'powers which a body possesses in virtue of the primary qualities of its insensible parts'. Neither the qualities proper nor the powers are to be confused with the ideas which they respectively cause, whereas the distinction 'which Locke was supposed by Berkeley and Reid to have drawn, is between qualities of bodies (these qualities being supposed to be perceptible) and ideas, sensations, or, in current terminology, sensibilia (supposed not to exist independently of the perception of them and to be the effect of the action of bodies on minds)'.[1] Again, the author says: 'Berkeley in *The Principles of Human Knowledge* understands Locke to mean by primary and secondary qualities not imperceptible qualities and powers but perceptible qualities and mind-dependent ideas'.[2]

In this note I wish to refute the charge so far as it concerns Berkeley. I am not concerned with Reid or any later philosophers.

It would be a surprising fact, if true, that Berkeley should have misunderstood Locke on this matter. Locke's

From *Mind*, Vol. XLIX (1940). Reprinted by permission of the author and *Mind*.

[1] *Op cit.*, p. 54.   [2] *Op cit.*, p. 71.

Did Berkeley Misunderstand Locke? 79

Essay formed his main philosophical reading, and we know that he paid particular attention to the chapter of the *Essay* in which the distinction between primary and secondary qualities is discussed by Locke, referring even to the particular section in which Locke most precisely defines his position.[3]

(i) Let us consider first the assertion that Berkeley held that by primary qualities Locke meant perceptible *qualities*, *i.e.*, that according to Locke we perceive the extension, motion, etc., of bodies. On a number of different occasions Berkeley presents the argument that it is absurd to talk of archetypes or patterns of our ideas existing in bodies: (*a*) *Commonplace Book*, 666, where Berkeley first put forward his contention that 'an idea can resemble nothing but an idea'; (*b*) *The Principles*, § 8; (*c*) *ibidem*, § 56; (*d*) *ibidem*, § 90; (*e*) *Three Dialogues*—Fraser, vol. 1, p. 465. All these passages are an attack on the theory that the ideas of sensible qualities have corresponding archetypes or originals in matter, and they presuppose that the view they are attacking makes a distinction between ideas and their archetypes, *e.g.*, between the idea of extension and the quality of extension in the body. If it is Locke's views that are under consideration it is clear that Berkeley's argument recognises them to imply a distinction between the *ideas* of primary qualities and the primary qualities themselves. But there is no very strong evidence that the argument is directed against Locke's theory, though it is usually supposed to be and I am inclined to think it is. Slight evidence, however, there is. In § 9 of the *Principles* the subject of primary and secondary qualities is introduced for the first time, and here Locke is obviously the object of criticism. In § 14, which continues this criticism, Berkeley uses the same argument about the absurdity of supposing archetypes with reference to Locke. If, then, these passages do refer to Locke, Berkeley obviously understood Locke to make a distinction between the primary

[3] *Commonplace Book*: 114. P. Round figure a perception or sensation in the mind, but in the body is a power. L.b. 2, c. 8, s. 8; 115. Mem. Mark well the later part of the last cited section; 338. P. Mem. Strictly to remark L.b. 2, c. 8, s. 8.

qualities (which exist in the body and are not perceptible) and the ideas of them (which are perceptible but have no existence in the body).

Curiously enough, the best evidence that Berkeley understood perfectly well that Locke by primary qualities meant imperceptible qualities and not perceptible qualities comes from a passage quoted by Mr. Jackson to prove exactly the opposite. It is from § 9 of the *Principles*. The first two sentences quoted by Mr. Jackson run as follows: "Some there are who make a distinction betwixt *primary* and *secondary* qualities. By the former they mean extension, figure, motion, rest, solidity or impenetrability, and number; by the latter they denote all other sensible qualities, as colours, sounds, tastes and so forth." If this passage stood alone I do not think we could have any doubt that Berkeley had misunderstood Locke. For it would then naturally be interpreted to mean that Locke supposed figure, motion, etc., to be sensible qualities. But the next sentence proceeds as follows: "The ideas we have of these last they acknowledge not to be the resemblances of anything existing without the mind, or unperceived; but they will have our ideas of the *primary qualities* to be patterns or images of things which exist without the mind, in an unthinking substance which they call Matter". This sentence elucidates the meaning of the previous two sentences. It makes clear that Berkeley understood correctly that, for Locke, our *ideas* of the primary qualities exist in the mind, whereas the qualities themselves are the archetypes existing in an unthinking substance.

(ii) Did Berkeley misunderstand Locke's view as to the nature of secondary qualities? Did he think Locke meant by them mind-dependent ideas, and fail to grasp that Locke's doctrine was in fact that the secondary qualities are powers in bodies?

In the *Principles*, § 10, Berkeley says: "They who assert that figure, motion and the rest of the primary or original qualities do exist without the mind, in unthinking substances, do at the same time acknowledge that colours, sounds, heat, cold and suchlike secondary qualities, do not; which they tell us are sensations, existing in the mind alone, that depend on and are occasioned by the different size, texture, and motion of the minute particles of matter."

I do not think it possible to deny that Berkeley here uses the term 'secondary qualities' in a misleading way. But even here it seems to me that what Berkeley does is not to *misunderstand* Locke's theory, but to give to the term 'secondary qualities' a meaning other than that which Locke, when he is speaking exactly, gives to it. This is certainly regrettable, considering that it occurs in a passage which is a statement of Locke's doctrine, but it does not necessarily mean that the doctrine has been misunderstood. Berkeley, I think, is here using the terms 'primary qualities' and 'secondary qualities' simply as shorthand expressions for two groups of phenomena, figure, etc., on the one hand, colour, etc., on the other, to save the trouble of enumerating the whole group. Read in this way the passage is a fairly good account of Locke's views. For it attributes to Locke the view that figure, motion, etc., exist without the mind (*i.e.*, as qualities in bodies *as well as* ideas in the mind); whereas colour, sound, etc., exist only as ideas in the mind, being caused by the figure, motion, etc., in the body. This seems the obvious meaning of the passage taken as a whole; and it represents quite fairly what Locke himself says.

(iii) There is, however, one further point which requires further defence. Locke, when he speaks exactly, applies the term 'secondary qualities' to *powers* in bodies to produce various sensations in us by their primary qualities. It is not easy to see what importance should be attached to the distinction between the statement that ideas of colour, etc., are caused by powers a body possesses in virtue of its primary qualities and the statement that they are caused by the primary qualities. But such as it is, Locke, in his exacter moments, made the distinction.

Although Berkeley is not guilty of attributing to Locke the view that secondary qualities are mind-dependent ideas, he does seem to have failed to make this distinction in the *Principles*, § 10, between the qualities bodies possess and the powers they possess in virtue of those qualities. How venial the offence is may be judged by considering that Locke himself slips into committing it immediately after he has made the distinction between powers and qualities.[4]

Nevertheless there are reasons for supposing that Berkeley was perfectly well aware of Locke's doctrine of 'powers'. He seems, in fact, to have proceeded from a modification of Locke's view concerning the external causes of our ideas to his own doctrine of "*esse* is *percipi*"; and, in doing so, to have reflected earnestly upon the doctrine of powers. Although he early realised that there could be no knowledge of the particular nature of the qualities or powers that cause our ideas he did not at once scrap the notion of powers. An early entry in the *Commonplace Book* reads:—

41. "Nothing corresponds to our primary ideas without but powers. Hence a direct and brief demonstration of an active powerfull being distinct from us, on whom we depend, etc."

It is worth noticing that Berkeley here refers to primary *ideas,* showing that he recognises a distinction between the ideas of extension, motion, etc., and their causes. But he has given up the notion that the causes in any way resemble the ideas and so calls them powers, not qualities. The same distinction between the ideas and the powers is found in:

52. "Bodies, etc., do exist even when not perceived— they being powers in the active being."

Yet another entry is obviously important in its reference to Locke, but is very difficult to interpret:—

81. "I am more certain of ye existence and reality of bodies than Mr. Locke; since he pretends onely to what he calls sensitive knowledge, whereas I think I have demon-

---

[4] *Essay*, II, 8, § 15: On secondary qualities Locke writes: "They are in the bodies we denominate from them, only a power to produce those sensations in us: and what is sweet, blue or warm in idea, *is but the certain bulk, figure and motion of the insensible parts in the bodies themselves which we call so*". My italics.

Did Berkeley Misunderstand Locke? 83

strative knowledge of their existence—by them meaning combinations of powers in an unknown substratum."

It appears that the last phrase refers to an early view which Berkeley held, *viz.*, that an object is a combination of powers inhering in a substance of which we can know nothing.[5]

If this interpretation is correct it seems that he later came to think that the notion of an unknown substratum was ridiculous; that there was no reason to suppose a special power to produce such idea, but that only one power, God, was necessary. It is perhaps significant that the fourth entry after the one quoted immediately above reads:—

85. "Powers. *Quaere* whether more or one onely?"

The development of Berkeley's thought is perhaps to be seen in the following entries of the *Commonplace Book:*—

130. "M. Matter tho' allowed to exist may be no greater than a pin's head."

133. "M. No active power but the Will: therefore Matter, if it exists, affects us not."

However, the notion of powers did not disappear very easily from Berkeley's thought, for a later entry reads:

290. "M. Bodies &c. do exist whether we think of them or no, they being taken in twofold sense—collections of thoughts and collections of powers to cause those thoughts. These later exist; tho' perhaps *a parte rei* it may be one simple perfect power."

Again in another entry:—

302. "The twofold signification of Bodies, *viz.*, Combinations of thoughts and Combinations of powers to raise thoughts."

[5] This is the interpretation of the passage adopted by Mr. G. H. Johnston in his edition of the *Commonplace Book* (p. 121). Another possible interpretation is that the last phrase refers to Locke's doctrine, not Berkeley's. But if this is so and Berkeley was at this time believing that the ideas *are* the object, it is difficult to see why he should claim that we have demonstrative knowledge of objects. He ought to claim, on Locke's terminology, that we have intuitive knowledge of objects. (The reference in these terms is to Locke's *Essay*, IV, 2, where intuitive, demonstrative and sensitive knowledge are compared.)

In Entry 515 Berkeley is moving away from the twofold signification of bodies, for he writes:—

515. "Qu. whether the substance of body or anything else be any more than the collection of ideas included in that thing?"

And finally:

814. "Not to mention the combination of powers, but to say the things—the effects themselves—to really exist, even when not actually perceived; but still with relation to perception."

The 'twofold signification' is Berkeley's attempt to make explicit Locke's doctrine concerning white, cold and round, which "as they are in the snowball, I call qualities, and as they are sensations or perceptions in our understandings, I call them ideas".

All these entries make it abundantly clear that Berkeley was well aware of the distinction which Locke drew between imperceptible powers and mind-dependent ideas. He was himself elaborating the distinction only to find that it had to be scrapped in the end.

Mr. Jackson attempts to clinch the matter by the contention that "the argument that the primary qualities 'are inseparably united with the other sensible qualities' . . . is valid only if secondary qualities are taken to mean mind-dependent ideas".[6] If this contention were sound it would be shattering to my defence of Berkeley. The whole passage in Berkeley is as follows:—

"Now, if it be certain that these *original* qualities are inseparably united with the sensible qualities, and not, even in thought, capable of being abstracted from them, it plainly follows that *they* exist only in the mind."[7]

Berkeley's use of the terms 'original qualities' and 'other sensible qualities' is, once again, a shorthand one. He is not using 'other sensible qualities' as Locke, when he speaks exactly, would use the term. But this difference in usage is not a misunderstanding of Locke. When Berkeley says that colour, taste, etc., exist *only in the mind* this is his way of saying that there is nothing like our ideas of

---

[6] Op cit., p. 72.   [7] *Principles*, § 10.

Did Berkeley Misunderstand Locke? 85

colour, taste, etc., in the body. This still allows of the existence in the body of powers which cause ideas of colour, etc., and is in harmony with Locke. But, of course, when Berkeley concludes in the course of developing his own theory that figure, motion, etc., exist only in the mind, this carries with it an implication concerning colours, tastes, etc., *viz.*, that there are no qualities of body at all and consequently no powers to cause ideas of colour, etc., and this separates him from Locke.

SUBSTANCE, REALITY, AND PRIMARY QUALITIES
JONATHAN BENNETT

Two bad mistakes have been taken over from Berkeley by most philosophers who have read and assessed him with the casualness usually accorded to the great, dead philosophers. Each mistake is in the nature of a conflation or running together of two philosophical doctrines which ought to be kept apart, and thus a conflation also of the problems which the doctrines offer to solve. The doctrines in question are all expounded in Locke's *Essay Concerning Human Understanding*. They are: (1) a certain account of what it is for a property to be instantiated by something; (2) a certain account of the distinction between appearance and reality, or between how it is with me and how it is with the world; and (3) a thesis about primary and secondary qualities. Locke certainly accepted (2) and (3). His scathing attacks on (1) have usually been taken as a defence of it—here Locke has suffered the usual fate of the ironist.

In the first part of my paper I shall discuss the conflation by Berkeley, and by most English philosophers since his time, of (1) with (2). This conflation is, specifically, an *identification*: Berkeley and others have actually failed to see that (1) and (2) are distinct. The conflation of (2) with (3)—which I shall treat in the second part of the paper—has not usually taken the extreme form of an identifying of the two doctrines with one another. Occasionally, (3) is described as a "version" of (2), but a more

From the *American Philosophical Quarterly*, Vol. 2 (1965). Reprinted, with minor corrections, by permission of the author and the *American Philosophical Quarterly*.

Substance, Reality, and Primary Qualities 87

common mistake is the milder one of treating (3) as being integrally connected with (2) in a way in which it is not.

In respect to both parts of the paper, I have been greatly helped by criticism from Peter Bell and Ian Hacking.

My interest in these conflations is philosophical rather than exegetical. If distinct false theories—such as (1) and (2)—are identified with one another, it will be harder to see why they are false and where the truth lies. Furthermore, I shall argue that there is something true and important which Locke, in his doctrine (3), was struggling to say about primary and secondary qualities. Yet his gestures in the right direction have not been followed up as they deserved; and it seems that post-Lockean philosophers' neglect of the primary/secondary distinction has been due to their thinking that what Locke says about the distinction is an integral part, or one formulation, of a single monolithic doctrine of which (1) and (2) are also essential ingredients. This has tarred the primary/secondary distinction with the same brush as some things which have rightly been rejected, and so something important has been overlooked.

Through all the Berkeleian commentaries which identify (1) with (2), and wrongly connect (2) with (3), there is inevitably an appreciable haze of vagueness and failure of grasp. This does especial harm by nourishing the assumption that the study of philosophers like Locke and Berkeley is only a marginally useful activity which may be adequately conducted with the mind in neutral. In fact, it can be one of the most rewarding and demanding of philosophical exercises.

PART I

1. *The Substance Doctrine*

The account of property-instantiation which I call "Lockean," meaning that Locke said a good deal about it, is a view about the logic of subject-predicate statements. What concepts—or, as Locke would put it, what *ideas*—

are involved in the subject of the statement that *The pen in my hand is expensive?* Certainly, the concepts of being a pen, and of being in my hand; but these are not enough, for the statement speaks of a *thing which* is a pen and is in my hand. What thing is this? I may answer that it is the purple thing which I now see before me; but when I say that the purple thing I now see is a pen and is in my hand, I speak of a *thing which* is purple, etc., and so my introduction of "purple" and "seen by me" still fails to capture the whole concept of the subject in the original statement. Even if I produce some non-trivial truth of the form "The . . . is purple, is seen by me, and is a pen in my hand," this can be only a delaying action. Sooner or later, I must admit that this kind of expansion is bound to omit an essential element from the concept of the pen in my hand. What is missing is the concept of a *thing which* . . . : this is an ingredient in the concept of a *thing which is F* for each value of *F*, and is therefore not identical with the concept of a *thing which is F* for any value of *F*. This omnipresent constituent of any subject-concept is the concept of a property-bearer, or of a possible subject of predication. Let us call it the concept of a *substance*. It appears then that if any subject-predicate—or any existential—statements are true, there must be two basic sorts of item: (a) substances, and (b) qualities or properties. It is the special privilege of substances that they can bear or have or support qualities, and cannot in the same way be borne by anything else. We commit ourselves to the existence of "substances" in this sense every time we affirm of some property that it is instantiated by something or other: for a property to be instantiated is for there to be some substance which has or bears it.

I offer the foregoing paragraph as a rational reconstruction of one strand in the substantialism which Locke discusses in *Essay* II, xxiii, 1–4. In § 2 he says: "The idea then we have, to which we give the general name substance, being nothing but the supposed but unknown support of those qualities we find existing, which, we imagine, cannot subsist *sine re substante*, without something to support them, we call that support *substantia*, which, according to the true import of the word is, in plain English, standing under, or upholding." It is usual for Locke to say that we cannot "imagine" how qualities or accidents can exist unsupported, but the substantialism in question is certainly based, at least in part, upon logical considerations: some awareness of this is shown by Locke in II, xii, 4 and III, vi, 21, though the latter is not quite consistent.

Leibniz made a good remark about the Lockean theory of property-instantiation: "In distinguishing two things in [any] substance, the attributes or predicates, and the common subject of these predicates, it is no wonder that we can conceive nothing particular in this subject. It must be so, indeed, since we have already separated from it all the attributes in which we could conceive any detail" (*New Essays* II, xxiii, 2). This suggests, though it did not to Leibniz, the following argument. Suppose a substantialist were to say that any given item counts as a substance if and only if it has a certain property S which is definitive of substantiality. In that case, his account of what it is for a property to be instantiated, viz., that P is instantiated if and only if some substance bears P, would say merely that P is instantiated if and only if some item is both S and P. His analysis of a statement about the instantiation of one property would thus yield, uselessly, a statement about the joint instantiation of two properties. A defender of the Lockean doctrine must therefore deny that substances are items of a certain kind: to be of a kind is to have the properties which define the kind, and the Lockean doctrine cannot allow that there are properties which substances must have in order to count as substances. But the claim that substances are items of a certain kind *is* the Lockean account of property-instantiation. The whole point and interest of the account lies in its claim that every subject-concept includes the concept of a certain kind of item whose special right and duty it is to bear properties.

The Lockean account must, therefore, be wrong. Its crucial error is the move from "There is a concept of a *thing which* . . . , which enters into every subject-concept" to "There is a kind of item about which nothing can be said except that items of that kind bear properties." There are many kinds of things, but things do not form a kind. There is, perhaps, a "concept of a subject in general," but it is to be elucidated in terms of the way in which more special concepts function in certain kinds of statement, and is not to be regarded as a concept which picks out a class of items.

2. *The Veil-of-Perception Doctrine*

Locke certainly did make a mistake about the distinction between what appears to be the case and what is really, or objectively, the case. His view is that the difference between seeing a tree, say, and being in a visual state as of seeing a tree though there is no tree to be seen, is the difference between having a sensory "idea" while in the presence of a real thing which is like the idea, and having such an idea while in the presence of no such thing. Sometimes he speaks only of a "correspondence," "agreement," or "conformity" between the sensory idea and the thing; and he also thinks that there is a causal relation between the two; but he speaks too of a "likeness," and of ideas as "copies" of real things. This exposed him to a damaging attack from Berkeley who said that "An idea can be like nothing but an idea," and that no sense attaches to the question whether human sensory states are informative of a real, objective world which is *like* them. This talk about ideas as like real things is associated with, and strongly reinforces, Locke's mistaken handling of the question "Might it not be the case that there are no real things at all outside my mind? Can I be sure that the whole course of my experience is not just a dream?" Locke tries repeatedly to lay these sceptical doubts: see IV, II, 14; IV, 4–5; and XI, 2–10. His arguments to this end are unsatisfactory, consisting as they do of *ad hominem* teasing of the sceptic and covert appeals to empirical evidence. Even opponents of phenomenalism would now hesitate, I think, to follow Locke in his calm assumption that the question "Might it not be that there is no real extra-mental world?" requires an answer but stands in no need of criticism. Locke criticizes the moral character of the questioner, but his picture of the real world as represented by sensory states which "copy" it precludes his criticizing the question. This aspect of Locke's thought may be summed up in the remark that Locke puts the real world on the other side of the veil of perception, which explains my phrase "veil-of-perception doctrine." The word "doctrine" is misleading, though. Locke's treatment of the appearance/reality distinction is not prominent in the *Essay*: it appears mainly as a by-product of the mishandling of a certain sceptical question, and it has little of the weight or the deliberateness which go with a properly doctrinal status. That the veil-of-perception doctrine is usually credited to Locke as a *doctrine*—which he was consciously concerned to expound and defend—is due mainly to certain blunders which it is my present purpose to correct.

3. *The Two Doctrines in Berkeley*

The two philosophical views which I have sketched are distinct: one addresses itself to the question "What concepts do we use when we say *Something is F*?" while the other tackles the question "What is the difference between saying that *It is as though I were seeing a tree* and saying that *I see a tree*?" Although these are as different as chalk from cheese, they have been confidently identified with one another by Berkeley and by many other philosophers. Before explaining why Berkeley makes this remarkable mistake, I shall show that he makes it and in what ways.

Sometimes he does not make it at all, but treats one of the two Lockean doctrines in isolation from the other. In *Principles* § 49 he discusses the logical doctrine of substance without bringing in the veil-of-perception doctrine: "In this proposition, A die is hard, extended and square, they will have it that the word *die* denotes a subject or substance, distinct from the hardness, extension, and figure which are predicated of it, and in which they exist. This I cannot comprehend: to me a die seems to be nothing distinct from those things which are termed its modes or accidents. And to say a die is hard, extended, and square is not to attribute those qualities to a subject distinct from and supporting them, but only an explication of the meaning of the word *die*." And in §§ 18–20, 86–88 there is a good part of the case against the veil-of-perception view, with no admixture of polemic against substance.

Nearly always, though, Berkeley welds the two doctrines together to form a single view about "material substance." Berkeley uses "matter" and its cognates to refer to Locke's purported "real things" which lie behind the veil of perception. (He also associates "matter" with Locke's views about primary qualities, but that raises issues which I shall discuss in Part II of this paper.) The word "substance," on the other hand, is especially associated with the Lockean account of property-instantiation. The phrase "material substance," then, which Berkeley uses lavishly and which hardly occurs in Locke, ensures that any discussion of one of the two doctrines has a good chance of becoming mixed up with a discussion of the other. Sometimes the mixture is fairly innocent: in *Principles* § 68, for example, Berkeley makes some shrewd remarks about substratum-substance, and, although he uses the word "matter" for what he is attacking, the attack itself is not seriously infected with anything which is appropriate to the veil-of-perception doctrine rather than the substance doctrine.

Often enough, however, the mixture is lethal. In *Principles*, § 16 Berkeley makes a point about substance, and not only refers to it as "matter" but also invokes "extension," which has nothing in particular to do with substratum-substance but does have to do with primary qualities and also with Locke's real world beyond the veil of perception: "It is said extension is a mode or accident of matter, and that matter is the substratum that supports it. Now I desire you that you would explain what is meant by matter's *supporting* extension. . . ."

Again, in § 17 Berkeley tries to locate the enemy: "If we inquire into what the most accurate philosophers declare themselves to mean by *material substance*, we shall find they acknowledge they have no other meaning annexed to those sounds but the idea of being in general, together with the relative notion of its supporting accidents." This is a fair enough report of what Locke says not about "material substance" but about "substance." Berke-

Substance, Reality, and Primary Qualities 93

ley adds that he does not understand the proferred account of the "meaning annexed to these sounds," and continues: "But why should we trouble ourselves any further in discussing this material *substratum* or support of figure and motion and other sensible qualities? Does it not suppose they have an existence without the mind? And is not this a direct repugnancy and altogether inconceivable?" He then launches off from "existence without the mind," etc., into an attack on the veil-of-perception doctrine! In this passage, a complaint against a wrong analysis of subject-concepts is jumbled together with a complaint against Locke's insufficiently idealist analysis of reality.

In § 37: "If the word *substance* be taken in the vulgar sense, for a combination of sensible qualities, such as extension, solidity, weight and the like: this we cannot be accused of taking away. But if it be taken in a philosophic sense, for the support of accidents or qualities without the mind; then indeed I acknowledge that we take it away, if one may be said to take away that which never had any existence, not even in the imagination." This might be taken to mean "Of course there are things which have properties, but in saying this we do not employ a concept of naked thinghood"; or it might be taken to mean "Of course there are real objects, but that statement can be analyzed purely in terms of mental states." There is no basis for preferring either interpretation.

In § 74: "But though it be allowed by the *materialists* themselves that matter was thought of only for the sake of supporting accidents. . . ."

Finally, in § 76: "If you stick to the notion of an unthinking substance, or support of extension, motion and other sensible qualities, then to me it is most evidently impossible there should be any such thing. Since it is a plain repugnancy that those qualities should exist in or be supported by an unperceiving substance."

These are some of the clearer expressions of the conflation; but the *Principles* and *Three Dialogues* contain many others which would suit my purpose even better if they did not also involve the further tangling of the two views so far discussed with Locke's view about primary qualities.

4. Why Berkeley Identified the Two Doctrines

This is not just a simple-minded blunder on Berkeley's part. His identification of the two Lockean doctrines flows naturally from his underlying assumption that the word "idea" can be used univocally to cover something in the nature of sensory states and something in the nature of concepts or meanings of words. This assumption enables Berkeley to use "ideas of things" in such a way as to identify *qualities of things* with *sensory states which we have when we perceive things*. An idea of white for example is a certain kind of visual field; but it is also what I must be able to have in my mind if I am to understand the word "white," i.e., it is the meaning of the word "white," i.e., it is the property or quality of whiteness.

Some recent writers, sensing Wittgensteinian insights in Berkeley's theory of meaning, have denied that he takes "idea" in one of the two ways I have indicated. This, in my view, is a serious misreading of what Berkeley explicitly says about meaning and understanding; and it rides roughshod over the many passages in which he handles specific questions about meanings *solely* in terms of the possibility of bringing appropriate ideas into one's mind.

Since Berkeley uses "idea" in these two ways, it is natural that he should fail to distinguish the two Lockean doctrines; for each doctrine purports to offer an anchor for free-floating "ideas," one relating sensory states to the objectively real, and the other relating qualities to the things which have them. Furthermore, Berkeley can say of each Lockean doctrine that it over-populates the world: one by postulating "real things" which are logically dissociated from ideas (= sensory states), and the other by postulating "substances" which are something over and above collections of ideas (= qualities). The rather Berkeleian sentence "Things are just collections of ideas, not something over and above them" can be interpreted, taking ideas as qualities, as denying the Lockean account of property-instantiation; or, taking ideas as sensory states, as denying the veil-of-perception doctrine.

Substance, Reality, and Primary Qualities

This diagnosis of the conflation is strongly confirmed in *Principles* § 78: "Qualities . . . are nothing else but *sensations* or *ideas*, which exist only in a mind perceiving them." Note also *Principles* § 9: "By matter therefore we are to understand an inert, senseless substance in which extension, figure, motion, do actually subsist, but it is evident from what we have already shown, that extension, figure and motion are only ideas existing in the mind, and that an idea can be like nothing but another idea, and that consequently neither they nor their archetypes can exist in an unperceiving substance."

Special note should be taken of the phrase "sensible qualities," in which Berkeley often embodies his double use of "idea." For example in § 38: "But, say you, it sounds very harsh to say we eat and drink ideas, and are clothed with ideas. I acknowledge it does so, the word *idea* not being used in common discourse to signify the several combinations of sensible qualities which are called *things* . . . But . . . the hardness or softness, the colour, taste, warmth and such like qualities which combined together constitute the several sorts of victuals and apparel, have been shown to exist only in the mind that perceives them; and this is all that is meant by calling them *ideas*. . . ."

5. *The Two Doctrines in Locke*

The source of Berkeley's identification of the two doctrines is his double use of "idea"; but this he shares with Locke. Yet Locke does not run the substance doctrine together with the veil-of-perception doctrine: the two are distinct in Locke, as well as in fact. Since their non-distinctness does more or less follow from a premiss which Locke accepts—namely that "idea of *x*" can without ambiguity mean both "quality of *x*" and "appearance of *x*"— it must be conceded that Locke keeps the two doctrines apart only by betraying his basic premisses. This picture of Locke, as saying something true which he is committed to denying, is confirmed by certain details in the relevant parts of the *Essay*. These parts are not extensive. Contrary to the impression given by Berkeley, Locke does not have much to say about the substance which supports properties, or about the real world beyond the veil of perception: in the one case because he regards it as embarrassing and trivial and perhaps as just wrong, and in the other because he does not see that it involves an important mistake on a difficult philosophical problem. However, Locke's few discussions of substratum-substance and of related matters show that, although he has no intention of identifying the substance doctrine with the veil-of-perception doctrine, he cannot help expounding the former in words which would also be appropriate to the latter. In Locke's handling of the two doctrines, they drift together of their own accord.

(1) In the opening sections of *Essay* II, xxiii, Locke speaks of substance as something which we invoke when we become aware of "a certain number of simple ideas which go constantly together," or as something which is supposed to uphold "such combinations of simple ideas as are by experience and the observation of men's senses taken notice of to exist together." These expressions have to do with the instantiation of properties only if "idea" is taken to mean something like "property." But then, it seems, Locke is here raising not the general question "What is it for a property to be instantiated?" but the much more special question "What is it for a number of properties which go constantly together to be jointly instantiated?" This shift is bewildering; but it becomes intelligible if we remember that "ideas" may also be sensory states. For if we take "idea" to mean "sensory state," the phrases "ideas which go constantly together" and "combinations of simple ideas [which] exist together" may be taken to refer to certain kinds of dependable order in our experience. On that interpretation, the passages in question do not concern a queerly restricted version of the substratum-substance doctrine but rather concern the problems about objectivity or "reality" which are the province of the veil-of-perception doctrine. Locke makes no attempt to exploit these ambiguous phrases in order overtly to connect substance with what lies behind the

veil-of-perception; but the basis for such a connection is there in the words he uses.

(2) In II, xxiii, 1, Locke says that when we note a number of sensory ideas going together, "not imagining how these simple ideas can subsist by themselves, we accustom ourselves to suppose some substratum wherein they do subsist and from which they do result; which, therefore, we call substance." Here again, substances are supposed to uphold "ideas"; and ideas must again be properties if the passage is to concern the substance doctrine at all. But, so construed, the passage says that substances are supposed to cause their own properties, and it is not clear why Locke should have thought that anyone believes that. Our puzzlement is removed if we remember that ideas can also be sensory states; for, on that reading of "from which [ideas] do result," it echoes that part of the veil-of-perception doctrine which says that real things cause our sensory states. As in the previous case, Locke here declines to cash in on this unhappy verbal overlap between the two doctrines in order explicitly to identify them with one another. On the contrary, in the very next section he tries to drag "ideas" apart from "qualities," and thus to free the substance doctrine of any talk about causal relations by asserting that substances support qualities and that qualities cause sensory states: "If anyone will examine himself concerning his notion of pure substance in general, he will find he has no other idea of it at all, but only a supposition of he knows not what support of such qualities which are capable of producing simple ideas in us." If Locke had held firmly and consistently to that presentation of the matter, nearly every page of the *Essay* would have required revision. In fact, though, he is no more explicit or deliberate in his attempt to separate the two doctrines, and the two uses of "idea," than he is in allowing them to run together. Where Berkeley confidently identifies the two doctrines, Locke sometimes nearly identifies them and sometimes implicitly resists this identification; but the consequent tensions in his writing are not those of a man who has consciously located a problem.

(3) In II, xii, 4–6, Locke first distinguishes between "ideas of modes" and "ideas of substances." He clearly intends this to correspond to a distinction between adjectives and nouns, or between what may be said of a thing and things of which something may be said. This purely logical interpretation of the mode/substance distinction reappears at intervals throughout the *Essay*, for example in II, xiii, 19: "They who first ran into the notion of accidents, as a sort of real beings that needed something to inhere in, were forced to find out the word substance to support them," a remark which contains no hint of a restriction to substances of the special kind which Locke calls "real things." In the preceding section, too, Locke shows his awareness that the substance doctrine is supposed to account for property-instantiation generally, when he asks demurely whether God, finite minds, and bodies are all supposed to be "substances" in the same or different senses of the word. Yet even in his first introduction of "ideas of substances" and of the allegedly associated "supposed, or confused, idea of substance, such as it is," there is a dangerous reference to "distinct particular things subsisting by themselves." This last phrase could be taken to mean "things which exist independently of any percipient," an interpretation which would connect "ideas of substances" with the veil-of-perception doctrine. Perhaps in that passage Locke is not taking "subsisting by themselves" in that way; but he certainly does so later. In II, xxx, 4, he says, in effect, that in constructing complex ideas of modes we are subject only to the laws of logic: "There is nothing more required to those kinds of ideas to make them real, but that they be so framed, that there be a possibility of existing conformable to them." In the next section, however, he says that ideas of substances are subject to a more stringent requirement: "Our complex ideas of substances being made, all of them, in reference to things existing without us, and intended to be representations of substances as they really are, are no farther real than as they are such combinations of simple ideas as are really united and co-exist in things without us." This is a mistake: the propriety of a general noun no more depends

upon its having instances than does the propriety of an adjective. My point, however, is that in making this mistake Locke very explicitly connects "ideas of substances" with questions about appearance and reality, and thus lays the foundation for connecting the latter with the doctrine of substratum-substance. I say only that he "lays the foundation" for this, because in this passage which so explicitly connects ideas of *substances* with "things without us" there is, interestingly, no mention at all of the idea of *substance*.

On this evidence, I think we may say that Locke did not wish to identify the two doctrines but was under pressure from his own presuppositions to do so. Had he thought to identify them he would, I think, have been deterred by the obvious absurdity of identifying the real world which may *resemble* our sensory ideas with the substratum-substances which may bear or uphold properties but which are in themselves *unqualitied*. This manifest contradiction appears in most accounts of Locke—for example in those of Berkeley and Warnock—but I have yet to find a commentator who notices this feature of what is generally taken to be Locke's position.

6. *Why Others Have Identified the Two Doctrines*

So much for Berkeley and Locke; but what of those philosophers who have collapsed the substance doctrine into the veil-of-perception doctrine without having the excuse of an underlying mistake about the use of "idea"? What—one cannot help asking—do they think is happening in Berkeley's pages when they read the passages in which two or even three totally distinct questions are discussed at once? If they read Berkeley attentively and critically, how do they think that his use of "material substance," etc., connects with Locke or with the truth? I cannot fully explain this propensity for taking Berkeley's problems at his own valuation of them; but the following hypothesis suggests how someone might come to accept the conflation without resting it directly on the double use of "idea."

One considers the distinction between appearance and reality and illustrates it by a situation in which one can say "It seems to me that I see something square, but is there really something square which I see?" One then puts this in the form: "I am in the presence of a manifestation, in my visual field, of squareness; but am I in the presence of something which is square?" The question whether what appears to be the case is really the case is thus quietly transmuted into the question whether a certain property has a possessor. One notes also that each question might—mistakenly but plausibly—be analyzed in terms of an elusive "something we know not what," and this further encourages one to believe that they are two versions of a single question of which Locke gave a single wrong analysis.

The train of thought indicated in my hypothesis is invalid. The question "Given that I seem to see something square, is there really something square which I see?" does not raise the question about property-instantiation which the Lockean doctrine of substance is supposed to elucidate. This is proved by a simple destructive dilemma.

(a) If we allow that my visual field contains a part which is square, then that part is the "thing which" is square, i.e., it bears the property of squareness with which I am confronted. It is a mistake to think that the Lockean concept of substance must be so handled that only physical or public or extra-mental objects are cases of substance-plus-properties. The whole point of the doctrine, as is often remarked even by those who perpetrate Berkeley's conflation, is that it separates the substance from *all* its properties and insists that for a property to be instantiated is for it to be borne by an item of which nothing can be said except that it bears that property. So: *if some part of my visual field is square, then I am not in the presence of a property for which I am seeking a bearer*, for the property in whose presence I am already has a bearer.

(b) If, more sensibly, we deny that anything in my visual field is itself square, and say only that my visual field is similar to ones which I often have when I see something square, then my agnosticism about whether I see a square thing is agnosticism about whether I am in the presence of a manifestation of squareness at all. My question "Is the world at this point really as it appears to be?" is therefore not of the form "Is there a bearer for this property?" So: *if no part of my visual field is square, then I am not in the presence of a property for which I am seeking a bearer,* for I am not, in the required sense, "in the presence of a property" at all.

7. Some Examples

Here is one passage where Berkeley makes the shift I have described from "Does something real correspond to this sensory state?" to "Does something have this property?"

It is worth while to reflect a little on the motives which induced men to suppose the existence of material substance. . . . First, therefore, it was thought that colour, figure, motion, and the rest of the sensible qualities or accidents, did really exist without the mind; and for this reason it seemed needful to suppose some unthinking *substratum* or *substance* wherein they did exist, since they could not be conceived to exist by themselves. . . . (*Principles* § 73.)

O'Connor sees that there is *a* doctrine about substance of a purely logical kind. But he brings it in as an afterthought; dismisses it as an impossible interpretation of "the substratum theory," for no reason I can imagine except that he has taken Berkeley as his source for Locke; and shows, by his use of "something" in the first sentence, that he has not seen how distinct the two doctrines are:

It is certainly not logically necessary, or even true, that colours, for instance, cannot occur except as properties of a coloured something. If I stare at a light for a few seconds and then turn my gaze away, I shall see an "after-image" in the form of a coloured patch which certainly does not inhere in any substance. The supporter of the substratum theory of substance has either to claim (i) that the after-image is itself a substance or (ii) that it inheres in my visual field. (i) is a *reductio ad absurdum* of the substratum theory, though a sense datum would qualify as a substance in the *logical* sense of the word: it has properties without being itself a property of anything. . . .[1]

With satisfying explicitness, Morris presents Berkeley's semi-phenomenalism as contradicting something said "largely on the credit of Aristotle's logic":

> Berkeley has little difficulty in showing that the conception of material substance was in the philosophy of Locke no more than an uncriticized survival. Philosophers had always taken it for granted, largely on the credit of Aristotle's logic, that qualities must be supported by some underlying permanent self-subsistent substance. . . . Berkeley [argues against this] that throughout our whole experience of the physical world we never apprehend anything but sensible qualities and collections of sensible qualities. All we know of things or can know of them is what we perceive by sense; if there were more in things than this, we could not know it. This at once becomes clear, he says, if we consider what is meant by the term "exists". . . . "There was an odour, that is, it was smelled; there was a sound, that is to say, it was heard; a colour or figure, and it was perceived by sight or touch. This is all that I can understand by these and the like expressions." This doctrine is evidently based on the argument that whenever we are aware of a physical object, introspective analysis shows that there is nothing present in our mind but a number or collection of simple ideas of qualities; and it is taken by Berkeley to prove that knowledge simply consists in the awareness of sensible qualities.[2]

Warnock mixes the substance doctrine with the veil-of-perception doctrine by sliding smoothly from "matter" to "the essential 'support' of qualities":

[1] D. J. O'Connor, *John Locke* (London, Penguin Books, 1952), pp. 80–81.
[2] C. R. Morris, *Locke, Berkeley, Hume* (Oxford, The Clarendon Press, 1931), pp. 74–75.

Substance, Reality, and Primary Qualities

We must seek to clarify Berkeley's disagreement with Locke about "matter" or "material substance." The central point of Berkeley's argument is that the expression "material substance" is *meaningless*, an empty noise. Locke, who held that our ideas are of qualities, had of course admitted that we do not "perceive" substance, that it is indeed "something we know not what"; but he thought that we must none the less accept this something, as being the essential "support" of qualities.[3]

On pp. 95–96 of his book Warnock tells us that according to Locke "there is a world of physical ('external') objects" which within certain limits "actually have the qualities which our ideas incline us to assign to them." Then on p. 109: "Locke had asserted the existence of 'matter', 'material substance', a *something* of which nothing could be either said or known." Does this introduce a second Lockean doctrine? Warnock seems not to think so. Is he then pointing out a flat inconsistency in a single Lockean doctrine? Apparently not: like Berkeley before him, Warnock presents as Locke's "doctrine" something which is flatly and obviously inconsistent, yet does not call attention to this inconsistency because, one presumes, he has not noticed it. The double metaphor with which Warnock places the Lockean duplicate world "somehow behind or beneath" the world of experience reflects nicely his uncertainty as to just what view he wishes to attribute to Locke.

Examples can be found in nearly every extended discussion of Locke or Berkeley—in Fraser, Stephen, Huxley, Alexander, Hicks, Luce, Broad, Russell, Randall, Copleston—but not only in them. Ayer uses the phrase "sensible properties" in high Berkeleian fashion to effect a slide from "the thing itself as opposed to anything which may be said about it" to "the thing itself [as opposed to] its appearances":

> It happens to be the case that we cannot, in our language, refer to the sensible properties of a thing without introducing a word or phrase which appears to

[3] G. J. Warnock, *Berkeley* (London, Penguin Books, 1953), p. 103.

stand for the thing itself as opposed to anything which may be said about it. And, as a result of this, those who are infected with the primitive superstition that to every name a single real entity must correspond assume that it is necessary to distinguish logically between the thing itself and any, or all, of its sensible properties. And so they employ the term "substance" to refer to the thing itself. But from the fact that we happen to employ a single word to refer to a thing, and make that word the grammatical subject of the sentences in which we refer to the sensible appearances of the thing, it does not by any means follow that the thing itself is a "simple entity," or that it cannot be defined in terms of the totality of its appearances. It is true that in talking of "its" appearances we appear to distinguish the thing from the appearances, but that is simply an accident of linguistic usage. Logical analysis shows that what makes these "appearances" the "appearances of" the same thing is not their relationship to an entity other than themselves, but their relationship to one another.[4]

PART II

Locke distinguishes between "primary" and "secondary" qualities. A thing's primary qualities are its shape, size, spatial location, velocity, and degree of hardness; its secondary qualities are its color, temperature, smell, taste, and sound. Locke's attempt in *Essay* II, viii, 9, to give a general definition of this distinction is unsuccessful, but for present purposes the above lists suffice.

According to Locke, the secondary qualities of things are not "of" or "in" them in the same full-blooded sense as are their primary qualities. To say of something that it "is purple," for example, is to employ a natural and permissible *façon de parler*; while to say of something that it "is spherical" may be to state a plain fact in a way which requires neither gloss nor apology. I shall try to show that

[4] A. J. Ayer, *Language, Truth and Logic* (London, Victor Gollancz, 1946), p. 42.

Substance, Reality, and Primary Qualities 105

something true and interesting is misexpressed by this Lockean thesis, and that Berkeley's conflation of it with Locke's veil-of-perception doctrine reflects Berkeley's total failure to see what Locke was getting at in his discussion of primary and secondary qualities.

1. *The Phenol Argument*

Phenol-thio-urea tastes intensely bitter to 75 per cent of humans; to the rest it is tasteless. With a 25 per cent block of "non-tasters," we cannot say outright that the stuff is bitter: it tastes bitter to more people than not, but there is no such thing as "the" taste of it. If the non-tasters comprised only .001 per cent of all humans, then we could describe phenol-thio-urea as bitter without qualification: perhaps lemons are tasteless to .001 per cent of humans, but lemons are sour for all that. Suppose a world where phenol-thio-urea is unqualifiedly bitter, i.e., tastes so to almost everyone. Suppose further that a dynasty of world dictators begins intensive breeding of non-tasters and gradually allows the tasters to die out. This is good genetics: some of the tasters' offspring will be non-tasters, while the mating of two non-tasters can produce only non-tasting progeny. After a few dozen generations, phenol-thio-urea is tasteless to everyone living, so that there are as good grounds for calling phenol-thio-urea tasteless as for calling water tasteless.

This describes a course of events in which something (a) is bitter at one time, (b) is tasteless at a later time, and (c) does not itself change in the interim. This, on the face of it, is a contradiction; and we can resolve it only by saying that the stuff's bitterness is not one of "its properties" in the full-blooded sense in which a thing's losing one of its properties *is* its changing.

Similar arguments could be developed for the taste of any given kind of stuff, and also for colors, sounds, and smells. A simple genetic control would not always be available; but mass microsurgery might bring it about that no human could see any difference in color between grass and blood, and to do this would be to bring it about that grass was the same color as blood. Similarly for other pairs of colors, and for tastes, sounds, and smells.

This is not one of those epistemological blockbusters which begins "Suppose that, as is logically possible, we were to wake up one morning and find that for some mysterious reason we were all . . . etc." The kind of story which I am telling is one in which, after the modification of the human frame has taken place, everyone knows just what has happened and how. Furthermore, the stories are more than just logically possible: we know how we could realize the tale about phenol-thio-urea, and the discovery of a surgical technique or a genetic control for any other discrimination which we make in respect of colors, tastes, sounds, or smells is scientifically well on the cards.

We may still call things green or sour or stinking or noisy, but philosophers should bear in mind the essentially relative nature of these adjectives and their like: "similar in color" means "looking similar in color to nearly everyone under normal conditions," and a careful metaphysic will take note of that fact.

The foregoing paragraphs contain what I shall for short call "the phenol argument." Before relating it to Locke and Berkeley, I should say at once that the argument is not valid. It depends upon the epitome which says that phenol-thio-urea is bitter at one time, tasteless at a later time, *and yet does not itself change in the interim.* The italicized clause is false: in the original story phenol-thio-urea does undergo a change, namely a change in respect of its taste. Admittedly it does not change its chemical structure, but to infer from this that it does not change at all is simply to beg the question in favor of primary qualities. The story shows that a thing may change in respect of its secondary qualities without changing its primary qualities; but this is not a contrast between primary and secondary qualities, for it is also true that a thing's primary qualities may change without any change in its secondary qualities. A fluid may have its primary qualities changed by the addition of a reagent, without changing in color, taste, or smell; and a knob of plasticine may be squashed flat.

Substance, Reality, and Primary Qualities 107

It is natural to protest that *that* does not show the argument to be invalid, because squashing a piece of plasticine is doing something to it in a way in which the selective breeding of humans is not doing something to phenol-thio-urea. The phenol-thio-urea in the story, one might say, does not change in itself. I shall try below to show what justice there is in these responses: to see the force of such phrases as "does not change in itself" is to see what the truth is about primary and secondary qualities.

2. Locke and Berkeley on Secondary Qualities

The phenol argument is mine, not Locke's: he does not suggest that a secondary quality of something might be altered by a species-wide physiological change. His discussions of primary and secondary qualities in II, viii, 9–26; xxiii, 11; and IV, iii, 11–13, 28–29 strongly suggest, however, that Locke would welcome the phenol argument as making his kind of point for his kind of reason. His own detailed arguments are more obviously unsatisfactory than the phenol argument; and yet even they give to some readers the impression that there is something true here which Locke is mishandling. I shall try to show that this impression is correct; but first let us see what Locke's arguments are, and what Berkeley does with them.

(1) Locke thinks that those of our sensory states which enable us to make secondary-quality discriminations between things can be explained in terms of the things' primary qualities: seen colors, for example, can be explained in terms of surface-textures, the impact upon our eyes of particles of light, and so on. But he stresses (II, viii, 11–13; IV, iii, 12–13, 28–29) that these explanations depend upon brute-fact, non-necessary, God-ordained correlations between our secondary-quality sensory states and the primary qualities which underlie and explain them. He seems to think—though he is reticent about this—that our seeings and feelings of the primary qualities of things have a necessary connection with the primary qualities themselves; perhaps because in that case there is supposed to be not only an explanatory or causal relationship but

also a resemblance (II, VIII, 15). Berkeley dismisses the talk about resemblances between ideas and bodies (*Principles* § 9); and argues that in any case there is only brute fact observed regularity in any of the connections ordinarily taken to be causal (§§ 25, 30–31). I assume that Berkeley is right on both these points, and that if Locke has got hold of a truth about primary and secondary qualities it must be sought elsewhere.

(2) In II, VIII, 20, Locke says: "Pound an almond, and the clear white colour will be altered into a dirty one, and the sweet taste into an oily one. What real alteration can the beating of the pestle make in any body, but an alteration of the texture of it?" Berkeley does not, I think, address himself directly to this; but he would have said that the beating of the pestle cannot make, or cause, any alteration whatsoever. His reasons for this lie outside my present scope, but this argument of Locke's is itself important, as I shall show. We may notice right away that the argument begs the question: Locke invites us to say that because the pestle can cause only primary-quality changes in the almond, the second-quality changes must therefore be primary-quality ones in disguise; but this can be rebutted by saying that beating something with a pestle can cause alterations other than primary-quality ones, as is proved by what happens to the color and taste of an almond when it is beaten with a pestle.

(3) In II, VIII, 21, Locke points out that the same water may at once feel warm to one hand and cool to the other, which "figure never does, that never producing the idea of a square by one hand which has produced the idea of a globe by the other." Berkeley concedes the point about the warm/cool water phenomenon, but claims that it has primary-quality analogues, as can be discovered "by looking with one eye bare, and with the other through a microscope." (*First Dialogue*, p. 153 in David M. Armstrong [ed.], *Berkeley's Philosophical Writings.*)

(4) In II, XXIII, 11, Locke says that to the naked eye blood looks "all red," but through a good microscope it is seen as "some few globules of red swimming in a pellucid liquor; and how these red globules would appear, if glasses

Substance, Reality, and Primary Qualities 109

could be found that could yet magnify them 1,000 or 10,000 times more, is uncertain." Again, Berkeley agrees (*First Dialogue*, pp. 148–49) but says that analogous considerations apply to size, which is a primary quality (pp. 152–53).

(5) In II, viii, 16–18, Locke says that no reason can be given for saying that the heat is "actually in the fire" which would not also be a reason for saying that the pain is actually in the fire; yet it is clearly wrong to say the latter. Berkeley agrees with this cordially (*First Dialogue*, pp. 141–44), but takes it that here again there is no difference between primary and secondary qualities.

In each of (3), (4), and (5) Locke says something about secondary qualities which he thinks will show that they sit looser to the world than is usually thought; and in each case Berkeley kidnaps Locke's remark and uses it to prise primary qualities off the world as well. Yet Locke is *wrong* in that part of each claim which Berkeley *accepts*. In (3), it does not follow—and should not even seem to follow—from the fact that we may err about temperatures that therefore things do not really have temperatures. In (4), the microscopic appearance of blood serves Locke's purpose only if it is possible that through a powerful enough microscope we should see the minute parts of blood as entirely colorless; and that is impossible since, for purposes of this argument, "colorless" must mean "invisible." In (5), it is not true that any grounds we could give for assigning temperatures to things would also be grounds for assigning pains to them.

Berkeley's view is not merely that what Locke says about secondary qualities is false unless it is so construed as to hold also for primary qualities, and that therefore Locke has failed to drive a wedge between the two sorts of quality. Berkeley genuinely agrees that things do not really have secondary qualities, and dissents only by saying that this is *also* true of primary qualities.

The explanation of this is as follows. Berkeley thinks that in agreeing with what Locke unclearly says about secondary qualities he is agreeing that a phenomenalist or idealist analysis ought to be given of statements about the secondary qualities of things, i.e., that talk about things' colors and smells and sounds, etc., is to be understood as shorthand for talk about certain sorts of sensory states. It is this thesis which he believes to hold also for talk about the primary qualities of things; it is the thesis which Berkeley offers as a rival to Locke's veil-of-perception account of the distinction between appearance and reality. Berkeley, in short, takes Locke's thesis about secondary qualities to be a *qualification* of his veil-of-perception doctrine. The latter says that there are facts about nonmental reality which are logically unconnected with facts about sensory states; and Berkeley takes the secondary-qualities doctrine to be an important rider to the effect that the genuinely extramental facts about reality are those which involve primary qualities only and do not include those which involve secondary qualities.

This account of what Berkeley is about explains the passages to which I have called attention as well as many more like them; and it is strongly confirmed by *Principles* § 14–15. If I am right about this, then Berkeley has completely misunderstood the kind of thing which Locke was trying to say; but I cannot justify this last claim without first saying what I think to be the truth about primary and secondary qualities. Only in the light of what is true about primary and secondary qualities can we understand what Locke wanted to say about them.

3. *Color Blindness and Size "Blindness"*

Locke calls attention to the ways in which our perception of secondary qualities may vary according to the bodily condition of the percipient and according to the state of the percipient's environment. Berkeley rightly says that such variations also infect our perception of primary qualities but wrongly implies that the two sorts of quality are on a level in this respect. To see that they are not on a level, and why, is to grasp the truth after which Locke is fumbling.

I shall contrast two kinds of sensory aberration: in one, someone sees two things as being of the same color when

Substance, Reality, and Primary Qualities   111

in fact they are not, and in the other someone sees and feels two things as being of the same size when in fact they are not.

Suppose, then, that someone who is confronted by a red thing and a white thing convinces us that he sees them as having exactly the same color. He may believe us when we tell him that the things do have different colors; and if they differ in no other way we can, without asking him to trust us, prove to him that there is some difference between the two things which we see and he does not. Also, we may show him—or he may discover for himself—that the two objects differ in respect of the wave lengths of the light they reflect, and that wave lengths usually correlate with seen colors. But if he ignores other people's talk about the two objects, and ignores esoteric facts of optics, he may never discover that his seeing of the two objects as having the same color arises from a sensory defect in him. A failure of secondary-quality discrimination, in one who is otherwise sensorily normal, can—and sometimes does—persist unsuspected through any variations in distance or angle of view, light-conditions, mouth-washing, cold-curing, and so on.

Contrast this with the case of a size-"blind" man who, going by what he sees and feels, judges a certain drinking mug to have the same size as a certain cup, although in fact the former is both higher and wider than the latter. In such a case, we can place the cup inside the mug; or fill the mug with water, and then fill the cup from the mug and pour the remaining water on the ground; or place both vessels on a horizontal surface and draw the size-"blind" man's hand across the top of the cup until it is stopped by the side of the mug; and so on. What are we to suppose happens when our size-"blind" man is confronted by these manipulations of the cup and the mug? There are just two relevant possibilities. (a) We may suppose that the size-"blind" man has a normal apprehension of what happens when we manipulate the cup and the mug, and therefore quite soon realizes that his original judgment about their sizes must have been mistaken. (b) We may suppose that in each case there is some supplementary inadequacy in his perception of what is done to the cup and the mug, or of the outcome of what is done, so that what he sees and feels still fits in smoothly with his original judgment that the two vessels are of the same size.

To adopt supposition (a) is just to admit that this case is radically different from that of color blindness. If the point of the latter were just that there are or could be aberrations in our perception of secondary qualities, then we could say the same of primary qualities; and we could add that it is absurd to deny that a certain kind of quality really is a quality of the things in the world, just because we do or might sometimes fail to discern it. What gives relevance and bite to color blindness, and to abnormality of secondary-quality perception generally, is the fact that any such abnormality can persist, not just for a few moments or under special conditions, without the victim's being given any clue to his abnormality by his other, normal sensory responses. The manipulations of the cup and the mug could be performed not by us but by the size-"blind" man himself: they involve ordinary commerce with familiar middle-sized objects, and are in a very different case from the color-blind man's attention to wave lengths or to other people's classifications of things by their colors.

If we want an analogy between size-"blindness" and color blindness, then, we must adopt supposition (b). But look at what this involves: the size-"blind" man must be unable to see or feel that the cup is inside the mug, or unable to see or feel that the mug has not momentarily stretched or the cup contracted; he must be unable to see or feel that the cup has been filled from the mug, or unable to see or feel that there is water left in the mug after the cup has been filled; he must be unable to see or feel that his hand is touching the cup as it moves across the top of it, or unable to see or feel his hand being stopped by the side of the mug. It will not do merely to suppose that as the manipulations are performed he sees and feels *nothing*. To preserve the analogy with color blindness we must suppose that what he sees and feels gives him no reason for suspecting that there is something wrong with

Substance, Reality, and Primary Qualities 113

him; and so his visual and tactual states through all the manipulations of the cup and the mug must present no challenge to his belief that he is handling an ordinary pair of drinking vessels which are of the same size. This is bad enough, but there is worse to follow. If the size-"blind" man is to be unable to see or feel the water which remains in the mug after the cup has been filled from it, this will require yet further sensory aberrations on his part: if the water is poured over a lighted candle, or used to dissolve a lump of sugar, or thrown in the size-"blind" man's face, his perception of any of these events must also be appropriately abnormal if his original judgment is to remain unchallenged. Similarly with any of the other sensory aberrations with which we must prop up the initial one: each requires further props which demand yet others in their turn, and so on indefinitely.

The desired analogy with color blindness has collapsed yet again. In the case of color blindness, the sensory abnormality was not clued by the victim's other sensory responses although these were normal; but to keep the size-"blind" man in ignorance of his own initial sensory abnormality we have had to surround it with ever-widening circles of further abnormalities.

Strictly speaking, it is not quite correct to say that the single failure of color-discrimination could well remain unclued by the victim's other, normal sensory responses. For if he detects no difference in color between R_1 which is red and W_1 which is white, what are we to suppose that he makes of the color of a second red thing, R_2, in relation to the color of W_1? If his only sensory aberration is to concern the comparison of R_1 with W_1, then we must suppose that he sees no difference of color between R_2 and R_1, and no difference of color between R_1 and W_1, and yet sees a *large* difference of color between R_2 and W_1. This is clearly unacceptable, and so we are in trouble here unless we suppose our man to be unable to see color differences between red things and white things generally. This, however, does not restore the analogy between color blindness and size "blindness." For the infectious spread of sensory aberrations around the single initial failure of size-discrimination does not involve merely other failures to discriminate sizes. The original aberration can remain unclued only if it is backed by failures of shape-discrimination, movement-detection, sensitivity to heat, and so on. The single red/white failure spreads to red/white failures generally, but need spread no further; but the failure to discriminate sizes spreads endlessly into all the victim's perceptions of his environment.

As well as losing our analogy, we are also losing our grip on the initial datum of the size "blindness" case, namely that we can agree with the size-"blind" man about the identity of a certain cup and mug, disagreeing with him only about their relative sizes. For it has turned out that there are countless visible and tangible aspects of our environment in regard to which the size-"blind" man does not agree with us, so that it is now by no means clear that we can still assume that we share with him a sensory awareness of a single objective world.

4. The Crucial Contrasts

The foregoing discussion of color blindness and size "blindness" illustrates two crucial and closely related contrasts between primary and secondary qualities.

(1) There are countless familiar, exoteric, general facts about the connections between a thing's primary qualities and its ways of interacting with other things: a rigid thing cannot be enclosed within a smaller rigid thing; a thing cannot block another thing's fall to the earth without touching it; a cube cannot roll smoothly on a flat surface; a thing's imprint on soft wax matches the outline of the thing itself; and so on, indefinitely. The analogue of this does not hold for secondary qualities. Admittedly, there are connections between a thing's color, say, and its ways of behaving in relation to other things: in general, a brown apple will be more squashable than a green one; a blue flame will boil a pint of water faster than a yellow flame of the same size; a thing's color will correlate with the wave lengths of the light it reflects: and so on. But neither for colors nor for any other secondary qualities can we

Substance, Reality, and Primary Qualities 115

make, as we can for primary qualities, an enormously long list of obvious, familiar, inescapable connections of the relevant kind.

(2) Just because of the numerousness and familiarity of the connections between the primary qualities of things and their ways of interacting with one another, no clear sense attaches to the suggestion that something might persistently fail to obey these general connections. If a thing's purported size is belied by enough of its ways of interacting with other things, there is no point in saying that it does have that size. As against this, there would be a point in saying that a thing was red even if this were belied by the wave lengths of the light reflected from its surface, or by its flavor, hardness, chemical composition, etc. If in sunlight a given thing were indistinguishable in color from other things which were agreed to be red, then this fact could sensibly enough be reported in the words "That thing is red," even if we had to add one or more riders such as ". . . though its light-reflecting properties are atypical for red," or ". . . though its taste is atypical for red wine," or ". . . though its temperature is atypical for red iron." There is in fact a tight correlation between wave lengths of reflected light and the colors seen by most people in sunlight, and we therefore do not have to decide either for or against defining color-words in terms of how things look and treating the associated wave lengths as mere empirical correlates of colors. If the need for a decision did arise, however, we could choose to give our color terminology a purely visual basis and still have it doing pretty much the work which it does for us now. Analogous remarks apply also to all other secondary qualities. Not so, however, for primary qualities. As the discussion of size "blindness" showed, the interrelations between things in respect of their primary qualities are numerous and various and tightly interlocked. There seems to be little chance of inventing a partial breakdown of them such that those which survive the breakdown could form a basis for a working vocabulary of primary qualities. So far as I can see, the only kind of breakdown over which we could hope to keep control would be one involving the collapse of all

but one of the normal correlates of some primary quality. For example, we might suppose a world in which things had reasonably reliable "sizes" if "the size of x" is defined solely in terms of the visual field presented by x when it is stationary and at some stated distance from the observer, and in which none of the other actual correlates of size continued to hold. This supposition does not, however, really provide us with a minimal sense of "size" analogous to the purely visual sense of "color"; for the supposition has cut away so much of what normally attends upon "size" that it almost certainly leaves no basis for a language of physical objects. It offers us a minimal sense of "size" while robbing us of everything which could have a size.

We can now see why the phenol argument is plausible, and why it really does show something about secondary qualities as against primary. We know what it would be like to be aware that the taste of phenol-thio-urea had been altered by means of a change of the human frame. But what could ever entitle us to say "Oranges, which used to be spherical, are now cubic; but this change has been brought about solely by a change in humans"? The difficulty here is not merely our ignorance of appropriate surgical or eugenic techniques, nor the scientific implausibility of suggesting that such techniques might be discovered: if the obstacles were only of that sort, then it would be historically impossible that the point brought out by the phenol argument should be one of which Locke was dimly aware. The trouble we meet in trying to reproduce a primary-quality analogue of the phenol argument is that we must either (a) allow the analogy to fail by supposing only that erstwhile spheres "look cubic" in some very restricted sense, e.g., in the sense of presenting visual fields like those now presented by sugar cubes when seen at rest (while in all other ways looking and feeling spherical); or (b) allow the analogy to fail by telling an astronomically complicated story in which not only the shapes of erstwhile spheres but also thousands of other aspects of the world were perceived differently; or (c) insulate shape from its present correlates by means of some radical conceptual revision which has no analogue in the phenol argu-

Substance, Reality, and Primary Qualities

ment and which no one can see how to perform anyway. Of these alternatives, (a) and (b) do not produce the desired analogy, and perhaps (c) does not either; while (b) and (c) involve conceptual and empirical complications which we have no idea how to handle.

This difference between primary and secondary qualities is closely connected with the fact that the former alone involve the sense of touch. How they involve it, and what this has to do with the contrast I have drawn, are matters which I cannot go into here.

5. The Relevance of This to Locke

Locke says nothing about color blindness: it seems not to have been generally recognized in his day. Yet I maintain that the contrast I have drawn between primary and secondary qualities, and which I have approached through a discussion of sensory abnormalities, is one which Locke saw dimly and was struggling to express and defend. My grounds for this contention are the following.

(1) The points which I have made could without absurdity be summed up in the Lockean remark that it is true of secondary qualities, in a way in which it is not of primary, that they are "merely" the powers which things have to affect us in certain ways.

(2) Locke was aware that primary qualities are all logically connected with solidity and extension, and these he regarded as definitive of "body" (II, iv, 1–2). Furthermore, he thought that the essentialness of "solid" and "extended" to "body" was connected with the different ways in which primary and secondary qualities are qualities "of" bodies, though he seems to have misunderstood the nature of the connection (II, viii, 9). My discussion indicates that Locke is right about the definition of "body," and right in his assumption that this is a deep conceptual fact which is not on a par with the dictionary definition of "brother" as "male sibling."

(3) Part of Locke's thesis about primary and secondary qualities is that if we knew enough we could give causal explanations, purely in primary-quality terms, for all our

secondary-quality discriminations. Over the possibility of a purely primary-quality science, Locke had an optimism which was not at all justified by the state of physiology in the seventeenth century: note his calm assumption that *of course* the pestle's effect on the almond must be describable purely in primary-quality terms. My discussion of primary qualities shows why someone in Locke's position should so confidently assume that the final, perfect science will require only a primary-quality vocabulary.

(4) Several of Locke's examples share with the phenol example an emphasis upon the notion of a thing's changing in respect of a secondary quality without changing *in itself*. When Locke said that porphyry in the dark has no color, he erred; but he seems clearly to have had in mind the fact that our main basis—he would have said our only basis—for attributing colors to things is such that our color-reports can vary without any change in the things themselves. My discussion shows why this is plausible and how far it is true.

6. *Berkeley's Blunder*

I submit, then, that I have presented a truth about primary and secondary qualities and that it is this after which Locke was groping. Now, the point which I have brought out has nothing to do with the veil-of-perception doctrine: it is not a version of that doctrine, or a qualification of or a rival to it. It operates on a different level altogether. One can state and explain what is interesting in the distinction between primary and secondary qualities—whether or not one goes so far as to say that secondary qualities are not "of" things as primary qualities are—only on the basis of normal assumptions about our entitlement to trust the evidence of our senses. What I have called Locke's "veil-of-perception doctrine" is really just his mishandling of a certain sceptical question, and the latter makes sense only if it asks whether the objective world is, really, *in any way at all* as it appears to be. An affirmative answer must be given to this question before one can present the contrast between primary and secondary qualities.

Substance, Reality, and Primary Qualities 119

To be fair, I must concede that the thesis about primary and secondary qualities can be taken as a qualification of the veil-of-perception doctrine in the following extremely minimal way. The veil-of-perception doctrine says that statements about objects are logically dissociated from statements about states of mind, and the primary/secondary thesis can be seen as conceding that this logical dissociation does not hold for statements attributing secondary qualities to objects but only for those attributing primary qualities to them. I think that it is because the relation between the two doctrines can be viewed like this that they are so often conflated; and it is therefore important to see what is wrong with this way of looking at the matter.

Considered as a qualification of the veil-of-perception doctrine, i.e., as a concession that not all statements about objects are logically dissociated from statements about states of mind, the primary/secondary thesis is just a bore. Even the most fervent super-Lockean would agree that some predicates of objects are connected with mental predicates; for example, that we commit ourselves to something about states of mind when we say that castor oil is nasty, that warm baths are soothing, that hair shirts are uncomfortable, or that the New York subway system is confusing. If Locke's thesis about secondary qualities were important only as a concession that some predicates of objects are logically connected with mental predicates, it would be without any importance at all since it would be "conceding" what no one has ever denied. What makes it interesting is not its saying (a) "Some predicates of objects have *some* logical connections with mental predicates," but rather its saying (b) "Secondary-quality predicates of objects have *these* logical connections with mental predicates." Now (b) does not offer any useful support to the view that there are logical connections between all predicates of objects and mental predicates: the Lockean view of the status of secondary qualities is no more a stage on the way to complete idealism or phenomenalism than is the Nazi valuation of Aryans a stage on the way to a belief in the worth and dignity of all men. In each case, the further step may consistently be taken; but in neither case is the taking of it just a further development of the line of thought by which the first stage was reached.

Just as the Lockean thesis about secondary qualities is not a significant *restriction* on the veil-of-perception doctrine, so the Lockean thesis about primary qualities is not —or need not be—a somewhat restricted *version* of the veil-of-perception doctrine. If to (a) "Some predicates of objects have *some* logical connections with mental predicates" we add the rider "but primary-quality predicates don't," then the result is indeed all of a piece with the veil-of-perception doctrine, and is thus in opposition to idealism or phenomenalism. But if to (b) "Secondary-quality predicates of objects have *these* logical connections with mental predicates" we add the rider "but primary qualities don't," the result says only that primary-quality predicates are not connected with mental predicates *in the way in which* secondary-quality predicates are. This presents no challenge at all to Berkeley or to any phenomenalist who knows what he is about: I have defended it myself, through my discussion of size "blindness," without conceding a thing to the veil-of-perception doctrine.

This difference of level between the two theses is fairly clear in Locke's own pages. In his battles with the sceptic, Locke does invoke empirical facts which are not legitimately available to him; but he does this covertly, and knows that he ought not to do it at all. As against this, his discussions of the primary/secondary contrast are riddled with open appeals to experimental evidence. (This is perfectly proper: a satisfactory treatment of the primary/secondary distinction must begin with empirical facts; though it ought, as Locke's does not, to connect these with the relevant conceptual points.) Locke notes this explicitly in II, viii, 22: "I have, in what just goes before, been engaged in physical inquiries a little farther than perhaps I intended . . . I hope I shall be pardoned this little excursion into natural philosophy, it being necessary, in our present inquiry, to distinguish the primary and real qualities of bodies, which are always in them . . . etc." Again, in IV, iii, 28, he denies that any "correspondence or connexion" can be found between our ideas of secondary qualities "and those primary qualities which (experience shows us) produce them in us." In the context of the battle against the sceptic, these references to "physical inquiries" and to what "experience shows us" would be merely grotesque. Still less do we find Locke mixing up the primary/secondary thesis with the question of substratum-substance. In his principal exposition of the former, II, VIII, 9–26, the word "substance" does not occur.

As with the other conflation, so here there are some invitations to error, and thus some excuses for Berkeley, in Locke's pages. In particular, he says that our ideas of secondary qualities do not, while those of primary qualities do, resemble things themselves; and resemblance is also invoked in connection with the veil-of-perception doctrine. But the most that this shows is that Locke was unclear about the relation between the two theses: it could not show that they are—or even that Locke consciously thought them to be—related as Berkeley thinks they are.

(My attention was drawn by one of the referees for this *Quarterly*, and by Professor H. H. Price, to the relevance here of Locke's theory about real essences. A thing's "real essence" is that microphysical primary-quality constitution of it which, according to Locke, is the causal basis for all its large-scale observable qualities, primary and secondary. Locke says that we know very little about real essences: "Though the familiar use of things about us takes off our wonder, yet it cures not our ignorance. When we come to examine the stones we tread on, or the iron we daily handle, we presently find that we know not their make; and can give no reason of the different qualities we find in them. . . . What is that texture of parts, that real essence, that makes lead and antimony fusible; and wood and stones not? What makes lead and iron malleable; antimony and stones not?" (III, VI, 9). What makes this important for Locke is just that since we do not *in fact* know much about real essences these cannot be the basis which we do now use for our classifications of physical things, and so the way is open for Locke to urge the candidacy of "nominal essences" as our actual basis for classification. But he sometimes (as in III, III, 17) gives the impression that he regards real essences as *necessarily* beyond the reach of our knowledge, and thus suggests that they have a "something we know not what" or a "beyond the veil" kind of status which smacks of both the substratum-substance and the veil-of-perception doctrines. I am sure that Locke did not hold as a considered opinion this strong view about the unknowability of real essences; but he undoubtedly does sometimes seem to hold it; and it is likely that Berkeley and others have in this way, as well as in the ways I have already discussed, been tempted to conflate the primary/secondary doctrine (of which the theory of real essences is an integral part) with one or both of the other two doctrines. This is the more probable since—as Professor Price has pointed out to me—the whole issue between Locke and Berkeley could be seen as a dispute between a proponent and an enemy of the microphysical approach to physical science. I find this last suggestion extremely illuminating—it captures Locke's picture of science as the minute *dissection* of large-scale objects, and Berkeley's picture of science as the intelligent *comparison* of large-scale objects with one another—but to follow it up here would take me too far afield.)

I conclude, then, that some things worth saying about the primary/secondary distinction are pointed to by Locke's discussion of it, and have no clear logical connection with the philosophical problem about the distinction between what appears to be the case and what is really the case.

It is for his insights into the latter problem that Berkeley is chiefly valued: he is rightly seen as a precursor of phenomenalism, and even those who hold no brief for phenomenalism agree that Berkeley taught us much about what goes wrong when the distinction between appearance and reality is divorced, as it is by Locke, from anything cashable in experience. But if we are to understand what is happening in Berkeley's pages, we must see through his appalling conflation of the question about the appearance/reality distinction with both the question about substance and that about the primary/secondary

Substance, Reality, and Primary Qualities 123

distinction. Consider for example the following passage from *Principles* § 9:

> . . . they will have our ideas of the primary qualities to be patterns or images of things which exist without the mind, in an unthinking substance they call *matter*. By matter, therefore, we are to understand an inert, senseless substance, in which extension, figure, motion and so forth do actually subsist, but it is evident from what we have already shown that extension, figure and motion are only ideas existing in the mind, and that an idea can be like nothing but another idea, and that consequently neither they nor their archetypes can exist in an unperceiving substance. Hence it is plain, that the very notion of what is called *matter*, or *corporeal substance*, involves a contradiction in it.

How can such a farrago as this be understood—how could anyone spell out in plain terms what it is that is being opposed here—except on the basis of an elaborate exposure of the two conflations? Many passages in *Principles* and *Three Dialogues* are similarly unintelligible until the two conflations have been understood and rejected; and Berkeley's writings are full of tensions which can be resolved only on that same basis. For example, according to the primary/secondary doctrine, things do have primary qualities in a way in which they do not have secondary; according to the veil-of-perception doctrine things may really have none of the properties we attribute to them; and of course substratum-substances cannot have, *qua* substances, any properties at all. And so, although "by matter, therefore, we are to understand an inert, senseless substance, in which extension, figure, motion and so forth do actually subsist," *Principles* § 47 tells us that "the matter philosophers contend for is an incomprehensible somewhat, which hath none of those particular qualities whereby the bodies falling under our senses are distinguished one from another." In these two passages taken together, Berkeley is not nailing down an inconsistency in Locke; he is indulging in an inconsistency which arises from his misunderstanding of Locke's problems.

The literature does not yield the same rich harvest of thorough, glad commission of this conflation as it does for the one discussed in the first part of my paper. Most commentators merely take Berkeley's word for it that the veil-of-perception doctrine is integrally connected with the thesis about primary and secondary qualities, and lurch somehow across the gap where the connection is supposed to be. In somewhat the same way, they accept but do not intelligently argue for Berkeley's demonstrably false claim that Locke's theory of abstract ideas is connected with the three-headed monster which Berkeley calls Locke's doctrine of material substance.

It is a disaster that the British empiricists, and Berkeley in particular, have received such cursory attention in recent years. There is so much in them that is boldly and energetically wrong that they can be enormously instructive as object lessons, if in no other way, to anyone who will attend *closely* to their thought. The wretched course of English epistemology over the past half-century illustrates, depressingly, the dictum that those who do not study history are in danger of reliving it.

LOCKE'S VERSION OF THE DOCTRINE OF REPRESENTATIVE PERCEPTION

REGINALD JACKSON

This is an attempt to carry out a programme to which I seem in the course of my article on "Locke's Distinction between Primary and Secondary Qualities" (reprinted in this volume, pp. 53–77 above) to have committed myself. The aim of that article was to challenge, on the ground that it conflicted with Locke's definitions of his terms, the tradition, established by Berkeley, which interprets the distinction as one between two groups of sense-data, namely, sensible qualities of bodies and sensible ideas which are mistaken, by the unsophisticated consciousness, for qualities of bodies, but which do not really exist independently of the sensing of them. An alternative interpretation was advocated, according to which Locke recognises Primary Qualities, Secondary Qualities, and Ideas of Sensation (including both Ideas of Primary Qualities and Ideas of Secondary Qualities) as three distinct groups of entities. By Primary Qualities Locke was said to mean qualities in the strict sense, contrasted with relations in belonging to a body in itself at least momentarily, and it was held that no Primary Qualities are sensible. By Secondary Qualities Locke was said to mean, not a kind of qualities, but a kind of relations, namely powers of bodies, dependent on their determinate Primary Qualities, to produce Ideas of Sensation in the mind of a percipient whose body is suitably situated. Ideas of Sensation were said to be the only sense-data, all of them numerically distinct from qualities of bodies. Accordingly, no difference was

From *Mind*, Vol. XXXIX (1930). Reprinted by permission of *Mind*.

admitted between the ontological status of Ideas of Primary Qualities and the ontological status of Ideas of Secondary Qualities. On the contrary, it was claimed that of all Ideas of Sensation, if of any, Locke shares Berkeley's opinion that their *esse* is *percipi*.[1] That this interpretation modified Locke's definitions of his terms in some important particulars was admitted; but an attempt was made to vindicate such modification as seemed inescapable, by reference to Locke's habitual use of the terms and to the exigencies which might have led him, in spite of the way in which he used them, to define them as he did.[2]

[1] See below, p. 146, note.

[2] The article was not concerned with the history of either the terms or the distinction itself. As I find, however, that I have stated that Boyle "was really the author not only of the terms but also of the distinction itself", I take this opportunity of saying that, though the terms, Primary and Secondary Qualities, had been previously used, they had not been previously—to judge by the citations of Hamilton and Baeumker—used in this sense. It must also be admitted that, though the distinction itself was not that said to have been drawn by Democritus, between what in Locke's terminology would be "primary qualities of insensible parts" and "ideas of secondary qualities," the peculiar feature of Locke's distinction was anticipated by Aristotle's distinction between παθητικαὶ ποιότητες and πάθη, which corresponds to Locke's distinction between "secondary qualities" and "ideas of secondary qualities" (Hamilton's *Reid*, pp. 826–827), while Locke's distinction between "ideas of primary qualities" and "ideas of secondary qualities" appears to correspond to Aristotle's distinction between αἰσθητὰ κοινὰ καὶ ἴδια (*ibid.*, pp. 828–830).

That Locke's Secondary Qualities are not sense-data but powers, was noticed by Hamilton (p. 839*b*) and recently by Baeumker in his article "Zur Vorgeschichte zweier Lockescher Begriffe" (*Archiv für Geschichte der Philosophie*, 1907–08). Baeumker seems, however, to have thought that Boyle did not anticipate Locke on this point. The Secondary Qualities are, he says, "bei Locke nicht, wie bei Boyle, die 'Ideen,' d.h. die Sinnesinhalte selbst; vielmehr versteht er darunter die realen Kräfte in den Dingen, welche jene Ideen bewirken, ihnen aber unähnlich sind" (p. 515, *cf.* pp. 507, 510). Erdmann, while citing Baeumker, seems not to have himself distinguished between Secondary Qualities and sense-data (*Berkeleys Philosophie im Lichte seines wissenschaftlichen Tagebuchs*, p. 44). Cook Wilson, in his "Letter in criticism of a paper on Primary and Secondary Qualities,"

But the article claimed further that Locke's distinction between Primary and Secondary Qualities, if interpreted in accordance with the Berkeleian tradition, is awkwardly related to his distinction between Qualities and Ideas, not only being rendered redundant, as a distinction between physical reality and sensible appearance, by the distinction between Qualities and Ideas, but also, in view of the different standpoint from which the distinction between physical reality and sensible appearance is drawn, being incompatible with the distinction between Qualities and Ideas. This claim assumed that Locke's distinction between Qualities and Ideas was an embodiment of the doctrine of Representative Perception. Now this assumption is not beyond controversy. If a commentator interprets Locke's distinction between Primary and Secondary Qualities in such a way as to imply that Locke did not hold the doctrine of Representative Perception, he may be prepared to acknowledge and defend this implication.

July, 1904 (in *Statement and Inference*, vol. ii., pp. 764–800), also notices (p. 764) that "the secondary qualities, which are qualities of the external object, are strictly speaking not the sensations . . . but the powers in the object to produce the sensations".

The criticism of Berkeley's argument that the primary qualities "are inseparably united with the other sensible qualities" (p. 72 of this volume) is confused, owing to my having first directed it against the argument, erroneously ascribed to Berkeley, that the primary qualities are inseparably united with the *Secondary Qualities*, and having at the last moment corrected the quotation without observing that the correction rendered the criticism inapplicable. It is, however, true that Berkeley uses "sensible quality" as a term covering both what he calls primary and what he calls secondary qualities, and he would have been prepared to accept, as an equivalent contention, Bradley's claim that "without secondary quality extension is not conceivable" (*Appearance and Reality*, p. 16).

On p. 54 the view that Locke thought primary qualities were sensible, is wrongly ascribed to Reid, as well as to Berkeley, instead of only to Berkeley. Reid, so far as I know, never treats Locke as other than a thorough-going Representationist, and his interpretation of Locke's distinction between Primary and Secondary Qualities is at variance with that of the article only in his failure to distinguish between "secondary qualities" and "ideas of secondary qualities".

Campbell Fraser did explicitly defend it in the face of the contrary interpretation of Hamilton, and his view has not been, so far as I know, subjected to criticism. For, although both Dr. Alexander[3] and Professor Gibson[4] have expounded Locke's view of our knowledge of the external world as a version of the doctrine of Representative Perception, they have neither directly challenged, nor endeavoured to refute, the Berkeleian tradition. In fact this tradition seems easily to be overlooked. For Reid, who always treated Locke as an exponent of the doctrine of Representative Perception, and even went so far as to claim that "all philosophers, from Plato to Mr. Hume, agree in this, That we do not perceive external objects immediately, and that the immediate object of perception must be some image present to the mind",[5] not unnaturally supposed that "Berkeley's system follows from Mr. Locke's, by very obvious consequence"[6] and that "a man who was firmly persuaded of the doctrine universally received by philosophers concerning ideas, if he could but take courage to call in question the existence of a material world, would easily find unanswerable arguments in that doctrine".[7] But Reid allows his own just view of the relation between Locke's position and Berkeley's thesis to blind him to the fact, that Berkeley did not recognise the full extent of the admission which Locke had made, but supposed that the view of Locke had first to be modified by proving that Locke's view of "certain sensible qualities", namely that they "have no existence in matter, or without the mind", is true "of all other sensible qualities whatsoever", before it could be made to agree with the doctrine of Representative Perception.[8] Since the Berkeleian tradition seems not to have been refuted and since Campbell Fraser revived the view that Primary Qualities are "called ideas in the mind, at one point of view, phe-

[3] *Locke*, in the series "Philosophies, Ancient and Modern".
[4] *Locke's Theory of Knowledge* (especially pp. 130, 172 *et seq.*, 222 *et seq.*).
[5] Hamilton's *Reid's Works*, 4th ed., p. 263a (all refs. to both Hamilton and Reid, are to this edition).
[6] P. 287a. [7] P. 282b. [8] *Cf.* this volume, p. 72.

nomena presented by the thing, at another",[9] the assumption made in the previous article about the nature of Locke's distinction between Qualities and Ideas requires vindication. Its defence involves questions, the discussion of which would have been disproportionate if presented as an incident in the course of an investigation of the distinction between Primary and Secondary Qualities; and so its defence was not attempted in the previous article. This omission the present article will try to make good.

The title is polemical, since what has to be attempted is to prove that Locke's view of our knowledge of the external world is a version of the doctrine of Representative Perception, and not, assuming this, to inquire in what form Locke held that doctrine.

In the attempt to support this thesis, it will be assumed that there are only two alternatives open to an interpreter of Locke's view of our knowledge of the external world. These alternative interpretations can be advantageously viewed as successive stages in a process of departure from Naïf Realism, common sense being supposed to be "naïvely realistic wherever it does not think that there is some positive reason why it should cease to be so".[10] In Locke's terminology Naïf Realism would be expressed by saying that all "simple ideas of sensation", that are presented "when our senses are actually employed about any object",[11] are qualities of bodies. Now nobody thinks that Locke held this view, it being generally agreed that not only philosophy and science, but even common sense, have reasons for refusing to identify certain "simple ideas of sensation" with any qualities of bodies. If one who has advanced so far neither recognises that the remaining "simple ideas of sensation" are exposed to similar objections nor perceives any inconsistency in assigning to each of two groups of "simple ideas of sensation" a different ontological status, the resultant view will be what may be called the Mixed View. This, unlike Naïf Realism, draws a distinction between appearance and reality, and the dis-

[9] Fraser's edition of Locke's *Essay*, Vol. I., p. 178.
[10] Broad, *Perception, Physics, and Reality*, chap. I.
[11] *Essay* IV., XI., 11.

tinction falls between two groups of "simple ideas of sensation". If, however, it is seen either that those "simple ideas of sensation," which the Mixed View declares to be qualities of bodies, are exposed to direct attack in the same way as those which the Mixed View pronounces to be appearances, or that the withdrawal from physical reality of the one group involves the withdrawal of the other group, the resultant view will be the doctrine of Representative Perception. This agrees with the Mixed View in drawing a distinction between appearance and reality, but the distinction now falls not between two groups of "simple ideas of sensation" but between all "simple ideas of sensation" and all qualities of bodies, so that one can speak of sensible appearance and physical reality as mutually exclusive. It agrees with Naïf Realism only in assigning to all "simple ideas of sensation" a common ontological status. The Mixed View is naïvely realistic with respect to some "simple ideas of sensation" and representationist with respect to others. It is the Mixed View which is attributed to Locke by Berkeley and by Campbell Fraser, and it is the doctrine of Representative Perception which is attributed to him by Reid and Hamilton and by Dr. Alexander and Professor Gibson.

On the assumption that these alternatives are exhaustive, it will still appear that, so far from needing no vindication, the thesis that Locke held the doctrine of Representative Perception is probably incapable of being conclusively proved, and must in any case be stated in carefully guarded terms. The difficulty is occasioned in part by the character of Locke's writings and in part by the peculiar relation between the two views that have been attributed to him.

For, to take the latter source of difficulty first, what has to be shown is that Locke accepted the doctrine of Representative Perception without any reservation in favour of Naïf Realism, and this has to be shown in the face of the claim that Locke's view was constituted in part by the doctrine of Representative Perception and in part by Naïf Realism. Now there is no doubt that Locke not only occasionally, but even habitually, uses the language of Naïf

Realism, and this admission might be supposed, if coupled with the claim that Locke sometimes uses the language of the doctrine of Representative Perception, to be tantamount to the recognition of the rival interpretation. In order to avoid misunderstanding in this matter, it will be necessary to distinguish two references in which a writer may be said to be inconsistent. The charge sometimes means that what is put forward by the writer as a single view is really made up of conflicting propositions. In this sense Kant would be said by many commentators to be inconsistent, in his argument that only objects of possible experience can be known, on the ground that the Subjective Deduction of the Categories is an indispensable part of the argument and that its claims to insight into the conditions which determine experience are incompatible with what Kant is trying to prove. But sometimes the charge means that, even if the writer does put forward an internally consistent view, he at times makes statements which conflict with one or more of the propositions which constitute his view. In this sense Kant would be said to be inconsistent in holding different views of the nature of Time in the Transcendental Æsthetic and in the Transcendental Analytic. If this kind of inconsistency is called *inconstancy*,[12] the term *inconsistency* may be restricted to the former kind. Now it is clear that inconstancy may involve inconsistency. Whether it does so or not depends on whether the occasions of inconstancy can be revised without prejudice to the view with which they conflict, and in the case of Kant's conflicting views about Time commentators disagree in their findings on this question. But it is also clear that inconstancy does not necessarily involve inconsistency; for the occasions of inconstancy may —where due to negligence or to the influence of habits formed before the central view was worked out—be readily amendable. Now, in terms of this distinction it may be said that what has to be shown is that Locke was a *consistent* Representationist, not that he was a *constant* Representationist. He is at times a Naïf Realist and possibly

[12] A term used by Locke (*Essay*, III., x., 5), to denominate vacillation in the use of words.

also at times he holds the Mixed View, but he does not in general hold a view which is made up of tenets selected from Naïf Realism and from the doctrine of Representative Perception.

But the admission that Locke is not a constant Representationist involves the other source of difficulty, which is the necessity of deciding which of the admittedly conflicting passages are the occasions of inconstancy. This difficulty is present in some degree whenever a commentator is engaged in interpretation as distinguished from criticism, in discovering what a writer means as distinguished from estimating the truth of his view. For the attempt to reveal what a writer means—unless it is mere explanation—presupposes that he does not always succeed in saying what he means, and that it is necessary in order to discern his 'real meaning' to reject or amend the passages in which he fails to express it. Now there may be no difficulty in showing that some passages in a philosophical work conflict with others, and no inconsequence in claiming that, inasmuch as the writer cannot be supposed to have intended to contradict himself, some at least of the conflicting passages do not express his 'real meaning'. But there remains the difficulty of selecting the passages which do express it. Moreover, since a writer presumably means what he says, at least at the moment at which he says it, it is necessary to vindicate and explain any reference to a 'real meaning'.

This difficulty is met by some commentators, who proceed on the Hegelian plan of treating all previous philosophies as imperfect expressions of the one true philosophy, by selecting from the treatise which they are professedly interpreting whatever passages seem to them most promising, and setting these down as the embodiment of the writer's 'real meaning'.[13] But, whatever may be the value

[13] *Cf.* Caird, *Critical Philosophy of Kant* (Preface), for the view that "the only valuable criticism is that which turns what is latent in the thought of a great writer against what is explicit, and thereby makes his works a stepping-stone to results which he did not himself attain" and that "to understand [Kant] . . . is to detect a consistent stream of tendency which, through all obstruction, is steadily moving in one direction; to discern the unity

Locke's Version of Representative Perception 133

of this proceeding, (and its value may be incalculable), it seems to be something more than interpretation. It seems clear, for example, that two people may dispute about the question whether Locke really held the Mixed View or the doctrine of Representative Perception, and that this question is distinct from the question which of the two views ascribed to him approximates the closer to the truth.

Perhaps the most satisfactory significance that can be given to the term 'real meaning' is given by defining it as the doctrine which a writer would have selected if his attention had been drawn to the conflicting passages.[14] In order to show that such a claim in behalf of any doctrine is probable, two points must be established. It must be shown that the passages which the interpreter prefers really do embody the doctrine; and it must also be shown that the conflicting passages, although they contradict the doctrine, can fairly be supposed to have been written, under the influence of certain factors, by one who would have surrendered them if he had been aware that they were likely to obscure the doctrine. But, even if these points can be established and if, as is obviously requisite, there is no other doctrine for which a similar case can be presented, the argument could hardly be allowed to prove that so vacillating a writer as Locke would have submitted to the proposed interpretative surgery. In view of this uncertainty it seems best to limit the thesis of this article to the contention that the doctrine of Representative Perception is certainly embodied in some passages of the *Essay*; that there were strong influences which might be fairly supposed to have led Locke, especially if he had never contemplated the Mixed View as a possible alternative to the doctrine of Representative Perception and so was not apprehensive of misunderstanding, to use the language of

---

of one mind which, through all changes of form and expression, is growing towards a more complete consciousness of itself". Whether or not Kant can be satisfactorily expounded in this way, it seems necessary, when dealing with a writer in whom one cannot "detect a consistent stream of tendency which, through all obstruction, is steadily moving in one direction", to distinguish between interpretation and criticism.

[14] *Cf.* Hamilton (p. 820) on the interpretation of Reid.

Naïf Realism on almost all occasions and especially with reference to the Ideas of Primary Qualities; and that it is difficult to understand how Locke could, on the supposition that he really intended the Mixed View, have come to write the passages which embody the doctrine of Representative Perception. Of these three claims, the last can hardly be argued until an explanation of the conflict, on the hypothesis that Locke held the Mixed View, is forthcoming. The argument will therefore be confined mainly to the first two claims.

The first of these claims, namely, that the doctrine of Representative Perception is certainly embodied in some passages, has to be made out in the face of the fact that those very passages, which according to this claim can only be an expression of that doctrine, have been regarded by Campbell Fraser as an expression of the Mixed View, and have been admitted by Hamilton to be unhappily worded. Commenting on Locke's statement that "the ideas of primary qualities of bodies are resemblances of them, and their patterns do really exist in the bodies themselves",[15] Fraser says, "This implies that what we are directly percipient of, *i.e.* the idea, belongs, in the case of the real or primary qualities of sensible things, to the things themselves, being *body itself manifested*, so far as a percept *can* present what is extended."[16] And Hamilton finds it necessary to "modify the obnoxious language," and maintains that Locke's meaning would be better expressed if we "instead of saying that the ideas or notions of the primary qualities *resemble*, merely assert that they *truly represent*, their objects, that is, afford us such a knowledge of their nature as we should have were an immediate intuition of the extended reality in itself competent to man".[17]

[15] II., VIII., 15.   [16] I., p. 173.
[17] P. 842a. Fraser seems to have supposed that in this passage Hamilton is conceding his view that "Locke treats primary qualities as 'real', or 'perfectly resembling the real', and virtually 'the same'; but called ideas in the mind, at one point of view, phenomena presented by the thing, at another" (*Essay*, I., p. 178). His supposition is apparently due to Hamilton's statement that, if the "obnoxious language" were modified as he suggests, "Reid's doctrine and theirs [not "his" as Fraser quotes. Hamilton

In the hope of showing that Locke's language neither implies what Fraser says nor requires the modification which Hamilton prescribes, it will be better to consider the Mixed View and the doctrine of Representative Perception at first, not in the form in which Locke would have had to hold them, but in the form which they assume when stated in terms of the current view that what is sensed is not a "simple idea" but a complex sensum which, though not recognised by the act of sensing as possessing qualities, is recognised as possessing qualities when judgment supervenes upon the act of sensing. Then, when the formulæ appropriate to the doctrine of Representative Perception have been examined, the effect, if any, of Locke's different analysis of the perceptual situation can be taken into account.

Of the Mixed View and of the difference between it

is referring not to Locke only, but to Descartes and Locke] would be found in perfect unison". But, while Hamilton regards both Descartes and Locke as exponents of the doctrine of Representative Perception, he thinks that Reid's "intended" doctrine of perception, "one of *immediate* cognition, under the form of *real presentationism*", is obscured by many statements appropriate to "one of *mediate* cognition under the form of *egoistical representationism*" (p. 820a). Accordingly, in saying that "Reid's doctrine touching the present distinction [that between Primary and Secondary Qualities] corresponds, in all essential respects, with that maintained by" Descartes and Locke (pp. 841–842), he is suggesting that the agreement consists in the acceptance not of a "form of real presentationism", but of a "form of egoistical representationism" which "rejected all representative entities different from the act itself of cognition" (p. 842a). His objection to Locke's language is not that it implies "representationism" but that it implies, he thinks, a crude form of "representationism". Hence he says that "the whole difficulty and dispute on this point is solved by the old distinction of *similarity in existence*, and *similarity in representation*" (p. 842a), which I take to imply that Locke should have said that the "idea" is similar, in its character as a representation, to the "quality," but that "idea" and "quality" are different in existence. Since Locke is clearly using "idea" to denote a content sensed and not an act of sensing, his language does not seem to need the modification which Hamilton proposes. But it may be admitted that Locke does not face the problem of the ontological status of "ideas of sensation".

and the doctrine of Representative Perception, Dr. Broad has given an account in his chapter on "The Theory of Sensa" in *Scientific Thought*.[18] He there contrasts what he holds to be "involved in the common scientific view of physical objects and their sensible appearances"[19] or "what the average person with a scientific training believes"[20] with what he calls the "Critical Scientific Theory", which is "an attempt to formulate clearly, in terms of the Sensum Theory of sensible appearance, the view about the external world which has been at the back of the scientific mind since the time of Descartes and Locke".[21] The aim of each view is "to assert the *physical* reality of shapes and sizes, and to deny the *physical* reality of colours, temperatures, noises, etc.".[22] But, while the crude view maintains that the physically real qualities are sensible and that the surfaces to which they belong are sensible, the more developed view denies that any physically real qualities are sensible and holds that the physically real qualities can be determined only by inference from physically unreal qualities, to which they are causally related and some of which resemble them. Dr. Broad contends that the Mixed View is inconsistent both with itself and with the facts.[23] It is internally inconsistent because it by implication both affirms and denies that what we sense are surfaces of bodies, by affirming that sensible shape is physically real and yet denying that colour is physically real.[24] It is inconsistent with the facts because the argument, based on variation of sensible qualities where the object body is supposed to undergo no change, which has been used to prove the physical unreality of some sensible qualities, has the same force when stated with reference to the supposedly physically real sensible qualities. It is an attempt to combine a naïvely realistic view of some sensible qualities with a "causal theory" of others, and it is necessary "to restate it in a completely causal form".[25]

[18] Pp. 272–283. [19] P. 272. [20] P. 273.
[21] Pp. 281–282. [22] P. 279. [23] Pp. 273–274.
[24] This is not quite the same as Broad's argument.
[25] P. 282.

When so restated the Mixed View is superseded by the doctrine of Representative Perception. It will be convenient to formulate the doctrine of Representative Perception in terms of a negative and a positive tenet. The negative tenet is that no physical reality is sensible. In current terminology this may be expressed by saying that no sensa are parts of bodies, and, on one view of the nature of a quality, it will follow that no sensible qualities are qualities of bodies. The positive tenet is that there is a physical reality and that it is represented[26] by sensible appearance. The statement that sensible appearance *represents* physical reality does not *mean* that sensible appearance *resembles* physical reality. But the statement can be defended only on the supposition that sensible appearance does resemble physical reality, since otherwise an exponent of the doctrine would be unable to give any account of the nature of physical reality, even to the extent of pronouncing it to be spatial. Nevertheless, all that is *meant* by saying that sensible appearance represents physical reality is that the apprehension of sensible appearance serves the percipient instead of the apprehension of physical reality. Thus the sensing of colour may lead the percipient to select appropriate food. The power of the food to produce a certain effect upon the body of the percipient is, according to Locke, conditioned by some of the determinate primary qualities of the food; and the secondary quality, or power to produce sensible colour, is also conditioned by some of the determinate primary qualities of the food. If, instead of sensing the colour, we sensed the determinate primary qualities by means of which the food produces the colour, we should, by associating these qualities with the

[26] What follows has nothing to do with Locke's use of the word 'represent'. He uses the word 'representation' (*Essay*, II., xxx., 2) as a synonym for 'image'. But we are concerned here only with the meaning of our claim that Locke accepted the doctrine of Representative Perception. An attempt was made in the previous article (this volume pp. 69–70) to show that the phrase "idea of a quality" could be interpreted to mean 'idea representing a quality'. Cook Wilson seems to have thought that 'represent' should mean 'resemble'. (*Statement and Inference*, vol. ii., p. 771.)

power to produce a certain effect upon our bodies, be able equally well to select appropriate food. Locke seems sometimes to think that if we could sense the primary qualities, including the so-called "qualities of the insensible parts", we should, instead of waiting on experiment, be able to predict the powers of a body, and so be able to establish a *Science* of Physics. But it is in any case clear that the qualities of the food might be reasonably supposed to be able to serve the purpose, if these qualities were sensible, which is in fact served by the physically unreal sensible qualities. It follows that, without holding that a sensible quality resembles a physical quality, we can intelligibly say that it represents, stands for, or serves instead of, a physical quality. It is necessary that some such account be given of the meaning of 'represent', as implied in such phrases as "idea of a quality", because if 'represent' were taken to mean 'resemble'—and it seems certain that the two words do not in general have the same meaning—the inevitable inquiry into the extent of the resemblance of sensible appearance to the physical reality which it represents would be anticipated. And, in fact, on Locke's view, resemblance by no means necessarily accompanies representation. For the statement that "the ideas of primary qualities of bodies are resemblances of them"[27] means that the "ideas" which represent the macroscopic primary qualities resemble those qualities, and this is clearly intended to be a synthetic judgment. And the claim, that "there is nothing like our ideas [of secondary qualities] existing in the bodies themselves",[28] means that the "ideas" which represent the microscopic primary qualities do not resemble those qualities, so that here representation and resemblance are unquestionably distinct.

Theories which agree in these two tenets may differ in detail, so that it is appropriate to speak of Locke's view, according to our thesis, as a *version* of the doctrine of Representative Perception. Thus the Cartesian version differs from the Lockian version in its account of the nature of

[27] II., VIII., 15.   [28] II., VIII., 15.

physical reality. But unless what is said to be represented by sensible appearance is at least spatial it is not properly described as physical reality. So a theory which maintains, with Berkeley, that only spiritual substances are represented by sensible appearance, or, with Hume, that the nature of what is represented cannot be determined, should not according to the above formulation be classified as a version of the doctrine of Representative Perception.[29] Then, again, different views may be taken of the nature of sensible appearance. It may be held to be either dependent on, or independent of, the sensing of it, and so on, provided that it is not identified with physical reality.[30] This is important for our purpose, because Locke does not seem to have made up his mind about the status of "ideas of sensation," and this article does not try to determine his view, or views, on that question. Lastly, the extent of the resemblance of sensible appearance to physical reality may be variously estimated without violation of the *sine quibus non* of the doctrine of Representative Perception. For our purpose, it is Locke's acceptance of the negative tenet that has to be made out; for it is the negative tenet that distinguishes the doctrine of Representative Perception from the Mixed View.

A special problem, which is easily seen to confront the doctrine of Representative Perception thus formulated, is presented by the tendency of the positive tenet to conflict with the negative tenet. For the negative tenet requires that physical reality should be numerically distinct from sensible appearance, that no physical reality should be any sensible appearance: but the positive tenet requires that physical reality should be *known* though not *sensed*, and this claim can be justified only by showing that sensible

[29] There is, so far as I know, no reason why the doctrine of Berkeley should not be called a version of the doctrine of Representative Perception, provided that the positive tenet is formulated in such a way as to include non-physical realities among the realities which sensible appearance may be held to represent.

[30] *Cf.* Hamilton (pp. 804–819) for various possible forms of Representationism in reference to the ontological status of the representative entities.

appearance can be the source of the knowledge of physical reality. This obligation is twofold. Not only must it be shown that sensible appearance is evidence for the existence of a physical reality of such a kind as the version of the doctrine of Representative Perception describes. It must also be shown that sensible appearance is the source of acquaintance with the qualities which are asserted on that evidence to belong to physical reality. The latter requisite offers a difficulty apart from the question of the cogency of the evidence, a difficulty which lies in the reconciliation of the numerical distinctness of physical reality and sensible appearance with the necessity of describing physical reality in terms of sensible appearance. On the one hand, there is a temptation to express the fact of numerical distinctness by saying that, just because no physical reality is any sensible appearance, no attribute of physical reality can be also an attribute of sensible appearance. On the other hand, the possibility of describing physical reality in terms of sensible appearance would be commonly defended by saying, that physical reality and sensible appearance have certain attributes in common, and that to describe physical reality it is necessary only to enumerate those attributes of sensible appearance which are also attributes of physical reality. The conflict is evidently due to different uses of the term 'attribute', and the different uses affect equally such terms as 'quality', 'property', and 'character'. When it is said that no attribute of physical reality can be also an attribute of sensible appearance, 'attribute' is treated as a particular. When it is said that physical reality and sensible appearance have attributes in common, 'attribute' is treated as a universal. Accordingly the formula which an exponent of the doctrine of Representative Perception selects for expressing the relation of sensible appearance to physical reality will be conditioned by his attitude towards the problem of the particularity or universality of attributes.

The settlement of this controversy about the propriety of the application to characteristics, whether attributes or relations, of the distinction between universal and particular is fortunately beyond the scope of this article.[31] But it is important for our purpose that the point at issue in this controversy should be recognised. The two views are defined by Prof. Stout in his lecture on 'The Nature of Universals and Propositions'.[32] The one view, which Prof. Stout attacks, he formulates as follows: "There is no plurality of particular qualities corresponding to the plurality of particular things. The common quality is regarded as indivisibly single. Two billiard balls are both round and smooth. So far as they are both round, the roundness of the one is the roundness of the other. . . . Abstract nouns, as standing for the quality in its singleness, without reference to any multiplicity of things qualified by it, are thus regarded as singular terms, like proper names".[33] "Qualities and relations, as such, are universals."[34] To this he opposes the view that "a character characterising a concrete thing or individual is as particular as the thing or individual which it characterises. Of two billiard balls, each has its own particular roundness separate and distinct from that of the other, just as the billiard balls themselves are distinct and separate".[35] "Abstract nouns are . . . not singular but general terms. Shape, for example, stands for 'all shapes as such'."[36] On this view "the phrase 'common character' is elliptical. It really signifies a certain general kind or class of characters. To say that particular things share in the common character is to say that each of them has a character which is a particular instance of this kind or class of characters." This claim has nothing to do with the claim that some qualities are determinables, and that one determinate form of a given determinable is different from another determinate form of the same determinable. The differ-

[31] Cook Wilson's distinction between 'attribute' and 'attribute-element' seems to afford an argument in support of the recognition of particular attributes. For if 'attribute' can be resolved into 'having an attribute-element', and if an 'attribute-element' is a particular, the 'having a particular attribute-element' must be itself particular (*Statement and Inference*, vol. i., p. 153 et seq.; p. 199).
[32] *Proceedings of the Brit. Acad.*, vol. x.   [33] P. 4.
[34] P. 3.   [35] P. 4.   [36] P. 5.

ence between particular instances of a class of characters is not a difference of kind, whether generic or specific. This may be seen by selecting a variant of a determinable of the lowest order, where differentiation into determinate forms is precluded, such as 'equilateral triangularity'. On Prof. Stout's view, the equilateral triangularity of one equilateral triangle is not identical with the equilateral triangularity of another equilateral triangle. But the equilateral triangularity of each is "a particular instance of the kind or class of" equilateral triangularities, which is coextensive with the class of equilateral triangles. It seems to follow that the relation of similarity can connect particular instances of a class of characters and not only particular instances of a class of things. On the other hand, those who hold that "qualities and relations, as such, are universal" must maintain the impropriety of the statement, that a quality of one substance is like a quality of another substance, except where the statement means that the resembling attributes are different determinate forms of the same determinable. Thus it would be right to say that the shape of one surface is like the shape of another surface, if, while each surface is triangular, one is a right-angled isosceles triangle and the other is an equilateral triangle. For this would mean that the single quality 'equilateral triangularity,' and the single quality 'right angled isosceles triangularity', the one of which belongs to the one surface (as well as to others not mentioned) and the other of which belongs to the other surface (as well as to others not mentioned), have in common the single character of being determinate forms of the single determinable, 'triangularity' (which single character is also common to other determinate forms). But, when two equilateral triangles are being compared, the proper statement is that the equilateral triangularity of the one is the equilateral triangularity of the other, and this statement would not, on this view, as it would on Prof. Stout's view, be incompatible with the numerical distinctness of the two triangles.

If, bearing in mind these two views about the nature of a character, we return to the distinction between the doc-

Locke's Version of Representative Perception 143

trine of Representative Perception and the Mixed View, we find that this would have to be expressed in one way by those who hold that a character is necessarily universal and in another way by those who hold that a character of a particular thing is itself particular. Let it be supposed that in some perceptual situations the sensible appearance is geometrically similar to the physical reality. According to the doctrine of Representative Perception, the situation would have to be described by those who hold that a character of a particular thing is itself particular, by saying that the particular shape of the sensible appearance is not identical with, but resembles, the particular shape of the physical reality. But, according to the Mixed View, the situation would be described, by saying that the particular shape of the sensible appearance is the particular shape of the physical reality. And the internal inconsistency of the Mixed View would be easily seen to arise from the fact that, while this implies that the sensible appearance is identical with the physical reality, the claim, that the particular colour of the sensible appearance is not a characteristic of the physical reality, which is not coloured at all, implies that the sensible appearance is not identical with the physical reality. Those who hold that a character is necessarily universal could not accept this account. But they could give an alternative account. They would have to describe the situation, according to the doctrine of Representative Perception, by saying that the sensible appearance and the physical reality are different instances of the same single determinate shape. According to the Mixed View, the sensible appearance and the physical reality would be the same instance of this single determinate shape, and the internal inconsistency of the Mixed View would arise from the fact that, while this implies that the physical reality is identical with the sensible appearance, the view that the sensible appearance is, while the physical reality is not, an instance of colour, implies that they are not identical. The important consideration for our purpose is that, whereas, on the view that a character is as such a universal, the statement, that the shape of the sensible appearance is the shape of the physical reality, would be in accordance with the doctrine of Representative Perception, on the view that a character of a particular thing is itself particular, this statement, unless recognised as an elliptical way of saying that the two particular shapes are two instances of a class of such shapes, would abandon the doctrine of Representative Perception, and would imply either the Mixed View or Naïf Realism.

Now there seems to be no doubt that Locke would have acquiesced in the view that "a character characterising a concrete thing is as particular as the thing or individual which it characterises". For he held that "general and universal belong not to the real existence of things; but are the inventions and creations of the understanding" and that when "we quit particulars, the generals that rest[37] are only creatures of our own making; their general nature being nothing but the capacity they are put into, by the understanding, of signifying or representing many particulars".[38] It is true that in these passages Locke is concerned rather with things than with qualities. But his attitude towards qualities is governed by the same principle. For, by way of illustration of the origin of universals as a means of avoiding endless names, he says, "Thus the same colour being observed to-day in chalk or snow, which the mind yesterday received from milk, it considers that appearance alone, makes it a representative of all that kind; and having given it the name whiteness, it by that sound signifies the same quality wheresoever to be imagined or met with; and thus universals, whether ideas or terms, are made."[39] The determination with which he clung to this view is strikingly evidenced in his criticism of Stillingfleet's distinction between nature considered as particular and nature considered as universal, or nature considered "as it is in distinct individuals" and nature "considered

[37] Gibson quotes "result" (pp. 322–323).
[38] *Essay*, III., III., 11. *Cf.* Gibson (pp. 322–323), and *Remarks upon some of Mr. Norris's Books*, § 12.
[39] II., XI., 9. That Locke's language betrays the awkward nature of his position is not a sufficient reason for doubting that this was his position.

abstractly, without respect to individual persons". Stillingfleet's distinction is clearly expressed, and he gives reasons for drawing it. On the one hand, "the nature of man, as in Peter, is distinct from the same nature, as it is in James and John; otherwise, they would be but one person, as well as have the same nature".[40] On the other hand "the nature itself remains one and the same; which appears from this evident reason, that otherwise every individual must make a different kind".[40] Now not only does Locke fail altogether, in his first letter, to grasp Stillingfleet's view, but in his second letter he details with approval the objection of a friend, that Stillingfleet's "sticking so close all along to that vulgar way of speaking of the same common nature, being in several individuals, has made him less easy to be understood. For to speak truly and precisely of this matter, as in reality it is, there is no such thing as one and the same common nature in several individuals; for all, that in truth is in them, is particular, and can be nothing but particular".[41] This being Locke's view, the appropriate statement for him to make in comparing two similar things is, not that they have a quality in common, but that a quality of the one resembles a quality of the other.

But, before examining Locke's attempt to meet the difficulty presented by the tendency of the positive tenet of the doctrine of Representative Perception to lead to a qualification of the negative tenet, it is necessary to notice a peculiarity of Locke's version of the doctrine. In the account given above of the relation between physical reality and sensible appearance, it has been throughout assumed that sensible appearance is made up of things with qualities, in accordance with the prevalent view that what is sensed is never a bare quality, such as colour, but always a complex sensum, to which qualities, such as shape and colour, belong. Now it seems pretty certain that Locke intended to denote, by "simple ideas of sensation", not what are denoted by 'sensa', but what are denoted by 'sensible qualities'. But what he intended to connote is far

[40] Works (1794), vol. iii., pp. 72–73.   [41] P. 175.

from clear. Despite his statement that the ideas produced "by the qualities that affect our senses" "enter by the senses simple and unmixed",[42] which suggests that we are supposed first to apprehend "simple ideas of sensation" and then by a subsequent synthesis to generate sensa, Campbell Fraser seems to be right in denying that Locke meant to assert that the simple ideas can be "received, or represented, in their simplicity",[43] and in claiming that the simple ideas are supposed to be original data only as constituents of aggregates—what Hume called "complex impressions"—in which they can be distinguished by subsequent analysis. Granted, however, that the simple ideas of sensation are always apprehended in groups, this does not require them to be qualities. Locke's usual expression is that they "exist in combination" or "accompany one another", and he never speaks of them as qualities of sensible appearance nor as qualities of anything except when he in his naïvely realistic language treats them as sensible qualities of bodies. He habitually regards them as dependent for their existence on the sensing of them, but he does not suppose that they are qualities of mind. Unfortunately, he never faces the problem of the ontological status of simple ideas of sensation.[44] If, however, Locke was in-

[42] *Essay*, II., II., 1.
[43] Vol. i., p. 144. Cf. *Essay*, II., XII., 1; XXII., 2; Gibson, pp. 47–49, 61–62.
[44] Cf. T. E. Webb, *The Intellectualism of Locke*, for the view that "the Idea of Locke, like the Idea of Arnauld, is the mere act of thought considered as an object of reflection" (p. 38). It is true that in many passages, such as "our ideas being nothing but actual perceptions in the mind, which cease to be anything when there is no perception of them" (*Essay*, II., x., 2), and perhaps generally in the *Essay*, Locke holds the view that "ideas" depend for their existence on the consciousness of them. But in his *Examination of Malebranche* and his *Remarks upon some of Mr. Norris's Books*, he seems not to recognise the extent of the ground common to him and to his opponents; and his unwillingness to admit that on his own view "ideas," being neither "modifications of the mind" nor physical qualities, are in God in the only sense in which they are in the mind of a percipient—as objects of consciousness—leads him into difficulties. Sometimes what is seen is "the marygold in the garden" (*Remarks*, § 2); at other times it is "the image . . . on the retina" (*Exam.*, § 10).

Locke's Version of Representative Perception 147

clined to treat them as substantival, in the sense that they are not qualities of anything, this would only strengthen his inclination to regard them as particulars. Viewed as an attempt, by one who regarded both "simple ideas of sensation" and qualities of bodies as particulars, to reconcile the two tenets of the doctrine of Representative Perception, Locke's distinction between Qualities and Ideas and his claim that some Ideas resemble Qualities present themselves as complementary requisites of that doctrine.

It is to preserve the negative tenet that the distinction between Qualities and Ideas is drawn. That Locke's language, even in the formulation of this distinction, is woefully confused, must be admitted.[45] Not only does he identify Qualities or "modifications of matter in the bod-

---

And he urges against Malebranche the difficulty of explaining how on Malebranche's view we can "know there is any such thing existing as body at all" (*Exam.*, § 52) without betraying the least suspicion that his own view is exposed to the same objection. In fact, he was justly "complained of for not having 'given an account of, or defined the nature of our ideas'" (*Remarks*, § 2), since, while willing to admit that "seeing a colour, and hearing a sound, is a modification of the mind", if this means "an alteration of the mind from not perceiving to perceiving that sound or colour" (*Exam.*, § 47), he never faces the necessity of determining the status, on his view, of the sound and the colour themselves. Webb's argument, that "in the Examination Locke denies that Ideas are 'Modifications of *Mind*', while in the Essay he consistently admits that they are 'Modifications of *Thinking*'" (p. 38), or that he denies "Ideas to be Modifications of the mental Substance," but holds they are "Modifications of the mental Energy, and, therefore, identical with the percipient act" (p. 37), does not seem to be capable of explaining these passages. And the passage which Webb cites, that in thinking "the mind observes a great variety of modifications, and from thence receives distinct ideas" (*Essay*, II., XIX., 1), is of no assistance. For Locke is there speaking of mental acts, and the "ideas" referred to are "ideas of reflection", and there is no objection to the claim that these are "modifications of the mental Energy". What is in dispute is how the "ideas of sensation", of which some of these "modifications" are the acts of apprehension, are related to the apprehension of them.

[45] *Cf.* Reid, p. 317. Hamilton finds that these "strictures on Locke are rather hypercritical". But the nature of the confusion must be considered if Locke is to be interpreted at all.

ies" with "the power to produce any idea in our mind",[46] which strictly belongs to the body "by reason of its insensible primary qualities".[47] He also introduces the distinction between Qualities and Ideas as a distinction between two kinds of "ideas".[48] Moreover, his choice of terms is unhappy and is an offence against his maxim to apply "words as near as may be to such ideas as common use has annexed them to".[49] For his distinction requires that the term "Quality" be restricted, in its application, to qualities of physical reality, and that what it would be in accordance with general usage to call qualities of sensible appearance or, at any rate, sensible qualities be called not "Qualities" but "Ideas". He may have been influenced in this by his habit of not regarding "simple ideas of sensation" as qualities of anything. But it is not surprising that he is unequal to the strain of constantly observing the breach with the general usage of so widely current a term as 'quality', and that he queers his distinction both by speaking of "sensible qualities" when his distinction requires "Ideas" and by references to "ideas in the things themselves" where he should say "Qualities". If we distinguish the technical use of the terms by means of initial capitals, we may say that Locke's distinction safeguards the negative tenet of the doctrine of Representative Perception by calling qualities of physical reality 'Qualities' and by calling what we call qualities of sensible appearance or sensible qualities 'Ideas'.

It is in order to reconcile with the distinction between Qualities and Ideas the implication of the positive tenet, that physical reality can be described in terms of sensible appearance, that Locke goes on to claim, not that physical reality resembles sensible appearance in the possession of certain common qualities, but that certain qualities of sensible appearance or certain "simple ideas of sensation" resemble certain qualities of physical reality. Had he held that "qualities and relations, as such, are universals," and had he also recognised that "simple ideas of sensation" are qualities of sensible appearance, he could, without jeop-

[46] II., viii., 7, 8.   [47] II., viii., 23.   [48] II., viii., 7.
[49] III., xi., 11.

Locke's Version of Representative Perception 149

ardising the doctrine of Representative Perception, have claimed that physical reality and sensible appearance have certain qualities in common. But since he held that "general and universal belong not to the real existence of things," and since he did not usually regard "simple ideas of sensation" as qualities of anything, such a claim would have been fatal to the numerical distinctness of Qualities and Ideas. On the other hand, the formula which he chooses both makes it possible for him to describe physical reality in terms of sensible appearance and, so far from involving any qualification in the direction of Naïf Realism of the negative tenet of the doctrine of Representative Perception, itself presupposes the integrity of the negative tenet. For his claim is that some Ideas, namely, "ideas of primary qualities", "are resemblances of them, and their patterns do really exist in the bodies themselves", while other Ideas, namely, "ideas of secondary qualities", "have no resemblance of them at all".[50] This claim clearly requires that the particular Qualities and Ideas, which either resemble or do not resemble one another, be numerically distinct.

·Now the whole purport of this proceeding is smothered when Locke is interpreted as if he accepted the Mixed View, and when the statement that "ideas of primary qualities" resemble Qualities is treated as if it identified "ideas of primary qualities" with Qualities. It has already been claimed "that it is difficult to understand how Locke could, on the supposition that he really intended the Mixed View, have come to write the passages which embody the doctrine of Representative Perception". It may be worth while to examine Campbell Fraser's handling of the problem. Commenting on the statement "that the ideas of primary qualities of bodies are resemblances of them, and their patterns do really exist in the bodies themselves; but the ideas produced in us by these second-

[50] II., VIII., 15. I take "them" to be, in the first statement, the Qualities represented by Ideas of Primary Qualities, and, in the second statement, the Qualities (microscopic) represented by Ideas of Secondary Qualities. See this volume (pp. 67–70).

ary qualities have no resemblance of them at all",[51] he says, "Locke, less subtle [than Berkeley], probably means, in his vague way, that the primary qualities are virtually the ideas we have of them, while of the other qualities there is nothing in the things that can be identified with what we feel. The alleged 'resemblance' in the former case is Locke's way of asserting the objective existence of the presented appearance or idea."[52] Why Locke, if this had been his meaning, should have expressed himself so oddly—and the oddity is by no means adequately recognised in the description of Locke's language as a "vague way" of speaking—is not explained. In point of fact, Locke's statement, vague though it may be in other references, is with reference to this issue sufficiently definite, and the objection to it, from the point of view of a commentator who attributes to Locke the view that some "ideas of sensation" are identical with qualities of physical reality, is not that it is vague, but that it is definitely incapable of being so construed. But it has already been argued that the statement, which Locke *should*, according to Campbell Fraser, have made, is incompatible with the distinction between Qualities and Ideas which he had just previously drawn, while the statement which Locke *did* make is exactly what is required to prevent that distinction from reducing Locke to silence on the subject of the nature of physical reality and at the same time requires that the distinction be maintained unimpaired. The interpretation, therefore, represents Locke as meaning something, which his statement cannot reasonably be supposed to mean, which he has no motive for saying, and which he has a sound motive for not saying.

With the truth or falsity of Locke's view this article is not directly concerned. But it is possible that the opinion of some of Locke's critics, that the claim that some Ideas resemble Qualities is not even plausible, has been in part responsible for the belief that Locke did not mean what he said. It must be admitted that Locke overstates the resemblance, since a determinate Quality is not, except per-

[51] II., VIII., 15.   [52] I., 173.

Locke's Version of Representative Perception 151

haps in unusual perceptual situations, an exact "pattern" of the Idea which represents it. Possibly, however, Webb is right in saying that, "in stating our Ideas of the Primary Qualities to be exact resemblances, Locke merely meant to assert that those Qualities exist in nature exactly as in thought we conceive them to exist".[53] But, in any case, the trouble is not removed by the substitution of identity for resemblance. The criticism offered by Berkeley seems, however, to have nothing to do with the variability of "ideas of primary qualities" where the Qualities are believed to be constant. He claims that "an idea can be like nothing but an idea; a colour or figure can be like nothing but another colour or figure".[54] Now Locke does not say that colour—an "idea of a secondary quality"—is like a Quality, but he does say that the "idea of shape" is like a Quality, and to this Berkeley's objection seems to be either that physical reality cannot have shape, or that a sensible quality cannot resemble a physical quality because the one is sensible and the other is physical—an objection which rests on a failure to recognise that resemblance, so far from precluding, presupposes difference.[55] And the criti-

[53] *The Intellectualism of Locke*, p. 30.   [54] *Principles*, viii.
[55] It almost looks as if Cook Wilson brings this objection against the doctrine, when he says, "Is Hs (*i.e.*, heat as sensed), representative of Hx (*i.e.*, Heat as in the body) as being like it? No: for then Hx as like a sensation in quality would itself have to be a sensation: and that, according to your own view, would be a 'flagrant absurdity' " (*Statement and Inference*, vol. ii., p. 773).
Again, "With you 'representative' means 'representing something other than itself'; it would be important to say what 'other than itself' exactly means, whether 'other' as one smarting pain is other than another such pain or different in kind as the smart is different from the thorn which causes it . . . your theory necessitates the latter kind of difference, for if Hs, which represents Hx in the body, were *like* Hx, what you call the flagrant absurdity would be committed of supposing the body had a sensation" (pp. 779–780). But it is, perhaps, impossible to understand his argument without access to the paper which he is discussing.
Berkeley, in bringing this criticism, inconsistently implies that Locke did hold the doctrine of Representative Perception. He seems not to have noticed that the argument, that what has been proved of "certain sensible qualities", namely, that they "have

cism offered by Reid seems also to have nothing to do with the fact that the resemblance is overstated, but to be conditioned by his curious[56] refusal to distinguish between 'act of sensing' and 'content sensed', which results in his first supposing that an "idea of a primary quality" is a "sensation" and then arguing that "no quality of an inanimate insentient being can have the least resemblance to it".[57]

Before considering the problem presented by the conflicting passages, we may observe that the view that Qualities and Ideas are numerically distinct, is by no means confined to the passages we have examined. It is clearly implied when Qualities are contrasted with "the ideas produced by them in the mind"[58] and when Ideas are contrasted with their "external causes", which may be "but a privation in the subject".[59] Even in a passage in which Locke, apparently overlooking the incompleteness of the resemblance of "ideas of primary qualities" to the Qualities which they represent, and so being in danger of substituting identity for resemblance, namely, in the statement that "a circle or square are the same, whether in idea or existence, in the mind or in the manna", the manna is still said to be "able to produce in us the idea of a round or square figure", while the "idea of motion represents it [the Quality] as it [the Quality] really is in manna moving".[60]

There are, however, numerous passages in which Locke uses the language of Naïf Realism. We have already seen that the distinction between Qualities and Ideas is introduced as a distinction among "ideas", and they are said to be distinguished "as they are ideas or perceptions in our minds; and as they are modifications of matter in the

---

no existence in matter, or without the mind", "may be likewise proved of all other sensible qualities whatsoever" (*Principles*, xiv.), could not be a criticism of the same doctrine as the argument that "an idea can be like nothing but an idea".

[56] Curious in view of his full recognition of the distinction between "thought and the object of thought" (*e.g.*, p. 277).

[57] P. 229. Reid is referring to 'pain,' but he claims that "what we have said of pain may be applied to every other sensation".

[58] II., VIII., 22.   [59] II., VIII., 1, 2.   [60] II., VIII., 18.

bodies that cause such perceptions in us". It is clear that the word "they" could grammatically refer to the same entities, but only at the cost of implying the identity of "ideas of secondary qualities" as well as of "ideas of primary qualities" with Qualities. But there are more definite instances. Thus "external material things" are identified with "the objects of sensation" in a context which demands that "objects of sensation" be interpreted as "objects sensed".[61] Again "simple ideas", without distinction between "ideas of primary qualities" and "ideas of secondary qualities", are said to be "conveyed in by the senses, as they are found in exterior things",[62] and, in the sections which follow, the language proper to the doctrine of Representative Perception, according to which Locke speaks of "qualities which are capable of producing simple ideas in us",[63] alternates with the language proper to Naïf Realism, until Locke, in a desperate attempt to be fair to everybody, takes refuge in the comprehensive geniality of the formula "qualities or simple ideas",[64] as if the terms were interchangeable. In one passage he refers to "the particular ringing sound there is in gold";[65] and, when he claims that there can be no "doubt to the eye (that can distinctly see white and black), Whether this ink and this paper be all of a colour",[66] he implies that an "idea of a secondary quality" is identical with a Quality. But there are also passages in which Locke identifies only "ideas of primary qualities" with Qualities. Motion and figure are said to be "really in the manna whether we take notice of them or no".[67] Primary Qualities are said to be "in them [bodies], whether we perceive them or not".[68] And the important term "insensible primary qualities",[69] applied to microscopic qualities, implies that macroscopic qualities are sensible, though the expression "every particle of matter which has bulk enough to be perceived"[70] can be corrected by reference to the more accurate "masses of matter, of a bulk sufficient to cause a sensation in us".[71]

[61] II., I., 4.   [62] II., XXIII., 1.   [63] II., XXIII., 2.
[64] II., XXIII., 6.   [65] III., XI., 21.   [66] IV., II., 5.
[67] II., VIII., 18.   [68] II., XXIII., 9.   [69] II., VIII., 23.
[70] II., VIII., 9.   [71] II., IV., 1.

There seems to be no difficulty in accounting for these passages on the view that Locke really intended the doctrine of Representative Perception and that the passages are, accordingly, occasions of inconstancy. The inaccuracy arises in part from the well-known difficulty of constantly adapting a language to meet the needs of a doctrine which was formulated long after the language had become firmly established, a difficulty intensified for Locke by his contempt for the traditional terminology of the Scholastics and by his sympathy with the plain man. It is also in part due to the fact that Locke is largely occupied in giving an account of the origin of our "complex ideas of particular substances", and, as these ideas are certainly acquired before the difficulties of Naïf Realism are felt, the consciousness whose development Locke traces does suppose qualities of bodies to be sensible. These considerations, together with the fact that Locke explicitly asks indulgence for such inconstancy,[72] and even chooses the term "secondary quality" as "accommodated to the vulgar notions, without which one cannot be well understood",[73] seem to justify the qualification of these passages in the light of what Locke says elsewhere. But the vital consideration, if we have to choose between the Mixed View and the doctrine of Representative Perception, is that the naïvely realistic passages have to be treated as occasions of inconstancy on either interpretation; and, in treating the passages in which "ideas of primary qualities" are identified with Qualities as also occasions of inconstancy, one can plead all the same influences in explanation, together with the additional factor of the resemblance of the entities thus inconstantly identified.

[72] II., VIII., 8.   [73] II., XXXI., 2. *Cf.* II., VIII., 10.

LOCKE AND THE PROBLEM OF PERSONAL IDENTITY

ANTONY FLEW

I. PREAMBLE

This paper attempts to do three main things. First, it outlines Locke's contribution to the discussion of the problem of personal identity, that is, the philosophical problem of what is meant by the expression "same person." Second, it attacks Locke's proposed solution, showing that it is quite irreparably wrong. Third, it enquires how Locke was misled into offering this mistaken yet perennially seductive answer.

II. LOCKE'S CONTRIBUTION

Locke's contribution to the discussion was fourfold. First, he saw the importance of the problem. Second, he realized that the puzzle cases, the "strange suppositions," were relevant. Third, he maintained that "same" had a different meaning when applied to the noun "person" from its meaning in other applications. And, fourth, he offered his own answer to the main question of the meaning of "same person."

1. Locke saw the importance of the problem. It is important because, "In this personal identity is founded all the right and justice of reward and punishment" (*Essay*, II, xxvii, 18). That is to say, it is never fair to blame nor

From *Philosophy*, Vol. XXVI (1951). Reprinted by permission of the author and *Philosophy*. The paper has been revised for this volume.

just to punish the prisoner in the dock for murdering his bride in her bath unless the prisoner is the same person as he who did the deed. The same is equally true of the ascription of responsibility at the Last Judgment. Furthermore and even more fundamentally, as Locke clearly saw but never so clearly stated, all questions of survival, pre-existence, and immortality, are questions of personal identity. The question "Is Cesare Borgia still alive, surviving bodily death?" is equivalent to "Is there a person now alive, surviving bodily death, who is the same person as Cesare Borgia?"

But it might still be argued (and certainly would be argued, by those numerous contemporary philosophers who pray, with the Trinity mathematicians, that their subject may never be of any use to anybody) that all that has been proved is that some important questions are or involve questions of personal identity, and that it has not been shown that these questions demand a solution of the philosophical problem of personal identity. Perhaps psychical research can proceed without benefit of any philosophical analysis of "same person" just as many other sciences proceed satisfactorily with the study of so-and-sos without feeling handicapped by the lack of philosophical analyses of the expression "so-and-sos." This analogy is misleading here. For it is precisely the cases studied by psychical researchers and parapsychologists, which raise both in them and in everyone who reads of their work, exactly those questions of meaning which it is the proper business of analytical philosophy to answer.

When we are presented with stories like that of the "Watseka Wonder," recorded by William James in Chapter x of *The Principles of Psychology*, we ask whether the patient Lurancy Vennum really was or became the same person as Mary Roff. Someone then is bound to ask what we mean by "same person," for this is pre-eminently the sort of question where "It all depends what you mean." Or take an example from Locke: "I once met with one, who was persuaded that his had been the *soul* of Socrates (how reasonably I will not dispute; this I know, that in the post he filled, which was no inconsiderable one, he passed

Locke and the Problem of Personal Identity 157

for a very rational man, and the press has shown that he wanted not parts or learning; . . ." (*Essay*, II, xxvii, 14: italics original). Perhaps this was a case which set Locke himself enquiring about personal identity. But for us it is sufficient if we have shown that the puzzle cases which are so characteristic of certain investigations inevitably and rightly raise philosophical questions about the meaning of "same person."

2. Locke seems to have been the first to appreciate the relevance of such puzzle cases. They present a challenge. Any solution to the problem must be able to do one of two things. Either it must consist in some sort of definition or set of rules, which will enable us to deal with all possible puzzles; either by telling us that "same person" is or is not correctly applicable; or by hinting to us what further factual information we require before we can know. Or else the solution must explain why the questions raised by the puzzle cases cannot be so definitively answered. Locke himself chose the first alternative, and answered all the puzzles he had invented in the light of his talismanic definition. For instance, he tells us what would decide the puzzle of the man who claimed to have the same soul as Socrates (*Essay*, II, xxvii, 19).

3. Locke maintained that "same" is systematically ambiguous: "It is not therefore unity of substance that comprehends all sorts of identity or will determine it in every case; but to conceive and judge of it aright, we must consider what idea the word it is applied to stands for" (*Essay*, II, xxvii, 8). It would not be relevant to discuss this general claim. It is enough to show that Locke is right at least in so far as he is maintaining that there are special and peculiar problems about "same" as applied to persons. And this can be seen to be the case by the example of Hume, who thought he could solve the problem of the identity of things, but confessed himself completely at a loss as to "the nature of the bond which unites a person."

4. Locke proposed a solution to the philosophical problem. It is that X at time two is the same person as Y at time one if and only if X and Y are both persons and X can remember at time two (his doing) what Y did, or felt,

or what have you, at time one. The parenthetical "his doing" has to go in since, as Professor Bernard Williams has pointed out, "we constantly say things like 'I remember my brother joining the army' without implying that I and my brother are the same person"; though it is worth stressing, as Williams does not, that all such utterances do still carry an implicit personal identity claim about the speaker —the claim that he was himself around and acquiring the information at the time in question. Certainly by making this insertion our reformulation becomes even more obviously exposed to "Butler's famous objection that memory, so far from constituting personal identity, presupposed it." Yet this is not a fault in the reformulation, considered as a representation of Locke's position. For that position actually is wide open to that objection. It is not, as Williams seems to be suggesting, only our present belated insertion which lends colour to it.[1]

A person is for Locke "a thinking intelligent being, that has reason and reflection, and can consider itself as itself, the same thinking thing, in different times and places" (*Essay*, II, xxvii, 11). This is distinguished from the idea of man since, "ingenious observation [*sic!*] puts it past doubt", that "the idea in our minds, of which the sound *man* in our mouths is the sign, is nothing else but of an animal of such a certain form" (*Essay*, II, xxvii, 9: italics supplied); although a very little later we are told that the same idea consists "in most people's sense" of the idea of "a body, so and so shaped, joined to" that of "*a thinking or rational being*" (*Essay*, II, xxvii, 10: italics supplied).

Locke's proposed solution, in his own words, is that: "That with which the consciousness of this present thinking thing *can* join itself, makes the same person, and is one self with it, and with nothing else; and so attributes to itself and owns all the actions of that thing, as its own, as far as that consciousness reaches, and no further; as everyone who reflects will perceive" (*Essay*, II, xxvii, 17: italics

---

[1] B. A. O. Williams, "Personal Identity and Individuation" in *Proceedings of the Aristotelian Society* 1956–57, p. 233: the objection itself is considered more fully in III (1), below.

original). One must here point out that the word "consciousness" is not used by Locke clearly and consistently. Sometimes it seems to mean self-conscious, in the tricky and curious sense in which to say that someone is self-conscious is not to say that he is embarrassed: for instance, we read that "a being that . . . can consider itself as itself . . . does so only by that consciousness which is inseparable from thinking . . ." (*Essay*, II, xxvii, 11). Sometimes it seems to be more straightforwardly the consciousness which is the opposite of anaesthesia: for instance, when "self" is defined as "a conscious thinking thing . . . which is sensible or conscious of pleasure or pain, capable of happiness or misery . . ." (*Essay*, II, xxvii, 17). But in his main statements of his position "consciousness" is simply equivalent to "memory," as can be seen from the words, "Could we suppose any spirit wholly stripped of all its memory or consciousness of past actions; as we find our minds always are of a great part of ours, and sometimes of them all . . ." (*Essay*, II, xxvii, 25). In the interests of both clarity and brevity we have used "remember" instead of "be conscious of" in our restatements of Locke's central thesis.

III. OBJECTIONS TO LOCKE'S SOLUTION

There are two lines of attack.
1. The first and simpler was classically taken by Bishop Butler in his dissertation *Of Personal Identity:* "And one should really think it self-evident, that consciousness of personal identity presupposes, and therefore cannot constitute, personal identity; any more than knowledge, in any other case, can constitute truth, which it presupposes" (§ 3).[2] It is absurd to say that "he is the same person" *means* that "he can remember that he is the same person." The absurdity is usually slightly masked, since expressions such as "I remember doing, feeling, seeing something" do not refer explicitly to the fact that what is

[2] *Works*, ed. W. E. Gladstone, Oxford University Press, 1897.

remembered is that the speaker is the same person as did, felt, or saw whatever it was.

2. The second line of attack is much more intricate, demanding very careful generalship. The crux is that Locke's criterion is at the same time both too strict in blackballing and too lenient in admitting candidates. Often his definition would not allow us to apply the expression "same person," where we certainly should think it properly applicable; whereas in other cases Locke's ruling would be that it did apply, when we should certainly judge it not correctly applicable.

Before developing this second attack two distinctions have to be made. Two of the terms in Locke's definition are relevantly ambiguous. "Can" may be either "can as a matter of fact" (hereafter referred to as "can [factual]") or it may be "can without self-contradiction be said to" (hereafter referred to as "can [logical]"). There is also a more subtle ambiguity in "remember," which is best brought out by symbolic examples. "I know p" entails "p," whereas "He said that he knew p, and he was not lying" does not entail "p." Similarly, "I remember p" entails "p," but "He said that he remembered p, and he was not lying" does not entail "p." For, just as it is possible to be honestly mistaken in a claim to know something, so it is possible to be honestly mistaken in making a claim to remember something. When someone challenges a knowledge claim or a memory claim he is not necessarily, or even usually, challenging the claimant's integrity. He is much more likely to be merely questioning the truth of the proposition said to be known or remembered. And, of course, if the proposition is in fact false this is sufficient to defeat the claim really to know or truly to remember. (Another possibility, mentioned only to be dismissed as here irrelevant, is that the critic is either challenging the adequacy of the grounds available to support the knowledge claim or challenging the implicit claim to have been in the past in a position which qualifies remembering now.) We have, therefore, to distinguish between genuine remembering, which necessarily involves the truth of the

Locke and the Problem of Personal Identity

proposition said to be remembered, and making honest memory claims, which does not.

It is now time and possible to ring the changes on these alternative interpretations of "can" and "remember."

(a) First, taking "can" as logical and "remember" as entailing the truth of what is remembered, Locke's definition could be made into a necessary truth, albeit a futile necessary truth. For it is manifestly true, though not an helpful definition of "same person," that X at time two is the same person as Y at time one if and only if X and Y are both persons and X can (logically) remember at time two (his doing) what Y did, or what have you, at time one. It is manifestly true since for it to be genuine memory the person remembering must necessarily be the same person as the person whose experience or activity he claims to be remembering as his own. On this interpretation what we have is of course not open to attack on the ground that it is too exclusive or too inclusive, only that it is an otiose only too truism.

(b) Second, taking "remember" in the same way as referring to genuine remembering and "can" as can (factual), Locke's definition is open to two objections. First, it excludes too much; for we often and rightly want to say that we must have done something or other though we cannot for the life of us remember doing it. We are even prepared to accept full responsibility for such forgotten actions, at any rate provided that they are not too important. Even if they are important, and even if we want to disown or diminish our moral or legal responsibility for them, we are prepared to concede that we are the same persons as did them, unless, mistakenly, we think that personal identity is not merely the necessary but also the sufficient condition of full moral and legal responsibility.

The second objection to the second interpretation is the famous paradox, The Case of the Gallant Officer. This objection seems to have been made first, but in a monochrome version, by Berkeley in the eighth section of *Alciphron* VII. Later it was reproduced by Reid in glorious Technicolor: "Suppose a brave officer to have been flogged when a boy at school, for robbing an orchard, to have taken a standard from the enemy in his first campaign, and also to have been made a general in advanced life."³ Then, if the young officer could remember the flogging, and the general could remember taking the standard but not being flogged as a boy, on Locke's principles we should have to say that the general both is and is not the same person as the orchard robber. He is not the same (because he cannot now remember the robbery), and yet he is the same (because he is the same as the young officer who was in turn the same as the boy thief).

(c) The third possibility is to take "can" as can (logical) and "remember" as involving only the making of an honest memory claim. The objection to this is that it will let too much in. This point too was, it seems, first made by Berkeley in the private *Philosophical Commentaries:* "Wherein consists identity of person? Not in actual consciousness; for then I'm not the same person I was this day twelvemonth, but while I think of what I then did. Not in potential; for then all persons may be the same, for aught we know. *Mem:* story of Mr Deering's aunt. Two sorts of potential consciousness—natural and preternatural. In the last section but one I mean the latter."⁴

It is surely our present point which Berkeley is making since his preternatural potential consciousness is obviously equivalent to ability to remember in the present interpretations of "can" and "remember." No one seems able to provide any informative gloss on his note: "*Mem:* story of Mr Deering's aunt." But presumably Berkeley is thinking of something which we should count as a puzzle case, and it looks as if he—unlike Locke's other early critics—appreciated the relevance of such cases.

(d) The fourth possible combination, that of "can" as can (factual) with "remember" as involving only the making of an honest memory claim, yields an interpretation open to all three objections made against the thesis in in-

---

³ *Essays on the Intellectual Powers of Man,* ed. A. D. Woozley, London, 1941, III, 6.
⁴ *Works,* ed. A. A. Luce & T. E. Jessop, Edinburgh, 1948–57, Vol. I, p. 26, Entries 200–2: spelling and punctuation slightly modified.

Locke and the Problem of Personal Identity

terpretations two and three. First, it leaves too much out, ignoring amnesia. Second, it lets too much in, ignoring paramnesia. Third it is internally inconsistent, being exposed to the paradox of The Case of the Gallant Officer. Since people seem more familiar with amnesia than with paramnesia it is just worth remarking that paramnesia is not just a logical possibility but a real phenomenon. The stock and pathetic example is the British King George IV, who in his declining and demented years "remembered" his dashing leadership at the Battle of Waterloo; notwithstanding that only a devoutly Lockean, or an unscrupulously flattering, courtier could have pretended that the King must therefore have been present on that decisive field. Vulgar cases are provided daily by those who press forward to claim sincerely but without factual foundation the discredit for committing the latest newsy murder.

3. This completes our direct case against Locke's proposed solution of the main philosophical problem. But here, as in the political trials in less happier lands, the direct case can be rounded off with a sort of confession. For despite his insistence that, "the same consciousness being preserved, whether in the same or different substances, the personal identity is preserved" Locke is nevertheless, reasonably but inconsistently, anxious lest "one intellectual substance may not have represented to it, as done by itself, what *it* never did, and was perhaps done by some other agent . . ." (*Essay*, II, xxvii, 13: italics original).

Locke's anxiety is indeed very reasonable, and, as F. H. Bradley said in a slightly different connection: "it may help us to perceive, what was evident before, that a self is not thought to be the same because of bare memory, but only so when the memory is considered not to be defective."[5] But, though reasonable, Locke's anxiety is entirely inconsistent with his official account of personal identity, which requires him to deny that there can (logical) be honest but falsidical memory claims. For if "being

[5] *Appearance and Reality*, London and New York, 1893, p. 85.

the same person as did that" *means* "being a person able to remember (his) doing, or being able to be conscious of (his) doing, that" then you cannot consistently say that a person may both be able to remember doing and yet not actually have done some particular thing. (Or, rather, to be absolutely strict, this can be made consistent only by interpreting "remember" to refer exclusively to genuine veridical memory; thus reducing this whole account of personal identity to vacuity.)

In his desperation Locke falls on his knees: "And that it never is so, will by us, till we have clearer views of the nature of thinking substances, be best resolved in the goodness of God; who as far as the happiness or misery of any of his sensible creatures is concerned will not, by a fatal error of theirs, transfer from one to another that consciousness which draws reward or punishment with it" (*Essay*, II, xxvii, 13). But the assistance for which Locke supplicates is beyond the resources even of Omnipotence. For on Locke's view there could be no sense in his own fear that people might lose or escape their deserts because they remembered doing what they had not in fact done: if anyone can remember doing something then necessarily—according to Locke's account—he is in fact the same person as did that deed. By making this desperate appeal, Locke both tacitly confesses the inadequacy of his own account of personal identity and provides one more example of a phenomenon already all too familiar to the student of religious apologetic—the hope that the sheer physical power of a postulated God can make contradictions consistent or by itself make utterances to which no sense has been given sensible.

IV. SOURCES OF TROUBLE

The question now arises how Locke managed to get himself into this confused and catastrophic position. This is a question of very much more than merely antiquarian interest, since in one form or another both that position itself and the mistakes which misled Locke into it seem to

Locke and the Problem of Personal Identity

have a perennial appeal. One first part of the answer lies in those possibilities of confusion about memory, which we have examined already. (See III, especially III(2), above.)

Second, as we have also seen, Locke uses the word "conscious" and its associates in several ways. He seems to slide from his definition of "person" as "a thinking intelligent being, that . . . can consider itself as itself, the same thinking thing, in different times and places", by way of talk of "that consciousness which is inseparable from thinking, and as it seems to me, essential to it," to the eventual conclusion that "and as far as this consciousness can be extended backwards to any past action or thought, so far reaches the identity of that person" (*Essay*, II, xxvii, 11). Here we seem in the first passage to be dealing with the sort of consciousness of self which is not the self-consciousness of embarrassment, in the second with that consciousness which is contrasted with complete unconsciousness, and in the concluding third with a consciousness which is identified with memory.

Third, Locke seems sometimes—like many others since—to have confused the epistemological questions, "How can we know, what good evidence can we have for, propositions about personal identity?" with the inseparable but not identical enquiry, "What do such propositions mean?" It is the latter which he is supposed to be pursuing. But what he offers would provide a partial answer to the former. Thus when he tells us that on the "Great Day" everyone will "receive his doom, his conscience accusing or excusing him," or that if he could remember "Noah's flood" as clearly as last winter's "overflowing of the Thames" he could no more doubt "that he was the same *self*" who saw both floods, he is clearly answering a question of the first sort; or perhaps one of the subtly but importantly different 'How can we convince ourselves' sort (*Essay*, II, xxvii, 22 and 16). But neither sort of question can be identified with that to which Locke's main problem belongs: "in this doctrine not only is consciousness confounded with memory but, which is still more strange, personal identity is confounded with the evidence which we have of our personal identity."[6]

Fourth, as we have seen, Locke defined "person" as "a thinking intelligent being, that has reason and reflection, and can consider itself as itself, the same thinking thing, in different times and places." Ignoring the possible danger of circularity which lurks in this talk of "the same thinking thing," the more radical objection must be made that this definition misses the ordinary meaning and use of the term "person." We learn the word "people," by being shown people, by meeting them and shaking hands with them. They may be intelligent or unintelligent, introspective or extraverted, black, white, red, or brown, but what they cannot be is disembodied or in the shape of elephants. Locke's definition would make it a contingent truth about people that some or all of them are either embodied in, or are of, human form. But in the ordinary use of the word "people," we do actually meet people and shake hands with them; we do not meet the fleshy houses in which they are living or the containers in which they are kept. Nor is it logically possible for cougars (or parrots!) to be people. It is in short a necessary truth that people are of human shapes and sizes; and, not a contingent fact that some or all people inhabit human bodies or are of human form.

This is not to say that all talk of disembodied people (or even parrot people) must always and necessarily be self-contradictory. It may perhaps be that the word "people" is being used in a radically unusual sense by those who wish to point out an analogy between the behaviour of people and some situations in which no people are present. This is a perfectly respectable method of adding to our language, a method which only becomes dangerous when it is not understood, when it is thought that "person" in the new sense has the same meaning, the same logical liaisons, as "person" in the old, familiar sense. Locke himself admitted that his distinction between "man," which he used in substantially its ordinary sense,

---

[6] Reid, *op. cit.*, III, 6.

and "person," which he wants to use in a sense which would allow the possibility of disembodiment or embodiment, in different (or even non-human) bodies, is not made in ordinary language: "I know that, in the ordinary way of speaking, the same person, and the same man stand for one and the same thing" (*Essay*, II, xxvii, 15). But though Locke did unguardedly admit this, he failed to realize how important this admission was and what its implications are. If you use "person" in a new sense, in a way other than the ordinary, then you wreck your chances of producing a descriptive analysis of "same person." And it was this which, most of the time, Locke has to be construed as trying to do: "we must consider what *person* stands for" he tells us, in introducing his definition of "person"; and he rounds off his account of the meaning of "same person" with the comment, "as everyone who reflects will perceive" (*Essay*, II, xxvii, 11 and 17).

V. PERSONS, UNLIKE MEN, THOUGHT OF AS INCORPOREAL

This attempt to make a fundamental distinction between "same man" and "same person" demands investigation. Why does Locke want to do it?
1. First, we can find certain nuances of English idiom which might suggest a distinction of this kind. For instance it would be slightly more natural to use "man" when referring to physical characteristics and "person" when referring to psychological ones: Charles Atlas and the Army offer to make a new man of you; the Pelman Institute, or your psychoanalyst, are more likely to promise that you would be an altogether different person after a course of their treatment. But this is the merest nuance, for when Robert Browning wrote:

> There they are, my fifty men and women
> Naming me my fifty poems finished!

he was dedicating a collection of character sketches. A slightly more promising temptation lies in phrases like "Our Claude is quite a different person since he went away to school." As we are quite sure that he is really the same boy, the same person, as in fact we should only say someone was quite a different person (in this sense) if we were sure he was the same person (in the ordinary sense), we may become inclined to make our point by saying that the same man may or may not be the same person.

Then again there are in our language, and in many others, the embedded traces of what was once a scientific hypothesis, the hypothesis of possession. This degenerated into a mere alternative idiom through the addition of so many qualifications ("But it is an *invisible* spirit," and so on) that it no longer risked falsification. It thus ceased to be an hypothesis at all. Instead of saying, "He drove wildly," or "Why on earth did he do it?" we can say "He drove like a man possessed" or "Whatever possessed him to do it?" And this sometime hypothesis and present dead metaphor has even now perhaps not altogether lost its seductive power. Certainly it had not when Locke wrote. For, noticing that we do not punish "the mad man for the sober man's actions" he thought that this, "is somewhat explained by our way of speaking in English when we say such an one is 'not himself', or is 'beside himself'; in which phrases it is insinuated, as if those who now, or at least first used them, thought that self was changed; the selfsame person was no longer in that man" (*Essay*, II, xxvii, 20).

2. This suggests a second reason for Locke's distinction between a man and a person. Locke seems to have assumed that there is one single necessary and sufficient condition of moral and legal responsibility. But he notices cases where he does not want to blame or punish someone who in some sense seems to have been the agent who did the wrong or criminal action. For instance, he does not want a madman to be punished for what he did before he went mad; and he does not want to blame people for actions which they simply cannot remember having done. So then, instead of saying that the person in question did

do whatever it was but he is not to be held responsible, or at least not fully responsible, because he is now amnesic or insane, Locke distinguishes the man from the person, announcing that the word "person" is a "forensic term, appropriating actions and their merit" (*Essay*, II, xxvii, 26). This opens up for him the possibility of saying in some troubling case that blame or punishment would be here improper because we have before us only the same man and not the same person as did the deed.

3. The third basis for Locke's distinction between the man and the person was his Platonic-Cartesian conviction that people essentially are incorporeal spirits, and that human bodies in fact are controlled by internal shadow beings in ways similar to, but much less intelligible than, that in which ships are directed by their captains or vehicles by their drivers: "For I presume it is not the idea of a thinking or rational being alone that makes the *idea of man* in most people's sense; but of a body so and so shaped joined to it . . ."; but, though the idea of man thus involves the body as well, the essential person is the thinking or rational being which is not necessarily of human shape or even corporeal (*Essay*, II, xxvii, 10: italics original). Or, again, "if the identity of soul alone makes the same man; and there be nothing in the nature of matter why the same individual spirit may not be united to different bodies, it will be possible that . . . men living in distant ages . . . may have been the same man: which way of speaking must be from a very strange use of the word *man*, applied to an idea out of which body and shape are excluded" (*Essay*, II, xxvii, 7: italics supplied). Which is all very well, but still takes for granted that people are souls; which, presumably, conceivably could thus transmigrate.

This is not the place either fully to characterize or generally to assail the Platonic-Cartesian view of man.[7] But it is worthwhile to devote some space to showing how fundamental and how important this view was for Locke,

[7] For such more thorough treatment see G. Ryle, *The Concept of Mind*, London, 1949, perhaps comparing A. G. N. Flew (editor), *Body, Mind, and Death*, New York, 1964.

and how little inclined he was seriously to question it. For it is a view presupposed by his whole account of personal identity; while the impossibility of that account should itself in turn be seen as one of the most powerful objections against that view of the nature of man.[8]

Locke's first concern in the *Essay* is to prove that we have no surreptitious access to black-market ideas, but are properly confined to getting our supplies through the official channels of post-natal waking experience. He claims at one point: "We know certainly, by experience, that we *sometimes* think; and thence draw this infallible consequence—that there is something in us which has the power to think" (*Essay*, II, 1, 10: italics original). The conclusion of this lamentable argument opens up precisely the possibility which Locke is most concerned to close. For the word "thinking" is being used in the Cartesian sense, in which to think is to have any sort of conscious experience. Now, if our thinking is done by some possibly incorporeal internal thinking thing, then it becomes natural to ask whether it can do any thinking without our knowledge; whether perhaps it may not sometimes slip out to have some experiences on its own, maybe taking up station for the purpose inside some alien body. All of which suggestions, colourfully presented as the hypothetical doings of Socrates, Castor, Pollux or their several souls are then duly considered by Locke (II, xxvii, 13–15).

Yet the "infallible consequence" which here sets off these bizarre speculations is not validly drawn. For though we do undoubtedly know that "we sometimes think" this has not the slightest tendency to show that this thinking is done by "something in us which has the power to think." Quite the reverse. The argument derives what little plausibility it has from the tacit assumption that everything we do is done with some special organ. But this is false. We write with our hands, certainly. But we do not decide, or sleep, or fret with special organs of deciding, sleeping, or fretting. It is the same with thinking, both in the ordinary

---

[8] Compare A. M. Quinton "The Soul," *The Journal of Philosophy*, 1962, and A. G. N. Flew " 'The Soul' of Mr. A. M. Quinton," *The Journal of Philosophy*, 1963.

and in the wide Cartesian sense. Thinking, like sleeping and deciding, is an "affection of the whole man." It would be pleasant to believe that Locke was beginning to realize this when he wrote: "But whether sleeping without dreaming be not an affection of the whole man, mind as well as body, may be worth a waking man's consideration . . ." (*Essay*, II, 1, 11).

4. One aspect of the Platonic-Cartesian view of man deserves special separate mention. It is that it provides something which may plausibly be held both to survive a man's death and to be accountable, on the "Great Day," for his deeds upon earth. Now to be justly accountable, here or hereafter, for a murder you have to be the same person as the villain who did the murder; that is the necessary, though by no means the sufficient, condition of full responsibility. But if you attach the customary sense to "person," this necessary condition can never be satisfied by anyone who died before the "Great Day." For he will simply not exist to be to any degree responsible. He will have died and been buried. Nor can the situation be saved merely by producing an indistinguishable person to stand his trial. For "one thing cannot have two beginnings of existence, nor two things one beginning . . . That, therefore, that had one beginning, is the same thing; and that which had a different beginning in time and place from that, is not the same, but diverse" (*Essay*, II, xxvii, 1).

Locke therefore, committed as he was to beliefs both in immortality and in a just reckoning on "that Great Day," had a very strong reason—or perhaps it should be called a motive, for insisting that "person" unlike "man" may refer to something incorporeal. For while it is immediately obvious that a person in the everyday sense, a person such as we can meet face to face in the streets, (logically) cannot survive bodily death and dissolution, it may perhaps seem at first sight conceivable that a person, in the sense of a series of experiences linked together in some subtle gap-indifferent way, or in the sense of a "thing which is sensible or conscious of pleasure and pain, capable of happiness or misery," might survive, and be the bearer of responsibility for what that same person (in a new and rather peculiar sense) did "in the body." There are appalling difficulties in the logic of such new senses of "person" and "same person," which we do not have to discuss here.[9]

Yet it is both relevant and worthwhile to draw attention to Locke's achievement in uncovering some of these difficulties. He himself did not see clearly what, or how great, or how numerous they are. This was partly because he thought he was defining the ordinary sense of "person." He therefore saw no difficulty in making a "disembodied person" (that is a person in some new sense) the same as (and thus possibly accountable for the actions of) some person who had lived at a previous date (some person, that is, in the old sense). Partly again it was because, since he thought he had successfully found in memory what Hume called the "uniting principle, which constitutes a person," he could scarcely be expected simultaneously to realize that memory can only discover and not constitute personal identity (in any sense of "person"). Partly, finally, it was for the simple reason that this territory Locke had entered was too vast and too difficult for any single explorer to open up immediately.

Locke had to struggle to his insights through a rank growth of baffling terms, such as, "immaterial substances," "selves," "thinking substances," "rational souls." The insights which he did achieve are the more remarkable inasmuch as a critic of the calibre of Bishop Butler failed to see that the subject presented difficulties, complaining of the "strange perplexities" that had been raised: "Whether we are to live in a future state, as it is the most important question which can possibly be asked, so it is the most intelligible one which can be expressed in language" (§ 1). Locke, had he lived to read the dissertation *Of Personal Identity* would have agreed about the supreme importance of the question. But he might, very reasonably, have asked for some solution of those "strange perplexities" of the puzzle cases before being prepared to concede that things really were all quite so straightforward as Butler thought.

[9] But see Quinton and Flew, *op. cit.*, n. 8.

Locke and the Problem of Personal Identity 173

5. A fifth source of Locke's unhappy analysis of personal identity lies in his un-Lockean assumption that we can find a definition such that, granted we are provided with all the relevant factual data, we shall be able to say in every actual or imaginable case whether or not the expression "same person" can correctly be applied. This assumption is mistaken.

(a) Doubt may be thrown upon it in three ways. First, it is unsettling to see the troubles of those who have tried to fulfil such a requirement. Locke offered one such candidate definition, with the unfortunate results already examined. Berkeley, more prudently, refrained deliberately from the attempt. In the *Philosophical Commentaries* he reminds himself "carefully to omit defining of Person, or making much mention of it" (Entry 713). This good advice he resolutely follows throughout his published works, with the significant exception of a passage in the eighth section of Book VII of the *Alciphron*. There he challenges the minute philosophers to, "untie the knots and answer the questions which may be raised even about human personal identity" before requiring, "a clear and distinct idea of *person* in relation to the Trinity": a very typical piece of Berkeleian intellectual judo.

(b) Second, this assumption overlooks the possibilities of vagueness, of the marginal cases in which we do not quite know where to draw the line. Most words referring to physical objects are vague in some direction; somewhere there is an undemarcated frontier; somewhere there is a no man's land of indeterminacy; often there is a complete encircling penumbra of perplexity. And this is and must be so because nature has no natural kinds: "God made the spectrum, man makes the pigeonholes." It was Locke himself who launched attack after attack on the superstitions of real essences and natural kinds. It is he himself who points again and again to the specimens which will not fit properly into any available category. It is he who points to the vagueness even of the term "man." It is he who draws attention to the changelings who are "something between a man and a beast," he too who tells us the story of the Abbot Malotru who was so monstrous at his birth that "he was baptized and declared a man provisionally," and Locke again who insists that "There are creatures . . . that, with language and reason and a shape in other things agreeing with ours, have hairy tails; others where the males have no beards, and others where the females have" (*Essay*, IV, IV, 13 and III, VI, 26 and 22).

Nevertheless, despite all this, Locke never seems to entertain the possibility that "person," "rational being," "soul," "Immaterial spirit," "self," and the rest of the words and expressions alleged to refer to the putative and elusive internal population of the body, may be affected in the same way. This failure shows up most strikingly when he argues that no external shape is an infallible sign that there is a rational soul inside: "Where now (I ask) shall be the just measure; which is the utmost bounds of that shape which carries with it a rational soul?" He points out once again "all the several degrees of mixture of the likeness of a man or a brute," and demands: "What sort of outside is the certain sign that there is or is not such an inhabitant within?" Finally he complains: "we talk at random of *man*; and shall always, I fear, do so, as long as we give ourselves up to certain sounds, and the imaginations of settled and fixed species in nature, we know not what . . . So necessary is it to quit the common notion of species and essences, if we will truly look into the nature of things . . ." (*Essay*, IV, IV, 16). Yet he himself is all the while assuming as it were a real essence of the rational souls, a fixed species or natural kind of the people who inhabit some, though we cannot always tell which, of these men and near men whom we meet.

(c) Third, since our ordinary language, and the concepts of ordinary language, have been evolved or introduced to deal with the situations which are ordinarily met with, and not with the extraordinary, we may reasonably expect some failures of adaptation when new and unexpected situations arise. And these do in fact occur. The old conceptual machinery breaks down. The old terminological tools fail to cope with the new tasks. These breakdowns are different from the cases in which indecision arises from the vagueness of a term. "Ship" is perhaps a vague term in that a whole spectrum of similarity stretches between things which are certainly ships, via the things which provoke linguistic hesitation, to other things which are undoubtedly boats. But when a court has to decide whether the word "ship" in a statute covers flying boats, the difficulty arises: not so much from the vagueness of the term "ship" (that would imply that the drafting of the statute was bad and could perfectly well have been improved); but from what has been called its open-texture. The concept which we have has in fact evolved to cover the situations that have arisen before or were thought likely to arise, and not the situations which have not arisen and could not have been foreseen. Vagueness could have been removed by prescribing that nothing under so many tons was to count as a ship within the meaning of the act: "To remove vagueness is to outline the penumbra of a shadow. The line is there after we have drawn it and not before." But it is not possible "to define a concept like *gold* with absolute precision, i.e. in such a way that every nook and cranny is blocked against the entry of doubt. That is what is meant by '*open texture*' of a concept."[10] It is this open texture much more than any actual vagueness in use which prevents the definition of "person."

By imagining, fully two centuries before the foundation of the Society for Psychical Research, a series of puzzle cases which leave us at a loss as to whether or not to apply the expression "same person," Locke revealed what he did not himself see, that it is not possible to define the meaning of "same person" descriptively and at the same time give a definition which will answer all possible problems of application. This is not possible because there is no usage established for many of these unforeseen situations. Therefore no such proper usage can be described. In cases such as Locke produces we can only admit that we don't know what to say; and then perhaps prescribe what is to be the proper usage if such cases do occur or recur. It is not possible to produce even a prescriptive definition which will give absolute security against all possibility of

[10] F. Waismann, "Verifiability" in *Logic and Language* (First Series), ed. A. G. N. Flew, Blackwell 1951.

surprise and indecision. Locke produced a definition of "same person" which enabled him to give an answer to all the puzzle cases which he imagined. Let someone appear who seemed to remember the Noah's flood as clearly and accurately as he remembered last year's overflowing of the Thames. If we accepted Locke's definition, then clearly we could and should say without hesitation that he had been present at Noah's flood: an answer which, assuming that he had been born in this century, would be false. But no prescription can give absolute determinacy. Locke did not, and could not, imagine all the possibilities. Suppose, what is not merely conceivable but imaginable, that a person splits like an amoeba—first into two Siamese twins—then separating into two identical twins. And suppose both twins, call them A1 and A2, can remember all that the original person, call him A, could remember before his unfortunate and disruptive experience. On Locke's definition A1 and A2 will both be the same person as A, and yet they will obviously be different people, just as are identical twins. Clearly we should not know what to say. This preposterous supposition will serve to show that it is not possible to produce either a descriptive or a prescriptive definition of "same person" which shall remove every possibility of linguistic perplexity. We can prescribe against vagueness, but then there is always the open texture through which forever threatens the insidious infiltration of the unforeseeable and the unforeseen.

VI. CONCLUSIONS

The search for the talismanic definition which shall solve all possible problems, the search for the real essence of personal identity, was therefore a mistake. Why did Locke make it? It involved, as we have seen, an abandonment of his greatest insight and a betrayal of the glorious revolution he was leading against the superstition of real essences and natural kinds. However, it is just as easy to fail to apply a new discovery consistently as it is to push it to absurd extremes. We smile at the man who tells us:

Locke and the Problem of Personal Identity 177

"I'm an atheist now, thank God!" But we all fall into similar inconsistencies. So there is every reason to expect with the notoriously inconsistent Locke, what we do in fact find, a failure to see all the implications of, and to apply thoroughly and systematically, his own discoveries.

Then we remember those long struggles that had to be fought, and which still drag on in some intellectual backwoods, before the doctrine of evolution was allowed to include, without reservation, our own species. We remember the bitter rear-guard actions, arguing for a special creation for this one most favoured species. We can see still in Rome the final forlorn hope to save the special creation of souls to inhabit the bodies which have at last been conceded to be the most recent results of the evolutionary process. In the light of all this, it no longer seems surprising that Locke, living two centuries before the famous Victorian battles over the origin of species, failed to take his great insight into the enclosure reserved for the ghostly company of "rational souls," "persons," and "thinking substances."

Another source of the inability to see that questions may be asked about personal identity to which there can be no true or false answer (until and unless a new decision, which may be wise or unwise, is made about what is to be proper usage) lies in the familiar fact that people often know things about their pasts which they conceal from other people. We tend, being aware of this familiar truth, to assume that all questions about the identity of persons are always wholly factual, susceptible of straight true or false answers, long after we have realized that questions as to whether this is or is not the same thing may sometimes not be so straightforward. We feel that the person in question must himself always know—yes or no—whether he is the same person as the man who broke the bank at Monte Carlo. Even if we cannot discover the answer because he will not tell us or because we do not trust him, even if he protests that he does not know, still we assume that if he could (seem to himself to) remember that would settle the issue definitively.

We are not, obviously, inclined to think that the thing

could tell us if it wanted to: but we do tend to think that the person could, and, if he did, that would be that: "Wherever a man finds what he calls himself, there, I think, another may say is the same person" (*Essay*, II, xxvii, 26). And "should the soul of a prince, carrying with it the consciousness of the prince's past life, enter and inform the body of a cobbler . . . everyone sees he would be the same person with the prince . . ." (*Essay*, II, xxvii, 15: italics original). And so, confident that the subject must always know whether or not he is the same person, just as he always has the last word as to whether or not he is in pain, Locke proceeds to give his disastrous definition of personal identity; quite overlooking the facts of amnesia and paramnesia which show decisively that personal identity is in this respect not like pain. The honest testimony of the subject is not with personal identity as it is with pain the last word. But the fact that it is such very good evidence, combined with the fact that we are all all too familiar with human reticence and deceit, misleads us into thinking that it is.

To sum up. We outlined Locke's contribution to the study of the philosophic problem of personal identity, and showed that his central answer was wrong. We then enquired at length into the sources of his mistakes, finding five; first, a series of confusions about memory; second, his muddled and slippery use of the term "consciousness"; third, the failure rigidly to distinguish the meaning of statements from, what is so inseparably connected with it, their methods of verification; fourth, the view that "person" refers to some bodiless and intangible inhabitant of the dark room of the understanding (*Essay*, II, xi, 17) rather than to people like those we meet in everyday life; and, fifth, the assumption that there is some real essence of personal identity, that it is possible to produce a definition and a definition furthermore which can guard us against every threat of future linguistic indecision. We neither began nor intended to begin to tackle the problem itself; it was a sufficient, and very Lockean, task to clear the ground of a few obstructions and to point out some of the dangers which beset the road.

LOCKE'S POLITICAL THEORY AND ITS INTERPRETERS
CHARLES H. MONSON, JR.

One of the more interesting phenomena of recent philosophical scholarship has been the interest shown in John Locke. More than a dozen major works have appeared during the past twenty-five years and the spate of articles, on all aspects of his thought, increases every year. But, coincidentally there has been a reassessment of the applicability of traditional democratic principles to a complex industrialized society; hence much of the interest in Locke, understandably, has centred on his political theory.

But some writers, when they return to Locke, have failed to find the natural rights, natural law, contract theory of the state so apparent to their eighteenth-century counterparts. Rather, they have found a theory they describe, variously, as advocating egoism, absolute subordination to majority rule, capitalism, anarchy, the denial of natural law, Hobbesianism, or the absence of natural rights. These writers, careful scholars and systematic thinkers all, challenge the traditional interpretation of Locke, and in a larger sense, the traditional justification for democratic government. Hence, a careful scrutiny of their reports on Locke's real, but as yet misunderstood, political theory seems to be in order.

From *Political Studies*, Vol. VI (1958), under the title "Locke and His Interpreters." Reprinted by permission of the author and the Clarendon Press, Oxford.

I

The most recent, the most scholarly, and the most defensible of the 'non-traditional' interpretations is in Leo Strauss's *Natural Right and History*.[1] For purposes of analysis, his account can be reduced to three assertions: first, Locke is not a natural law theorist; second, he is a Hobbesian; and third, his egoism is also demonstrated by his account of property rights.

Strauss argues that Locke cannot be a natural law theorist, for he gives no account of how men know the law of nature. He could have said either reason or revelation, but there are no philosophical theories in the *Second Treatise*[2] and his other works provide no definite answers either. Moreover, the first alternative is unacceptable because rational knowledge also requires proof of God's existence and human immortality, proofs which Locke says are not demonstrable, hence 'natural reason is unable to know the law of nature as a law'.[3] At best, he accepted a 'partial' law of nature, moral rules which correspond to Scriptural injunctions, but his rules, when analysed, are not identical with those of Jesus. Hence, Locke does not adequately account for man's knowledge of natural law and this shows that he 'cannot have recognized any law of nature in the proper sense of the term'.[4]

In the last analysis this argument asserts that you can tell *what* one knows only if he tells you *how* he obtained his knowledge; an interesting, if dubious, assumption which Strauss makes no effort to justify even though his whole argument rests on its validity. But, no matter; grant the assumption and, moreover, grant that Locke did not provide an adequate explanation, still it does not follow that he was not aware of the problem. In the *Second Trea-*

---

[1] University of Chicago Press, 1953. A condensed version appeared in *The Philosophical Review*, Oct. 1952.
[2] Ibid., p. 220.
[3] Ibid., pp. 203–4. But see *Essay*, Book IV, chapter 10.
[4] Ibid., p. 220.

tise he explicitly asks himself how the law of nature can be known and he answers:

> Yet, it is certain there is such a law and that, too, as intelligible and plain to a rational creature and a studier of that law as the positive laws of commonwealths; nay, possibly plainer, as much as reason is easier to be understood than the fancy and intricate contrivances of man.

And again: the law of nature can be understood by men 'who will but consult reason'. Or again: by men 'who will not renounce reason'. And still again: by men 'who live according to reason'.[5] Locke, then, did provide an explanation and his answer makes Strauss's extended criticisms of knowledge by revelation both irrelevant and misleading.

But Strauss, a careful scholar, no doubt was aware of the many places in which Locke says that natural law can be known by reason. Why, then, did he reject these explicit statements? The answer seems to be: they are not enough. We must know more about reason's competence and in *The Reasonableness of Christianity* Locke says that reason cannot prove God's existence. Therefore, Strauss's argument seems to be: reason cannot know of God's existence, and natural law comes from God, so reason cannot know natural law, and Locke cannot have meant what he said.

This method of argument requires several comments. First, Strauss goes outside the *Treatise* because he is convinced that it contains no philosophical theories, only 'civil' ones; a highly debatable point which, again, he makes no attempt to justify. Second, his choice of the *Reasonableness* as the main source for defining reason's competence is unfortunate, for the work is not primarily concerned with this problem (as was the *Essay*, for instance) and it was a product of Locke's later life, a time when he was more interested in religion than political theory. But, most important, it does not reflect the posi-

[5] *Second Treatise on Civil Government*, Appleton Century edn., 1937, secs. 12, 6, 11, 19. See also secs. 30, 32, 56, 57, 63, &c.

tion Locke takes in the *Treatise*, for there he asserts, more than twenty times, that reason can know natural law. Yet not once does he suggest that one must prove God's existence in order to have this knowledge.

Locke himself points backwards, not forwards, from the *Treatise* for the fuller explanation. He does not say that he will examine the subject more carefully at some future time; rather, he quotes from Hooker and other natural law writers and he suggests, in both the *Treatise* and the early *Essays*, that they have dealt with the subject more or less satisfactorily. If the *Treatise* lacks philosophical cogency, this results from unstated assumptions rather than undeveloped omissions, for Locke believed that when God created man, He gave him the means, natural law and natural reason, as guides and, if man 'will but use his reason, he will know [the law of nature] which directs a free and intelligent agent to his proper interest'.[6]

Strauss contends that Locke is really a Hobbesian because he recognizes no normative law of nature and, on the contrary, frequently asserts egoism and selfishness as men's primary motivation. In the *Essay* Locke says: 'Nature has put into man a desire for happiness, and an aversion to misery; these are, indeed, innate practical principles.' Or, as Strauss restates it: 'The desire for happiness and the pursuit of happiness have the character of an absolute right, a natural right.' This 'right of nature is more fundamental than the law of nature' and since each person is interested in his own happiness, 'the most fundamental of all rights is the right of self-preservation'. Hence, 'Locke's theory can be understood perfectly, if one assumes that the laws of nature are, as Hobbes put it, "but conclusions or theorems concerning what conduces to the conservation and defence" of man over against other men.'[7]

This line of argument raises no question of scholarship, for Locke does make such statements; the important question is whether these statements are of central impor-

[6] *Treatise*, sec. 57. For a further analysis, see Locke's *Essays on The Law of Nature*, Oxford University Press, 1954.
[7] Strauss, op. cit., pp. 226, 227, 229.

tance. Here again we must note Strauss's impatience with the *Treatise*, for he prefers other statements, this time principally from the *Essay*, as the true indicators of Locke's political theory.[8] The procedure, of course, is all right *if* the same information could not be obtained from the *Treatise*. But this claim cannot be supported, for, as Strauss himself recognizes, the *Treatise* contains many descriptive ethical statements.[9] However, all of them do not stress egoism. Some do, for instance: 'the sacred and unalterable law of self-preservation'; 'the individual's unalterable right to preserve his own property'; and his obligation to help others 'only when his own perservation comes not in competition'.[10] But others do not, for instance: each individual agrees to establish a government where 'the legislative will make laws as the public good of the society shall require', and he obeys a government only when it 'rules for the public good of the people'.[11] From a strictly textual analysis, then, Locke does not have a consistent descriptive theory and it might have been this very inconsistency which drove Strauss to conclude that the fundamental premiss is outside the *Treatise*.

But the evidence also indicates another conclusion, one closer to Locke's own teaching. Every person *should* follow 'the law of nature which willeth the peace and preservation of all mankind' and some men do what they should while others, indeed, 'the greater portion of mankind', do not.[12] Thus, descriptively some men are egoists, others are not, and Locke's account of human motivation is accurate, although inconsistent. But, in a more important sense, normatively, none should be merely egoists, for each has a natural obligation to preserve others, and a state can

[8] But even this hedonism is but a part of the more complex (and confusing) ethical theory of this work. See Sterling Lamprecht, *The Moral and Political Philosophy of John Locke*.
[9] See Strauss, pp. 227–30.
[10] *Treatise*, secs. 87, 123, 6. Also see secs. 25, 50, 94, 123, 137, 138, &c.
[11] Ibid., secs. 87, 131, 183. Also see secs. 88, 96, 97, 99, 129, 130, &c.
[12] Ibid., sec. 7.

exist only if its legislators follow 'that eternal rule to all men [which requires] the preservation of all mankind'.[13] The ethical theory in the *Treatise*, then, is both consistent and coherent; it is Strauss's method which is in error.[14]

Strauss considers Locke's few statements about property rights 'the central part of his political teaching' and added evidence for his Hobbesianism, for 'the natural right of property is a corollary of the fundamental right of self-preservation'.[15] He concludes that Locke sanctions 'unlimited appropriation without concern for the needs of others' because the only limitation to appropriation, that property should not be allowed to spoil, is removed in a civil society, where 'with the invention of money . . . each man can rightfully and without injury possess more than he himself can make use of'. 'According to the Natural Law [*sic*!]—and this means according to the moral law—man in civil society may acquire as much property of every kind and in particular as much money as he pleases.' Thus, Locke's doctrine 'is directly intelligible today if it is taken as the classic doctrine of "the spirit of capitalism", for by building society on the low but solid ground of selfishness

[13] Ibid., sec. 135.
[14] Others have argued that Locke's normative law of nature sanctions egoism, for in sec. 6, and elsewhere, Locke says one should help others 'only when his own preservation comes not in competition'. This interpretation has the advantage of combining selfish interests with prudential obligations, the doctrine Strauss explicitly rejects but implicitly accepts; but two considerations can be brought against this position. First, there are only a few statements in which the law of nature is said to justify selfishness but there are over fifty references to its justifying concern for all mankind; hence, the latter must represent Locke's considered judgement and the former his inaccurate expression of it. Second, on this view, an individual would never join a civil society if he believed that most of his rights would be violated; but when he does join, Locke says he agrees that 'the fundamental natural law which is to govern even the legislative itself is the preservation of society and (as far as will consist with the public good) of every person in it' (sec. 134). Hence, an individual might have some, or most, or even all his rights violated and still accept the action as justified because it preserves the society. Men's obligations, then, are moral, not merely prudential.
[15] Strauss, op. cit., pp. 234–5.

one will achieve greater public benefits than by futilely appealing to virtue which is by nature unendowed'.[16]

The validity of Strauss's conclusion hinges on his establishing two points: first, that the right to acquire money is removed from the spoilage principle; and second, that this right is the archetype—and justification—for all property rights.

Locke's comments on money always have presented difficulties, for, on the one hand, he speaks of 'laying up', 'hoarding', 'heaping up', 'keeping', and 'possessing' money rather than 'investing', 'increasing', or 'acquiring' it as a good capitalist would. Moreover, he says money's chief function is to facilitate the exchange of goods, for it is 'some lasting thing that man would take in exchange for the truly useful but perishable supports of life'. And the spoilage principle still operates, for 'a man may rightfully and without injury possess more than he can make use of because it may continue long in his possession without decaying'.[17] So, clearly, Locke did not intend to be a capitalist.

Yet, one can rightfully ask what Locke would do with his 'heaped up' money, and answer, with him, use it for 'a disproportionate and unequal possession of the earth'; for 'continueing and enlarging his possessions'.[18] And other tracts, written during the same period, espouse a remarkably cogent capitalist theory.[19] So, clearly, Locke can be made, quite easily, into a capitalist.

The evidence, then, is not conclusive and hence Strauss's conclusion is not justified. But, the important point is not textual, whether there are limits to the accumulation of money; rather, it is philosophical, whether this account, now assumed to be correct, acts as prototype and justification for all property rights. Is the right to appropriate and retain property limited in any way?

If Locke on money is used to justify Locke on property,

[16] Ibid., pp. 240, 241, 243, 246–7.
[17] *Treatise*, op. cit., secs. 47, 50, 36.   [18] Ibid., secs. 48, 50.
[19] See C. B. Macpherson's 'Locke on Capitalist Appropriation' in *Western Political Quarterly*, 1951, pp. 550–66, for an interesting exposition of this view.

it is not remiss to note that money is mentioned in only five of 'On Property's' twenty-six sections suggesting, thereby, that Strauss is letting the tail wag the dog. Moreover, Locke frequently discusses property rights in other chapters but never again refers to money; perhaps the tail is wagging an elephant. Furthermore, it is simply not true that Locke sanctions unlimited appropriation and inalienable property rights. Again, he is quite explicit. When the legislature is not in session, the ruler may make laws for the common good,

> for many accidents may happen wherein a strict and rigid observation of the laws may do harm (as not to pull down an innocent man's house to stop the fire when the next to it is burning) . . . the end of government being the preservation of all, as much as may be.
> It is fit everyone who enjoys a share of protection should pay out of his estate his proportion for the maintenance of it. But still it must be with his own consent, i.e. the consent of the majority giving it either by themselves or their representatives.
> [When a man leaves the civil society] he must quit the right which belongs to him by the laws of it and leave the possessions there descending to him from his ancestors.[20]

Thus, an individual *agrees* to have his house destroyed, his property confiscated, and his taxes decided by the majority because these acts preserve civil society. Locke makes these assertions because he believes men have obligations as well as rights, but Strauss ignores all such statements because he is convinced that a 'civil society merely creates the conditions under which individuals can pursue their productive-acquisitive activity without obstruction', i.e. men have no obligations.[21] Strauss's theory is interesting; unfortunately, it is not Locke's.

This does not exhaust Strauss's account of property rights or his total report on Locke, but it should be sufficient to show that his interpretation is both misleading

---

[20] *Treatise*, op. cit., secs. 159, 140, 191.
[21] Strauss, op. cit., p. 246.

and mistaken. Why has such a competent scholar made such grievous mistakes? The answer is as simple as it is obvious. The author of the definitive work on Hobbes's political theory must have found it easy to assume that Locke's presentation would be as rigorous and complete as Hobbes's, so when he failed to find precise definitions,[22] logical acumen, or complete analyses in the *Second Treatise* he felt compelled to scurry to Locke's other writings to patch together a theory Locke *might* have used. And when Locke's reconstructed natural law theory turned out to be inadequate, what better premiss to assert as basic than one which Locke occasionally suggests, and one which Strauss already knew intimately—Hobbes's egoism.

II

Two other 'non-traditional' interpretations warrant brief consideration. According to Willmoore Kendall, Locke's fundamental premiss is in his account of community life, for

> whenever men live in a community with one another, the relations between them can be described in terms which, in addition to assigning to the whole community unlimited power, assigns to its numerical majority a *right* to make decisions which are binding upon all.[23]

Since 'the majority rule principle is, in a word, implicit in the logic of community life', it follows that 'the commonwealth's judgments are the individual's judgments *whether he agrees with them or not, i.e. they are the individual's judgments even when he consciously disagrees with*

---

[22] For instance, Locke stipulatively defines 'property' as: (1) 'estate'; (2) 'lives, liberties, and estates'; (3) 'the property which men have in their persons as well as their goods'; (4) 'life, liberty, health, limb, and goods'; and (5) 'life, liberty, and limb'. See secs. 123, 87, 173, 6, 137, 171.

[23] *John Locke and the Doctrine of Majority Rule*, Illinois University Studies in Social Sciences, Urbana, Illinois, 1941, vol. 26, p. 112. Italics in text.

them'.²⁴ Men's rights, then, 'are such rights as are compatible with the public good which, in turn, is determined by the majority' and Locke is *really* advocating an extreme majority rule theory 'so authoritarian that no individualist could conceivably accept it'.²⁵

As with all 'nothing but' interpretations, the adequacy of Kendall's account can be measured in two ways: is there any important aspect of Locke's thought which cannot be subsumed under the governing principle; and, does he consistently maintain his own interpretation? On both counts Kendall fails.

Consider the status of natural law. According to Kendall, 'men have an unlimited competence to modify the law of nature by agreement; for example: the agreement among men "to put a value on" money means, if it means anything at all, that the law of nature can be changed by unanimous agreement'.²⁶ Of course, the reference to unanimity does not necessarily support the claim for majority rule, for an action may be binding under the latter but not under the former. Moreover, this interpretation ignores such explicit statements as: 'The law of nature does not depend on the express consent on any of the commoners.'²⁷ Finally, Kendall confuses man's interpretation of the law with the law itself, man's understanding with God's understanding; for Locke does not suggest that human agreements, even unanimous ones, can alter pre-existent principles.

Or again, Kendall claims that when there is conflict between the individual's right to retain property and the community's right to use it, the spoilage principle requires that one 'unhesitatingly sacrifice the former to the latter'.²⁸ Textually, Kendall is in error, for Locke makes no such statement in the sections cited; in fact, in these sections Locke repeatedly refers to a condition of plenty, hence there would be no conflict of rights. And even if there were, there is nothing in the spoilage principle to

---

²⁴ Ibid., pp. 66, 105. Italics in text.
²⁵ Ibid., pp. 112, 113. Also see pp. 58, 71, 78.
²⁶ Ibid., pp. 84–85.   ²⁷ *Treatise*, op. cit., sec. 28.
²⁸ *Treatise*, secs. 31–36; Kendall, op. cit., p. 71.

suggest that Locke 'unhesitatingly' accepts the alternative Kendall attributes to him. Indeed, why accept the spoilage principle at all? Kendall does not claim that majority rule is authoritative here; why, then, should one recognize its authority? In fact, Kendall does not really believe that Locke can be squeezed into one principle. He begins his critique with the pronouncement: 'We are not, be it noted, denying that both elements, indefeasible individual rights (which are, of course, only a shorthand expression for objective moral standards) and decision making power in the majority are present in Locke's system.'[29] And this dualist interpretation seems to reflect his more considered judgement, for his last chapter explains how the two elements can be 'reconciled'.[30] But if there are two, then the majority rule principle alone is not sufficient: the best disproof for Kendall's interpretation is Kendall himself.

Kendall sees Locke as asserting obligations and denying rights; Charles E. Vaughan finds the positions reversed. He considers Locke's account of natural law most important, and since this law

> proclaims itself to the heart of every individual, man comes into the world with a ready made knowledge of good and evil, a knowledge of his rights and obligations before he ever enters a civil society. [Therefore], each person is entitled to dictate his will to the state; to refuse his assent—and we can only conclude, his obedience also—to any law or executive act which does not square with the divinely ordained code which each man finds written in his heart and which he alone has the right to interpret.[31]

Thus, Locke is 'The Prince of Individualists', for he claims that individuals are bound by only those obliga-

[29] Ibid., p. 54.
[30] Ibid., pp. 133–5. His answer, for what it is worth, is that Locke held a 'latent premise' that the proposition 'right is that which the majority wills' is equivalent to the proposition 'the majority always wills what is right'.
[31] *Studies in the History of Political Philosophy*, Manchester University Press, 1925, vol. i, pp. 164, 171–2.

tions they choose to recognize. Or, to restate but two of the implications:

> Taxation, as commonly understood, is in no way to be justified.
>
> The only kind of war which can be justified on Locke's premises is the war *pro aris et focis*: the war waged by the individual against a savage invader in defense of bare life and personal property. All other forms of war demand the sacrifice of individual life and property to the welfare of the state. And this is a demand which no state framed on Locke's principles has a right to make; and which, if made, no individual in his senses would dream of accepting.[32]

Vaughan is more shrewd than Kendall, for instead of reinterpreting every statement as an instance of the basic principle, he simply admits Locke's diversity—and then accuses him of inconsistency. When Locke says a citizen should pay taxes, join others in fighting a war, agree to have his house destroyed, or abide by majority rule, Vaughan reports the claimed obligations and then says Locke did not clearly understand his own doctrine. Accordingly one cannot dispute Vaughan with documentation; he claims that these instances have nothing to do with Locke's *real* theory. But one can point out the implication: if men have no civil obligations, and fully three-fourths of the *Second Treatise* is concerned with man's rights and obligations in civil society, then most of Locke's political philosophy never should have been written or, since it was, should never be read, if his real theory is to be understood.

However, Vaughan's basic candour leads him to state, succinctly, the crucial problem for his interpretation. Locke is the Prince of Individualists *only* if every individual *qua* individual has complete knowledge of the law of nature, for

> either the law of nature is not so effective an instrument as you would have us believe for curbing the

---

[32] *Treatise*, pp. 183, 198.

passions of man and securing his peace and welfare, or the change from the state of nature to the civil society is an unnecessary, and therefore, an unwarranted revolution.[33] Vaughan accepts the second alternative, for if every person has the sole right to interpret the law, he has no obligation to obey a civil society which interprets it for him; therefore, Locke's civil society is unnecessary and unwarranted.

But Locke's own account is closer to the first. The state of nature is full of 'fears and continual dangers', 'great inconveniences', 'mutual grievances, injuries, and wrongs'; in fact, without government, the law of nature is largely ineffectual.[34] Some people do not understand its provisions; others cannot apply the rules to specific cases; still others are torn between conflicting obligations; and many simply do not do what they should. There is no 'common and uniform' interpretation of the law, no clear understanding of one's rights and obligations, hence men do not come to civil society with 'a fully developed moral sense', but precisely because they *lack* that sense. Hence, civil society is both necessary and justified; indeed, if it were not, political philosophy would be futile.

Vaughan's writing is persuasive, his logic tenacious, but he commits one fundamental error: he confuses the *how* with the *what*. He argues that since the law of nature is known only *by* an individual, the individual's interpretation is justified—and inalienable. But the argument is purely formal, for if natural law sanctioned watching sunsets or eating gollywompus meat, Vaughan's conclusion still holds, since only an individual can decide how many sunsets or how much meat. For Locke, however, the *content* of natural law, the moral rules men *should* recognize, is of most importance, for these injunctions provide the basis for understanding the rights and obligations necessary to a civil society.

[33] *Studies*, pp. 165–6. Also see pp. 158–61, 201.
[34] *Treatise*, op. cit., secs. 90, 91, 127.

III

In addition to their specific errors, these interpreters share a common misconception: that Locke's theory can be reduced to a simple 'nothing but' principle. Actually, his theory is exceedingly complex. This can be seen best by reducing all his assertions to their logical components.

1. *Consent.* Locke tells us that his purpose is to 'justify' the revolution restoring Parliamentary rule to England. To do so, he denies that the *right* to rule comes from God, the Divine Right of Kings theory, but affirms that it does come from the voluntary consent of the governed. His chief purpose, then, as many writers have said, was to establish a democratic theory of sovereignty whereby government would be made responsible to its citizens and hence not rule 'arbitrarily'.

1.1. However, this claim requires the prior assumption that citizens have a right to choose their rulers. How is this right justified? Obviously it is not a right granted by existent rulers, for they might not rule with consent; *de facto* is not identical with *de jure* rule. The right, therefore, must exist independently of political authority; it is a 'natural' right, a claim that man *qua* man enjoys.

1.2. Man, therefore, must have a logical, if not physical, pre-political existence: the 'state of nature'. In this condition each individual has the right to seek his own preservation, but he also has the obligation to help to preserve, or at least not to hinder, the preservation of other men.

1.3. These 'natural' rights and duties are justified in two ways:

1.31. All life is created, and destroyed, by God; hence He must desire the continued existence of all living beings.

1.32. By means of eternal moral rules, 'laws of nature', He has told men how they should treat each other: they should seek the preservation of all mankind.

Locke's Political Theory and Its Interpreters 193

1.4. Government by consent, then, is simply the best way for an individual to fulfil his 'natural' rights and obligations.

1.5. Any government so established has the right to interpret the law of nature for specific cases and every citizen has an obligation to obey its laws.

2. *Freedom.* In addition to the existence and authority of independent moral principles, Locke utilized several meanings of 'freedom'.

2.1. If men should not, but can, ignore the dictates of natural law, they have the ability to choose: in traditional terms, men possess 'free will'.

2.2. The right of self-preservation allows each freely to 'appropriate' property. Each may justifiably aggregate as much as he desires, provided only that he should neither acquire it by 'invading' his neighbour's share nor allow it to spoil. The right to free appropriation leads to:

2.21. The labour theory of value, for nature's bounty acquires value only when someone 'mixes' his labour with it; and

2.22. A *laissez faire* economic theory, for the right to property depends upon one's own efforts, each being responsible for his own preservation. Government has no obligation to provide for the slackers.

2.3. The distinction between *de facto* and *de jure* rule requires an opportunity to choose if the right is not merely formal. Locke attaches such importance to this that he provides for three such opportunities.

2.31. Men must believe that the limitations imposed by government are less onerous than anarchy. Most will reach this conclusion because of past experience, but those who choose anarchy when their neighbours form a government are not bound by the others' decision.

2.32. Those who prefer government still must choose its form. This involves:

2.321. An agreement about procedures, for until all can concur in a method for making decisions, no justified decisions can be made. Locke identifies this agreement with majority rule (although he says other mutually acceptable procedures could be justified) and, presumably, it is a unanimous accord, for nothing in 2.31 makes the majority's decision to accept majority rule binding upon all. And,

2.322. An agreement about people. Once the procedures have been accepted by all, the particular legislators can be chosen.

2.33. But even these two instances of voluntary consent are not sufficient, for the final test of any government is experience. In time, some may prefer the terrors of anarchy to the tyranny of the majority; hence the government's right to rule must be measured, continuously, against its purpose for ruling; government by consent allows the perpetual potential right to revolution.

2.34. For those born after government's establishment, the first two opportunities are supplanted by the doctrine of implied consent, but the continual right to reassess the government's achievements remains unaltered.

2.4. These agreements are identical with a contractual relation wherein the parties' rights and obligations are clearly recognized and mutually accepted.

3. *Equality.* Locke's theory also uses the concept of equality; again, in several senses.

3.1. Since God makes no distinctions among men, He must consider all to be of equal moral worth, hence His law admonishes men to seek both their own preservation and the preservation of others. This rule applies:

3.11. When there is no governmental force to ensure its recognition, and

3.12. When government does exist and the law can be enforced.

3.121. Legislators should always recognize this general moral rule when making laws and hence should not rule 'arbitrarily' or against the 'public good'.

3.122. An individual cannot justify revolution by claiming abrogation of his own rights; only a claimed violation of the rights of the majority gives sufficient reason for one to consider rebellion.

3.2. Each man's right to self-preservation allows him to appropriate property; his obligation to others limits his appropriation to what will not spoil. All, then, have an equal right to some degree of property and each has an obligation to see that the right is fulfilled.

3.3. Majority rule assumes that each person counts for one and only one vote in making political decisions and choosing legislators. Also, presumably, each should have an equal opportunity to become a legislator.

Consent; freedom; equality: these are the concepts from which Locke's political philosophy is made. Each is distinct: freedom to consent also implies freedom not to; economic freedom is different from (and incompatible with?) economic equality; consent does not necessarily imply the assumed equality of majority rule. Yet each is necessary: without consent the denials in the *First Treatise* and the affirmations in the *Second* would be incomprehensible; without freedom to exercise choice, the right to consent would be empty; without a theory of obligations, the establishment and continuance of government would be impossible. So, Locke's theory really involves three distinct, but interrelated, ideas; hence all attempts to explain it with a single 'nothing but' principle are doomed, *a priori*, to failure.

IV

If this brief analysis is even approximately correct, several conclusions seem justified.

One should not be surprised at the extent and assortment of differences which mark the writings of Locke's interpreters; his theory allows, indeed encourages, diverse explanations. Here he has been reported to be an anarchist and an authoritarian, a denier and an affirmer of natural law, an egoist and a majority rule advocate—and each writer can document his report with explicit statements. And this does not exhaust the possibilities. Others have seen Locke as a revolutionary, a traditionalist, a Whig, or a defender of inalienable rights and there is no reason why some shrewd observer, and competent scholar, should not see Locke's *real* theory as advocating Marxism, secession, or preserving the *status quo*. Actually, Locke's theory is so complex that writers can assert a variety of principles as basic—and with sufficient ingenuity find justification for their interpretation.

And this leads to a second conclusion. One does not need to be particularly astute to discover inconsistencies, for when statements originating from different basic concepts are laid side by side, incompatibilities become evident. Locke's theory requires both obedience to the state and the right to revolt: consent *v.* freedom. He sanctions unlimited appropriation, yet an obligation to help to preserve others: freedom *v.* equality. He relies upon majority rule, yet affirms the inalienability of an individual's consent: equality *v.* consent. It is no wonder, then, that some writers have concluded that Locke is 'a blundering incompetent' or 'a man whose problem exceeds his powers'.

Yet, these inconsistencies are not as serious as one might suppose. For one thing, a complex theory involves a number of different questions and some supposed inconsistencies have resulted from the failure to distinguish, for example, statements about the origin of government from statements concerning its moral efficacy, or descriptions of men's motivations from prescriptions of their rights. Moreover, as previously mentioned, Locke is not a careful writer,[35] hence one does not get at the heart of his theory by documenting isolated snippets and minutiæ. An interpreter's scholarship must seek out the frequently repeated assertions and the broad outlines of the theory if he is to escape the inconsistencies resulting from Locke's carelessness.

But even after using appropriate scholarship, one will still find paradoxes, for the basic principles, themselves, are partially incompatible. Yet it should be pointed out that these inconsistencies form the basis for many of the haunting dilemmas in modern democratic governments. Should we grant Communists freedom of speech when we know that, in power, they abolish government by consent? Which would you deny, freedom or consent? Should the proceeds from a progressive income tax be used for slum

[35] See n. 25.

clearance or farm subsidies; which is more important, freedom or equality? Should a conscientious objector be punished for refusing to support a war sanctioned by the majority; consent or equality? Each side justifies itself by appealing to basic democratic principles, hence we have no clear and ready answer to these problems. But if Locke's theory has inconsistencies precisely because it involves *all* these principles, we can conclude that criticisms of his theory are applicable far beyond the *Second Treatise* and that his unresolved difficulties still remain unresolved—and difficult.

One final point can only be suggested. Locke's theory actually involves a series of tensions, for these concepts supplement—and limit—each other both in theory and in history. Unlimited freedom is anarchy, but government initially established by consent can become tyrannical, hence, freedom must be restricted by consent; consent continually supplemented by freedom. Unlimited appropriation can lead to injustice, but total reliance upon the majority's beneficence can lead to apathy, so freedom is circumscribed by equality; equality complemented by freedom. Majority rule can be tyrannical, but a state with no commonly recognized procedures would be chaotic, so equality is countered by the right to review consent; freedom of conscience completed by equality. And in history, *laissez-faire* capitalism was challenged on the grounds of inequality and injustice; New Deal egalitarianism because it destroyed initiative and freedom; equal voting rights for negroes because those whites most affected will not consent. Locke's theory, then—and democratic government—have limits built into their framework, for when the consequences of any one concept become too important, an appeal to either, or both, the other two can be used to restore the balance.

Thus, both Locke's theory and democratic government's practice, are conducive to endless discussion and perpetual confusion, but also they have an inner source of vitality which makes the practice perenially adaptable and the theory continually interesting. Locke's theory, then, merely anticipates the problems of modern democratic government, so that in an even larger sense than the eighteenth-century writers realized, John Locke was the philosopher of democracy.

THE SOCIAL BEARING OF LOCKE'S POLITICAL THEORY

C. B. MACPHERSON

SOME UNSETTLED PROBLEMS OF LOCKE'S POLITICAL THEORY

The reference in the title of this paper is to be taken in a double sense. It marks a concern both with the social assumptions that carry the weight of Locke's political theory and with the type of society to which that theory pointed the direction. Not enough attention has been given to either of these problems, especially the first—the social assumptions. It is not entirely surprising that these assumptions have been neglected. The renewed discussion of Locke's political ideas in recent years is part of a revival of interest in natural law and in the meaning and possibilities of liberal democracy. But the current revival of interest in liberal-democratic principles contains its own dangers. It is, directly or indirectly, part of the Western defenses against communism. The consequent preoccupation with the broad validity of liberal democracy has inhibited any substantial notice of the class content of even seventeenth century liberal theory. Attention has thus been diverted from the social assumptions of Locke's theory, insofar as they are assumptions about the class character of society, in a way which is unlikely to be conducive

From *The Western Political Quarterly*, Vol. VII (1954). Reprinted by permission of the author, and of the University of Utah, copyright owners. A fuller treatment is to be found in the author's *The Political Theory of Possessive Individualism*, Oxford paperbacks, 1964, ch. V, "Locke: The Political Theory of Appropriation."

to a valid understanding either of his theory or of liberal-democratic principles.

The neglecting of social bases alone might not call for a reinterpretation of Locke, were it not that current interpretations leave at the heart of his political theory serious unexplained inconsistencies. Neglect of Locke's social assumptions and failure to explain contradictions in his political theory are not unrelated. This paper attempts in part to show that a closer analysis of these assumptions may render Locke's political theory more intelligible.

The prevailing view, it might fairly be said, is that Locke was primarily the theorist of the liberal state, of constitutional or limited government as opposed to arbitrary or absolute government, of government conditional on the consent of the governed, or of majority rule qualified by individual rights. It is usually implied that the problem Locke had set himself was either to build a universally valid general theory of political obligation or to provide a general validation of a particular constitutional position. In either of these versions, little attention is given to the social, as distinct from the constitutional, content of Locke's theory.

Such abstraction from social content has not always prevailed. A more realistic quality was given to the constitutional interpretation by those who saw Locke's state as, in effect, a joint-stock company whose shareholders were the men of property. This was the view taken by Leslie Stephen in his *English Thought in the Eighteenth Century* (1876), by C. E. Vaughan in his *Studies in the History of Political Philosophy* (1925), by Laski in his *Locke to Bentham* (1920) and his *Rise of European Liberalism* (1936), and by Professor Tawney in his *Religion and the Rise of Capitalism* (1926). There is one great difficulty in this view. Who were the members of Locke's civil society? If they were only the men of property, how could the social contract be an adequate basis of political obligation for all men? Yet undoubtedly the purpose of the social contract was to find a basis for all-inclusive political obligation. Here is an outstanding difficulty. That eminent historians of thought did not see it as such is probably

The Social Bearing of Locke's Political Theory

because their interpretation was mainly in the constitutional tradition:[1] it emphasized the limits Locke put on government in the interests of property, rather than the very great power Locke gave to the political community (his "civil society") as against individuals. Another view, with opposite emphasis, has made some headway in the last ten years, following the publication of Professor Kendall's study.[2] There a strong case is made that Locke's theory confers something very close to complete sovereignty on civil society, that is, in effect, on the majority of the people (though not, of course, on the government, which has only fiduciary power). Against this sovereignty of the majority, the individual has no rights. Impressive evidence can be shown for this reading of Locke. It leads to the striking conclusion that Locke was not an individualist at all, but a "collectivist" in that he subordinated the purposes of the individual to the purposes of society. He is made a forerunner of Rousseau and the General Will.[3] The case is a strong one. However, in concluding that Locke was a "majority-rule democrat," this interpretation overlooks all the evidence that Locke was not a democrat at all. It reads into Locke a concern with the democratic principle of majority rule, which was to be the focus of much American political thinking in the late eighteenth and early nineteenth centuries, as it is now. And it leaves a major problem: Does not majority rule endanger that individual property right which Locke plainly sought to protect? Moreover, it proposes a resolution of Locke's many inconsistencies by imputing to him an assumption ("that the chances are at least 50 plus out of 100 that the average man is rational and just"),[4] which

[1] Professor Tawney's, of course, was not, and he did draw attention to the decisive seventeenth century assumption that the laboring class was a race apart (R. H. Tawney, *Religion and the Rise of Capitalism* [Harmondsworth and New York: Penguin Books Ltd., 1940], pp. 175, 241, to which reference is made below, p. 204). However the implications for the political theory of the period, not being central to his argument, were not explored.
[2] Willmoore Kendall, *John Locke and the Doctrine of Majority-Rule* (Urbana, Illinois: University of Illinois, 1941).
[3] *Ibid.*, pp. 103–6. [4] *Ibid.*, pp. 134–35.

Locke certainly did not hold unambiguously and which he specifically contradicted more than once.⁵

More recently, attempts have been made, notably by J. W. Gough,⁶ to bring Locke back into the liberal-individualist tradition. However, these efforts are not conclusive. In trying to rescue Locke from the abstract logical treatment he has had at some hands and to restore his theory to its historical context, the emphasis is again put on his constitutionalism. But the context of political history overshadows that of social and economic history. At most, what is proposed is a compromise between Locke's individualism and his "collectivism," and major inconsistencies are left unexplained.

Indeed, almost all interpretations fail to account for radical contradictions in Locke's postulates. Why should Locke have said, and what could he have meant by saying, both that men on the whole are rational and that most of them are not; both that the state of nature is rational, peaceable and social, and that it is not essentially different from Hobbes's state of war?⁷ To make consistency the first rule of interpretation is as unrealistic as to take comfort in the allegation that great minds are not consistent. Yet the contradictions that lie on the surface of the *Second Treatise of Civil Government* deserve more explanation than they have had. The fact that they cannot be resolved by logical analysis, or explained by constitutional historical analysis, suggests that they are the outcome of a deeper social contradiction. Therefore we may look to Locke's view of his own society for insight into the meaning of his political theory.

⁵ *Second Treatise of Civil Government*, sections 21, 123; and see below, pp. 218–19.

⁶ J. W. Gough, *John Locke's Political Philosophy: Eight Studies* (Oxford, 1950).

⁷ *Rational* is used here in Locke's sense of governing oneself by the law of nature or law of reason (e.g., *Second Treatise*, § 6: Reason *is* the law of nature; § 8: To transgress the law of nature is to live by another rule than that of reason and common equity). For Locke's contradictory views of man's rationality, see below, pp. 216–19.

The Social Bearing of Locke's Political Theory

We shall find that his conception of that society, especially of its class differentiation, entered into his abstract postulates about the nature of society and man in a way that has not generally been noticed. This view goes far to account for the contradictions in Locke's political theory, and for the outstanding problems of its interpretation.

LOCKE'S SOCIAL PRECONCEPTIONS

Locke did not make all his social assumptions explicit. There is no reason why he should have done so. The assumptions which he and his contemporary readers absorbed from the thinking of their own time, and from their understanding of their own society, he could take for granted.

Here I want to direct attention to two preconceptions which Locke, in common with many others of his class and time, entertained about his own society. As assumptions about the nature of seventeenth century society they are explicit in various writings of Locke; as assumptions about society in general they are implicit in the *Treatise* and had a decisive influence in his political theory.[8]

These are (1) that while the laboring class is a necessary part of the nation, its members are not in fact full members of the body politic and have no claim to be so; and (2) that the members of the laboring class do not and cannot live a fully rational life. "Laboring class" is used here to include both the "laboring poor" and the "idle poor," that is, all who were dependent on employment or charity or the workhouse because they had no property of their own by which, or on which, they might work.

That these people were not, in fact or by right, full members of political society was the prevailing view in

[8] These two are not necessarily Locke's most fundamental social assumptions. First place should be given to his belief that every man is the sole proprietor of his own person and capacities. But as this is explicit in the *Treatise*, it does not demand the same attention here. (See below, pp. 213–14, 226–28).

England in the second half of the seventeenth century. They were regarded not as citizens but as a body of actual and potential labor available for the purposes of the nation. Professor Tawney has summarized their position in the observation that the prevailing attitude of English writers after 1660 "towards the new industrial proletariat [was] noticeably harsher than that general in the first half of the seventeenth century, and . . . has no modern parallel except in the behaviour of the less reputable of white colonists towards coloured labour."[9] The working class was, in effect, in but not of civil society.

This attitude may be seen as a secularization, not only of the Puritan doctrine of the poor, but also of that Calvinist view in which the church, while claiming to include the whole population, held that full membership could be had only by the elect. The nonelect (who were mainly, though not entirely, coincidental with the nonpropertied) were at once members and not members of the church: not full members sharing in the government of the church, but sufficiently members to be subject, rightfully, to its discipline.[10] This Calvinist position tended to exclude beggars, vagrants, and all unemployed poor from full citizenship, an implication of their exclusion from full membership in the church.

The secular view that came to prevail during the Restoration went much further. Not only the unemployed but also the employed poor were treated, not as citizens but as objects of state policy. Economic writers of the day admitted, even insisted, that the laboring poor were the ultimate source of any nation's wealth, but only if they were compelled to continuous labor. That the arrangements for extracting this labor were not regarded as entirely satisfactory in 1688 is evident from Gregory King's famous statistical estimate of the population and income of England in 1688 (which, as Unwin has said, affords

---

[9] Tawney, *op. cit.*, pp. 240–41.
[10] For expressions of this view in English Calvinism, see Christopher Hill, "Puritans and the Poor," *Past & Present*, II (November, 1952), 41.

"better evidence of the common assumptions of the directing classes than of any objective social facts").[11] He divided the whole body of the people into those increasing and those decreasing the wealth of the kingdom, and put not only "cottagers and paupers" and "vagrants," but also the "labouring people and outservants" among the occupational classes, each of which decreased the wealth of the kingdom.[12]

The estimated size of the propertyless wage-earning and unemployed classes in 1688 need not be emphasized, though it is striking enough: King and D'Avenant put more than half the population in this category. What is more important is the assumption that the laboring class is to be managed by the state in order to make it productive of national gain. The laboring class's interests were not subordinated to the national interest; the class was not considered to have an interest. The ruling-class view of the national interest was the only one.

This attitude towards the working class, generally explicit in the economic writings of the period from 1660, is nicely exemplified in William Petyt's statement:

> People are . . . the chiefest, most fundamental and precious commodity, out of which may be derived all sorts of manufactures, navigation, riches, conquests and solid dominion. This capital material being of itself raw and indigested is committed into the hands of the supreme authority in whose prudence and disposition it is to improve, manage and fashion it to more or less advantage.[13]

[11] George Unwin, *Studies in Economic History* (ed. by R. H. Tawney, London, 1927), p. 345.
[12] King's estimate is conveniently reproduced in Dorothy George, *England in Transition* (Penguin edition, 1953), pp. 150-51. It is partially reproduced in G. N. Clark, *The Wealth of England from 1496 to 1760* (London, 1946), but without the division into those increasing and those decreasing. The full table is in D'Avenant's *Works* (1771), II, 184.
[13] William Petyt, *Britannia Languens* (1680), p. 238. This and similar passages from various writers of the period are quoted in E. S. Furniss, *The Position of the Laborer in a System of Nationalism* (New York: Houghton, 1920), pp. 16 ff.

The view that human beings of the laboring class were a commodity out of which riches and dominion might be derived, a raw material to be worked up and disposed of by the political authority, was fully shared by Locke. The evidence leaves no doubt that he regarded the working class as subject to, but without full membership in, the political society of seventeenth century England. He assumed this not only as a matter of fact but as a matter of right. The moral assumption was that the laboring class does not and cannot live a rational life.

Evidence of these assumptions is scattered throughout Locke's writings. His proposals for the treatment of the able-bodied unemployed are fairly well known, although when they are mentioned by modern writers it is usually to deprecate their severity and excuse it by reference to the standards of the time. What is more to the point is the view which these proposals afford of Locke's assumptions. Masters of workhouses ("houses of correction") were to be encouraged to make them into sweated-labor manufacturing establishments; justices of the peace were to make them into forced-labor institutions. Children of the unemployed "above the age of three" were unnecessarily a burden on the nation; they should be set to work, and could be made to earn more than their keep. All this was justified on the explicit ground that unemployment was due not to economic causes but to moral depravity. The multiplying of the unemployed, Locke wrote in 1697 in his capacity as a member of the Commission on Trade, was caused by "nothing else but the relaxation of discipline and corruption of manners."[14] There was no question in his mind of treating the unemployed as full or free members of the political community; there was equally no doubt that they were fully subject to the state. The state was entitled to deal with them in this way be-

---

[14] Quoted in H. R. Fox Bourne, *The Life of John Locke* (London, 1876), II, 378. Locke seems to have regarded the idle poor as depraved by choice, in contrast to the laboring poor, whom he considered incapable of a fully rational life because of their position. (See below, pp. 220–21.)

cause they would not live up to the moral standard required of rational men.

Locke's attitude towards the employed wage-earning class has been noticed less often, though it is plain enough in various passages of his economic writings, particularly in *Some Considerations of the Consequences of the Lowering of Interest and Raising the Value of Money* (1691). There, incidentally to his technical arguments, Locke takes for granted that the wage-laborer constitutes a normal and sizable class in the nation,[15] that he has no property but is entirely dependent on his wages, and that, of necessity, his wages are normally at a bare subsistence level.[16] Such a person "just lives from hand to mouth." One passage in particular deserves quotation:

> ... The labourer's share [of the national income], being seldom more than a bare subsistence, never allows that body of men, time, or opportunity to raise their thoughts above that, or struggle with the richer for theirs (as one common interest), unless when some common and great distress, uniting them in one universal ferment, makes them forget respect, and emboldens them to carve to their wants with armed force: and then sometimes they break in upon the rich, and sweep all like a deluge. But this rarely happens but in the male-administration of neglected, or mismanaged government.[17]

It is hard to say which part of these remarks is the most revealing. There is the assumption that the laborers are normally kept too low to be able to think or act politically. There is the assertion that maladministration consists not of leaving them there, but of allowing such unusual distress to occur as will unite them in armed revolt. And there is the conviction that such revolt is improper, an offense against the respect they owe to their betters.

Now the question: Who has the right of revolution? is a decisive question with Locke. The revolutionary right is to him the only effective test of citizenship, as he makes

[15] *Considerations*, in *Works* (1759 edition), II, 13–16.
[16] *Ibid.*, p. 29.
[17] *Ibid.*, p. 36.

no provision for any other method of overthrowing an unwanted government. Although he insists, in the *Treatise,* on the majority's right to revolution, it does not seem to cross his mind here that the laboring class might have the right to make a revolution. Indeed there is no reason why such a thought should have occurred to him, for to him the laboring class was an object of state policy and of administration, rather than fully a part of the citizen body. Such a class was incapable of rational political action, but the right to revolution depended essentially on rational decision.

The assumption that members of the laboring class are in too low a position to be capable of a rational life—that is, capable of regulating their lives by those moral principles Locke supposed were given by reason—is evident again in *The Reasonableness of Christianity.* The whole argument of that work is a plea that Christianity be restored to a few simple articles of belief "that the labouring and illiterate man may comprehend." Christianity should thus again be made

> a religion suited to vulgar capacities; and the state of mankind in this world, destined to labour and travel. . . . The greatest part of mankind have not leisure for learning and logick, and superfine distinctions of the schools. Where the hand is used to the plough and the spade, the head is seldom elevated to sublime notions, or exercised in mysterious reasoning. 'Tis well if men of that rank (to say nothing of the other sex) can comprehend plain propositions, and a short reasoning about things familiar to their minds, and nearly allied to their daily experience. Go beyond this, and you amaze the greatest part of mankind. . . .[18]

This is not, as might be thought, a plea for a simple rationalist ethical religion to replace the disputations of the theologians. On the contrary, Locke's point is that without supernatural sanctions the laboring class is incapable of following a rationalist ethic. He only wants the

[18] *The Reasonableness of Christianity,* last two pages; *Works* (1759), II, 585–86.

sanctions made clearer. The simple articles he recommends are not moral rules, but articles of faith. Belief in them is all that is necessary, for such belief converts the moral rules of the gospel into binding commands. Locke's problem is to frame the articles so that they will appeal directly to the experience of the common people, who can thus believe.[19] The greatest part of mankind, he concludes, cannot be left to the guidance of the laws of nature or of reason; they are not capable of drawing rules of conduct from them. For "the day-labourers and tradesmen, the spinsters and dairy-maids . . . hearing plain commands, is the sure and only course to bring them to obedience and practice. The greatest part cannot know and therefore they must believe."[20]

Of course, Locke was recommending this simplified Christianity for all classes, as may be seen in his ingenuously mercantile observations on the surpassing utility of the Christian doctrine of rewards and punishments.

> The [ancient] philosophers, indeed, shewed the beauty of virtue; . . . but leaving her unendowed, very few were willing to espouse her. . . . But now there being put into the scales on her side, 'an exceeding and immortal weight of glory'; interest is come about to her, and virtue now is visibly the most enriching purchase, and by much the best bargain. . . . The view of heaven and hell will cast a slight upon the short pleasures and pains of this present state, and give attractions and encouragements to virtue, which reason and interest, and the care of our-

[19] The essential articles of belief are that there is a future life and that salvation can only be had by believing that Christ was raised from the dead to be the divine savior of mankind. Locke argues that this is a plain notion which, along with miracles, can readily be grasped by the illiterate in terms of their common experience: "The healing of the sick, the restoring sight to the blind by a word, the raising, and being raised from the dead, are matters of fact, which they can without difficulty conceive, and that he who does such things, must do them by the assistance of a divine power. These things lie level to the ordinariest apprehension: he that can distinguish between sick and well, lame and sound, dead and alive, is capable of this doctrine." (*Ibid.*, II, 580.)

[20] *Ibid.*, II, 580.

selves, cannot but allow and prefer. Upon this foundation, and upon this only, morality stands firm, and may defy all competition.[21]

No doubt Locke's readers would appreciate this recommendation of Christianity more than would the laborers, who were not in a position to think in terms of making "the most enriching purchase." However, Locke regards as only a secondary advantage the ability of his fundamental Christian doctrine to satisfy men of higher capacities. His repeated emphasis on the necessity of the laboring classes being brought to obedience by a belief in divine rewards and punishments leaves no doubt about his main concern. The implication is plain: the laboring class, beyond all others, is incapable of living a rational life.

Clearly, then, when Locke looked at his own society he saw two classes with different rationality and different rights. It would have been strange had he not done so. Locke was no Leveller. His was not the democratic puritanism that had appeared during the Commonwealth, but the puritanism which had encountered no difficulty in accommodating itself to the exigencies of class rule in 1660. Locke had welcomed the Restoration not only because it had put an end to the turbulence of the Commonwealth,[22] but also because it had restored something that was positively good,

> the protection of those laws which the prudence and providence of our ancestors established and the happy return of his Majesty hath restored: a body of laws so well composed, that whilst this nation would be content only to be under them they were always sure to be above their neighbours, which forced from the world this constant acknowledgment, that we were not only the happiest state but the purest church of the latter age.[23]

[21] *Ibid.*, II, 582.
[22] See the passages quoted from Locke's MS treatise of 1660 on the Civil Magistrate, in Gough, *op. cit.*, p. 178.
[23] Preface to the treatise on the Civil Magistrate, 1660; Bodleian Library, MS Locke C 28, fol. 2 verso.

From this unreserved approbation of the pre-Commonwealth constitution—not, of course, the constitution (of Church and State) as understood by James I and Charles I, but as understood by the Parliamentarians—he went on to state as a matter of principle that "the supreme magistrate of every nation what way soever created, must necessarily have an absolute and arbitrary power over all the indifferent actions of his people."[24] Locke showed himself to be truly conservative in 1660. From then on, his view of society was that of the men of substance.

THE SOCIAL PRECONCEPTIONS GENERALIZED

It would be surprising if Locke's preconceptions about his own society did not somehow affect his premises about society and man as such. His unhistorical habit of mind presented no obstacle to his transferring assumptions about seventeenth-century society into a supposed state of nature. As he took his assumptions about his own society

[24] *Ibid.*, fol. 3 recto. The difference between this and the position Locke took three decades later in the *Second Treatise* is not in the amount of power granted to the civil authority but in the locus of that power. The "absolute and arbitrary power" of 1660 is only over "indifferent actions." Indifferent actions he defined as those not comprehended in the law of nature or divine revelation; in other words, those matters as to which man is naturally free. (See Locke's premises, quoted in Gough, *op. cit.*, p. 179.) These are precisely the matters which in the *Second Treatise* Locke has the individual hand over to the supreme civil authority, there the civil society itself.

But in 1660 Locke was willing to consider a monarch—or was it only the king-in-parliament?—as the supreme authority; the "magistrate" is defined as "the supreme legislative power of any society, not considering the form of government or number of persons wherein it is placed" (MS treatise on Civil Magistrate, Bodleian Library, MS Locke, e. 7, fol. 1, sidenote); whereas in 1689 Locke reserved supreme authority to the civil society itself. He was consistent throughout in wanting a civil authority which could secure the basic institutions of a class society. In 1660 this required the recall of the Stuarts and the doctrine of the magistrate's absolute and arbitrary power in things indifferent; in 1689 it required the dismissal of the Stuarts and the doctrine of the *Second Treatise*.

so much for granted that he felt no need to argue them, they could easily be carried into his premises without any consciousness of a problem of consistency. I shall argue that both of the assumptions about his own society—that of a class differential in rationality, and that of a class differential in rights—were generalized in Locke's thinking into implicit assumptions about human nature as such and about individual *natural* rights, and that these assumptions modified his explicit postulates about human nature and natural rights.

In Locke's initial statement of his postulates in the *Treatise* (and in his analysis of human nature in the *Essay Concerning Human Understanding*, which has to be considered also for a full statement of his general theory of human nature), there is nothing to suggest an assumption of class differentiation. However, before he used these postulates to deduce the necessary character of civil society, he put forward other arguments, especially in his treatment of property rights, which imply that he had already generalized his differential assumptions about his own society into abstract implicit assumptions of differential human nature and natural rights.

(1) Differential Rights. We have seen that Locke found in seventeenth-century society a class differentiation so deep that the members of the laboring class had very different effective rights from the classes above them. They lived, and must live, "from hand to mouth," could never "raise their thoughts above that," and were unfit to participate in political life. Their condition was a result of their having no property on which they could expend their labor; their having no property was one aspect of the prevailing inequality which was grounded in "the necessity of affairs, and the constitution of human society."[25]

What Locke saw in his own society he considered typical of all civil society. But how did this become an assumption of differential *natural* rights, and where does it, as such an assumption, enter into the argument of the *Treatise?* It is certainly not present in the opening state-

[25] *Considerations, Works* (1759), II, 19.

The Social Bearing of Locke's Political Theory 213

ments about natural rights; there the emphasis is all on the natural equality of rights (§§ 4, 5).[26] The transformation of equal into differential natural rights comes to light in Locke's theory of property. In the chapter on property in the *Treatise*, he went out of his way to transform the natural right of every individual to such property as he needed for subsistence and to which he applied his labor, into a natural right of *unlimited* appropriation, by which the more industrious could rightfully acquire all the land, leaving others with no way to live except by selling the disposal of their labor.[27]

This transformation is not an aberration in Locke's individualism but an essential part of it. The core of his individualism is the assertion that every man is naturally the sole proprietor of his own person and capacities (§§ 4, 6, 44, 123)—the absolute proprietor in the sense that he owes nothing to society for them—and especially the absolute proprietor of his capacity to labor (§ 27). Every man is therefore free to alienate his own capacity to labor. This individualist postulate is the one by which Locke transforms the mass of equal individuals (rightfully) into two classes with very different rights, those with property and those without. Once the land is all taken up, the fundamental right not to be subject to the jurisdiction of another is so unequal between owners and nonowners that it is different in kind, not in degree: those without property are dependent for their livelihood on those with property and are unable to alter their own circumstances. The initial equality of natural rights, which consisted in no man's having jurisdiction over another (§ 4) cannot last after the differentiation of property. In other words, the man without property in things loses that proprietorship of his own person which was the basis of his equal natural rights. Locke insists that disparity in property is *natural*, that is, that it takes place "out of the bounds of society,

---

[26] This and subsequent references in the text are to the section numbers of the *Second Treatise of Civil Government*. Quotations are from the 1764 edition of the *Treatises*.
[27] "Locke on Capitalist Appropriation," *Western Political Quarterly*, IV, 550–66.

and without compact" (§ 50). Civil society is established to protect unequal possessions, which have already in the natural state caused unequal rights. In this way Locke has generalized the assumption of a class differential in rights in his own society into an implicit assumption of differential *natural* rights. This implicit assumption, as will be seen, did not replace the initial theory of equality: both were in Locke's mind at the same time.

(2) Differential Rationality. We have seen that Locke assumed in his own society a class differential in rationality which left the laboring class incapable of a fully rational life. The questions are: How did this become an assumption of differential rationality in general? And where did this enter the argument of the *Treatise*? It is clearly not present in the opening statements of postulates. There, rationality and depravity are dealt with abstractly and although rational men are distinguished from depraved men,[28] there is no suggestion that the distinction is correlated with social class. But as the argument proceeds and the postulates have to be made more specific, it becomes apparent that Locke has something else in mind. When he has to relate depravity and rationality to man's political needs, these qualities turn out to have meaning only in the setting of a particular kind of property institutions and to be closely related to ownership.

Whatever man's inherent depravity may be, Locke thinks it does not require any but the most rudimentary political society until there is extensive property. Where there was "the equality of a simple poor way of living, confining [men's] desires within the narrow bounds of each man's small property," there would be few controversies and few trespasses, and consequently no need of many laws or magistrates; there would be more fear of outsiders than of each other, and the main purpose of setting up government would be for security "against foreign force" (§ 107). A fully civil society of the kind which is the main concern of the *Treatise*, a society for the internal security of individual property, is required for the protec-

[28] See below, p. 218.

tion not of small equal properties but only of extensive unequal ones, not of a modest store of consumables or perhaps a few acres of land but of a substantial accumulation of resources. It is the propensity to accumulate property beyond the requirements of subsistence that necessarily leads rational men to establish civil society.

Here we reach the crux of the matter. The propensity to accumulate, although it leads to quarrels, is itself not depraved but rational. Not only is the desire for accumulation rational, according to Locke, but accumulation is the essence of rational conduct. More precisely, the true nature of rational behavior is to expend labor improving the gifts of nature for subsequent enjoyment of greater real income or of greater power or prestige. This procedure, in Locke's view, requires private possession; and the measure of rational industriousness is the accumulation of possessions.

All this can be seen in the famous chapter on property in the *Treatise*, the burden of which is that the truly rational man is the industrious man. Rational behavior in temporal affairs is investing one's energies in the accumulation of real property and capital. "God gave the world to men in common; but . . . he gave it them . . . for . . . the greatest conveniences of life they were capable to draw from it. . . ." Therefore, He "gave it to the use of the industrious and rational," who would "improve" it (§ 34). Improvement without ownership is impossible: "The condition of human life, which requires labour and materials to work on, necessarily introduces private possessions" (§ 35). Not everyone in the state of nature could acquire property, for wherever money is introduced—and it is introduced in the state of nature (§ 50)—the land is all appropriated (§ 45). That the appropriation leaves some men without any possibility of getting land does not disturb Locke because the day-laborer in a society where the land is all appropriated is better off than the greatest man in a primitive economy (§ 41).

Thus "the industrious and rational" are not all laborers, but only those who acquire property and improve it by their labor.[29] A further effect of the introduction of money is that the rational goal of a man's industry becomes accumulation beyond any requirements of consumption. "Different degrees of industry" give men different amounts of property, and the invention of money gives the more industrious man the opportunity "to enlarge his possessions beyond the use of his family, and a plentiful supply to its consumption" (§ 48). In short, rational conduct, in the state of nature, consists in unlimited accumulation, the possibility of which is open only to some. It follows that there was, in Locke's view, a class differential in rationality in the state of nature, inasmuch as those who were left without property after the land was all appropriated could not be accounted fully rational. They had no opportunity to be so. Like day laborers in civil society they were not in a position to expend their labor improving the gifts of nature; their whole energies were needed to keep alive. They could not "raise their thoughts above that," for they just lived "from hand to mouth."

THE AMBIGUOUS STATE OF NATURE

From the foregoing analysis it may be concluded that Locke read back into the state of nature, in a generalized form, the assumptions he made about differential rights and rationality in existing societies. Although the generalized assumptions modified in his own mind the initial postulates of the *Treatise*, they did not displace them. Locke entertained both at the same time, at different levels of consciousness. Hence, the postulates on which he was operating were confused and ambiguous. All men were on the whole rational; yet there were two distinct classes of rationality. All men were equal in natural rights; yet there were two distinct orders of possession of natural

[29] The same conclusion is reached, from a different starting point, by Leo Strauss, in a penetrating recent article on natural law: "On Locke's Doctrine of Natural Rights," *Philosophical Review*, XLI (October, 1952), 495–96.

The Social Bearing of Locke's Political Theory 217

rights. The source of the extraordinary contradiction in Locke's presentation of human nature is found here. We customarily think that Locke held men to be essentially rational and social. Rational, in that they could live together by the law of nature, which is reason, or which at least (though not imprinted on the mind) is knowable by reason without the help of revelation. Social, in that they could live by the law of nature without the imposition of rules by a sovereign. This conception, indeed, is usually said to be the great difference between Locke's and Hobbes's views of human nature. If there is a significant difference it is here that one expects to find it, rather than in the theory of motivation. For Locke, like Hobbes, held that men are moved primarily by appetite and aversion; the appetites are so strong that "if they were left to their full swing, they would carry men to the overturning of all morality. Moral laws are set as a curb and restraint to these exhorbitant desires."[30] It is usually maintained that the difference between this and Hobbes's view is that Locke thought men capable of setting these rules on themselves, by perceiving their utility, without installing a sovereign.

The general theory presented at the opening of the *Treatise* affirms that men are naturally able to govern themselves by the law of nature, or reason. The state of nature, we are told, has a law of nature to govern it, which is reason (§ 6). The state of nature is contrasted flatly to the state of war: the two are "as far distant, as a state of peace, goodwill, mutual assistance and preservation, and a state of enmity, malice, violence and mutual destruction, are from one another. Men living together according to reason, without a common superior on earth, with authority to judge between them, is properly the state of nature"

[30] *Essay Concerning Human Understanding*, I, 3, § 3. Cf. Locke's Hobbesian reflection in 1678 that "the principal spring from which the actions of men take their rise, the rule they conduct them by, and the end to which they direct them, seems to be credit and reputation, and that which at any rate they avoid is in the greatest part shame and disgrace," and the consequences he draws for government. (Quoted from Locke's MS journal in Fox Bourne, *op. cit.*, I, 403–4.)

(§ 19). It is no derogation of this view of the state of nature to allow, as Locke does, that there are some men in it who will not follow the law of nature. Nature's law teaches only those who will consult it (§ 6); some men transgress it and, by so doing, declare themselves "to live by another rule than that of reason and common equity" and in this way become "dangerous to mankind" (§ 8); a man who violates the law of nature "becomes degenerate, and declares himself to quit the principles of human nature, and to be a noxious creature" (§ 10). The whole picture of the state of nature in chapter ii of the *Treatise* is one of a people abiding by natural law, with some natural criminals among them: Locke even uses the word criminal to describe the man in the state of nature who violates its law (§ 8).

But this representation is only one of two quite opposite pictures Locke has of the state of nature. As early as chapter iii of the *Treatise*, only a page after the distinction between the state of nature and the state of war, we read that where there is no authority to decide between contenders "every the least difference is apt to end" in the "state of war," and that "one great reason of men's putting themselves into society, and quitting the state of nature" is "to avoid this state of war" (§ 21).[31] The difference between the state of nature and the Hobbesian state of war has virtually disappeared. Some chapters later, we read further that the state of nature is "very unsafe, very unsecure"; that in it the enjoyment of individual rights is

[31] This passage is not in the Everyman edition of the two Treatises (ed. by W. S. Carpenter) nor in the Appleton-Century edition of the *Second Treatise* and *Letter Concerning Toleration* (ed. by C. L. Sherman, New York, 1937). Each of these follows, at this point, a printing of the first edition of the *Treatises* which did not contain any § 21, and each has covered up the deficiency by arbitrarily dividing another section into two. (Sherman divides § 20; Carpenter divides § 36, so that all the sections in the Everyman edition from 21 to 35 are wrongly numbered.) The particulars of the two printings of Locke's first edition, and of their handling by modern editors, are given in Peter Laslett's "The 1690 Edition of Locke's *Two Treatises of Government*: Two States," *Transactions of the Cambridge Bibliographical Society*, IV (1952), 341–47.

"very uncertain, and constantly exposed to the invasion of others," and that it is "full of fears and continual dangers." All this danger occurs because "the greater part [are] no strict observers of equity and justice" (§ 123). What makes the state of nature unlivable, according to this account, is not the viciousness of the few but the disposition of "the greater part" to depart from the law of reason.

The contradiction between Locke's two sets of statements about natural man is obvious. It is a central contradiction in the explicit postulates on which his political theory is built. It will not do to say he simply echoes the traditional Christian conception of man as a contradictory mixture of appetite and reason. Locke no doubt accepted that view; and within it there is room for a considerable variety of belief as to the relative weights (or potentialities) of the two ingredients of human nature. Different exponents of Christian doctrine could take different views. What has to be explained is how Locke took not one position in this matter but two opposite positions.

One might say that he had to take both in order to make his case against Hobbes; he had to make men rational enough not to require a Hobbesian sovereign, yet contentious enough to necessitate their handing over their natural rights and powers to a civil society. However, to say this would be to accuse Locke, unjustly and unnecessarily, either of intellectual dishonesty or of extraordinary superficiality; besides, it would imply an underestimate of the extent to which Locke did subordinate the individual to the state.[32]

It seems more reasonable to conclude that Locke was able to take both positions about human nature because he had in mind simultaneously two conceptions of society, which, although logically conflicting, were derived from the same ultimate source. One was the seventeenth-century atomistic conception of society as a mass of equal, undifferentiated beings. The other was the notion of a society composed of two classes differentiated by their

[32] See below, pp. 226–28.

level of rationality—those who were "industrious and rational" and had property, and those who were not, who labored, indeed, but only to live, not to accumulate.

Locke was unconscious of the contradiction between these two conceptions of society because both of them (and not merely, as we have already seen, the second one) were elements transferred to his postulates from his comprehension of his own society. Ultimately it was Locke's comprehension of his own society that was ambiguous and contradictory. It could not have been otherwise, for it was the comprehension of an emerging bourgeois society, reflecting the ambivalence of a society which demanded formal equality but required substantive inequality of rights.

As a bourgeois philosopher, a proponent of seventeenth-century individualism, Locke had to regard men as equal, undifferentiated units, and to consider them rational. The bourgeois order justified itself by assuming, first, that all men were intellectually capable of shifting for themselves, and secondly, that rational behavior in this sense was morally rational, in accordance with the law of nature. Thus a necessary part of the bourgeois vision pictured man in general in the image of rational bourgeois man. Locke shared this view, which gave him the account of the state of nature as rational and peaceable.

At the same time, as a bourgeois philosopher Locke necessarily conceived abstract society as consisting of two classes with different rationality. The two classes in Locke's England lived lives totally different in freedom and rights. The basic difference between them in fact was the difference in their ability to live by the bourgeois moral code. But to the directing class this appeared to be a differential capacity in men to live by moral rules as such. This conception of society gave Locke the picture of the state of nature as unsafe and insecure. For to say, as he did, that most men are incapable of guiding their lives by the law of reason, without sanctions, is to say that a civil society with legal sanctions (and a church with spiritual sanctions) is needed to keep them in order. Without these

The Social Bearing of Locke's Political Theory 221

sanctions, i.e., in a state of nature, there could be no peace.

Both views of the state of nature flowed from the bourgeois concept of society, and both were necessary to it. Their common source obscured their contradictory quality. There was no question of Locke's basing his theory on an Aristotelian concept of two classes—masters and slaves—whose relative positions were justified by a supposed inherent difference in rationality. With Locke the difference in rationality was not inherent in men; it was socially acquired by virtue of different economic positions. But since it was acquired in the state of nature, it was inherent in society. Once acquired, that is to say, it was permanent, for it was the concomitant of an order of property relations which Locke assumed to be the permanent basis of civilized society. His notion of differential rationality justified as natural, not slavery,[33] but the subordination of one part of the people by their continual contractual alienation of their capacity to labor. In the bourgeois view men were free to alienate their freedom, and Locke, at least, thought that the difference in rationality was a result rather than a cause of that alienation. But the difference in rationality, once established, provided a justification for differential rights.

THE AMBIGUOUS CIVIL SOCIETY

We may now inquire how Locke's ambiguous position on natural rights and rationality enters and affects his theory of the formation of civil society. Men enter into civil society, Locke asserts, to protect themselves from the inconveniences, insecurity and violence of the state of nature. Or, as he declares repeatedly, the great reason for men's uniting into society and putting themselves under

[33] Locke did, of course, justify slavery also, but not on grounds of inherently differential rationality. Enslavement was justified only when a man had "by his fault forfeited his own life, by some act that deserves death" (§ 23). Locke appears to have thought of it as a fit penalty for his natural criminals.

government is to preserve their property, by which, he says, he means their "lives, liberties and estates" (§ 123, cf. § 173). When property is so defined, everyone has a reason to enter civil society, and everyone is capable of entering it, having some rights which he can transfer. However, Locke did not keep to this definition. He used the term in two different senses at points where its meaning was decisive in his argument. The property for the protection of which men oblige themselves to civil society is sometimes (e.g., §§ 123, 131, 137) stated to be "life, liberty and estate," but sometimes (e.g., §§ 138–140) it is clearly only goods or land.[34] Consequently, men without estate or goods, that is, without property in the ordinary sense, are rightfully both in civil society and not in civil society.

When the property for the protection of which men enter civil society is taken to be life, liberty and estate, all men (except slaves) are eligible for membership; when it is taken to be goods or estate alone, then only men who possess them are eligible. Locke interprets it both ways, without any consciousness of inconsistency. What has happened is understandable in the light of our analysis. Locke's recognition of differential class rights in his own society, having been carried into his postulates as an implicit assumption of differential natural rights and rationality, without displacing the formal assumption of general rationality and equal rights, has emerged at the level of the social contract in a crucial ambiguity about who are parties to the contract.

The question as to whom Locke considered to be members of civil society seems to admit only one answer. Everyone, whether or not he has property in the ordinary sense, is included, as having an interest in preserving his

[34] A striking instance of the latter use is in § 138, where, after arguing that men in society must have property (since the purpose of their entering society was to preserve property), he concludes that "they have such a right to the goods which by the law of the community are theirs, that nobody hath a right to take their substance or any part of it from them without their own consent; without this they have no property at all."

life and liberty. At the same time only those with "estate" can be full members, for two reasons: only they have a full interest in the preservation of property, and only they are fully capable of that rational life—that voluntary obligation to the law of reason—which is the necessary basis for full participation in civil society. The laboring class, being without estate, are subject to, but not full members of, civil society. If it be objected that this is not one answer but two inconsistent answers, the reply must be that both answers follow from Locke's assumptions, and that neither one alone, but only the two together, accurately represent his thinking.

This ambiguity about membership in civil society by virtue of the supposed original contract allows Locke to consider all men as members for purposes of being ruled and only the men of estate as members for purposes of ruling. The right to rule (more accurately, the right to control any government) is given only to the men of estate; it is they who are given the decisive voice about taxation, without which no government can subsist (§ 140). On the other hand, the obligation to be bound by law and subject to the lawful government is fixed on all men whether or not they have property in the sense of estate, indeed, whether or not they have made an express compact. When Locke broadens his doctrine of express consent into a doctrine of tacit consent, he leaves no doubt about who are obligated. Tacit consent is assumed to have been given by "every man, that hath any possessions, or enjoyment, of any part of the dominions of any government . . . whether this his possession be of land, to him and his heirs forever, or a lodging only for a week; or whether it be barely travelling freely on the highway; and in effect, it reaches as far as the very being of any one within the territories of that government" (§ 119). Locke is careful to say (§ 122) that this does not make a man a full member of civil society, but only subjects him rightfully to its government: the men of no estate are not admitted to full membership by the back door of tacit consent.[35] Of course, Locke had to retreat to tacit consent because it was impossible to show express consent in the case of present citizens of an established state. However, his doctrine of tacit consent has the added convenience that it clearly imposes obligation, reaching to their "very being," on those with no estate whatever.

It appears from the foregoing analysis that the result of Locke's work was to provide a moral basis for a class state from postulates of equal individual natural rights. Given the seventeenth-century individualist natural-rights assumptions, a class state could only be legitimized by a doctrine of consent which would bring one class within, but not make it fully a part of, the state. Locke's theory achieved this end. Its accomplishment required the implicit assumptions which he held. These assumptions involved him in the ambiguities and contradictions that pervade his argument. It is difficult to see how he could have persisted in such contradictions had he not been taking the class state as one desideratum and equal natural rights as another.

Locke did not twist deliberately a theory of equal natural rights into a justification for a class state. On the contrary, his honestly held natural-rights assumptions made it possible, indeed almost guaranteed, that his theory would justify a class state without any sleight of hand. The decisive factor was that the equal natural rights Locke envisaged, including as they did the right to unlimited accumulation of property, led logically to differential class rights and so to justification of a class state. Locke's confusions are the result of honest deduction from a postulate of equal natural rights which contained its own contradiction. The evidence suggests that he did not realize the contradiction in the postulate of equal natural right to unlimited property, but that he simply read into the realm of right (or the state of nature) a social relation which he

[35] We may notice incidentally that in his discussion of tacit consent, as well as in that of the supposed express entry into civil society by the contract, Locke lumps together life, liberty and estate under one term, and here the term is not even "property" but "possession" (§ 119, quoted above).

The Social Bearing of Locke's Political Theory 225

accepted as normal in civilized society. The source of the contradictions in his theory is his attempt to state in universal (nonclass) terms, rights and obligations which necessarily had a class content.

UNSETTLED PROBLEMS RECONSIDERED

When Locke's theory is understood in the sense here ascribed to it, some outstanding difficulties of its interpretation may be resolved.

(1) The problem inherent in the joint-stock interpretation of Locke's state is now no problem, for we have seen how Locke considers that the state consists both of property-owners only and of the whole population. He has no difficulty, therefore, in thinking of the state as a joint-stock company of owners whose majority decision binds not only themselves but also their employees. The laboring class, whose only asset is their capacity to labor, cannot take part in the operations of the company at the same level as the owners. Nevertheless, the laboring class is so necessary to the operations of the company as to be an organic part of it. The purpose of the company is not only to keep the property it has, but also to preserve the right and conditions which enable it to enlarge its property; one of these conditions is a labor force effectively submitted to the company's jurisdiction. Perhaps the closest analogue to Locke's state is the joint-stock company of merchants trading with or planting in distant lands, whose charter gives them, or allows them to take, such jurisdiction over the natives or the transplanted labor force as the nature of the trade requires.

(2) The implicit contradiction in that interpretation of Locke's theory which emphasizes the supremacy of the majority is also explained. The inconsistency, it will be remembered, was between the assertion of majority rule and the insistence on the sanctity of individual property. What would happen if the propertyless were a majority? This was no fanciful problem. It had been raised in the debates between the Levellers and the Independents in

the parliamentary army during the civil wars.[36] It was a real difficulty in Locke's day, for it was thought that the propertyless were a majority.[37] We can now see that there is no conflict between the assertion of majority rule and of property right inasmuch as Locke was assuming that only those with property were full members of civil society and thus of the majority.

(3) Various inconsistencies left unexplained in Locke by the liberal-individualist interpretation can also be resolved. Mr. Gough asks, for instance, whether Locke can really have believed, as he did (§ 140), "that the consent of a majority of representatives was the same as a man's own consent, from which it is, in fact, twice removed?"[38] Locke can easily have thought so if he was thinking primarily of the defense of property owners as a whole. His equation of a man's own consent with the consent of the majority makes sense only if he was thinking in this way. Locke was very well aware that there were differences of interest between the landed men, the merchants, and the monied men, differences which he saw sharply demonstrated in struggles over the incidence of taxation.[39] In these circumstances, the fact that he could identify individual and majority consent to taxation indicates that he was thinking of the defense of property as such. Locke could assume, as a man of property himself, that the common interest of propertied men was more important than their divergent interests as owners of land, or of money, or of mercantile stock.

(4) The debate about whether Locke was an individualist or a "collectivist," whether he put the purposes of the individual or the purposes of society first, now appears in a new light. When the fundamental quality of Locke's individualism is kept in mind, the controversy becomes meaningless. His individualism does not consist entirely in maintaining that individuals are by nature free and equal

[36] A. S. P. Woodhouse, ed., *Puritanism and Liberty* (London: Dent, 1938), esp. pp. 53-63.
[37] Cf. King's estimate, cited above, n. 12.
[38] *Op. cit.*, p. 69.
[39] *Considerations*, in *Works* (1759), II, 36, 29.

and can only be rightfully subjected to the jurisdiction of others by their own consent. The main significance of Locke's individualism is that it makes the individual the natural proprietor of his own person and capacities, owing nothing to society for them.

Such an individualism is necessarily collectivism (in the sense of asserting the supremacy of civil society over every individual). For it asserts an individuality that can be realized fully only in accumulating property, and, therefore, realized only by some at the expense of the individuality of the others. To permit such a society to function, political authority must be supreme over individuals; if it is not, there can be no assurance that the property institutions essential to this kind of individualism will have adequate protection. Individuals who have the means to realize their personalities (that is, the propertied) do not need to reserve any rights against civil society, since civil society is constructed by and for them, and operated by and for them. All they need to do is insist that civil society, or the majority of themselves, is supreme over any government, for a particular government might otherwise get out of hand. Locke did not hesitate to allow individuals to hand over to civil society all their natural rights and powers, including specifically all their possessions and land (§§ 120, 128, 136), or, what comes to the same thing, to grant all the rights and powers necessary to the ends for which society was formed (§§ 99, 129, 131), the majority being the judge (§ 97). The wholesale transfer of individual rights was necessary to get sufficient collective force for the protection of property. Locke could afford to propose this transfer because the civil society was to be in the control of the men of property. Under these circumstances individualism must, and could safely, be left to the collective supremacy of the state.

The notion that individualism and "collectivism" are the opposite ends of a scale along which states and theories of the state can be arranged, regardless of the stage of social development in which they appear, is superficial and misleading. Locke's individualism, that of an emerging capitalist society, does not exclude, but on the contrary demands, supremacy of the state over the individual. It is not a question of the more individualism, the less collectivism; rather, the more thoroughgoing the individualism, the more complete the collectivism. Hobbes's theory is the supreme illustration of this relation, but his denial of traditional natural law and his failure to provide guarantees for property against the sovereign (whether a majority of the people or an absolute monarch) did not recommend his views to those who thought property the central social fact. Locke was more acceptable because of his ambiguity about natural law and because he provided some sort of guarantee for property rights. When the specific quality of seventeenth-century bourgeois individualism is seen in this light, it is no longer necessary to search for a compromise between Locke's individualist and collectivist statements; they imply each other.

(5) Locke's constitutionalism now becomes more intelligible; it need not be minimized or emphasized. It can be seen for what it is, a defense of the rights of expanding property rather than of the rights of the individual against the state.

We may notice, in this respect, that Locke did not think it desirable (whereas the Levellers in the Agreement of the People had thought it essential) to reserve some rights to the individual against any parliament or government. Locke's state does not directly protect any individual rights. The individual's only safeguard against arbitrary government lies in the right of the majority to say when a government has broken its trust to act always in the public good, never arbitrarily. Locke could assume that this supremacy of the majority constituted a sufficient safeguard for individual rights because he thought that all who had the right to be consulted were agreed on one concept of the public good: maximizing the nation's wealth, and thereby (as he saw it) its welfare. This agreement could be postulated only because he thought that the laboring class had no right to be consulted. Locke's constitutionalism is essentially a defense of the supremacy of property—not that of the yeoman only, but more especially

The Social Bearing of Locke's Political Theory

that of the men of substance to whom the security of unlimited accumulation was of first importance. Locke's insistence that the authority of the government ("the legislative") is limited and fiduciary, dependent on the consent of the majority of taxable persons, or on that majority's interpretation of the government's faithfulness to its trust, is not the primary part of his whole theory. He had to develop limitations on government because he had first constructed the other part, i.e., the total subordination of the individual to civil society. Both parts were necessary for any theory which sought to protect and promote the property institutions, and thereby the kind of society, to secure which a civil war, a restoration, and a further revolution had been necessary. If in 1689 the confinement of arbitrary government had a more obvious immediacy, subordination of the individual to the state had at least as lasting a significance. The Whig revolution not only established the supremacy of parliament over the monarchy but also consolidated the position of the men of property—specifically of those men who were using their property in the new way, as capital employed to yield profit—over the laboring class. Locke's theory served the Whig state in both respects.

We have seen how Locke, by carrying into his postulates the implicit assumptions of class differential rationality and rights (derived from his comprehension of his own society), reached an ambiguous theory of differential membership in civil society, a theory which justified a class state from postulates of equal individual natural rights. Ambiguity about membership concealed from Locke himself the contradiction in his individualism, which produced full individuality for some by consuming the individuality of others. Locke could not have been conscious that the individuality he championed was at the same time a denial of individuality. Such consciousness was not to be found in men who were just beginning to grasp the great possibilities for individual freedom which lay in the advancement of capitalist society. The contradiction was there, but these men could not recognize it, let alone resolve it. Locke was at the fountainhead of English liberalism. The greatness of seventeenth-century liberalism was its assertion that the free rational individual was the criterion of the good society; its tragedy was that this very assertion necessarily denied individualism to half the nation.

LOCKE AND THE DICTATORSHIP OF THE BOURGEOISIE[1]

ALAN RYAN

It is a commonplace, but true, that the two terms on which Locke rests the greatest weight of doctrine in the *Second Treatise* are 'consent' and 'property'. It is with the second of these terms that we are here concerned, and in particular with the use which Locke makes of his doctrine that:

> 'The great and *chief end* therefore, of Mens uniting into Commonwealths, and putting themselves under Government, *is the Preservation of their Property.*'[2]

There has been a good deal of criticism levelled at Locke's account of property from one direction or another. Complaints of wild and absurd individualism[3] contrast with assertions of his collectivist leanings.[4] Complaints about his obsession with history that never happened[5] contrast with assertions of his intense interest in, and the great importance to his theory of, sociology, history and anthropology,[6] in as genuine a form as the seventeenth century knew them. Here we shall concentrate on a different issue, namely on the extent to which it is true that Locke's ac-

From *Political Studies*, Vol. XIII (1965). Reprinted by permission of the author and of the Clarendon Press, Oxford.

[1] I should like to say how much I owe to the late G. A. Paul in this paper; it amounts to a good deal as to doctrine, and all but everything as to method.
[2] See 124, cf. 134 (all refs. to Laslett edition).
[3] Vaughan: *Studies in the History of Political Philosophy.*
[4] Kendall: *John Locke and Majority Rule.*
[5] Gough: *John Locke's Political Philosophy.*
[6] Cox: *Locke on War and Peace.*

count of property, and his resultant account of natural rights, political obligation, and the proper functions of government, form an ideology for a rising capitalist class. My question is How far does what Locke says in the *Second Treatise* substantiate Macpherson's[7] thesis that he was providing—perhaps no more than half-consciously—a moral basis for the dictatorship of the bourgeoisie?

One initial clarification of the scope of my discussion of this question is needed. Macpherson uses a good deal of material from outside the *Second Treatise* to substantiate his view of it. Indeed his working assumption seems often enough to be that we should look for Locke's political theory outside the *Second Treatise* and then see if previously ambiguous passages in that work (numerous enough on anyone's reading) will square with the theory obtained elsewhere. This may be a method appropriate to a historical inquiry into Locke's political intentions; it may yield the historian a coherent and convincing answer to the question of what Locke *really meant*. Here, however, I take the alternative path of attempting to find within the *Second Treatise* alone some coherent doctrine of political right and obligation, based on what Locke says there about property. Such an account may perhaps be in danger of refutation by the historian as an account of *what Locke intended*. It is in less, even no, danger of contradiction from such a quarter as an account of *what Locke said*. And in case this is thought too small a claim, let me point out that we usually hold people to what they say, rather than to what they may suppose to follow from what they meant to say.

The essence of Macpherson's account is that Locke intends to supply the moral basis of that stage of economic advance which we have called the dictatorship of the bourgeoisie; this is a state of unrestrained capitalism, brutal in its treatment of the labouring classes, ruthless in its de-

---

[7] Macpherson: *Political Theory of Possessive Individualism*, ch. V. cf. "Locke on Capitalist Appropriation," *Western Political Quarterly*, Vol. IV (1951), pp. 550–66 and "The Social Bearing of Locke's Political Theory," reprinted in this volume, pp. 199–230 above.

Locke and the Dictatorship of the Bourgeoisie   233

struction of traditional values, of all social ties that impede the advance of the propertied classes. Locke is thus arguing for nothing less than the rightful absolute power of the propertied classes, for a morally justified tyranny of the employers over the employed. Indeed, the labouring and the unemployed classes have their rights so ruthlessly eroded that their status is to be subject to civil society without being full members of it; they are in it but not of it. The state of nature that Locke envisages must therefore be such that these elements of the bourgeois state follow from it. Crediting Locke as no-one has done before, with a logically rigorous deduction of civil society from the state of nature, Macpherson argues that everything in the state of nature conceived by Locke was put there by him for the purpose of generating some feature or other of bourgeois society. The misery, the viciousness, and the instabilities of the resulting society are attributed to 'contradictions' put into the state of nature by Locke. I need not emphasize how different is this Locke from the one we have met before.

I

The twin pivots upon which Macpherson's account turns are the premises he ascribes to Locke of the natural proprietorship of one's own labour, and the dependence of freedom and morality, and hence of citizenship, upon the possession of rationality. These are, of course, important elements in Locke's political theory; to Macpherson they account for the whole of this theory. They are central, vital, and closely connected. Rationality is evinced by (sometimes it seems that Macpherson is saying it is identified with) the ability to acquire goods and go on acquiring them up to the limits set by the Law of Nature. A rational man is one who obeys the law of Reason, and the law of reason is in turn the Law of Nature, and this is the will of God. Given such a gloss on what it is to be rational, the argument clearly runs that it is morally excellent to accumulate, that success in accumulating is a moral virtue, and hence that the man of property is of greater moral worth than the man without property. In the state of nature before the invention of money the title to property is given by labour, for in the state of nature each man is originally the unconditional owner of his own labour. This doctrine is, on Macpherson's account of it, an important and indeed a decisive break with medieval attitudes to labour and property, which were concerned to emphasize the obligations of a man to society and to his fellows, not his rights against them. So the rational man sets about accumulating property, and because his right to it is derived from his absolute right to his own labour, this right is absolute, too.

> 'If it is labour, a man's absolute property, which justifies appropriation and creates rights, the individual right of appropriation overrides any moral claims of the society. The traditional view that property and labour were social functions and that the ownership of property involved social obligations, is thereby undermined.[8]

Thus Locke secures the right to unlimited accumulation. But in the state of nature before the invention of money there are two limitations upon the exercise of this right. The first is that 'enough and as good' must be left for others,[9] which one may call the *sufficiency limitation*. The second is that nothing may spoil in the hands of the person who gathers it:

> 'As much as any one can make use of to any advantage of life before it spoils; so much he may by his labour fix a Property in. Whatever is beyond this, is more than his share, and belongs to others. Nothing was made by God for Man to spoil or destroy.'[10]

This we may call the *spoliation limitation*. There is a third apparent limitation imposed by the labour criterion of ownership, namely that a man must mix his labour with whatever he appropriates.[11] This limitation lies at the heart of what one might call 'radical' labour theories of

[8] Macpherson p. 221.   [9] Secs. 27, 33, 35.
[10] Secs. 31, 37, 38, 46.   [11] e.g. at sec. 27.

value, where the intention is to deny any title to property other than the title of manual labour. The obvious similarity between Locke's premises and those of all labour theorists leads many writers to suppose that he shares, or at any rate should have shared, this conclusion; but as we shall see, it is an important part of Macpherson's case that Locke never intended such a limitation at all. The two initial limitations are transcended by the invention of money. They are not broken or cast aside; rather, the sort of conditions under which they are applicable no longer obtain. The invention of money is seen by Locke as the discovery of:

> '. . some lasting thing that Men might keep without spoiling, and that by mutual consent Men would take in exchange for the truly useful, but perishable Supports of Life.'[12]

Although a man may by purchase acquire more land than he can use the immediate product of, he still leaves enough and as good for other men. It is true that this is not enough *land* and as good as that appropriated—though Locke seems at times to want to argue that even this is true—but rather that the standard of living is at least as good as before for everyone else.[13] That is, even when all the land is appropriated, the general standard of living is improved for everyone, even for the landless, because the invention of money has enabled the rational capitalist to apply his skills and labour to land and raw material that were formerly of little or no value to mankind. Locke puts a good deal of stress on this:

> 'For I aske whether in the wild woods and uncultivated wast of America left to Nature, without any improvement, tillage or husbandry, a thousand acres will yield the needy and wretched inhabitants as many conveniences of life as ten acres of equally fertile land doe in Devonshire where they are well cultivated.'[14]

Besides this transcending of the sufficiency limitation, there is now no risk of infringing the *spoliation limitation*.

[12] Sec. 47.   [13] Secs. 37, 41.   [14] Sec. 37.

For money does not decay, so however much of it a man has, he has no fears of it perishing uselessly in his possession. A man may heap up gold and silver *ad infinitum*:

> '... he might heap up as much of these durable things as he pleased; the exceeding of the bounds of his just *Property* not lying in the largeness of his *Possession*, but the perishing of anything uselessly in it.'[15]

As for the third limitation, Locke never meant it to hold. The crucial point about Locke's calling labour a form of property is not that it is a peculiar and sacred form of property, but that being property it is alienable; in the state of nature as elsewhere, men must be supposed free to exchange their labour for subsistence or for a wage. (Indeed they must, if Locke's fantasy of a pre-political market economy is to make any sense.) In his support Macpherson quotes Locke's equation of 'my' labour with the labour of my servant. The passage runs:

> 'Thus the Grass my Horse has bit; the Turfs my Servant has cut; and the Ore I have digg'd in any place where I have a right to them in common with others, become my *Property*, without the assignation or consent of anybody. The *labour* that was mine, removing them out of that common state they were in, hath *fixed* my *Property* in them.'[16]

The only meaning that such a passage will bear indicates that Locke never doubted that one man could appropriate the labour of another and thus become the owner of it. 'My' labour includes the labour of anyone I employ; hence the requirement that we mix 'our' labour with whatever we appropriate imposes no limits on the right to appropriate.

Given that it is morally excellent to accumulate property, whether consumable or durable, but particularly the latter, and given that the invention of money enables such accumulation to go on indefinitely, certain consequences for Locke's political theory may be drawn. Macpherson

[15] Sec. 46.   [16] Sec. 28.

Locke and the Dictatorship of the Bourgeoisie 237

not only goes on to draw them, but holds that Locke drew them too, and, further that Locke regarded them as the most important parts of his theory. The first is that Locke's wide definition of property as: 'Lives, Liberties, and Estates, which I call by the general Name Property'[17] is not the one usually adhered to, and is not the one involved in the crucial sections of the *Second Treatise* dealing with the limits on the authority of any government and with the right of the people to rebel against governments which they find oppressive.[18] In these passages, says Macpherson, 'property' means what we normally mean by the term, and refers particularly to property in fixed capital goods. From this it follows that 'the people' to whom Locke entrusts the right of rebellion cannot be the whole population, but must be the propertied classes only. The grounds of revolt are comprised under the heading of the government failing to preserve the property of its citizens; since very few people have any property, only this small number have any right to rebel. Labourers without property are in any case not fully rational—as demonstrated by the fact that they have no property—and therefore have no claim to full membership of civil society.

> 'While the labouring class is a necessary part of the nation its members are not in fact full members of the body politic and have no claim to be so . . Whether by their own fault or not, members of the labouring class did not have, could not be expected to have, and were not entitled to have full membership in political society.'[19]

As something less than full members of political society, they are objects of administration rather than citizens. This part of Macpherson's case is a crucial one, and my criticism of Macpherson's interpretation of Locke is largely concerned with this part of his account. An added merit Macpherson claims for his account is that it disposes of such riddles as Locke's basing obligation upon consent. If 'the people' are in fact the propertied classes,

[17] Sec. 124.   [18] Macpherson pp. 198, 230–1, 247–50.
[19] Macpherson pp. 221, 227.

then they will readily give their consent to whatever the legislative enacts, since what it enacts will always be in their class-interest, and the interest of the class against the rest of society is more vital to each member of it than is his own interest against other members of his class. The state has thus become a committee for managing the common interests of bourgeoisie. Naturally this also solves the clash between the individualist and collectivist elements in Locke's thought. To behave as an extreme individualist is to behave as a successful capitalist, and this is to achieve moral excellence; it is however a form of moral excellence only possible at the expense of those against whom one competes successfully, and of those whose labour one uses to enrich oneself. Hence what is needed by the individualists is a strong government which will hold the ring for their competition. Its strength is no threat to them, since it is a blatant instrument of class-rule; the tough capitalist does not require protection from his fellows.

> 'The individuals who have the means to realize their personalities (that is, the propertied) do not need to reserve any rights as against civil society, since civil society is constructed by and for them, and run by and for them.'[20]

The propertied class has a coherent, cohesive interest in maintaining its position vis à vis the labouring classes. Individual rights thus disappear; the labouring classes have none, the propertied class needs none. Similarly the oft noted analogy between Locke's civil society and a joint-stock company takes on a new aspect. Locke

> '... would have no difficulty in thinking of the state as a joint-stock company of owners whose majority decision binds not only themselves, but also their employees.'[21]

The only shareholders in the firm are the board of directors. The workers are employed to maximize the wealth of the firm, but have no say in the running of the company. Thus the domination of the state by the rising bourgeoisie is complete; its goals are their goals; its machinery is their

[20] Macpherson p. 256.   [21] Macpherson p. 251.

Locke and the Dictatorship of the Bourgeoisie 239

machinery; its decisions are their decisions. Their power over the labouring proletariat is absolute, and it is rightly so.

II

Macpherson supports this account of the ideological Locke with a good deal of quotation from the *Second Treatise*; but it will be appreciated by anyone familiar with that work and the variety of interpretation to which it has given rise, that no conclusive argument emerges from these quotations alone. The establishing of Locke as a capitalist lackey rests heavily, therefore, on his economic writings, where his attitude to the labouring poor, and even more to the unemployed, is indubitably severe. Similarly Locke's disparagement of the rationality of the poor is drawn from the *Reasonableness of Christianity*. In the light of a theory drawn from these sources it is not difficult to put the appropriate gloss on the ambiguous passages of the *Second Treatise*. (My objections to Macpherson are all based on the *un*ambiguous passages to which I fear he pays less careful attention.) About these outside sources I am sceptical. For one thing they cover a period of forty years, and one may doubt both Locke's consistency over that period and his remaining interested in precisely the same problems for so long. For a second thing, the *Reasonableness of Christianity* was largely written to point out that the detailed disputes of the sects were beyond the scope of *anybody's* reason, and its moral hardly seems to be that the working class is peculiarly irrational. It may be an ungracious response to so exciting an account as Macpherson's, but the impression made by his welding together of all this disparate evidence into a tough, lucid, and consistent theory is that of an interpretative *tour de force* rather than of a natural or convincing account of Locke.

Confining ourselves to the *Second Treatise*, there is ample room for doubt about Macpherson's account, and some plainly unambiguous statements by Locke that flatly contradict it. On the issue of rationality, for example, it is true that this is Locke's basis for knowledge of the moral law and hence the basis for being able to obey it. But it is quite incredible that Locke intends us to believe it is the property of one class only, or that he thinks it is chiefly displayed in the acquisition of capital goods. It is stated explicitly by Locke that very nearly all men are rational enough to know what the Law of Nature requires of them, though most men are little enough inclined always to obey it:

> 'The *State of Nature* has a Law of Nature to govern it, which obliges everyone; and Reason which is that Law teaches all mankind who will but consult it . . .'[22]

The problem is not that some people have not the ability to know what the Law requires of them, but that they will not take the trouble to think that they are morally obliged to do, or if they do take that trouble they will not take the trouble to do what they are morally obliged to. The reason, in general, why the Law of Nature is not enough is human selfishness and not human intelligence. In fact the only qualification Locke places on the general possession of rationality is that of age or mental defect:

> '. . . we are born Free, as we are born Rational; not that we have actually the exercise of either; Age that brings one, brings with it the other too.'[23]

The only persons other than the young who are not qualified by rationality are

> 'Lunaticks and Ideots. . . . Madmen'[24]

who hardly seem to be coextensive with the whole class of the labouring poor whom Locke is said to have written off as non-rational. Moreover, this statement by Locke comes only one chapter after the account of property rights in which the erosion of the rationality of the propertyless is supposed to have occurred. The total absence of any sign that Locke was sliding into the doctrine which is

[22] Sec. 6 cf. 12 &c.   [23] Sec. 61.   [24] Sec. 60.

Locke and the Dictatorship of the Bourgeoisie 241

said to be his considered opinion leaves us with no grounds for supposing that the mere absence of property in the sense of capital goods is sufficient to deny citizenship to persons who, by all normal tests, are sane and rational when they reach years of discretion.

Moreover, there is a good deal of confusion in Macpherson's account of what is supposed by Locke to be the distinctively rational feature about capitalist accumulation. There is initially a good deal of confusion in Locke too, but Macpherson does not so much clear this up as ignore it in favour of a doctrine which he attributes to Locke, apparently for no better cause than that it is the doctrine which a moralizing capitalist ought to have held. The only consistent line for Locke to take is fairly simple, and the elements of it are at least hidden in the account of property rights he does give. The Will of God, which he identifies with the Law of Nature and the demands of Reason, requires all men to be preserved as far as possible. The man who appropriates land, employs his skill upon it, and thus enriches mankind, is thereby obeying the demands of reason, that is, he is being rational. This is Locke's argument in a number of places. He refers initially to the right that each man has of preserving all mankind[25]—a 'right' which is better termed a duty. He argues that the man who encloses land and works it confers a benefit upon mankind; almost everything required for a civilized existence is due to the skill and effort which men have lavished upon the raw materials supplied by nature. In one passage he begins with the assertion:

> 'I think it will be but a very modest Computation to say, that of the *Products* of the Earth useful to the Life of Man nine out of ten are the *effects of Labour.*'[26]

Just how modest he thinks this computation to be appears soon enough:

> '. . . nay, if we will rightly estimate things as they come to our use, and cast up the several Expences about them, what in them is purely owing to *Nature,*

[25] e.g. sec. 11.   [26] Sec. 40.

and what to *labour*, we shall find, that in most of them ninety-nine out of one hundred are wholly to be put on the account of *labour*.'[27]

And a moment later the proportion becomes 999 parts in 1,000.[28] The invention of money allows this process to be carried to the lengths typical of a developed economy. Thus the labourer, along with society generally, benefits from the activities of the capitalists. And this is the rationale of capitalism. But, what is the incentive for the capitalist himself? According to Macpherson, Locke holds that capitalists develop their personalities in capitalism; but Locke says nothing of the sort, and in any case, it is both an unconvincing and vacuous account of the matter. What does it amount to beyond the assertion that people who want to become capitalists gratify their wish if they do become capitalists? Locke in fact is confused. At one point he suggests that nothing more than a fanciful liking for gold is at the bottom of it—but the rationality of piling up prettily coloured stones and metals is not clear. The value of money, of course, is a fancy value not in the sense of being a *fanciful* value, but in the sense of being an agreed or conventional value. But Locke does sometimes equate this with having no value at all. When he refuses to allow the conqueror the right to the conquered's territory, he excludes money thus:

> 'For as to Money, and such Riches and Treasure taken away, these are none of Natures Goods, they have but a Phantastical imaginary value: Nature has put no such upon them . . .'[29]

This clearly confuses conventional value and no value at all. The explanation of the good sense of capitalism that Locke hints at elsewhere, which makes a sound case, had three elements in it. The first is that men have come to have more wants than nature gave them; they desire more than they absolutely need; clearly the day labourer living at English subsistence level is much better off than the Indian king living at a high standard for a savage; a ra-

[27] Sec. 40.   [28] Sec. 43.   [29] Sec. 184 cf. sec. 46.

tional man will clearly join in this better consumption—an explanation of the inducement to become a capitalist which Macpherson rejects, but which makes good sense. But, on occasion Locke identifies the desire of having more than we need with simple greed, and suggests that the pre-monetary state of nature was a Golden Age.[30] In which case, the capitalist is not merely not rational, not morally excellent, but positively corrupt. (Macpherson's defence[31] that the condemnation of greed applies not to the capitalist but to the property-less who covet the capitalists' goods is clever, but is impossible to reconcile what Locke says about the earliest governments ruling a simple society. It is the whole state of society, not that of a single class which Locke commends or disapproves, and he clearly places the arrival of greed at the time of the invention of money.)[32] The second element is that we have already discussed, namely the argument that the capitalist is morally bound to promote the well-being of society; and Locke tends—as we noted in the case where he terms a duty a 'right'—to equate being bound by reason with wanting to do what reason tells one. So for Locke doing what is right can be something the capitalist gets out of being a capitalist. The third element is Locke's suggestion that a man will want to provide for other people to whom he feels an obligation or perhaps for those to whom he simply wants to give his goods. Giving away is a recognized form of use.[33] Of these three elements, only the first is a genuine prudential consideration which would allow us to say that the capitalist was being rational in the prudential sense rather than in the moral sense. It is plainly the account which Locke ought to have taken to match his conventionalist account of money. For if money has a conventional value within some society or other, then the whole point of getting rich is to be able to share the advantages of that society's economy to an increased extent. It seems that Macpherson confuses further what Locke confuses sufficiently. The only consistent line to be found in Locke is that capitalism is rational—morally—because it

[30] Sec. 111.   [31] Macpherson pp. 236–7.   [32] Sec. 108.
[33] Sec. 46.

is a step to the betterment of society, and that being a capitalist is rational—prudentially—because it enables one to enjoy a greater share of the betterment. A man's share in the greater social product is both his incentive and his reward. But so simple a doctrine as this is far indeed from fulfilling the requirements of Macpherson's theory.

This becomes clearer when we examine Macpherson's curious assertion that property rights are absolute because labour rights are so. The labour theory of proprietorship has been much misunderstood by Macpherson. It begins not as a theory of proprietorship but as theory of identification.[34] Locke says of the diet of the Indian:

> 'The Fruit, or Venison, which nourishes the wild *Indian*, who knows no Inclosure, and is still a Tenant in common, must be his, and so his, i.e. a part of him, that another can no longer have any right to it, before it can do him any good for the support of his Life.'[35]

But the sense in which food must belong to a man before it can do him any good is a biological one—namely he has to eat it; and the sense in which an Indian's nourishment is *his* is a logical one—namely that we can only identify nourishment by identifying the man nourished. This is not to talk of rights at all, and particularly not to talk of absolute rights. It is a very dangerous way of talking, for it swiftly confuses the 'his' of identification with the 'his' of ownership or rightful possession. Thus, there is a perfectly good sense in which: 'The *Labour* of his Body, and the *Work* of his Hands we may say, are properly his.'[36] But this sense needs elucidating. In one sense it is bound to be 'his', as it is a truth of logic that only *he* can do *his* labouring, and in this sense, whomever he labours for, it is still 'his' labour. But this does not establish that the only person entitled to benefit from his labour is himself. It is moreover impossible to reconcile Locke's concern for the rights of wives and children with the right to be absolutely selfish which Macpherson ascribes to Locke's natural man.

[34] See J. P. Day's review of Macpherson's book, *Philosophical Quarterly*, Vol. 14 (1964), pp. 266–68.
[35] Sec. 26.   [36] Sec. 27.

Locke and the Dictatorship of the Bourgeoisie 245

The confusion may be as much Locke's fault as anyone's, but it is fair to point out that Locke never talks of an 'absolute' right to anything at all. Customarily accepted moral obligations are not mentioned—or not often—but this might well be because Locke took them for granted, not because he did not accept them. Locke's concern after all was to defend men against royal force and robbery, and this is not a category which includes the demands of friends and family. The point of Locke's initial account of the right to goods given by labour is surely negative. He is faced with the question of how undifferentiated goods become the exclusive property of some one man; and the answer is that where there is plenty for everyone, acquisition and ownership need not be distinguished. If a man acquires something without breaking the laws of nature in the manner of his acquiring it, that is enough. The answer to the question 'Who has it?' serves as the answer to the question 'Who has it?'. Macpherson's emphasis on the absence of obligation to society is odd in view of the fact that at this point the conditions which create social ties do not exist at all; and the minimal obligation of leaving enough and as good for whomever may chance along is surely some sort of obligation, while obligations to one's family presumably exist at this rudimentary stage too. And Locke says clearly enough that when a man enters society he has his social title to his goods on society's terms[37]—a pre-echo of Rousseau. This after all is Locke's consistent line; we enter society to protect our property, so we must be prepared to contribute our fair share of whatever is required for this defence, and society must judge what it needs for the successful performance of its functions. If property includes life, limb, liberty, and possessions, then some pay taxes, but all forgo their natural liberty, and all are liable for the defence of the country from enemies external and internal.[38]

If we are correct in arguing that talk of 'absolute' property is seriously misleading and that no sort of absolute ownership is involved in either life, liberty or goods, on all

[37] Sec. 120.   [38] Secs. 128–30.

of which there can be claims, then there seems less reason than ever to suppose that Locke restricts the meaning of 'property' to fixed property in goods, or to suppose that he is engaged in an attempt to deprive the proletariat of all political rights for the benefit of the employing classes. The only essential characteristic that property possesses is that property is that of which a man cannot be deprived without his consent; for example, Locke says of the rights of the conquered under the conqueror:

> '... whatsoever he grants them, they have so far as it is granted, *property* in. The nature whereof is, that *without a Man's own consent* it *cannot be taken from him*.'[39]

And elsewhere, it is the absence of this characteristic that removes a possession from the position of actually being a man's property:

> 'For I have truly no *Property* in that, which another can by right, take from me, when he pleases, against my consent.'[40]

This characteristic applies for Locke to all goods both bodily and mental, save one's own life, which one cannot dispose of by contract, but which one can lose the right to by a sufficient breach of the natural law. It is significant that Macpherson's view of the power exercised over the property-less is that of Locke; it is despotic power, absolute and arbitrary, a power which Locke explicitly contrasts with political power. And it is crucially important to notice that the only case of despotic power allowed by Locke, and hence by inference the only case he allows of a man without property, is power over the renegade against reason and society:

> '... *Despotical Power* is an absolute, arbitrary power one man has over another, to take away his life, whenever he pleases. This is a power, which neither nature gives . . . . nor compact can convey . . . . but it is *the effect only of forfeiture*, which the aggressor makes of his own life, when he puts himself into the state of war with another.[41]

[39] Sec. 195.   [40] Sec. 138.   [41] Sec. 172.

Locke and the Dictatorship of the Bourgeoisie 247

Of political power he says in the next paragraph:

> '(By *Property* I must be understood here, as in other places, to mean that property which men have in their persons as well as goods.) *Voluntary Agreement gives* . . . . *Political Power to Governours* for the benefit of their subjects, to secure them in the possession and use of their properties.'[42]

And this power is immediately contrasted with power over the property-less:

> 'And *Forfeiture* gives the third, *Despotical Power to Lords* for their own benefit, over those who are stripp'd of all property.'[43]

And finally he sums up:

> '*Paternal Power* is only where minority makes the child incapable to manage his property; *Political* where men have property in their own disposal; and *Despotical* over such as have no property at all.'[44]

This seems to me conclusive enough against Macpherson's thesis that 'property' is to be read as if it referred only to property in goods. An obvious consequence, however, that we must draw is that if we accept Locke's wide reading of property as *bona civilia*, or 'life, liberty, health, and indolency of body; and the possession of outward things such as money, lands, houses, furniture, and the like,'[45] then it is clear that we must accept the whole population who have reached years of discretion as being the 'people' for the purposes of entrusting them with the right of revolution. That Locke did so is shown clearly by what he considers as a possible objection to his doctrine:

> 'To this perhaps it will be said, that the people being ignorant, and always discontented, to lay the foundation of Government in the unsteady opinion, and uncertain humour of the people, is to expose it to certain ruine.'[46]

His reply does not matter: what is important is how this contradicts Macpherson's picture of Locke. Locke is hardly

[42] Sec. 173.   [43] Sec. 173.   [44] Sec. 174.
[45] Laslett's note to sec. 3.   [46] Sec. 223.

likely to think it a plausible criticism of the rising capitalists that they are ignorant or unsteady of opinion or uncertain of humour. One verbal point that might lead one into accepting Macpherson's account is Locke's talk of 'deputies' and 'representatives'; it is easy enough to slip into thinking that this involves electing M.P.s—and of course no-one suggests that Locke is advocating universal suffrage. But, if we recall that Locke counts a monarch, ruling without a council, or a permanent oligarchy, as legislatives in precisely the same sense as the English King-in-Parliament is a legislative, it becomes clear that to be represented is not necessarily to have voted.[47] Macpherson may still be willing to argue that the labourer is not a 'full member' of civil society—but the trouble here is that Locke talks only of members, and never distinguishes between full and any other sort of membership. The passage Macpherson rests his case on is an oddity, and is anyway concerned with distinguishing the status of foreigners residing in a country from that of genuine subjects:

> 'And thus we see, that *Foreigners*, by living all their lives under another Government, and enjoying the priviledges and protection of it, though they are bound, even in conscience, to submit to its administration, as far forth as any Denison; yet do not thereby come to be *Subjects or Members of that Commonwealth*. Nothing can make any man so, but his actually entering into it by positive engagement, and express promise and compact.'[48]

Here it is the foreigner who is being contrasted with the member or subject; Macpherson's contrast is between the labourer who is a subject but not a member, and the propertied man who is both, a contrast of which the text is innocent. The obligation that the labourer and the foreigner incur, they incur along with the capitalist, for they have all given their tacit consent by enjoying property:

> '. . . whether this his possession be of land to him and his heirs for ever, or a lodging only for a week; or whether it be barely travelling freely on the highway.'[49]

[47] Sec. 138.   [48] Sec. 122.   [49] Sec. 119.

If this puts the labourer on a level with the foreigner it does so only by putting him on a level with his employer too. Locke never solves the problem of why a man's first country is thought to be his only country, but it is surely implausible to suggest that he anticipated Marx in holding that the proletarian has no country, only a class. It would be a foolish doctrine for Locke to hold, since it would have involved him in releasing labourers from the obligation to defend their country against external enemies, and would have meant that they could not be held guilty of such crimes as treason. We cannot but conclude that if labourers can be said to have a property—and we have seen no reason why they cannot be—then they are members of civil society. They receive benefits and accept corresponding obligations. They may pay no taxes, but they lend their labour and their strength to the defence of their society against enemies internal and external:

'... the *Power of Punishing* he wholly *gives up*, and engages his natural force (which he might before imploy in the execution of the Law of Nature, by his own single Authority, as he thought fit) to assist the executive power of his society, as the law thereof shall require.'[50]

Men allow society to regulate their lives, their liberties and their possessions; all who have need of protection for any of these things can receive it from civil society and thereby become obliged by its rules. The state exists not for a class but for all who are willing and able to use it on equitable terms.

III

Although Macpherson's theory about Locke's doctrine is thus falsified in so many details, it still presents a challenge to any critic. For its overall coherence and interest is extremely impressive, even though its foundations are shaky; and some of the detail—for example the exposition

[50] Sec. 130 cf. 136.

of Locke's defence of unequal property rights—is superior to anything yet produced on Locke. All discounting made of the ideological overtones which Macpherson hears in every word of Locke, the force of Macpherson's account challenges one to produce some alternative picture that fits the text better than his, but which takes notice of what is most valuable in his account. Let us then agree that the chapter *Of Property* is intended to justify the achievement of the capitalist, and the reward he reaps. As we argued above, the simplest argument for this is based on God's will that all mankind should flourish. Given fair distribution, the greatest social product is the will of God, and the dictate of reason. Locke never argues explicitly that the distribution is fair, though the elements of the argument required are there. They lie in the insistence that even the worst off in modern society is better off than he would be outside it, a thesis backed up by the ubiquitous American Indian; these latter it will be remembered:

> '. . . have not one hundredth part of the Conveniences we enjoy: And a King of a large and fruitful Territory there feeds, lodges and is clad worse than a day Labourer in *England*.'[51]

And they lie too in the suggestion that it is the superior ability and greater efforts of the capitalist that leads to his greater wealth:

> 'And as different degrees of Industry were apt to give Men Possessions in different proportions, so this *Invention of Money* gave them the opportunity to continue and enlarge them.'[52]

And perhaps, finally, in the suggestion that even now there is some surplus land left:

> 'in some inland, vacant places of America.'[53]

Thus, the capitalist is worthy of his profit; that he is worthy of all his profit Locke does not argue; perhaps his *laissez-faire* inclinations were not so strong that he thought it was true; perhaps they were so strong that he thought it

[51] Sec. 41.   [52] Sec. 48.   [53] Sec. 36.

Locke and the Dictatorship of the Bourgeoisie 251

needed no proving. The basic point, however, is simple enough; since all men have profited by entering a market society, there is no cause for complaint if some men have done better than others. But, here we part company with Macpherson. In Macpherson's account, Locke now proceeds to pile political oppression on top of inequality of possessions. A more convincing picture is that of Locke moving from the negative point that the labourer and the capitalist were not at odds to the positive task of showing that they have a shared interest, a common ground of political obligation, and a common right to see to the maintenance of their interests. It is indubitable that both are bound by the law; therefore the law must give something to them both, in return for which they are bound to obey it. And it is this something which Locke calls:

'. . . the Preservation of their Property'[54]

or else:

'. . . the mutual *Preservation* of their *Lives, Liberties and Estates* which I call by the general Name, Property.'[55]

A common interest requires one term to describe it, even though the most disparate things come as a result to shelter under the name of 'property'. All the inhabitants of a well-governed and well-organized country benefit from its government—even resident foreigners—so they all have a share in something; and whatever it is that they have a share in Locke calls property. Peace and security are also said by Locke to be the ends of government; men enter civil society:

'. . . by *stated Rules* of Right and Property to secure their Peace and Quiet.'[56]

All men require peace and security to lead tolerable lives, so all men have so much property as requires government for its preservation. It is, of course, odd to talk of all the

[54] Sec. 124. [55] Sec. 123. [56] Sec. 137.

things that society protects as property, but the effect is surely not that of setting up a bourgeois dictatorship so much as finding some common interest shared by both the proletarian and the bourgeois in a state which must often have seemed to give nothing save to those who were rich and powerful enough to need nothing from it. And the importance of giving the proletariat and the bourgeoisie a common interest is surely that their interests are opposed to absolute monarchy; nothing could be clearer than that the target of the *Second Treatise* is not the peaceful and docile proletariat, but the doctrine that a monarch has an absolute, and more particularly an arbitrary, power over his subjects. This is a recurring theme of the whole treatise, which might indeed have been subtitled a treatise against arbitrariness and in favour of relevance in political power. A large part of the chapter *Of the Dissolution of Government* is a defence of regicide as a last measure against a king who claims to have an absolute and arbitrary authority over his people.[57] Despite occasionally light-hearted manner in which he discusses the question of how we are to join reverence with a knock on the head, Locke commits himself to views which abundantly explain why he did not wish to be known as the author of the work during the lifetime of James II. Locke's bitterest attacks are always on absolute monarchy, as when he says:

> 'Hence it is evident that *Absolute Monarchy*, which by some men is counted the only Government in the world, is indeed *inconsistent with Civil Society.*'[58]

or that:

> 'Absolute, arbitrary power, or governing without *settled standing Laws,* can neither of them consist with the ends of society and government.'[59]

or that:

> '*Absolute Dominion*, however placed, is so far from being one kind of civil society, that it is as incompatible with it, as slavery is with property.'[60]

[57] Secs. 232–9.   [58] Sec. 90.   [59] Sec. 137.   [60] Sec. 174.

Locke and the Dictatorship of the Bourgeoisie

It seems quite incredible that anyone should not take it as an attack on the pretensions made by James II (or those which he was suspected of being about to make) to the position of a recipient of divinely granted power, and thus to freedom from all human law and control. Locke's target is arbitrariness rather than absoluteness; he goes into some detail about martial law, which allows summary execution for disobedience even to lethally dangerous orders, but which will not allow a general to touch one penny of a soldier's goods; the reason given by Locke is that this is:

> 'Because such a blind Obedience is necessary to that end for which the Commander has his Power, *viz* the preservation of the rest; but the disposing of his Goods has nothing to do with it.'[61]

Locke generalizes the argument that authority is limited in its scope to what is necessary to secure the ends for which the authority is set up to cover the case of parliament, the monarch and any other sort of authority. All rights are limited by the ends they are meant to secure, and the right to our obedience vested in our rulers is in exactly the same case. Royal authority, in other words, depends not on the person of the monarch, but on the good of the society. The quarrel is not between bourgeoisie and proletariat, but between king and people. No doubt the people are but rarely justified in revolution; but there is no question that they have the right to rebel *in extremis*.

Even on this reading of Locke, his theory is still a bourgeois one. It is beyond doubt a bourgeois mind which envisages all rights as property rights; it is also, more importantly for the political philosopher, a perceptive sort of confusion that leads to such an identification. For 'property' is not an inapt general name for the class or rights and obligations that enter into social theory—quasi-contractual rights and duties as they are. For in many ways property rights, in the ordinary sense of 'property', are paradigms of the rights that are exchanged and protected by contract. But only a bourgeois mind could fail to see that they are paradigmatic rather with respect to procedure than with

[61] Sec. 139.

respect to the importance of the ethical values involved. They are paradigmatically contractual, but they are not the most important contractual rights. But this still goes no way towards justifying Macpherson's attributing to Locke a ruthless, dictatorial programme of class-domination. In the joint-stock company that is Locke's state, all men are shareholders. Some men hold shares of life, liberty, peace, and quiet alone, while others hold shares of estate as well; these latter may receive more of the benefits and play a greater part in the running of the state, but there is no reason to suppose that in the eyes of God or Nature (or even in the eyes of John Locke) their shares have a peculiar importance. Few or no practical conclusions follow readily from Locke's account of political obligation; Macpherson's conclusions follow even less readily than the more egalitarian and humane ones that have been drawn in the past.

BERKELEY'S DENIAL OF MATERIAL SUBSTANCE
C. D. BROAD

1. *Preliminary Clarification.* Before considering Berkeley's arguments it will be wise to ask what is commonly understood by 'material substance,' and in what sense Berkeley denied its existence. For he always maintains that he is denying only the theories of certain scientists or philosophers, e.g., the Newtonians, Descartes, and Locke. He asserts that his own view admits the existence of all that plain men understand by 'bodies' or 'material things'. It will also be wise to clear up beforehand the notions of 'perception' and 'sensation'. These preliminaries will take up a considerable part of the paper.

1.1. *What do we understand by a 'material thing'?* It is always dangerous for philosophers to dogmatise about the opinions of plain men. What one ascribes to them is in fact an inference, drawn partly from one's introspection of oneself in one's 'plainer' moments, and partly from the phraseology of everyday speech in the few languages with which one is familiar. There is always a risk of putting into the mouths of babes and of sucklings what could have occurred only to the wise and prudent. But, provided that one is alive to the risks that one is taking, there is no great harm in taking them.

It seems to me that a plain man means by a 'solid body' or a 'bit of matter' something which has all the following characteristics. (1) It is literally extended. It is bounded by a closed surface and has an outside and a front. (2) It

From *The Philosophical Review*, Vol. LXIII (1954). Reprinted by permission of the author and *The Philosophical Review*.

is literally pervaded throughout its volume and over its surface with certain extensible qualities, e.g., colours, temperature, roughness or smoothness, and so on. (3) It is a centre from which there emanate certain sensible 'atmospheres', which form a kind of aura about it, e.g., a characteristic field of sound in the case of a tolling bell or a waterfall, a characteristic field of odour in the case of an apple, a field of sensible warmth in the case of a radiator, and so on. (4) Some of the qualities mentioned under headings (2) and (3) are revealed by some of our senses and others by others. But the very same part of the same body, e.g., the upper face of a certain coin, has at the same time qualities proper to various senses, e.g., colour, temperature, and textural qualities. It has temperature and texture when one is looking at it and not touching it and therefore is sensibly aware only of its colour; and it has colour when one is touching it and not looking at it and therefore is sensibly aware only of its temperature and its texture. Moreover, it has temperature, when one is only looking at it, in precisely the same sense in which it has temperature when one is feeling it; and when one is only touching it it has colour in precisely the same sense in which it has colour when one is looking at it. Lastly, it may have extensible qualities which none of our senses are fitted to reveal to us. (5) Beside having extensible qualities, which it may present to us sensibly, a bit of matter has certain causal or dispositional properties, active or passive. Among these may be mentioned inertial mass, impenetrability, greater or less elasticity and so on. (6) The *same* person can perceive the same part or different parts of the same bit of matter on *various* occasions by means of the same sense or different senses. (7) *Different* persons can perceive the same part or different parts of the same bit of matter, by means of the same sense or different senses, on the *same* occasion. (8) A bit of matter can exist, and change or remain unaltered, and act upon or be acted upon by other bits of matter, at times when no one is perceiving it. None of its extensible qualities or its powers is altered or abolished or reinstated by its becoming or ceasing to be perceived.

I do not say that all or any of these common sense beliefs are *true*. But I do say that, unless there be particulars which answer to all these eight conditions, then there are no 'bodies' or 'material things' in the plain straightforward sense of these phrases.

It is worth while to notice that philosophers who have explicitly or implicitly denied that there are material things, have done so for one or another of two fundamentally different reasons. One of these is much more radical than the other. The more radical line is to argue that the notion of one or more of the characteristics which enter into the notion of 'material thing' involves a contradiction, and therefore that nothing could possibly have that characteristic. This is the line taken, e.g., by Leibniz and by McTaggart. They argue that nothing could possibly be *extended*, because to be extended would entail consequences —e.g., being composed of parts which are themselves composed of parts and so on without end—which are palpably absurd. The other way is to argue that, although each of the characteristics involved in the notion of 'material thing' may *severally* belong to something or other, yet, *collectively* they could not be combined in *any one* particular. This is in fact the line which Berkeley takes. According to him, there are particulars which are extended, particulars which are coloured, particulars which have sensible hotness, and so on. But, in the first place, no particular which had colour could possibly have temperature, none which had temperature could possibly have colour, and so on. And, secondly, every such particular is confined in its existence to some one particular occasion in the mental history of some one particular person. He calls such particulars 'ideas'. Then again, according to him, there are also particulars which are persistent, capable of acting and being acted upon, and which exist independently of being perceived. But these are all *unextended*, and it is meaningless to ascribe to them colour, temperature, motion-or-rest, etc., or to suppose that they could be perceived by means of any conceivable *sense*. They are in fact minds or spirits; their activity consists in volition, and their passivity in being caused to have sensations or images by telepathic or immanent action.

1.2. *Perception and Sensation.* Berkeley unfortunately uses the one word 'perceive' to cover two quite different, though closely interconnected, kinds of experience. One is the non-inferential cognition which we take ourselves to have of material things and of certain physical events by means of sensation. This is the kind of experience which one would naturally express by saying: 'I see a cow over there', 'I am touching a bit of ice', 'I see a flash of lightning', 'I hear a bell tolling', and so on. The other kind of experience is having a sensation or quasi-sensation. When Berkeley is being careful he no doubt intends to mark this distinction by the use of the phrases 'perceive' and 'immediately perceive' respectively. When he uses 'perceive' in the wide sense it includes, besides what he calls 'immediate perception', a great deal of what he would call 'suggestion'. He takes the latter to consist of images, evoked through association by an immediate perception. But generally he uses 'perceive' for what he should describe as *'immediately* perceive'. This is a dangerous practice, and it is well to avoid it altogether. I shall use 'perceive' *only* in the usual sense, in which the proper grammatical object of the verb is the name or a description of some material thing or physical event, e.g., 'a cow', 'a brown, round, flat bit of copper', 'a flash of lightning', and so on. I shall use the technical word 'sense' as equivalent to what Berkeley in his more careful moments would describe as 'immediately perceive'.

Even if we confine ourselves to using 'perceive' in the way just mentioned, there is still a tiresome ambiguity about it, which we must now notice. 'Perceive', when so used, is a general name for seeing, hearing, touching, etc. Now it is customary to use such words as 'see', 'hear', 'touch', etc., only with the implication that the following two conditions are fulfilled. (i) That the experience is *veridical,* at any rate in its main outlines, i.e., that there is in fact a certain one body or physical event, answering pretty clearly to the description which the experient would naturally give of the object which he claims to be perceiving at the time. (ii) That the experience is *normally evoked.* In the case of visual perception this means that it is evoked by light coming to the experient's eyes directly or indirectly from a region outside his body. In the case of auditory perception it means that it is evoked by sound-waves coming to the experient's ears directly or indirectly from an external source. And similarly *mutatis mutandis* for other cases. If we believe that *either* of these conditions is unfulfilled, we should not commonly say that a person is 'seeing' or 'hearing' or in general 'perceiving'. Suppose, e.g., that I knew or believed that a person, who claimed to be seeing an oasis in the desert or to be hearing a voice, was dreaming or hallucinated. Then it would be contrary to usage for me to say: 'He is seeing an oasis' or 'He is hearing a voice'. I might say: 'He *seems to himself* to be seeing an oasis' or 'He *seems to himself* to be hearing a voice'. Or, if I were making my statement in writing, I might put the words 'see' or 'hear' in inverted commas. Suppose, again, that I knew or believed that a person's visual or auditory experience corresponded to a certain distant scene or event so closely as to exclude all question of chance-coincidence. And suppose that I knew that the experience could not possibly have been evoked in him directly or indirectly by light-waves or sound-waves coming to his body from the region of that distant scene or event. Then, again, it would be contrary to ordinary usage for me to say: 'He saw such and such a scene' or 'He heard such and such a sound'. I should say: 'He seemed to himself to see it' or 'He seemed to himself to hear it'; and I should add: 'But really it must have been a case of telepathy or clairvoyance or clairaudience'. Here the experience is veridical, but not normally evoked.

It is evident, then, that we need a word which shall be purely descriptive and shall not carry with it any implications either of veridicality or of normal evocation. We want a word which will cover, e.g., normal waking sense-perceptions, waking hallucinations (both delusive and veridical), and dreams. I propose to use the phrase '*ostensible* perception', and the corresponding phrases '*ostensible* seeing', '*ostensible* hearing', etc., for its various specific forms. With this terminology 'to *see*' is to have an ostensible visual perception which is both veridical in its main outlines and normally evoked. And similar remarks apply *mutatis mutandis* to the words 'to *hear*', 'to *touch*', and so on.

Now, whenever a person is having an ostensible perception he is *ipso facto* having a certain sensation or *quasi*-sensation. (I introduce the second alternative in order to cover the case of dreams and of certain kinds of waking hallucination. In these cases it might well be denied that the experient is having *sensations*, if that word is used so as to imply that the experiences are due to the stimulation of his external sense-organ. But he is certainly having colour-experiences, sound-experiences, and so on, which very clearly resemble in their intrinsic character sensations which are normally evoked.)

To illustrate these terms let us suppose, e.g., that a person has an experience, whether veridical or delusive, normally or abnormally evoked, which would correctly be described as 'ostensibly seeing a cricket-ball'. An essential part of that experience would consist in having a colour-sensation or a colour-quasi-sensation of a certain characteristic kind. The precise character of this could vary within certain ill-defined limits according to circumstances. If it were a normal waking perception, e.g., the details of the sensation would vary according to the part of the ball facing the percipient, according to his distance from it, the state of his eyesight, the lighting, and so on. But it would certainly be a sensation of a round-looking, convex-looking, brownish expanse.

But, although a colour-sensation or a colour-quasi-sensation of this kind is an essential factor in any experience which could properly be called 'ostensibly seeing a cricket-ball', it is not the whole of it. By a 'cricket-ball' we mean something which is solid and spherical; which has coldness and smoothness and hardness as well as brownness; which has parts which are not at the moment manifesting themselves to the observer's senses; and which has causal properties, such as mass, impenetrability, hardness, and elasticity. By 'ostensibly seeing a cricket-ball' we do not mean just having a sensation of a round-looking, convex-looking, brownish expanse. We mean (i) having

Berkeley's Denial of Material Substance 261

such a sensation, and (ii) being led by it, without any explicit process of inference and without even any experience of associative transition, to take oneself to be facing an object answering to the description which I have just given.

It would be *logically* possible to have such a sensation without being led by it to take for granted anything of the kind. It might be suggested that that would be the case with a young baby, looking at a cricket-ball for the first time. If so, it would be incorrect to say that the baby was ostensibly seeing a cricket-ball, and it might well be incorrect to make even the vaguer statement that it was ostensibly seeing a globular body. But I would not like to commit myself to the statement that a young baby would or even could (in the *causal* sense of possibility) have a visual sensation precisely like that which a grown person would have in a similar situation. It is possible, and it seems to me likely, that the character of the visual sensation itself is subtly modified by the associations which it comes to evoke. Then, again, it is quite possible, both logically and causally, for a grown person to have such a sensation and *not* be led by it to take himself to be facing a cricket-ball or even a body of any such kind. He might know or have reason to believe that he was subject to an optical delusion or a hypnotic suggestion. But in his case there would certainly be a strong incipient tendency to take himself to be facing a cricket-ball, and, unless he made and kept up a pretty deliberate effort, he would find himself slipping into that state of mind. Lastly, a grown person might be dreaming or hallucinated and be at the time quite unaware of the fact. In that case he *would* ostensibly be seeing a cricket-ball, but his ostensible perception would be wholly delusive.

1.3. *Analysis of Sensation.* I come now to the analysis of sensation or *quasi*-sensation. At any rate in the case of those visual and tactual sensations which occur when one ostensibly perceives a body of definite outline and selectively attends to it, the following analysis seems plausible. It seems plausible in such cases to say that having a sensation consists in being immediately aware of a particular, which *has* certain characteristics, e.g., a certain colour spread out within a certain contour, and which *manifests* those characteristics to one in and through the sensation. Take, e.g., the visual sensation which a person has when he is ostensibly seeing a cricket-ball. It seems highly plausible to say that having this sensation consists in being immediately aware of a particular which is, and *sensibly presents itself to one* as being, round and convex and brown. On the assumption that this kind of analysis is correct, I shall give the name 'sensing' to the act or process of being immediately aware of a particular as having certain qualities, e.g., colour in visual sensation, temperature in tactual sensation, and so on. I shall call any particular which is capable of being sensed a 'sensibile'. So the assumption which we are making, and which is embodied in this terminology, is that to have a visual or tactual sensation is to be sensing a sensibile which *has* certain sensibile qualities and to be *sensing it as having* some at least of the qualities which it has.

I can now define the word 'sense-datum'. I shall say that a sensibile is a 'sense-datum' for a certain person on a certain occasion, if and only if he is sensing that sensibile on that occasion.

Before going further I want to make it quite clear that these phrases are intended to leave all the following questions quite open. (1) Whether or not one and the same sensibile can combine qualities which can be sensed *only by different senses*, e.g., whether one and the same sensibile could have both sensible colour and sensible temperature. (It will be noted that, if this question should be answered in the affirmative, then a sensibile which is being sensed by a certain person on a certain occasion may have sensible qualities *beside* those which he then senses it as having.) (2) Whether or not one and the same sensibile could be sensed by the same person on *more than one occasion*, either by the same sense or by different senses. (3) Whether or not one and the same sensibile could be sensed by two *different* persons, either on the same or on different occasions, and either by the same or by different senses. (4) Whether or not there could be sensibilia which

Berkeley's Denial of Material Substance 263

are *sometimes* not sensed by anyone, or again sensibilia which are *never* sensed by anyone. (5) Whether the sensibile which a person senses when he ostensibly sees or touches a certain part of the surface of a body is sometimes or is never *identical with* that part of the surface of that body.

To all these questions Berkeley would unhesitatingly give a negative answer. In our terminology he would assert the following proposition:—Any sensibile is necessarily a sense-datum for some one and only one person on some one and only one occasion, and it could not conceivably have any characteristics *beside* those which that person senses it as having on that occasion.

Now I strongly suspect that this assertion of Berkeley's rests upon a certain other proposition, which is more fundamental than it. We may approach this in the following way. I defined a 'sensibile' as a particular which *has* certain sensible characteristics, e.g., sensible redness and sensible coldness. Again, I said that having a sensation consists in sensing a sensibile, and that an essential factor in this is sensing it *as having* certain qualities, e.g., as round or as red or as cold, and so on. Now these statements plainly leave open a further question, which I have not as yet mentioned, viz., whether or not a sensibile could be sensed as having a quality which it did *not in fact have*. Could it, e.g., be sensed as red when in fact it had no colour at all? or could it, e.g., be sensed as elliptical in contour when it was in fact circular? I have kept this question separate from the others, because nearly everyone who has accepted the analysis of visual and tactual sensations which is embodied in the present terminology has explicitly or tacitly answered it in the negative.

We are now in a position to state the more fundamental proposition which I suspect Berkeley to have held. I think that he would deny the distinction between *having* a sensible quality and *being sensed as having* a sensible quality. I think he would hold that no meaning whatever can be attached to *being* sensibly red or *being* sensibly round or *being* sensibly cold except *being sensed by someone* as red or as round or as cold, as the case may be. In fact, to *be* sensibly red just is to *look* or *sensibly appear* red to someone; to *be* sensibly cold just is to *feel* cold to someone; and so on for any sensible quality. It would follow at once from this that to talk of a sensibile which was not a sense-datum to anyone would be a contradiction in terms. For to describe something as a 'sensibile' is to imply that it *has* some sensible characteristic or other, and to deny that it is a sense-datum to anyone is to deny that it is *sensed by anyone as having* any sensible characteristic. Now, if the only meaning that can be attached to *'having* a sensible characteristic' is *being sensed by someone* as having that characteristic, this assertion and this denial contradict each other. It would also be meaningless to suggest either (a) that a sense-datum could have any quality which it is not sensed as having, or (b) that it could be sensed as having any quality that it does not have.

It should be noted that the proposition, which I have supposed to be at the back of Berkeley's mind, would not in itself entail that one and the same sensibile could not be sensed by different persons, either simultaneously or successively. All that it entails is that a sensibile must always be a sense-datum to *someone or other*. Again, it does not, strictly speaking, exclude the possibility that one and the same *particular* might sometimes be sensed and sometimes not sensed. All that it entails is that, if that were so, that particular could not possibly be called a 'sensibile' except at the times when it is a sense-datum to someone or other.

Now there is another, and still more radical, proposition, which would entail all the negative propositions which Berkeley maintains. It is this. Perhaps the suggested analysis of having a sensation, e.g., of a round, convex, brown expanse, is altogether mistaken. Perhaps it does not consist in sensing a certain particular as round and convex and brown. That analysis implies that there are two factors, viz., an act or process of sensing and a particular which is sensed, and that the latter might conceivably exist without being the object of the former. But might not a sensation be a completely unitary occurrence, not analysable into act of sensing and object sensed, but just having

Berkeley's Denial of Material Substance 265

two radically different but inseparable aspects? In respect of one of these aspects, viz., its being a state or modification of the percipient's mind, it is called a *'sensation of his'*, and counts as an event in his mental history. In respect of the other aspect it is called a 'sensation of so-and-so', e.g., of a brown, round, convex expanse. On this view the fundamental mistake is to suppose that 'of' here has the same kind of meaning as 'of' in such phrases as 'memory *of* so-and-so', 'thought *of* so-and-so', etc. In these latter phrases it certainly does denote the relation of a *cognitive act or process* to a *cognised object*, and the latter always is in principle existentially independent of the former. The mistake, it would be said, is to treat a sensation as a kind of cognition, and to regard the 'of' in the phrase 'sensation *of* so-and-so' as denoting the relation of a cognitive act or process to a cognised object. We might talk, on this view, of the 'content' of a sensation, but not of its 'object'. This view was held, e.g., by Prichard.

If this view were accepted, the negative Berkeleian propositions follow at once. What we have called a 'sensibile' would simply be a sensation considered in *one* of its two inseparable aspects. In its other aspect a sensation is an occurrence in the mental history of some one and only one person at some one and only one date. That, I suspect, is what Berkeley ought to have held and perhaps did hold. But, if so, his language often tends to disguise his meaning.

2. *Berkeley's Arguments.* We can now consider Berkeley's own explicit arguments. We may divide them into three groups, viz., (1) direct arguments for his view, (2) attacks on certain alternative views, and (3) discussion of certain possible objections to his view. I shall confine myself here to the direct arguments against the existence of material substance. These may be divided into (i) the *'esse'* = *'percipi'* argument, and (ii) a pair of supplementary arguments. We will now consider these three in turn.

2.1. *The* '*esse*' = '*percipi*' *argument*. At the end of Section 4 of the *Principles of Human Knowledge* Berkeley asks three rhetorical questions, and they constitute his main positive argument on this topic. I will now deal with them in the light of our preliminary clarification.

The questions are these: (1) "What are" houses, mountains, etc., "but the things which we perceive by sense?" (2) "What do we perceive beside our own ideas or sensations?" (3) "Is it not plainly repugnant [i.e., internally inconsistent] that any of" our ideas or sensations "or any combination of them, should exist unperceived?" Berkeley evidently expects us to answer the first two questions with 'nothing', and the third with 'yes'. If we do so, the argument would then run as follows: 'Houses, mountains, etc., are nothing but things which we perceive with our senses. Things that we perceive with our senses are nothing but our own ideas or sensations. But it is plainly self-contradictory to suppose that any one of our ideas or sensations, or any combination of them, should exist unperceived. Therefore, it is self-contradictory to suppose that houses, mountains, etc., should exist unperceived'. I will now take the three rhetorical questions in turn.

(1) If there are such things as 'houses', 'mountains', etc., they are certainly things which we can and often do perceive with our senses. But they would be a great deal more than that. They would be particulars which, even when we are perceiving them, have many parts and many qualities which they are not directly manifesting to our senses. For they would have insides as well as outsides, backs as well as fronts, temperatures and textures as well as colours, and so on. Again, each of them would be a thing which can be perceived by several persons simultaneously or successively, and by the same person on many different occasions, from various points of view and by means of various kinds of sensations. Lastly, they would be things which have characteristic powers and dispositions, which interact with each other, and which unfold their various histories whether anyone happens to be perceiving them or not. Berkeley is arguing from the common meanings and usages of ordinary words and sentences. If so, he ought to take into account their *full* meanings and implications, and not just a small selection which specially favours his case.

Berkeley's Denial of Material Substance 267

(2) Either the word 'perceive' is being used in the same sense in the second question as in the first, or in a different sense. If it is used in a different sense, the argument collapses through having an ambiguous middle term. But, if it is used in the same sense, it is simply untrue that what a person perceives is 'his own ideas and sensations'. What we ostensibly perceive is houses, mountains, rivers, etc. To apply the phrase 'one's own' to these, in the sense in which it is used in the phrase 'one's own sensations', is quite meaningless. It can be applied to them only in the quite different and irrelevant sense of legal ownership, as when one talks of 'my umbrella' or 'your bicycle'. You and I may perceive St. Paul's Cathedral; it is quite meaningless to say that you perceive *your* St. Paul's and I perceive *mine*.

There is one and only one interpretation which I can put on the second question which would enable me to answer it affirmatively. I should have to transform it as follows: 'What does a person *sense*, on any occasion when he is perceiving a material thing, but a sensibile? Is it not plain that this cannot be identified with the thing as a whole, and doubtful whether it can be identified even with a part of the thing's surface? Is it not plain, in any case, that it does not manifest to the percipient all the qualities which he takes to be possessed by the part of the thing which he is perceiving? And is not the fact that a person senses such and such a sensibile on a certain occasion, and that it then manifests to him such and such sensible characteristics, always determined to some extent by his position and orientation and by the sense-organs which he is using at the time?' I think that the answer to *these* questions is: 'Yes'. But an affirmative answer to them does not help Berkeley's argument.

(3) The third question is equivalent to the following: 'Is it not self-contradictory to suppose that there might be unsensed sensibilia?' In Section 3 of the *Principles* Berkeley says that the statement: 'There was a sound' just ·means: A sound was heard'; 'There was an odour' just means: 'An odour was smelled'; and so on. He sums this up by saying that 'to exist', as applied to sensible objects,

just means 'to be perceived'. (For reasons which I have already given, I shall substitute 'to be *sensed*' for 'to be perceived'.)

It is plain, however, from what he says elsewhere that Berkeley would wish to modify this at least in one or other of the following two ways. (i) 'There was a sound' means: '*Either* a sound was actually heard by some man or animal, *or* one would have been heard if certain conditions, wholly describable in terms of sensations, had been fulfilled'. (ii) 'There was a sound' means: '*Either* a sound was heard by some man or animal, *or*, if not, a sound was in some way present to the mind of God'. I think it is fairly plain that Berkeley really took the *second* alternative. In Section 48 of the *Principles* he writes as follows: "For, though we hold . . . the objects of sense to be nothing . . . but ideas which cannot exist unperceived; yet we may not then conclude that they have no existence except only when perceived by us, since there may be some other spirit that perceives them, though we do not. Wherever bodies are said to have no existence without the mind, I would not be understood to mean this or that particular mind, but all minds whatsoever." Again, in Dialogue II of the *Dialogues between Hylas and Philonous* he makes the following explicit statement: ". . . I conclude, not that they have no real existence, but that, seeing that they depend not on my thought and have an existence distinct from being perceived by me, there must be some other mind wherein they exist." The fact is that Berkeley himself was not a phenomenalist, though phenomenalism is a very natural alternative line of development from his principles.

Now I think it is fantastic to suggest that any proposition about God is part of the *meaning* of such a statement as: 'There was still a hooting sound going on when the ship's foghorn continued to blow after all the ship's company had moved away out of earshot in the lifeboats'. Let us, then, ignore this alternative here, and consider the other, i.e., the phenomenalist one. According to this, the only meaning which can be attached to this statement, although it is in the indicative mood, is the *conditional*

Berkeley's Denial of Material Substance 269

proposition that, *if* a man or other suitably equipped animal *had* been within earshot, he *would* have heard a hooting sound. What are we to say of this kind of contention?

(1) I think that many people would find it almost self-evident about odours and tastes, and highly plausible about sounds. But I would remark that the antecedent of the conditional involves the notion of being *within earshot* or some similar notion, i.e., the notion of an observer having a *body* which conditions his sensations and of that body being in a certain kind of *spatial relation* to another *body* which is supposed to be emitting the sound or the odour. I think that the plausibility and even the intelligibility of the proposed analysis vanish, if we try to analyse these features in the antecedent of the conditional in the way in which we have analysed the original proposition that there was a hooting sound.

(2) However that may be, does anyone find this kind of analysis in the least plausible, if applied to sensibilia of the kind which a person senses when he ostensibly sees or touches a body and when there is no ordinary commonsense reason to think that his ostensible perception is delusive? So far from it seeming obvious to me, it does not seem *prima facie* to be even plausible. When I look at a cricket-ball, e.g., I automatically take what is being sensibly presented to me, viz., a certain round convex brown expanse, to be part of the surface of a certain body. I unhesitatingly take for granted that the rest of its surface, which is *not* now being sensibly presented to me, is *now* round and convex and brown, in precisely *the same way* in which my present immediate object is so. I unhesitatingly take for granted that my present immediate object existed before I began to sense it and that it will continue to exist after I have ceased to do so. I assume that it then was and then will be round and convex and brown in precisely the way in which it now is so. I unhesitatingly take for granted that my present immediate object *now* is smooth and hard and cold, although I am not now sensing it as such; and that, if I were to touch it, I should *sense it as having* these qualities, which it *already has* but is not sensibly presenting itself to me as having.

Arguments may be produced to show that these instinctive beliefs are *false* or highly *doubtful*. But when I am told that I cannot possibly have them, because all this is meaningless nonsense which I cannot even *think*, and that I must instead be believing some conditional proposition about what I or someone else *would* sense under certain unfulfilled conditions, I remain wholly unconvinced.

Why is it that Berkeley's contention seems so obvious about odours, so plausible about sounds, and so unconvincing about the colour-expanses which one senses when one ostensibly sees bodies? We may begin by noting the following fact. The cases in which it seems *obvious* are those in which the percipient has no tendency to regard the sensibile which he senses as part of the material thing which he ostensibly perceives. The cases where it seems *unplausible* are those in which he naturally takes for granted that the sensibile which he senses is part of the surface of the material thing which he ostensibly perceives. Now in the former cases the percipient also has no tendency to believe that the sensibile which he senses has other qualities or parts or spatio-temporal continuations besides those which it sensibly presents itself to him as having. In the later cases, as we have seen, he always takes such things for granted about the sensibile which he senses. It is worth noticing that, even in the case of *visual* sensations, the Berkeleian contention is by no means unplausible for those vague, peripheral, or unusual sense-data which the percipient does *not* automatically and uncritically take to be a part of the surface of some body which he is looking at more or less directly. Take, e.g., the case of a visual after-sensation experienced with closed eyes, or the 'stars' which a person 'sees' when a blow is struck on his eye. It seems plausible, rather than shocking, to suggest that each of these exists only as sensed by a certain one person on a certain one occasion. And in the case of what are called 'mental *images*' of the visual kind, I suppose that everyone would find Berkeley's contention *prima facie* obvious, and the doctrine that such a coloured extended particular could exist except as imaged by a cer-

Berkeley's Denial of Material Substance 271

tain one person on a certain one occasion extremely paradoxical.

The fact is that Berkeley leads his readers 'up the garden path' at this point by the following two devices. (1) He discusses explicitly the case of an *unheard sound*, i.e., a sensibile of a kind which no one regards as a part of a body or of its surface even when it is sensed in connection with ostensibly perceiving a body, e.g., hearing a bell tolling. (2) He assimilates the sensibile which one senses when one is ostensibly seeing a body, to a visual *mental image* or to the sense-datum of a visual *after-sensation*. He takes for granted that it has and can have only the qualities which it is now sensed as having, viz., a certain colour and a certain extension and figure; whereas the instinctive belief of common-sense is that it can and does have others besides, viz., a certain texture and a certain temperature, which it is not now sensed as having simply because the appropriate sense-organ is not in operation.

It is fair to say that he had already argued elaborately in the *New Theory of Vision* against the possibility that any particular prehended by sight should be identical with any particular prehended by touch. We must therefore briefly consider the argument at this point. For, if it were valid, it would justify Berkeley in holding that the visual sensibilia sensed when one ostensibly perceives a body resemble visual mental images and the sense-data of visual after-sensations in having none but *purely visual* qualities. The argument occurs in Section 49 of the *New Theory of Vision*. He assumes there as a premiss something which he claims to prove considerably later on, viz., in Section 121 and those that immediately follow it. The premiss is that no characteristic which a particular is visually sensed as having can be identical with any characteristic which a particular is tactually sensed as having, and conversely. Thus, e.g., if I say and say truly: 'This *looks* round' and 'That *feels* round', the word 'round' must stand in the one sentence for a determinate under one determinable and in the other sentence for a determinate under a wholly different determinable. We need not here discuss whether this is true or false, well established or ill established. Let us grant it for the sake of argument.

Berkeley says that the correct conclusion to draw from this premiss is that a visually sensed particular and a tactually sensed one could never be the same particular. It seems to me quite plain that this does not follow from the premiss. In order to prove the conclusion the premiss needed is that characteristics which can be visually sensed are *incompatible* with those which can be tactually sensed. He has made no attempt to show this. And the more you insist that they fall under radically different determinables, the less reason you have to accept this. If the word 'round' in the sentence 'This feels round' and the word 'elliptical' in the sentence 'This looks elliptical' denote qualities which fall under quite different determinables, there is no obvious reason why a particular which feels round and a particular which looks elliptical should not be one and the same particular. A *fortiori* there is no obvious reason why a particular which looks brown and a particular which feels cold and smooth and hard should not be one and the same particular.

I have now examined in turn the three steps in Berkeley's *'esse'* = *'percipi'* argument. It is time to draw together the threads and examine the argument as a whole in the light of our comments on the parts. What Berkeley claims to prove is that it is self-contradictory to suppose that houses, mountains, and other bodies should exist unperceived. It is plain that in order to do this it is not enough to prove that it is self-contradictory to suppose that sensibilia should exist unsensed. It is necessary to add to this the premiss that a body is a sensibile, or a set of interrelated sensibilia, and nothing besides. What emerges from my comments is that Berkeley is faced with the following dilemma. There certainly are sensations with regard to which it is highly plausible to hold *either* (a) that the analysis into act of sensing and sensibile sensed does not apply to them, or (b) that, if it does, then it is obvious that no such sensibile could exist except as a sense-datum to a certain one person on a certain one occasion. Examples are sensations of smell, auditory sensations, and visual after-sensations. But in the case of none of *these* sensations would it be at all plausible to maintain that the sensibilia sensed are in any way parts of the bodies ostensibly perceived, or of any other bodies. On the other hand, there are sensibilia, viz., those which a person senses when he ostensibly sees or touches a body, which *are* taken by the percipient to be parts of the surface of the body seen or touched. But in the case of none of *these* sensibilia is it all obvious that the supposition that they might exist unsensed is intrinsically absurd. It can be made to seem absurd only by assuming, contrary to what common sense takes for granted, that they can have no qualities beside those which the person who senses them at any moment then senses them as having. This amounts to assuming that it is absurd to suppose that one and the same sensibile could be sometimes a purely visual sense-datum, sometimes a purely tactual sense-datum, and sometimes both a visual and a tactual sense-datum. I have tried to show that Berkeley's argument in the *New Theory of Vision* to show that this is absurd is quite inconclusive. But it would not help his case even if it were conclusive. For, just in proportion as we assimilate these sensibilia to visual images or the sense-data of visual after-sensations, so does it become increasingly unplausible to identify any *body* with any one of these sensibilia or any collection of them.

I conclude, then, that the argument is a failure. But I am sure that, like the ontological argument, it is a most interesting and important failure and far more valuable philosophically than most successes. Moreover, there are other arguments, based on certain specific features of ostensible sense-perception and on its physical and physiological conditions, which claim to show that the sensibile which a person senses, when he ostensibly sees or touches a body, cannot in fact be a part of the surface of that or any other body, and probably exists only in so far as it is a sense-datum to that person on that occasion. I find the cumulative effect of these arguments very convincing, and the attempted rebuttals very weak, though I admit that the arguments are neither severally nor collectively coercive.

2.2. *Supplementary Arguments.* Berkeley uses two supplementary arguments against the existence of material substance. One occurs in Sections 16 and 17 of the *Principles of Human Knowledge*, and the other in Sections 18, 19, and 20. I will now take these in turn.

(A) The first of these arguments is an attack on the notion of material substance as a substratum in which extension and other qualities inhere. Berkeley brings much the same objection as Locke did when he said that the notion of substance is the notion of 'a something I know not what' which supports qualities. This line of argument is logically independent of the *'esse' = 'percipi'* principle, and it might consistently be used by a person who rejected that principle.

Now Locke saw that, if there is anything in this objection, it applies equally to mental and to material substance. If there is a difficulty in the notion of a substratum in which sensible qualities inhere and physical events occur, surely there will be exactly the same difficulty in the notion of a substratum in which mental qualities inhere and mental events occur. Locke's conclusion is simply that we have a very inadequate notion of substance. But Berkeley rejects the possibility of *material* substance on the ground of these difficulties, while he is perfectly convinced that each person's mind is a *mental* substance. The question arises whether this is a consistent position to hold.

Berkeley was well aware that he might be twitted with inconsistency on this point. In Dialogue III of the *Dialogues between Hylas and Philonous* he makes Hylas argue as follows: "It seems to me that . . . in consequence of your own principles it should follow that *you* are only a system of floating ideas, without any substance to support them. . . . As there is no more meaning in 'spiritual substance' than in 'material substance', the one is to be exploded as well as the other." To this he makes Philonous answer as follows: ". . . I know or am conscious of my own being, and that *I myself* am not my ideas, but somewhat else, a thinking active principle that perceives, knows, wills, and operates about ideas. . . . Further I know what I mean when I affirm that there is a spiritual

Berkeley's Denial of Material Substance 275

substance or support of ideas, i.e., that a spirit knows and perceives ideas". Hylas professes himself satisfied with this answer, but ought we to be? We must remember that Berkeley means by 'ideas' sensibilia and mental images, and by 'knowing or perceiving ideas' sensing sensibilia and imaging images. Also he holds that it is nonsense to talk of a sensibile which is not a sense-datum to some one particular person on some one particular occasion and that the same holds *mutatis mutandis* for images. We must distinguish two parts in Hylas' contention. (1) That Berkeley is committed to holding that a person's mind is nothing but a system of interrelated ideas, i.e., sensed sensibilia and imaged images. (2) That on Berkeley's principles there is no more meaning in the phrase 'spiritual substance' than in the phrase 'material substance'. It is really only the second contention which directly concerns us at present.

Now the first part of Philonous' answer is addressed only to the first part of Hylas' contention. He argues that that which *senses* sensibilia and which *images* mental images, which exercises volition, and so on, cannot just be a system of sensed sensibilia and imaged images, however interrelated. That may very well be true. It amounts, in fact, to saying that the notion of a mental substance is the notion of something which wills, senses, images, and so on, which has a certain characteristic kind of unity at each moment, a certain kind of identity throughout time, and so forth. But the question remains whether to talk of that which performs these acts and *has* these properties, as distinct from the acts which it performs and the properties which it has, is not to talk of a 'something we know not what'.

I suppose that Philonous must be addressing himself to this question when he says: "Further I know what I mean when I affirm that there is a spiritual substance or support of ideas . . ." I think that Berkeley must mean that each of us is acquainted with his self as substratum, as well as with his own mental acts and with the sensibilia which he senses and the images which he images, and so each of us knows by acquaintance the relation of the former to the latter. He is presumably contrasting this with the fact that no one has ever pretended to be acquainted with the substratum of a material thing, as distinct from the qualities that it has and the events and processes which go on in it. So no one can pretend to know by acquaintance the relation of the former to the latter in *that* case. If this is Berkeley's position, I think it is *self-consistent*. Whether the positive part of it is tenable is another question. It would of course have been denied by Hume, for what that is worth. But it would no less have been denied by Kant and by James and by Stout, who were not professional sceptics and were explicitly reflecting on the question.

(B) Berkeley's second supplementary argument is directed to prove that, even if *per impossibile* there were bodies existing independently of being perceived, it would be impossible for anyone to know of the existence of any such body directly or to prove it demonstratively or even to establish it as a probable hypothesis.

I do not think that anyone would claim, with regard to any body which he was *not* ostensibly perceiving at the time, to know *directly* that it exists. So I think we may fairly discuss the question under the following two headings. (1) The case of a person who is ostensibly perceiving a certain body and who claims, with respect to it, that he knows directly or by demonstration or has good reasons for believing that it exists independently of being perceived. (2) The case of a person who claims, with respect to a body which he is *not* at the time ostensibly perceiving, that he knows by demonstration or has good reasons for believing that it exists independently of being perceived. Now I do not think that anyone would make the latter claim except on one or other of the following two bases: (i) Testimony from another person that he is perceiving or has perceived the body in question. (ii) A causal argument to the existence of the body in question from certain observed features in some body which he is perceiving or has perceived or which some other person testifies to perceiving or having perceived. Suppose that no one ever knows directly or by demonstration or has good reasons for believing, with regard to any body which *he is ostensibly*

Berkeley's Denial of Material Substance 277

perceiving, that it exists independently of being perceived. Then *a fortiori* no one would know or have good reasons for believing this with regard to any body which he is *not* ostensibly perceiving. So we may confine our discussion to Berkeley's attempt to establish the *former* negative proposition.

In order to do so profitably it is desirable to begin by drawing some distinctions which Berkeley does not explicitly recognize. I shall use the word 'know' in such a way that what is known is always a *fact* and not a particular existent. On this understanding we can distinguish *prima facie* at least the following kinds of knowing. (1) Knowing a fact about a presented particular by inspecting it and noting the characteristics which it presents itself as having. In this way a person knows, with regard to the sensibile which is presented to him when he looks at a penny in ordinary daylight, that it is brown and approximately circular. And he does *not* know at the time in this way that it is cold or that it is hard or that it is smooth. This may be called 'knowledge by acquaintance'; (2) Knowing a general fact by reflecting on the nature of certain terms and intuiting that terms of that nature *must be* or *cannot be* interrelated in a certain manner. In that way, e.g., a person knows that anything that had shape would have extension. He does *not* know in that way that triangles on the same base with their vertices on a line parallel to that base must be equal in area. This may be called 'knowledge by *internal evidence*'. (3) Knowing a fact by seeing that it is a logical consequence of another fact or of a conjunction of several other facts which one knows. This may be called 'knowledge by *demonstrative inference*'. (4) Knowing, by means of an experience which does *not* itself consist in knowing a fact and seeing its logical implications, a fact which is other than the fact that that experience is occurring and is of such and such a kind. A plausible example would be memory-knowledge by means of a present image that one has had a certain experience in the past. This may be called 'knowledge by *non-logical mediation*'. We can group together knowledge by acquaintance and knowledge by internal evidence under the head of 'unmediated knowledge'; and we can group together knowledge by demonstrative inference and knowledge by non-logical mediation under the head of 'mediated knowledge'.

In the case of *grounded belief* we can draw a *prima facie* distinction analogous to that which we have drawn between the two kinds of mediated knowledge. A person's justification for believing a proposition with a certain degree of conviction may be that he sees it to be more or less probable relative to some fact which he knows or to some other proposition which he strongly believes. This might be called 'belief grounded on *probable inference*'. But there seems *prima facie* to be another possibility. Might not a person in some cases be justified in believing a proposition with a certain degree of conviction, merely because he was having an experience of a certain kind, which did *not* consist in knowing a fact or believing another proposition and seeing that the proposition in question is more or less probable relative to this known fact or believed proposition? This might be called 'belief grounded on *non-logical mediation*'. Memory would again provide a plausible example. It might be said that the presence in a person's mind of a certain kind of image in a certain kind of context not only causes but also *justifies* a more or less strong conviction that he has had a certain experience in the past, even though it may not enable him to *know* that he has done so.

It should be noted that there is an ambiguity in the words 'immediate' or 'direct', as commonly used in connexion with knowledge or belief. What I have called 'knowledge by non-logical mediation' would sometimes be asserted to be 'immediate' or 'direct', because it is *not mediated by inference*; and it would sometimes be *denied* to be 'immediate' or 'direct', because it *is mediated by something*.

We can now deal fairly briefly with Berkeley's present contention. (1) On his principles it is quite obvious that a person who is ostensibly perceiving a body cannot know, with regard to the sensibile which he is then sensing, that it could exist independently of being sensed. For anything

Berkeley's Denial of Material Substance 279

that can be *known* must be a *fact*, and Berkeley claims to have shown that no sensibile could possibly exist except as a sense-datum for some one person on some one occasion.

(2) Suppose that Berkeley were mistaken on this point. Suppose that in fact a sensibile which a certain person senses on a certain occasion can and does exist also when neither he nor anyone else is sensing it. Even so, it is plain that merely to sense a certain sensibile on a certain occasion does not give to a person *knowledge by acquaintance* that it existed before he began to sense it or that it will exist after he shall have ceased to sense it. The only knowledge by acquaintance that it supplies is knowledge that the sensibile *now* exists and that it *now* has at least those qualities which it is sensed as having.

Still less does merely sensing a certain sensibile on a certain occasion supply *knowledge by acquaintance* that it is part of a more extensive and persistent particular, having other parts and other qualities which are not at the moment being presented to one's senses, and possessing also various dispositional properties.

(3) Berkeley argues that one could never infer demonstratively, from the mere fact that one is ostensibly perceiving a body answering to such and such a description, that there now is or ever has been or will be a body answering to that description, or indeed any body at all. His argument may be put as follows. If such a demonstrative inference were valid, its conclusion would always have to be true whenever its premiss, viz., that one is ostensibly perceiving a body answering to such and such a description, is true. But it is notorious that there are cases, e.g., dreams and waking hallucinations, where the premiss is true and the conclusion would be false.

This contention seems to me to be true but trivial. If the premiss of the supposed demonstrative inference is assumed to be rigidly confined to the fact that a person is having such and such an ostensible perception at a certain moment, Berkeley's objection is valid. But why should it be so confined? Why should not the minimal premiss include facts about the antecedents, the sequels, and the context of the ostensible perception? After all, there are certain tests by which we claim to distinguish dreams and waking hallucinations from normal waking ostensible perceptions, and Berkeley must be assuming the validity of these tests. He ought therefore to have considered carefully whether an ostensible perception *which passes all these tests* could be delusive in principle, even if it might be more or less so in points of detail.

Nevertheless, I entirely agree with Berkeley's conclusion. I do not see how the existence of any particular body, or of bodies in general, could possibly be *demonstrated* from any premiss, however extended, about the occurrence, the characteristics, and the interrelations of ostensible perceptions. Plainly some *universal* premiss would be needed in addition. Now I cannot imagine what this could be and I cannot believe that we could plausibly claim to know it.

Would the case be improved, if we were to substitute what I have called 'non-logically mediated knowledge' for knowledge by demonstrative inference? The allegation would be as follows. Whenever a person has an ostensible perception, occurring in a certain kind of sequence of ostensible perceptions and in a certain kind of experiential context, he thereby *knows without inference* that he is in the presence of a *body,* answering more or less closely to the description which he would naturally give of what he is ostensibly perceiving. I think that this is less vulnerable to criticism than the former contention. But it may be invulnerable only in so far as it remains too vague and general for the critic to come to grips with. If he were to insist on our specifying the kind of sequence and the kind of experiential context, we might have a difficulty in doing so, and he might be able to point out plausible counter-instances to every attempt that we might make.

(4) In considering whether one could justify a belief in the existence of bodies as a probable inference, Berkeley assumes that the argument would have to be from ostensible perceptions as mental events to bodies and events in bodies as their probable causes. He accepts as self-evident the principle that every event must have an

Berkeley's Denial of Material Substance 281

efficient cause. Two of his objections rest on propositions about causation.

(i) He held it to be self-evident that the only possible efficient causes are *minds* and that they can produce effects only by *volition*. If that be so, even if there were bodies they could cause nothing, and therefore no inference to them by way of the principle of universal causation could be valid. I do not propose to discuss this argument here.

(ii) Even if it be admitted that events in bodies could be efficient causes of events of *some* kind, viz., in other bodies, it is generally admitted that the causation of a mental event, e.g., a sensation, by a bodily event, e.g., the vibration of a particle in a person's brain, is completely unintelligible. But any causal argument, from the occurrence and interrelations of ostensible perceptions of bodies to the existence of bodies, would presuppose this kind of causal transaction. Berkeley evidently regards this as a serious objection. But it is not clear to me that it would be so, even if we granted the premiss that there is some special difficulty in the notion of a physico-psychical transaction. The objection would no doubt be fatal, if the alleged difficulty were supposed to show that the notion of such a transaction is *self-contradictory* and therefore that no such transaction is possible. But it seems to me that the utmost that could be granted is that no law of physico-psychical causation can have any trace of self-evidence, while some laws of physico-physical causation (e.g., the modification of motion by impact) might plausibly be alleged to be self-evident.

Berkeley's remaining argument may be put as follows. Even if there could be bodies, and even if events in bodies could cause mental events, still it must be admitted that we *could* have had exactly the same ostensible perceptions as we now have, even though no bodies had existed. Now, if that had been the case, we should have had precisely the same grounds for the causal inference from ostensible perceptions of bodies to the existence of bodies as we now have. And by *hypothesis* the inference would have been mistaken. So it might be mistaken if we were to make it now.

This assertion is doubtless true. But it is surely irrelevant here. For we are no longer considering the contention that the existence of bodies could be *demonstrated* from the fact that we have such and such ostensible perceptions of bodies and that they occur in such and such sequences and experiential contexts. What we are considering now is the contention that, relative to that fact, the proposition that there are bodies is highly probable, and therefore that we are justified in believing it fairly strongly. Whether that be so in fact, Berkeley's objection that nevertheless the belief may be mistaken is surely completely irrelevant.

But no doubt there are serious difficulties in the contention. One is the question: Whence did we get the notion of bodies, if the only particular existents which we are ever acquainted with are such that no one of them could conceivably exist except as a sense-datum for a certain one person on a certain one occasion? Another is this: Ability to explain known facts can make a hypothesis probable only if the hypothesis has some finite degree of probability antecedently to the facts to be explained. But what is *meant* by the probability of the existence of bodies antecedently to the fact that we ostensibly perceive bodies and that our ostensible perceptions occur in certain sequences and experiential contexts? And, if this notion be intelligible, what ground is there for assigning a finite value to this antecedent probability?

Finally we must consider a possibility which Berkeley did not envisage, viz., the possibility of what I have called 'belief grounded on non-logical mediation'. Might it not be claimed that whenever a person has an ostensible perception, occurring in a certain kind of sequence of ostensible perceptions and in a certain kind of experiential context, he not only *does believe*, but is thereby *justified in believing* with considerable confidence, that he is in presence of a *body*, answering more or less closely to the description which he would naturally give of what he is ostensibly perceiving? Obviously this is even less vulnerable to criticism than the stronger claim to knowledge by

Berkeley's Denial of Material Substance 283

non-logical mediation, which we have already considered. Moreover, since no question of *premisses*, and therefore no question of *causal* premisses, would arise, it is not open to objections based upon difficulties in the notion of causation in general or in the notion of mental events being caused by bodily events. I do not think it can be refuted, but I do not know how it could be recommended to anyone who was disinclined to accept it.

BERKELEY'S EXISTENCE IN THE MIND[1]
A. A. LUCE

We find existence in the mind asserted and existence outside the mind denied scores of times, probably more than a hundred times, in the *Principles*.[2] In the earlier portion of the work there is scarcely a section without a reference to the doctrine. The term *in the mind* is clearly a hinge of Berkeley's system, and it has been persistently misunderstood, in my opinion, from his day to ours.

Kant took it to mean that 'the objects in space are mere products of the imagination'.[3] Critics to-day are reluctant to attribute such nonsense to a sensible thinker; but many of them make much the same mistake as Kant. They put the charge less bluntly and more broadly; for Kant's words 'products of the imagination', they would substitute 'products of our faculties'; but that change would not affect the gravamen of the charge, *viz.*, that Berkeley's existence in the mind is mental existence.

My task is to show that by existence in the mind Berkeley does not mean mental existence, but does mean non-mental existence, perceived or perceivable by the mind.

If by existence in the mind Berkeley had meant mental existence, he would have said so, we may be sure. He was not the man to use four words habitually where two would

From *Mind*, Vol. L (1941). Reprinted, with minor corrections, by permission of the author and *Mind*.

[1] References to the *Three Dialogues* (abbrev. *Hyl.*) give the page number of Fraser's edition (1901) of the *Works*. References to the other works give the section number. For the *Commonplace Book* (CPB) I use Johnston's numbering of the entries.

[2] The *Three Dialogues* is equally insistent on the point from start to finish.

[3] *Refutation of Idealism*.

Berkeley's Existence in the Mind

do. The term *mental* occurs in Locke. Berkeley uses it in his *Commonplace Book* (740, 805, 821), and occasionally in his published works (e.g., *Princ. Intro.*, 9), but always in its proper meaning, *i.e.*, 'of or belonging to the mind'. He nowhere applies it, or, as far as I have observed, any equivalent term, to objects of sense.[4] No, Berkeley's key phrase does *not* mean mental existence.

What it does mean is clearly stated at the first occurrence of the term in the *Principles*, section 2.[5] In the previous section Berkeley has described his first type of created reality, *ideas*, and now he turns to his second type, *mind, spirit, soul* or *my self*, and says, 'By which words I do not denote any one of my ideas, but a thing entirely distinct from them, wherein they exist, or, which is the same thing, whereby they are perceiv'd'. This is official doctrine, explicit, decisive, and often repeated. To exist in the mind, for Berkeley, is to be perceived by the mind, and yet to be entirely distinct from the mind. From this definition he never deviates. This is his axiom, his New Principle, the positive aspect of his denial of matter. There is no matter, he teaches, because 'we eat, and drink, and are clad with the immediate objects of sense which cannot exist unperceiv'd or without the mind' (38). Objects seen, touched, heard, tasted, or smelled, sensible

---

[4] I have carefully verified this statement with regard to the *Principles* and the *Three Dialogues*, which together constitute the proper field of Berkeleian exegesis. The only doubtful terms, to my mind, are *notions* and *passions*. The former is applied to things of sense in *Princ.* 5 and perhaps, 74, the latter in *Princ.* 89. Both designate the object of knowledge, not the subject. *Notion* is one of the vaguest terms used by Berkeley. *Passion* is the equivalent of *passive entity*, and does not mean emotion. Both terms may be relics of the early stage of his thought (reflected in the first part of the *Commonplace Book*), when *mind*, for him, was passive, and not distinguished from its contents. The nearest approach to *mental existence* is *notional existence*, which in *Hyl.* 426 is opposed to *real existence*, real existence being repeatedly in the context predicated by Berkeley of things of sense. On *notional*, as used by the Objector in *Princ.* 34, see below, p. 290.

[5] Many other sections, notably 7, 14, 23, 24, 33, 38, 41, 82, 86, 87, 90, 94, 124, may be cited in evidence, but I shall here concentrate upon sections 2, 34, 45–48, and 49, because in them Berkeley is expressly expounding the meaning of the term.

qualities or things or ideas, sensations, *sensa*, or *sense-data*, call them what you please or what fashion dictates, they, one and all, when I perceive them, are in my mind, only in my mind, and are entirely distinct from my mind; and *that*, says Berkeley, is what I mean by existence in the human mind.

Now *mind*, in Berkeley, may also mean the divine mind; and this and other ambiguities, or should I say obscurities, in the key phrase require to be cleared up before we go further.

Berkeley's term *in the mind* is flexible, at times indefinite, but it is not intentionally ambiguous; if it is ambiguous to us, we must not blame Berkeley. It is an elastic term, and to a certain extent it takes its colour from its context, and the reader has to be on the alert about it. Take first the preposition. The *in* is the equivalent of *in relation to*;[6] but the full phrase is too awkward for general use. In our idiom 'I have it in mind' is a neat expression for the cognitive relation in general, and Berkeley is correct linguistically in using 'in the mind' as an abbreviation for 'in direct cognitive relation to the mind'. The phrase is not to 'be understood in the gross literal sense'.[7] The preposition implies, not situation in, not forming part of, but apprehension by.[8] Thus the British Museum is in my mind when I am in the British Museum, provided I am perceiving it or thinking about it. Things are not in my mind as the brain is *in* the head or as Monday is *in* the week or as the act of synthesis is *in* conception.

Then analyse the noun. *Mind*, in the *Principles*, is a very flexible term. It may mean the divine mind or the human mind, or it may be the negation *not-matter*. When Berkeley is merely the controversialist, attacking materialism, his *in the mind* means *not in matter*. Matter, *ex hypothesi*, is outside the mind and beyond its range. Berkeley says there is no such thing; he has looked; the

[6] *Cf. CPB*, 814; *Princ.* 3; and *Hyl.*, pp. 384, 453.
[7] *Hyl.*, p. 470. This passage is perfectly explicit, and deserves careful study.
[8] *Ibid.* 'My meaning is only that the mind comprehends or perceives them.'

things he sees and touches are in his mind and not outside. But of course he does not long remain at the stage of denial; *mind* soon becomes to him positive and a substance. It may be only mind in general, at the outset; for he can go a long way on that road without being specific; but sooner or later he has to distinguish sharply between the mind of God and the mind of man. And he does so. When he is drawing the line between sense and imagination, or between the perceived and the perceivable, the contrast between mind infinite and mind finite steps into the centre of the stage. Idealists to-day may think of mind as a vague, impersonal ether of spirit; but to Berkeley mind was minds, the mind of God or the minds of men.[9]

Having cleared up these ambiguities I return to my point that existence in the mind is *not* mental existence. I shall be met with the argument that Berkeley called things of sense *ideas*, which is equivalent to calling them mental. He does call them *ideas* of course; in his early books[10] he tried to establish the usage, because *idea* implies immediacy and 'a necessary relation to the mind'. It was a young man's experiment in technique, reasonable enough in its day, defensible by experts, but doomed to failure at the bar of average opinion. It was like trying to get the man in the street to-day to call shoes and ships and sealing wax *sense-data*. They are *sense-data*, but the term is too technical to make good. The Berkeleian idea of sense is exactly the *sense-datum*; but to apply either term to things opens the door to misunderstanding and to ridicule. But we must not make the wrong inference from this mistake in tactics. In calling things *ideas* Berkeley did not mean that they are mental; for he meant the opposite.

Mind and idea are sharply distinguished in Berkeley's philosophy. Mind is active; the idea is passive. He was an

[9] Berkeley moved in circles keenly alive to this distinction. His Provost in T.C.D., Peter Browne, made analogy without identity the cornerstone of his philosophy. His archbishop, William King, carried the distinction to the extreme, virtually denying all resemblance, and making divine thought and will as metaphorical as divine hands and feet.
[10] *Hyl.*, p. 453. Berkeley never quite abandoned this technique; even in *Siris* he once or twice calls things of sense *ideas*.

uncompromising dualist; he takes the thing into the mind, but does not let it become the mind, nor infect the mind, nor merge with the mind. He takes it in, but keeps it at arm's length. The thing of sense is *so* in the mind as to remain distinct from the mind. This distinctness is formally stated at the first mention of existence in the mind (*Princ.* 2), and is repeated with growing emphasis at several turning-points of the argument (*e.g.*, sect. 27, 86, 89, 139). Berkeley seems to have become, as he worked, more and more conscious of the activity of active mind and the passivity of passive idea. They are 'two kinds entirely distinct and heterogeneous, and which have nothing in common but the name' (thing or being, sect. 89); they are 'natures perfectly disagreeing and unlike' (sect. 139). He taught the same thing ten years later, 'Duo sunt summa rerum genera, corpus et anima'.[11] Within the truth of the creation Berkeley was a convinced dualist. He believed that God made the finite spirit and the sensible world, creating the one for the other, giving man's mind to know and the things of sense to be known, but not giving to either the power to produce or generate the other. The key phrase must be interpreted by the key doctrines; when Berkeley says a thing is *in the mind*, and calls it an *idea*, he thereby says that it is not a mental existence.

The root of the trouble is the assumption, natural but mistaken, that to an immaterialist things must be mental, because there is nothing else for them to be. If there is no matter, then all is mind; so argues the average man, because he starts from the equation, All reality is mind and matter, and, on subtracting matter, he is left with the equation, All is mind. Now there is no subtraction sum of that sort in the *Principles*; Berkeley nowhere says that all is mind, and he says things[12] quite incompatible with that wild fancy. The more firmly he asserts the mind and its rights, the more firmly he asserts the not-mind too.

[11] *De Motu*, 21.
[12] *E.g., Princ.*, 35. 'That the things I see with my eyes and touch with my hands do exist, really exist, I make not the least question. The only thing whose existence we deny, is that which philosophers call matter or corporeal substance.'

There is nothing outside the range of mind, for him, but there is much that is not mind. There is, to take a striking instance, the brain. Berkeley says that the brain 'being a sensible thing, exists only in the mind'.[13] Of course he does not mean that the brain is the mind, or is mental; he means that it is immediately perceived or perceivable.

Berkeley *so* denied the material as to assert the sensible. Giving up matter he held on to sensible things and the sensible world. His phrase *in the mind* was the war-cry, not of monism, nor mentalism, nor subjectivism, nor solipsism, but of direct awareness. He maintained a two-term theory of perception, and was up against thinkers, notably Locke, who held a three-term theory and put reality outside the mind. Knowledge is not knowledge, argued Berkeley, if the real be outside the mind, and only a pale copy thereof within. He insists, quite sensibly, that sensible reality is in the mind, is not outside the mind, exists only in the mind, and has neither absolute nor twofold existence. Existence in the mind is the elimination of the third term from knowledge, the removal of the cataract from mental vision, and the assurance that we see what we see, and not a *tertium quid*.

A river in brown flood builds its banks, while appearing to break them down. Berkeley's thought is like that river. It breaks matter, but builds the sensible. It destroys absolute existence, but establishes relative existence. It abolishes twofold existence in order to lay well and truly the foundation for the simple existence of the thing perceived. Thus Berkeley restores our native confidence in our senses, assuring us that what we actually sense is there, is given, is in our minds when we are minding it, and that when we are not minding it, it is still there, still offered, still in the mind of God.

Berkeley had the dramatic talent; he was able to think and feel with the other man, and he knew just where his opponent would misunderstand him. He foresaw the three main misrepresentations of his philosophy, and he deals with them as, respectively, the first, the fourth, and the

[13] *Hyl.*, p. 421.

fifth Objections to it.[14] In each of these passages he makes important statements about existence in the mind. We will consider them in order.

'By the foregoing principles, all that is real and substantial in nature is banish'd out of the world; and instead thereof a chimerical scheme of ideas takes place. All things that exist, exist only in the mind, that is, they are purely notional.'[15] That is the first Objection, Kant's objection, and the gist of it is that Berkeley gives things of sense only a mental existence, and thereby obliterates the distinction between real and imaginary. Berkeley, in reply, refers to sections 29, 30, and 33 to prove that on his principles, (1) the things we see, hear, touch, etc., really exist; (2) there is a *rerum natura*; and (3) the distinction between real and imaginary retains its full force.

In other words, Berkeley requires us so to understand existence in the mind as to preserve intact the real existence of the sensible world, the laws of nature, and the contrast between real and imaginary.

Can it be done? I do not see why not. I, for one, have no difficulty at all about it. I hold existence in the mind, in what I take to be Berkeley's sense of that term, and I believe in the reality of the sensible world, and in laws of nature, and I can tell the difference between real and imaginary; but, of course, one has to accept *ex animo* Berkeley's contention that the realities of sense are significant entities (*ideas*), produced and sustained by omnipresent Deity, and 'that they are not fictions of the mind perceiving them' (sect. 36).

Turn now to the fourth Objection (sects. 45–48). It is vividly summarised in the objector's cavil, 'Upon shutting my eyes all the furniture in the room is reduc'd to nothing, and barely upon opening 'em it is again created'.[16] The

---

[14] *Princ.* 34, 45–8, 49.
[15] The words, 'that is, they are purely notional' are not Berkeley's, but the objector's gloss; *cf. CPB*, 540, which contains this passage in brief.
[16] Some readers have taken these words as representing Berkeley's own views; and I grant that these sections are not as carefully written as most; but the words are *not* his views, and the fact becomes quite plain, if sections 45 and 48 are read contin-

objector is urging that on Berkeley's principles things are every moment annihilated and created anew, that sensible things, being ideas, must have only an intermittent existence, dawning in and fading out like the Cheshire cat in *Alice in Wonderland*, or like the fairy, Tinkabell, in *Peter Pan*. After stating the objection in section 45a, giving it its full force, Berkeley (sect. 45b) replies in effect; well, even if that charge be a true bill, it shall not move me from my primary intuition, nor make me assent to meaningless propositions. I actually perceive the tree; therefore it exists; and to claim for it an existence outside all mind at bottom has no meaning.

At this point Berkeley digresses; in sections 46 and 47 he points out that intermittency is accepted by Lockeans and Cartesians in respect of the 'secondary qualities', and that annihilation and continual creation are taught by the Schoolmen, and are assumed by the materialism of his day, notably in the infinite divisibility. These are *ad hominem* arguments only, designed to secure side-wind for his sails; for he did not accept Locke's 'secondary qualities', nor Malebranche's 'modifications of the soul', nor the 'matter' of scholastic and mathematician. He makes his position plain when he returns to his main argument at the opening of section 48. He says that we are not to conclude that objects of sense 'have no existence except only while they are perceiv'd by us, since there may be some other spirit that perceives them tho' we do not'. He then expressly denies that annihilation, continual creation and intermittency follow from his principles. As to whether they can be held along with his principles, he is silent; he does not commit himself one way or the other. But he clearly dissociates himself from those tenets, when he speaks of some other spirit perceiving the objects of sense 'tho' we do not'. Without a doubt then Berkeley's official teaching on existence in the mind is that objects of

---

uously. The insertion of sections 46, 47 has obscured the main sequence of thought.

(For a more careful exposition of Sections 45–8, although without substantial alteration, see the author's *The Dialectic of Immaterialism*, Hodder and Stoughton, 1963.)

sense may go in and out of the small circle of the mind of man, but do not thereby go in and out of existence; for they are conserved in the great circle of the mind of God. Therefore the furniture in the room is not reduced to nothing when I shut my eyes.

Now to the fifth Objection, our third and final passage (sect. 49), 'If extension and figure exist only in the mind, it follows that the mind is extended and figured'. This is a damaging criticism on the traditional view of the Berkeleian philosophy, but does it no harm on a true view. The objector raises the searching question, What does existence in the mind involve for the mind itself? If the divine mind be in view, Berkeley is charged with Spinozism and the deification of space; if the human mind be in view, he is charged with the denial of the distinction between mind and body. Berkeley's reply takes us right away from traditional Berkeleianism. He states positively what he means, and negatively what he does not mean, by existence in the mind. Extension and figure, he says, 'are in the mind only as they are perceiv'd by it, that is not by way of *mode* or *attribute* but only by way of *idea*'. The way of *mode* or *attribute* is Spinoza's way, the way of pantheism and mentalism, and the way back to materialism. Berkeley rejected that way; for him there can be no confounding of distinct natures, no fusion of mind and not-mind, no infecting of subject by object. He substituted the way of *idea*,[17] explaining it to mean that things 'are in the mind only as they are perceiv'd by it'.

Why should not Berkeley be taken at his word? In view of his plain, reiterated and common-sense statements, what is the point of making the man into a mystic, and his chairs and tables into mental entities? 'My meaning is only that the mind comprehends or perceives them' (*Hyl.*,

[17] The phrase deserves more attention than it has received. It is quite technical with Berkeley; it occurs again, *Princ.* 142, 'our souls are not to be known in the same manner as senseless, inactive objects, or by way of *idea*', and by implication in *Hyl.*, p. 455, 'in which they exist, not by way of mode or property, but as a thing perceived in that which perceives it'. See also *Hyl.*, p. 470, for the same contrast, and *Hyl.*, p. 458, for the impassibility of the divine mind.

p. 470). Why not give the speaker credit for ordinary sincerity? It is no compliment to try to make him mean something subtler than he says he means. Berkeley simply takes his stand on the facts of perception, and bids his readers understand perception, if they would understand his existence in the mind. 'The way of *idea*' is the way of the object which is not subject, the way of the immediate object which is the only object, the way of direct awareness, and that is the only way, for Berkeley, in which things are in the mind, because it is the only way in which things are perceived. His ideas of sense are sensible ideas, passive entities in the active mind, not mental, nor partaking in the nature of mind, not modes or attributes or properties of mind; they belong to a different *genus*. Often unknown by man, they are always knowable; they can be perceived and known, as trout can be angled for and caught. Berkeley nowhere teaches that the human mind is creative, constitutive or generative; he just teaches the common-sense doctrine that when a man minds a thing, that thing is in his mind, and therefore is not in matter.

We have studied Berkeley's direct statements about existence in the mind, his answers to objections, and the general tenor of his philosophy, and the results of all three lines of study agree. Before I sum up and have done, I must make a brief reference to the 'development' of Berkeley's thought; for some would blunt the edge of my argument by asserting that there were two Berkeleys, and that I have concentrated upon the realist aspect of his teaching, and have ignored the idealist aspect, "refuted" by Kant. I reply that the statement that there were in fact two Berkeleys cannot be substantiated. I believe, after close study of the question, in the unity of the Berkeleian philosophy. There were not two Berkeleys, at any rate during the period that matters, from 1710 to 1713 inclusive, the period during which he published his full philosophy. My first quotation on existence in the mind was from the opening of the *Principles*, my last was from the closing pages of the *Three Dialogues*, and the two quotations are in complete agreement. Over that period, about existence in the mind there is not a shadow of turning. I am prepared to admit a marked change of view before that period began,[18] a change which enhances the significance of his final decision. Berkeley had faced the issue; he had hesitated and deliberated; he had toyed with subjectivism, and had learned to distinguish *in the mind* from *of the mind*. When he was making the opening entries in the *Commonplace Book*, he did, I think, entertain the view that existence in the mind is mental existence; but the later entries tell a different story,[19] and before he finished the *Commonplace Book* and months before the *Principles* went to the press, his monism had given place to dualism, and the way of *mode* was replaced by the way of *idea*.

Let me summarise the conclusions of this article. Berkeley's key phrase has three shades of meaning, negative, psychological, and metaphysical. His *in the mind* may mean, (1) not in matter, (2) perceived by the human mind, or (3) perceived by the divine mind only. No hard and fast line can be drawn between these meanings; the reader must go by the context. In many passages the assertion of existence in the mind is, primarily, a denial of the existence of matter, and the distinction between mind human and mind divine does not arise; but in some passages the distinction becomes of cardinal importance. A sensible object, actually being perceived by you or me, is actually in the mind of man; but a sensible object, strictly so called, *i.e.*, one not being actually perceived by you, me, or other finite mind, exists, Berkeley teaches, in the mind of God, and in the mind of God alone.

These three shades of meaning correspond to Berkeley's three philosophical interests. He needed a flexible term for his varied tasks. First he was the controversialist, denying matter, 'the founder of a sect called the Immaterial-

[18] See my *Development within Berkeley's Commonplace Book*, MIND, Vol. XLIX, N.S., No. 193.
[19] See especially No. 24, 'Nothing properly but persons, *i.e.*, conscious things do exist, all other things are not so much existences as manners of ye existence of persons'. With which contrast No. 434, 'Impossible anything Besides that which thinks and is thought on should exist', also No. 820.

ists',[20] and he said *in the mind* meaning *not in matter*, as poets say *in heaven* meaning *not on earth*. Secondly, he was the psychologist, author of a new theory of vision; he believed in immediacy and direct awareness; he believed that what he saw, he saw, and not another thing or pale copy; and he expressed that belief by saying that the thing sensed was in his mind and not elsewhere. Thirdly, he was the metaphysician seeking ultimate answers to ultimate questions. He wanted to fathom the distinction between the perceived and the perceivable, between man's grasp and man's reach; he wanted to know the cause of change and the principles of human knowledge. He found the final solution of his problems in 'the vision of all things in God', and therefore existence in the mind, in Berkeley's last analysis, is existence in Him 'in whom we live and move and have our being'.[21]

[20] Swift to Lord Carteret, 3rd Sept., 1724.
[21] It is so stated in *Hyl.*, p. 453.

THE MIND AND ITS IDEAS: SOME PROBLEMS IN THE INTERPRETATION OF BERKELEY

S. A. GRAVE

The problems of interpretation with which I shall be concerned are set by what Berkeley says (1) about the relation of ideas to the mind, (2) about the mind itself.

I

The mind and its ideas, Berkeley states, are "entirely distinct."[1] This, I think, is the basic text for the unparadoxical Berkeley presented by Professor A. A. Luce; it states, at any rate, a position presupposed by this Berkeley's other opinions. He still maintains, of course, that physical things are "collections of ideas" and that ideas are "in the mind." But what does "in the mind" mean? It will mean something consistent with the entire distinction of ideas from the mind. "My meaning," Berkeley says, "is only that the mind comprehends or perceives them. . . ."[2] By "in the mind," Luce says, Berkeley means (with some colouring according to its context) "in direct

From the *Australasian Journal of Philosophy*, Vol. 42 (1964). Reprinted by permission of the author and the *Australasian Journal of Philosophy*. The paper has been revised for this volume.
[1] *The Principles of Human Knowledge*, § 2. Cf. § 89 ("entirely distinct and heterogeneous"). All quotations from Berkeley are taken from the edition of his *Works* by A. A. Luce and T. E. Jessop (Nelson, 1948–57). Section references only are given for the *Principles*.
[2] *Three Dialogues between Hylas and Philonous*, III (*Works*, vol. 2, p. 250). Cf. *Principles*, § 2.

The Mind and Its Ideas

cognitive relation to the mind."[3] There is nothing in this relationship which anchors the being of ideas to their being perceived by anyone in particular rather than by someone else. The things they constitute are therefore freed from dependence on any of us, being denied merely an existence "exterior" to all minds. Different perceivers can perceive the same things, which, in our absence, are sustained in existence as objects of God's never-failing "perception."

Berkeley has supplied all the materials for this unparadoxical Berkeley, whose doctrine is indeed so little extraordinary that, apart from making all agency volitional, it differs only in queer expression from the assertions of ordinary theism. The physical world has no existence independently of God. But this is equally true of finite minds. The dependence of every physical thing on being perceived subsides, when no perceiver is indispensable except God, into the dependence of everything on God.

Shortly after declaring the mind and its ideas to be entirely distinct, Berkeley asks of "the things we see and feel": "what are they but so many sensations, notions, ideas or impressions on the sense; and is it possible to separate, even in thought, any of these from perception?" And he answers: "For my part I might as easily divide a thing from it self."[4] The identity of an idea with the perception of it welds ideas to individual perceivers, with the following consequences.[5] The "same idea which is in my mind, cannot be in yours"—as Berkeley's Hylas says;[6] since things are collections of ideas, you and I therefore never perceive the self-same thing. The things each of us perceives have an intermittent existence with the intermit-

[3] "Berkeley's Existence in the Mind," reprinted in this volume (pp. 284–95 above), p. 286.
[4] *Principles*, § 5. Cf. "wherein . . . does the perception of white differ from white?" (*Philosophical Commentaries*, No. 585, Works, vol. 1, p. 73).
[5] As we shall see later on, there are devices which will enable a philosopher to hold the principle from which these consequences are derived and to emancipate himself verbally from them.
[6] *Three Dialogues*, III (Works, vol. 2, p. 247).

tency of our perception and no existence before our perception of them or after this has ceased. The possibility of a physical world to which God's "perception" is necessary and all other perception indifferent, is quite ruled out.

We have, then, as regards the perceptual access of different individuals to the same object, and as regards the conditions under which physical things exist, two sets of opinions, both of which might very plausibly be ascribed to Berkeley on the basis of what he asserts or implies. We shall be asking presently whether Berkeley inconsistently held both sets of opinions; if not, which of them he really held, and how the illusory presence of the other is to be explained.

Corresponding to these two sets of opinions are the two principles which I am calling, respectively, the "distinction" and "identity" principles. The "distinction-principle" would permit the unparadoxical opinions; the "identity-principle," itself paradoxical, would require the paradoxical opinions. Nothing would be more valuable in Berkeleian commentary than a reconciliation of these principles, an interpretation of Berkeley's words about the entire distinction of minds and ideas, which would show that he had a meaning for them consistent with what he says about the identity of an idea and its perception. I regret having no suggestions to offer. The positions seem to me quite irreconcilable, and I think Berkeley was driven into them by two conflicting desires: one, to oblige men to see that if there were no minds there would be nothing at all; the other, to meet the demands of common sense.

"Mem: To be eternally banishing Metaphisics &c & recalling Men to Common Sense," Berkeley wrote in his Note Books.[7] He will not allow, of course, that his own metaphysical enterprise runs into difficulties with common sense; he thinks he can always secure the non-resistance of common sense when he cannot have its aid. But good relations with common sense require that the objects of sight, touch, hearing, etc. be kept distinct from the mind. An entry in the Note Books reads fairly plainly as giving

[7] *Philosophical Commentaries*, No. 751 (*Works*, vol. 1, p. 91).

The Mind and Its Ideas 299

the necessary assurance: "I will grant you that extension, Colour etc. may be said to be without the Mind in a double respect i.e. as independent of our Will & as distinct from the Mind."[8]

I have suggested that a concern for common sense demanded from Berkeley the distinction-principle.[9] His metaphysical enterprise could not do without the identity-principle. Why do physical things have to be perceived in order to exist? The distinction-principle, which would counter any answer, has dropped out of sight when the question is raised. Berkeley's sustained effort to prove that physical things have no being unperceived, is to be found in arguments designed to reduce physical things to sensible things, sensible things to arrangements of sensible qualities, sensible qualities to sensations or ideas, in which what one is aware of can no more be separated from one's awareness of it than a thing can be detached from itself.

Let us now remind ourselves of the consequences of the identity-principle. It requires each of us as different perceivers to perceive different things. It prohibits the things that each of us perceives from existing before our perception of them and imposes on them an intermittent existence with the intermittency of our perception. It rules out the possibility of a physical world sustained by God alone. Some sense of Berkeley's commitment to these consequences rarely escapes his readers, but though he occasionally gives them oblique expression, he does not avow them; on the contrary, he appears repeatedly, in explicit words or by implication, to represent them as misunderstandings of his position; the opinions that he appears to declare are the unparadoxical ones that the

[8] *Philosophical Commentaries*, No. 882 (p. 104).
[9] The principle crystallizes also the extreme dualism of Berkeley's contrast between the properties of a physical thing and those belonging to a mind: minds and physical things are "entirely distinct and heterogeneous." Common sense, one can safely say, would not endorse a contrast which gave minds a monopoly of "power or agency," nor would it go along with what is presumably Berkeley's opinion that ideas of the imagination are as distinct from the mind as things that are seen and handled.

distinction-principle would sanction. Thus there appear to be two Berkeleys in Berkeley, one of them—discernible largely by inference and interpretation—conforming to the prescriptions of the identity-principle, the other—very visible—availing himself of the permissions of the distinction-principle. The first principle, it might be suggested, would operate in the construction of Berkeley's theory, the second in its defence against commonsense objections.

I shall try to show that these appearances are altogether deceptive: that Berkeley never repudiated any of the consequences of the identity-principle; that the distinction-principle is in complete abeyance when the question is asked whether the perception of different individuals can have a common object, and when issues are raised as to the conditions under which physical things exist; that the illusion of two conflicting sets of opinions is generated by the expression of paradoxical opinions in unparadoxical language.

Berkeley argues in the Third Dialogue[10] that he maintains nothing that would prevent us from saying that different persons are perceiving the same thing, whenever this is what we would ordinarily say: the word "same" is applied "where no distinction or variety is perceived," and he is not altering anyone's "perceptions."

> Let us suppose several men together, all endued with the same faculties, and consequently affected in like sort by their senses, and who had yet never known the use of language; they would without question agree in their perceptions. Though perhaps, when they came to the use of speech, some regarding the uniformness of what was perceived, might call it the *same* thing: others especially regarding the diversity of persons who perceived, might choose the denomination of different things. But who sees not that all the dispute is about a word? to wit, whether what is perceived by different persons, may yet have the term *same* applied to it?

These imaginary men suddenly endowed with speech are presented as speaking like ordinary men; the point of

[10] *Works*, vol. 2, pp. 247-48.

The Mind and Its Ideas

the conjectural experiment is that what they say might naturally be said by anybody in their situation. The first group say: "We all perceive the same thing." (That they are really no ordinary men is indicated by the fact that, as Berkeley has it, this is only what they *might* say.) The second group are astonishingly disposed to affirm that different things are perceived—not because of any feature of what is perceived, for they are all "affected in like sort by their senses," but because there are several perceivers. This consideration, together with Berkeley's comment that "same" or "different" here is a matter of words in the choice of which one can please oneself, shows how what the first group say is to be construed: different persons can perceive the same thing in the sense in which they can have the same headache (or the same idea, in the ordinary sense of "idea"). Neither group is composed of ordinary men: the second consists of Berkeleians voicing paradox, the first of Berkeleians concealing it.[11]

Berkeley concludes the discussion of his problem with a casual gesture towards divine "archetypes," not themselves perceived by us but corresponding to the objects of our perception. He points out that the objection that "no two see the same thing" bears no more hardly on him than on the philosophers who hold the kind of theory Locke held. They acknowledge that we immediately perceive only our own ideas. "But they suppose," he has Hylas say, "an external archetype, to which referring their several ideas, they may truly be said to perceive the same thing." Hylas is assured that the "principles" he is being invited to accept also allow the supposition that our ideas have external archetypes. External to our minds, located in the divine

[11] It is perhaps worth mentioning that Berkeley could have avoided this paradoxical account of the sense in which different perceivers can perceive the *same* thing by attempting a more complicatedly paradoxical reconstruction of the notion of a *thing*. He could have set about representing a thing as a collection of systematically related ideas not in X's mind alone, or in Y's, but in the minds of any number of perceivers. X's ideas would indeed never be objects to Y but the things they partially constitute, the things which Y's ideas also partially constitute, would be objects to both.

mind, they serve "all the ends of identity" as effectively as if they had absolute externality. A poor recommendation, as Hylas must have known unless he had quite forgotten the close of the First Dialogue.

Samuel Johnson, Berkeley's American correspondent, wrote to him raising difficulties about a number of matters and wanting to be sure that he always had Berkeley's meaning. On the basis of deliberate remarks which we shall be considering presently, he had understood Berkeley to be assigning a doubt-aspect existence to things, giving them an archetypal being as ideas in the divine mind, and an ectypal being in finite minds as ideas "copying" or "imaging" or "resembling" in some way these exemplars. "When therefore," Johnson wrote, "several people are said to see the same tree or star, etc. . . . it is (if I understand you) *unum et idem in archetypo,* tho' *multiplex et diversum in ectypo,* for it is as evident that your idea is not mine nor mine yours when we say we both look on the same tree, as that you are not I, nor I you."[12] Berkeley's reply to Johnson is silent on this point.

How are we to understand Berkeley's assurances that our perception does not affect the existence of things? We have to go on hints and obscure statements, but there is enough to let it be seen that Berkeley is not repudiating any of the consequences of the identity-principle, that he is speaking with the vulgar, however reluctantly he may be only speaking with them. Several ways of thinking are open to the learned in this matter, as they are when different perceivers are said to perceive the same thing. One of them, which reappears fugitively but without disguise in the *Principles,* is indicated in the Note Books, with Berkeley's reminder to himself of the need for undisturbing words:

> Mem: to allow existence to colours in the dark, persons not thinking &c but not an absolute actual existence. 'Tis prudent to correct mens mistakes without altering their language. This makes truth glide into their souls insensibly.

[12] Second letter to Berkeley (Berkeley's *Works,* vol. 2, p. 286).

Colours in ye dark do exist really *i.e.* were there light or as soon as light comes we shall see them provided we open our eyes. & that whether we will or no.[13]

There is another suggestion in the Note Books. It is directly applicable to Berkeley's insistence that things have an existence "exterior" to our minds in the mind of God: "+ Bodies etc do exist even w^n not perceiv'd they being powers in the active Being."[14] One has to avoid propping up an interpretation of Berkeley with anything doubtful from his Note Books, anything that he could plausibly be regarded as having repudiated during their composition. Entries inconsistent with later entries come into this class, along with those bearing the + sign which Berkeley might have intended as a cancelling mark.[15] Most of the entries reducing, or appearing to reduce, unperceived objects to powers carry the + sign, but a self-admonition towards the end of the Note Books removes any disqualification on this score: "Not to mention the Combinations of Powers but to say the things the effects themselves to really exist even w^n not actually perceiv'd but still with relation to perception."[16] The most natural construction to be put on this remark would seem to be that Berkeley has decided against revealing an opinion which he has not rejected.[17]

We are to say that the things we perceive exist independently of our perception of them. The suggestions just mentioned provide possibilities of meaning for our words when we are speaking not only with strict propriety but

[13] *Philosophical Commentaries*, Nos. 185, 185a (*Works*, vol. 1, p. 25). Cf. *Principles*, § 3 (". . . I should say it existed, meaning thereby that if I was in my study I might perceive it . . ."); § 58.
[14] *Philosophical Commentaries*, No. 52 (*Works*, vol. 1, p. 13). Cf. Nos. 41, 282, 293, 293a (pp. 11, 35, 36).
[15] See Luce's introduction to his *editio diplomatica* of the *Philosophical Commentaries* (Nelson, 1944), pp. xxv–xxvi.
[16] *Philosophical Commentaries*, No. 802 (*Works*, vol. 1, p. 96).
[17] In *Three Dialogues*, III (*Works*, vol. 2, pp. 239–40) it is argued that there must be both powers and ideas in the being which "imparts" ideas to us. As always, the relation between the ideas pre-existing in God and the ideas imparted is left wholly obscure.

also according to the truth of things. Berkeley suggests yet a further possibility: the things we perceive exist independently of us in their divine archetypes. He cannot, of course, allow us to perceive the divine archetypes themselves. To suppose that anything we perceive is identical with anything in God is to corporealize deity. And so he says, repudiating Malebranche's "notion" of our *"seeing all things in God"*: "I do not understand how our ideas, which are things altogether passive and inert, can be the essence, or any part (or like any part) of the essence or substance of God, who is an impassive, indivisible, purely active being."[18] Berkeley goes on to state what he declares to be his own position:

> Take here in brief my meaning. It is evident that the things I perceive are my own ideas, and that no idea can exist unless it be in a mind. Nor is it less plain that these ideas or things by me perceived, either themselves or their archetypes, exist independently of my mind, since I know myself not to be their author, it being out of my power to determine at pleasure, what particular ideas I shall be affected with upon opening my eyes or ears. They must therefore exist in some other mind, whose will it is they should be exhibited to me.

It is an odd statement. The things one perceives are one's own ideas, Berkeley says. We draw the inferences: therefore no one else's (in virtue of the identity-principle, necessarily no one else's), therefore with no existence independently of their perceiver's mind. These things, Berkeley says, or their archetypes (as though it didn't matter which) exist independently of their perceiver in some other mind. We do not take the alternatives seriously: it is of course the archetypes which exist in another mind, and are "exhibited" when things are perceived. Whatever this word might mean, it cannot, consistently with Berkeley's criticism of Malebranche, mean "exhibited."

We perceive objects of sense; the divine archetypes can-

[18] *Three Dialogues*, II (*Works*, vol. 2, pp. 213–14). Cf. *Principles*, § 148.

The Mind and Its Ideas 305

not become objects to our senses. What we perceive was brought into existence: the divine archetypes are eternal and uncreated. Arguing in the Third Dialogue for the compatibility of his opinions with the scriptural account of creation,[19] Berkeley sets up a "two-fold state of things, the one ectypal or natural . . . created in time," "the other archetypal and eternal." This, he implies, will give everybody all he can intelligibly want. We are bound in theological orthodoxy to assert that "all objects are eternally known by God." Berkeley asserts it, with the remark that to say that they have "an eternal existence" in the mind of God, is to state the same truth. According to the doctrine of creation, the things that make up the physical world have a beginning. And according to Berkeley also, they have a beginning—relatively to finite perceivers, for "nothing is new, or begins to be, in respect of the mind of God."[20] The creative decree, by which the physical world was brought into existence, made "perceptible" to creatures what was previously hidden in deity.

Berkeley has Hylas put the objection that he is allowing things which in the Mosaic history of creation precede man, "no actuality of absolute existence" but only "hypothetical being," before there were men to perceive them. There is no inconsistency between his opinions and the Mosaic history, Berkeley replies: these things might have existed before men in the minds of "other created intelligences."

> I say farther, in case we conceive the Creation, as we should at this time a parcel of plants or vegetables of all sorts, produced by an invisible power, in a desert where no body was present: that this way of explaining or conceiving it, is consistent with my principles, since they deprive you of nothing, either sensible or imaginable: that it exactly suits with the common,

[19] *Works*, vol. 2, pp. 250–56. Cf. Letter to Percival, *Works*, vol. 8, pp. 37–38.
[20] The theological doctrine which Berkeley puts into these ambiguous words maintains that God's knowledge of His creatures does not begin with the (absolute) beginning of their existence.

natural, undebauched notions of mankind . . . I say moreover, that in this naked conception of things, divested of words, there will not be found any notion of what you call the *actuality of absolute existence.*

Berkeley's contention here seems to be this: for men of plain, uncorrupted common sense, a thing exists if it could be perceived by anyone suitably circumstanced; they have no use for, and find no meaning in, talk about "actuality of absolute existence."

To sum up. Berkeley did not hold two sets of conflicting opinions, governed by the identity and distinction principles respectively; he held the opinions prescribed by the identity-principle. He would like to have been, and was willing to be thought, a theistic realist; he was a theistic phenomenalist. These are the metaphysical facts as Berkeley sees them: without God nothing at all would exist; without creatures capable of perception nothing physical would exist, for physical things are constituted by ideas of sense which God "excites" in the mind or "imprints" upon it; without X nothing that X perceives would exist, for the things he perceives are constituted by his ideas. But there are correspondences between X's ideas and Y's, and between their ideas and the divine archetypal ideas. The metaphysical facts have no implications for our actual or possible experience. Accordingly, Berkeley thought, acceptance of his opinions called for no paradoxical language: we are to continue to say in the ordinarily appropriate circumstances that different perceivers perceive the same thing, and to speak in a manner that implies that things are unaffected by our perception of them.

II

I now turn to problems of interpretation that arise in connection with some features of Berkeley's conception of the mind.

Besides our ideas, there is "something which knows or perceives them, and exercises divers operations, as willing, imagining, remembering about them. This perceiving,

The Mind and Its Ideas

active being is what I call *mind, spirit, soul* or *my self*."[21] "A spirit is one simple, undivided, active being: as it perceives ideas, it is called the *understanding*, and as it produces or otherwise operates about them, it is called the *will*."[22] We shall be particularly concerned with the elucidation of these statements which represent the mind as a substance, as something, that is, to which its actions and passions belong, which is single, simple, and enduring, while they are various and transitory. The substantival mind (the soul, the self) is not, for Berkeley, an occult entity whose existence is merely a suppositional necessity. It is not an unknowable substratum of experience but something of which one is, or can become, "conscious." The word "substance" does not appear in either of the passages before us. If Berkeley rather tended to avoid speaking of the mind as a substance—except, curiously, in relation to ideas which he did *not* think of as modifications of a substance—it was perhaps because the word with its Lockean associations so strongly suggested an unknowable substratum.

Berkeley asserts that the qualities which constitute physical things, deprived of the impossible "support" of material substance, have instead the "support" of immaterial substance, that the mind is their "subject" or "substratum."[23] All the familiar metaphysical words, and all their familiar implications are cancelled or radically changed. "It is therefore evident there can be no *substratum* of those qualities but spirit, in which they exist . . ." The distinction-principle, usually inert when the dependence of ideas upon the mind is in question, now controls Berkeley's meaning and he completes his sentence with the words "not by way of mode or property, but as a thing perceived in that which perceives it."[24] Not by way of mode or property, because, as he explains, if such were the manner of their presence, extension, colour, etc., would

[21] *Principles*, § 2.   [22] *Principles*, § 27.
[23] *Principles*, §§ 89, 91; *Three Dialogues*, III (*Works*, vol. 2, pp. 233, 237).
[24] *Three Dialogues*, III (*Works*, vol. 2, p. 237).

be predicable of the mind;[25] the mind could be red and round.

Now if we look for the reasons Berkeley gives for holding the mind to be a substance, I think that, apart from one short argument and the vague and perfunctory experiential claim that he is "conscious" of his being, that he knows it by "a reflex act," we shall not find anything other than fragmentary expression of the need for a "support" or "subject" of ideas. And we have just seen that, for Berkeley, the mind does not stand to its ideas as a substance to its modes and qualities; that to say that the mind supports its ideas or is their subject is merely to say that ideas, in order to exist, must be perceived. It seems so far an open question whether ideas must be perceived by what has the monadic unity of a substance, or whether it is sufficient that they occur as items in a "congeries of perceptions." We might profitably at this point consider Berkeley's short argument.

Your denial of material substance, Hylas says to Philonous, should commit you, in consistency, to the opinion that you yourself are "only a system of floating ideas, without any substance to support them". The answer he gets is this: material substance cannot be perceived, is not even conceivable. But "I know or am conscious of my own being . . . I know that I, one and the same self, perceive both colours and sounds: that a colour cannot perceive a sound, nor a sound a colour: that I am therefore one individual principle, distinct from colour and sound; and, for the same reason, from all other sensible things and inert ideas."[26]

Though Berkeley speaks metaphorically[27] when he asserts that ideas and the things they constitute have their "support," "subject" "substratum" in the mind, he is clearly not dealing in metaphor in this argument for the

[25] *Principles*, § 49.
[26] *Three Dialogues*, III (*Works*, vol. 2, pp. 233–34).
[27] Cf. C. M. Turbayne, "Berkeley's Two Concepts of Mind," *Philosophy and Phenomenological Research*, September 1959 and June 1962. Turbayne regards the substantialist language in Berkeley's account of the mind as metaphorical throughout.

The Mind and Its Ideas

mind or self as a substance, as something unifying its experience itself an uncompounded unity, not a "system" but "one individual principle." And the literal truth of a substantialist account of the mind seems to be presupposed in his argument for the immortality of the soul: "indivisible, incorporeal . . . an active, simple, uncompounded substance," the soul is invulnerable to the decay and dissolution which affects bodies and is therefore immortal by nature.[28]

Once again, however, we have to consider the possibility of a divided, or of a disguised, Berkeley. The functions of the mind as substance are certainly more abridged for Berkeley than is often supposed: he does not regard the mind's ideas as its "accidents." But the actions and passions of the mind must belong to it as accidents belong to their substance, if the word "substance" ever retains its standard meaning as a metaphysical term when he applies it to the mind. A characterization of the mind which is to be found in both the *Principles,* and the *Three Dialogues,* some entries in the Note Books, and an evasiveness in the correspondence with Johnson suggest that he might be merely retaining the word while holding a conception of the mind which would properly be called antisubstantialist.

". . . all the unthinking objects of the mind agree, in that they are entirely passive, and their existence consists only in being perceived: whereas a soul or spirit is an active being, whose existence consists not in being perceived, but in perceiving ideas and thinking."[29] How are we meant to understand the parallel asserted here between the relation of an object to its being perceived and the relation of a subject to its perceiving? When *esse est percipi* is construed according to the identity-principle, there is not both the object *and* its being perceived—these are one and the same. Are we to construe *esse est percipere*

[28] *Principles,* § 141.
[29] *Principles,* § 139. Cf. § 71 (". . . the question is no longer concerning the existence of a thing distinct from *spirit* and *idea,* from perceiving and being perceived."); § 81; *Three Dialogues,* II (*Works,* vol. 2, p. 223).

similarly; or are we to apply an equivalent of the distinction-principle and take Berkeley to mean not that "perceiving ideas and thinking" constitute the being of their subject, but that their subject has no inert being, that it is always perceiving and thinking?

If we turn to the Note Books for illumination, we find Berkeley in a late entry toppling the substantival pronoun into the verb: "Substance of a Spirit is that it acts, causes, wills, operates, or if you please (to avoid the quibble y^t may be made on ye word it) to act, cause, will, operate . . ."[30] On the other hand, the set of "Humian" entries (" . . . Mind is a congeries of Perceptions . . .")[31] is marked with the + sign. And there are several late entries which more or less clearly assert the mind to have a being not constituted by its willing and perceiving. This is the most explicit of them: "I must not Mention the Understanding as a faculty or part of the Mind, I must include Understanding & Will etc in the word Spirit by wch I mean all that is active. I must not say that the Understanding differs not from the particular Ideas, or the Will from particular Volitions."[32] Two entries occurring well on in the Note Books present a specific problem of interpretation:

> Certainly the mind always & constantly thinks & we know this too In Sleep & trances the mind exists not there is no time no succession of Ideas.
>
> To say the mind exists without thinking is a Contradiction, nonsense, nothing.[33]

Is it a contradiction to suppose that the mind exists without "thinking" because the mind *is* its thinking, or because to exist it must persist through time, and there is no time without the succession of ideas in thinking? When Berkeley asserts in *Principles*, § 98, "that the soul always thinks," the reason given is one which connects the "dura-

---

[30] *Philosophical Commentaries*, No. 829 (*Works*, vol. 1, p. 99).
[31] Nos. 579–81 (p. 72).
[32] No. 848 (p. 101). Cf. Nos. 849 (p. 101), 871 (p. 103).
[33] Nos. 651, 652 (pp. 79–80).

tion" of finite minds with this succession, and we are not helped towards an understanding of *esse est percipere* when Berkeley adds that anyone attempting to "abstract the *existence* of a spirit from its *cogitation*" will find it a difficult task.

If "*esse* be only *percipere*," Samuel Johnson wrote to Berkeley, he could not understand how Berkeley framed the argument for the immortality of the soul. And wouldn't the soul have more being at one time and less at another, corresponding to variations in the intensity of its "thinking"? And "if *esse* be only *percipere*, upon what is our consciousness founded? I perceived yesterday, and I perceive now, but last night between my yesterday's and today's perception there has been an intermission when I perceived nothing. It seems to me there must be some principle common to these perceptions, whose *esse* don't depend upon them, but in which they are, as it were, connected, and on which they depend, whereby I am and continue conscious of them."[34] Since "any degree of perception" is "sufficient to Existence," Berkeley replied, it does not follow that we have more existence at one time than at another; a thousand yards of snow is not whiter than a yard. He contrasted Locke who "holds an abstract idea of existence; exclusive of perceiving and being perceived" with Descartes who "proceeds upon other principles."[35] He did not mention the argument for the immortality of the soul. He directed Johnson to examine carefully what he had said in various places about abstraction.

What he had said about abstraction does nothing to determine whether or not its "absurdity" is incurred in supposing the soul to be other than its perceptions and volitions, though never without some one or other of these. To try to separate the being of sensible things from

[34] Second letter to Berkeley, Berkeley's *Works*, vol. 2, p. 290. In his earlier letter (ibid. p. 277) Johnson had asked: "Can actions be the *esse* of anything? Can they exist or be exerted without some being who is the agent?" Berkeley gave Johnson no answer to these questions.
[35] Second letter of Berkeley to Johnson (ibid. p. 293).

their being perceived is to attempt an impossible abstraction, but we attempt it also if we try to imagine extension without any of the secondary qualities—though extension is different from these qualities. Yet if Berkeley did hold a substantialist doctrine of the soul, how are we to explain the evasiveness of his replies to Johnson? If he did not, how are we to understand his argument for the immortality of the soul?[36] And how are we to interpret the description of the soul or mind as "an active, simple, uncompounded substance," as "one simple, undivided, active being"?[37]

Esse est percipere, on one interpretation of this formula, resolves the mind into the complexity of its active and passive experience. *Esse est percipi*, intended to define the existence of bodies, has consequences for the mind that are more radical. The ideas of sense which constitute corporeal things have no being unperceived because their being is their being perceived. These ideas, Berkeley explains, are not in the mind "by way of mode"; their presence in that manner would corporealize the mind; that they are "in the mind" means only that they are perceived. If, however, an idea and the perception of an idea are identical, it is impossible for perception to be a modification of the mind. Unless *esse est percipi* is understood according to the distinction-principle, so that being and being perceived are merely (and gratuitously) hyphenated,

---

[36] What is in question are the grounds on which Berkeley infers the immortality of the soul. One of the earliest entries in the Note Books records the opinion that immortality is easily thought of without reference to any metaphysics of the soul: "+ Eternity is onely a train of innumerable ideas. hence the immortality of ye Soul easily conceiv'd. or rather the immortality of the person, y^t of ye soul not being necessary for ought we can see" (*Philosophical Commentaries*, No. 14, *Works*, vol. 1, p. 9).

[37] The statement, "I am therefore one individual principle", which concludes Berkeley's argument against the notion of the self as "only a system of floating ideas", impenetrably disguises his opinion if he held the self to have only the unity of a system. The passage in which the argument occurs was added to the third edition of the *Three Dialogues* which was published in 1734. The correspondence between Johnson and Berkeley falls between September 1729 and March 1730.

The Mind and Its Ideas

perception seems to sheer off from its subject and to collapse into its objects. "Wherein," to repeat Berkeley's question, "does the perception of white differ from white?" If an idea and its perception are held to be identical, and the mind is thought of not as a substance but as a system, a place for perception can be found within this system, but ideas will have to become "part of the mind."[38] It was Berkeley's doctrine that the mind and its ideas are entirely distinct and heterogeneous. Behind some very curious entries in the Note Books lies, at least in part, I think, a sense of the disruptive impact made on the mind by the identification of the *esse* of an idea with its being perceived:

> The soul is the will properly speaking & as it is distinct from Ideas.

> The Spirit the Active thing that wch is Soul & God is the Will alone . . .[39]

One wants if possible a unified Berkeley. The primary aim of this paper is to draw attention to the need for harmonizing interpretations of statements which are fundamental in his philosophy.

[38] Cf. D. M. Armstrong, *Perception and the Physical World* (Routledge & Kegan Paul, 1962), pp. 71–72.
[39] *Philosophical Commentaries*, Nos. 478a, 712 (*Works*, vol. 1, pp. 60, 87). Cf. Nos. 708 (p. 86), 814 (p. 97), 847 (p. 101).

BERKELEY'S SENSATIONALISM AND THE *ESSE EST PERCIPI*-PRINCIPLE

KONRAD MARC-WOGAU

In the following pages I am going to discuss two propositions and an argument of great importance in Berkeley's philosophy. I shall try to state the propositions and the argument as exactly as possible, and to analyze their mutual relations. This seems to me of interest both from a historical and a systematical point of view. The problem is partly in what way the propositions in question and the premisses of the argument are related in Berkeley's own thinking, i.e. in what way he has used them in his own system, and partly in what way they are logically related. These two questions are intimately connected with each other, and I shall begin with some remarks on this connection.

Berkeley undoubtedly belongs to the kind of philosophers who strive to think as consistently as possible, and who also have a pronounced sense of logical consistence and clearness. His train of thinking can be said to be conditioned by the logical relations between the propositions composing it. Now, suppose that a proposition *q* can be shown to follow logically from a proposition *p*, and suppose further that Berkeley takes *p* as a premiss from which follows *q*, then the assumption is reasonable that Berkeley's belief in *q*, at least in part, is determined by his belief in *p*. (I say "at least in part", since also other considerations and, perhaps, even feelings may have been relevant in this connection.)

The situation is, however, very seldom so simple. Most

From *Theoria*, Vol. XXIII (1957). Reprinted, with minor corrections, by permission of the author.

frequently a proposition *q*, which a philosopher of Berkeley's type vindicates, and which he deduces from a proposition *p*, does not follow logically from *p* only, but from *p* and other premisses which are not explicitly mentioned. Berkeley did not always endeavour to state explicitly all the premisses of his arguments. In the cases where an argumentation is such that it will be conclusive only if several not mentioned premisses have to be added, one is therefore faced with an awkward problem. Then the question is admissible: did Berkeley believe that the proposition *q* follows from the proposition *p* only, without the aid of other premisses, or did he mean that other premisses need not be mentioned explicitly? In other words: is his argumentation a false conclusion or is it a correct conclusion with one or several tacitly implied premisses? As a rule Berkeley's utterances do not tell how these questions are to be answered. The choice of either alternative depends on one's more or less favourable attitude towards Berkeley. A rigorous critic may perhaps deny the argumentation to be conclusive, if account is to be taken to the explicitly mentioned premisses only, and consider that as an objection to Berkeley; a more favourably disposed interpreter, on the other hand, will argue that Berkeley, since the explicitly mentioned premisses are not sufficient to make his argumentation conclusive, must have presupposed one or several premisses without mentioning them explicitly. It seems to me that the last-mentioned attitude ought to be applied by a historian of philosophy to the utmost limit, if his interpretation shall be of any interest. Surely, the claim of consistency must not be exaggerated. Some degree of obscurity and inconsistence can be expected even in philosophers who endeavour to think consistently. A lack of clearness which we discover in a philosopher, e.g. from the beginning of the eighteenth century, can easily be explained by the fact that some important distinctions, which are commonplace to us, had not been made at that time. The progress in philosophy consists indeed, to a large extent, in the introduction of new, previously neglected distinctions. Berkeley, e.g., did not ask whether a statement is analytic or synthetic, whether it is logically necessary or merely factual. It is therefore not astonishing that he can use a thesis sometimes as a logically necessary, sometimes as a factually true proposition. Also inconsistencies of another kind can be found. Different theses of a system may appear more or less evident to the philosopher, and he does not, perhaps, pay attention to the fact that some consequences of one thesis contradict some consequences of another. The detection by a critic of such inconsistencies does not contradict the assumption that the philosopher tried to think as consistently as possible. The situation is, however, quite different, when one has to do with a limited argumentation, which appears inconsistent in spite of the fact that the philosopher assumed it as consistent. My discussion aims only at such cases. Even then the claim of consistency must, certainly, not be exaggerated. Sometimes, when explaining an argumentation, it may be reasonable to speak about a false conclusion, an inconsistency, or a gap in a chain of proof. Yet, as a rule it is preferable to avoid such a kind of explanation, provided the argumentation can, without much construction, be explained by the introduction of tacitly presupposed premisses.

The historian of philosophy has then to find these presupposed premisses. This is, however, connected with great difficulties as every argumentation, however unreasonable it may seem from the beginning, can be made conclusive, if it is allowed to add a sufficient number of presupposed premisses. The method of making an argumentation conclusive by supplying it with tacitly presupposed premisses has, therefore, only a very restricted application. The decision of the question whether, in a given case, any unmentioned premiss may reasonably be presupposed must be left to the judgment of the historian of philosophy. It is rather difficult to lay down some general guiding rules.

Now, if it is decided to apply the method in question to a given case, another problem presents itself. It is easily seen that an argumentation can be made conclusive by adding different tacitly presupposed premisses or sets of such premisses. None of the different explanations may be

The Esse est percipi-*Principle*

absurd or improbable. In such cases the historian of philosophy has to make a choice between the different available explanations. Also here much depends on his judgment. Sometimes it may suffice to add as a presupposed premiss some trivial proposition which has never been doubted. The explanation may then seem convincing. This, however, is an exceptionally simple situation. In most cases premisses must be added, which are not at all self-evident or generally accepted. Then the choice between the different explanations may be guided by some general considerations. Some of them may be suggested here:

(a) If there are utterances by the philosopher showing him to have believed in a proposition p which can explain an argumentation, then it may seem reasonable to choose p as additional premiss. Objections can, however, be raised against this method. It is not at all sure that p, if unfamiliar to commonsense, may be preferred as a presupposed premiss to a proposition q which expresses a commonsense belief. The situation seems not to be uncommon that a philosopher in many contexts unconsciously starts from commonsense beliefs, although in other contexts he holds quite a different point of view. But suppose that a proposition p does not express what commonsense believes, and clearly contradicts what the philosopher utters in other contexts. Can then p be accepted as a supplementary premiss? By the addition of p as a premiss the argumentation may, perhaps, be made conclusive; but, at the same time by this explanation you impute to the philosopher an inconsistency in another respect. An explanation of this kind may, nevertheless, often appear convincing. The fact that a philosopher, in different parts of his system, starts from different premisses which contradict each other is less astonishing than an inconsistency or a faulty reasoning in the case of a brief, carefully worked out argument. Of course, if it is assumed that the philosopher starts from incompatible premisses in different contexts, the explanation of this inconsistency also is a desideratum. (One argumentation, e.g., may be an inheritance from a period, when the philosopher started from other premisses.)

(b) As a rule it is reasonable to choose the weakest of two propositions both of which, if chosen as supplementary premisses, can make an argumentation conclusive. If p_1 and p_2 are such propositions, and if p_2 involves p_1 plus something more, the explanation by the addition of the premiss p_1 is preferable. Psychologically this rule is perhaps not obvious. In many argumentations we surely start from unnecessarily strong premisses. Yet, it seems more cautious and fairer not to impute to the philosopher an assumption which implies more than is absolutely necessary for the explanation of a given argument.

(c) A premiss is preferable, if it also can explain other argumentations found in the same philosopher.

These remarks on the method of explanation appear perhaps self-evident and uncomplicated, but their application to a given concrete material implies many problems. The situation becomes more complicated when the different principles, suggested here, have to be weighed one against the other. From the following examination of some of Berkeley's theories it will become evident that often one and the same argumentation can be explained in different ways; at least it may be very difficult to see the reason for giving preference to one over the others.

A cornerstone in Berkeley's philosophy is his thesis of the infallibility of sense-perception. We meet it already in Berkeley's *Philosophical Commentaries* (=PC). One ought, he says, to trust the senses as people generally do. It is absurd to put aside the senses (entries 740, 539). In the published writings this idea is taken up with the same decisiveness. What "makes philosophy ridiculous in the eyes of the world" is that philosophers doubt of everything they see, hear, or feel (A *Treatise concerning the Principles of Human Knowledge* [=Pr.], § 88). And with a point directed against Cartesianism, Berkeley reiterates: "That what I see, hear, and feel does exist, . . . I no more doubt than I do of my own being" (Pr. § 40). "Away then with all that scepticism, all those ridiculous philosophical doubts. What a jest is it for a philosopher to question the existence of sensible things, till he has it proved to him from the veracity of God . . . I might as well doubt of my own being, as of the being of those things I actually see and feel" (*Three Dialogues between Hylas and Philonous* [=D.], Works of George Berkeley edited by Luce and Jessop, II 230). And he adds: "That a thing should be really perceived by my senses, and at the same time not really exist, is to me a plain contradiction" (*ibid.*).[1]

This assumption that the object of sense-perception necessarily is real or exists is a basic idea of sensationalism. Certainly, it would be wrong to call Berkeley sensationalist, if sensationalism means the doctrine that all knowledge consists in, or originates from, sense-perception. He assumes, as is well known, a special kind of knowledge which has nothing to do with sense-perception, viz. the knowledge of minds and relations. It is, however, possible to speak about the sensationalistic thesis in Berkeley's philosophy in respect to the above mentioned idea, that every sense-perception is a perception of something real. Berkeley, however, maintains a thesis of considerably wider

[1] Very instructive in this respect are Berkeley's brief remarks at the end of § 22 of the *Introduction to Pr.* (II 39), where he discusses the possibility of mistake in respect to what is directly perceived. Like many adherents of the theory of sense-data in modern time Berkeley maintains that only verbal errors are possible in respect to the objects of perceiving. "So long as I confine my thoughts to my own ideas divested of words"—he says—"I do not see how I can easily be mistaken." He mentions different possibilities. (a) "The objects I consider, I clearly and adequately know" (cf. the doctrine that a sense-datum cannot be otherwise than it is perceived to be); (b) "I cannot be deceived in thinking I have an idea which I have not"; Berkeley thus rejects here the possibility of the situation that one believes to perceive something, e.g. to hear a sound, though in reality he has no such perception (cf. my book *Theorie der Sinnesdaten*, p. 428 f.); (c) every judgment about my ideas (the directly perceived), both a judgment in which I compare two ideas and a judgment in which I analyze a given compound idea, is based upon my attention to the content of my consciousness, i.e. is "knowledge by acquaintance", a knowledge which is founded upon direct awareness, and therefore does not contain a mistake.

scope. The infallibility of sense-perception is due to the fact that perception is a direct awareness of the object, i.e. an awareness which does not imply any inference or associative transition from something to something else. Yet, according to Berkeley, all kind of perceiving, not only the perceiving of ideas of sense, has this nature of direct awareness. Also the perceiving of ideas of imagination and memory is direct awareness in this sense, and therefore free from mistake.[2] Thus the thesis that the perceived is undoubtedly real or exists is applicable not only to the objects of sense-experience, but to the objects of every kind of perceiving. I shall call this thesis the *extended sensationalistic thesis* in Berkeley, and shall express it as a formal implication:

$$(x) \ (x \text{ is perceived} \supset x \text{ exists}) \qquad (1)$$

(Following an abovementioned principle I choose this weaker formulation, although a stronger one, e.g. in the sense of a strict implication, is quite possible; it is very difficult to know exactly, how much Berkeley attaches to his own formulations. This is, however, irrelevant to the following argumentation.)

Another basic thesis in Berkeley's philosophy is the *esse est percipi*-principle. It holds true of all ideas that their *esse* is their *percipi*. In *PC* this thesis is introduced as a new principle of great importance. "This I think wholly new. I am sure 'tis new to me", Berkeley writes in entry 491. And in his published books he repeatedly returns to the principle in question, and uses it as an important premiss in many argumentations.

Though this fundamental principle is referred to and commented in many contexts, it is very difficult to interpret its meaning. The comparison of different utterances gives the impression that Berkeley, without observing it, takes the principle sometimes in one, sometimes in another sense. My first problem is to distinguish some of the possible senses of the principle between which the inter-

---

[2] Cf. *D*., II 238: "it being a manifest contradiction to suppose he should err in respect of that", i.e. what he perceives immediately.

The Esse est percipi-*Principle*

preter has to choose. I ask first what "*esse*", then what "*percipi*", and lastly what "*est*" can mean in the phrase "*esse est percipi*".

1. Berkeley translates the word "*esse*" sometimes by "being", but most often by "existence" (or "reality"). In *Pr.* § 6 he says that the "being" of the sensible things "is to be perceived or known". In § 3 and often elsewhere, in commenting the principle, he asks, on the other hand, what is meant "by the term exist when applied to sensible things". This different translation may correspond to a difference in respect to what Berkeley intends to say. It is well known that the term "*esse*" has been used in mediaeval philosophy both for "*essentia*" and "*existentia*". If "*esse*" is taken in the former sense, the principle could be interpreted as a statement to the effect that the property to be perceived is essential to ideas or sensible things or is implied by their very being, i.e. that it belongs to the notion *idea* or *sensible thing*.[3] If, on the other hand, "*esse*" is taken in the latter sense, the principle must mean that the existence of ideas, which is a property not belonging to the notion *idea,* involves their being perceived. Between these two interpretations there exists a fundamental difference. According to the former the principle is an analytic statement the truth of which follows from Berkeley's definition of the terms "idea" and "sensible thing" as object of perceiving. The principle means that the property of being perceived necessarily belongs to the idea, in virtue of this definition. According to the latter interpretation of "*esse*" the principle may be non-analytic. It only states that there is, in respect to ideas, an intimate relation between their property to exist and their property to be perceived, a relation which does not necessarily follow from the meaning of the word "idea".

Berkeley considered his *esse est percipi*-principle as a

[3] Cf. e.g. *Pr.* § 25, where Berkeley expresses the doctrine that passiveness is essential to ideas by the words: "the very being of an idea implies passiveness". In the same manner, but using now the word "existence", he says in the third Dialogue (II 236) "every unthinking being is necessarily, and from the very nature of its existence, perceived by some mind".

demonstrable principle. "Newton begs his principle, I demonstrate mine", he says in *PC*, entry 407. It could then be concluded that the principle is not meant as an analytic statement in the given sense. There seems to be stronger evidence for the interpretation of the principle as a statement the truth of which does not follow from the definition of the term "idea". But it is, of course, also possible that Berkeley, without observing it, gave his principle different senses in different contexts.

Some evidence for the interpretation of the principle as an analytic statement in the given sense can be found at the beginning of the first dialogue. It is worth while to examine Philonous' argumentation in these pages. Here the discussion turns about the meaning of the term "sensible thing"; Philonous introduces the definition: "sensible things are those only which are immediately perceived". He then demonstrates that only sensible qualities, like light, colour, shape, sound, etc., are sensible things. In spite of the fact that he nowhere makes an explicit statement to this effect, his conclusion seems to be that the property of a sensible quality to be immediately perceived follows from the definition of the term "sensible thing".[4] Thus the statement that the quality of being immediately perceived is indispensable to a sensible thing seems to be analytic. It must, however, be observed that this argumentation is based upon a wholly unwarranted transition from the definition of "sensible things" as those objects, "which *can* be perceived immediately by sense" to the definition: "sensible things are those only which *are* immediately perceived by sense" (II 174; italics mine). In this context Philonous really shifts from one definition to the other, Hylas not observing the trap. The two definitions are indeed entirely different: that a sensible thing

[4] The last sentence of *Pr.* § 4 may, perhaps, be considered as such a conclusion. "For what are the forementioned objects (i.e. sensible objects) but the things we perceive by sense, and what do we perceive besides our own ideas or sensations; and is it not plainly repugnant that any one of these or any combination of them should exist unperceived?" This repugnance is, Berkeley seems to mean, a consequence of the definition of "sensible things" as things immediately perceived by sense.

The Esse est percipi-*Principle*

must be actually perceived, follows from the latter, but not from the former. Not before the third dialogue (II 234) does Hylas quite legitimately raise the objection: "I grant the existence of a sensible thing consists in being perceivable but not in being actually perceived". But by this time Philonous is able to refer to earlier alleged reasons that an idea cannot exist without being actually perceived. Thus, while at the beginning of the first dialogue the *esse est percipi*-principle, viz. that ideas exist only when actually perceived, is introduced as an analytic statement the truth of which follows from the definition of "sensible thing", the argumentation which follows clearly shows that the principle is not meant as an analytic statement of this kind. Only the assumption that the principle is not an analytic statement makes it also explainable why Berkeley felt a need of its demonstration.

2. The terms *"percipi"* (to be perceived) and *"percipere"* (to perceive) Berkeley uses in a very wide sense. As has already been indicated "perceiving" means direct awareness of ideas, i.e. an apprehension which does neither contain nor presuppose any inference or transition from one mental act to another. It is the opposite to "reason" or demonstrative knowledge. As awareness of ideas, it is also opposite to the knowledge of minds and relations which, according to Berkeley, is a special kind of knowledge, introduced in the later editions of *Pr.* and *D.* as "notion". Perceiving seems to comprise both sensuous and unsensuous cognition, not only the apprehension of sensible things and of ideas of memory and imagination, but also a kind of unsensuous knowledge of what something is. Berkeley e.g. uses the expression "to perceive the table" not only in respect to the apprehension which I or other finite minds have of the table, but also to God's perception of the table though "His ideas are not convey'd to Him by sense, as ours are" (II 241). According to one of Berkeley's letters to S. Johnson, it is easy to think of the mind freed from the body as having ideas of colour without an eye and of sounds without an ear (II 282). In these cases the perception might be understood in analogy to what Berkeley says about God's having the idea of pain.

God does not suffer pain, but he knows "what pain is, even every sort of painful sensation" (II 240). His perceiving of ideas is a kind of knowledge of what they are.— In *PC* Berkeley's mode of expression is more differentiated. There he speaks about "being perceived, imagined, thought on". In his published writings the term "to perceive" is a comprehensive term for all these different kinds of apprehension. When the *esse est percipi*-principle is discussed, the different kinds of apprehension are only seldom enumerated. The expression in *Pr.* § 6 that the being of ideas "is to be perceived or known", is one of the few exceptions.

It has been maintained that Berkeley's term *"percipi"* does refer not only to the actual, but also to a possible awareness of an idea. *"Esse"* is also *"posse percipi"*.[5] This interpretation can be supported by a clear utterance in § 3 of *Pr.*, where Berkeley says: "The table I write on, I say, exists, that is, I see and feel it; and if I were out of my study I should say it existed, meaning thereby that if I was in my study I might perceive it, or that some other spirit actually does perceive it". Thus the existence of the table means that it can be perceived, or that it is actually perceived by a mind.[6] According to the theory of creation, worked out by Philonous in the third dialogue, things partly have absolute existence, as far as they are (actually) perceived by God, partly "relative or hypothetical" existence, as far as they have been made accessible by God's creation to possible perception of finite minds. The creation consists in God's decision that "they should become perceptible to intelligent creatures, in that order and manner which he then established and we now call the laws of nature" (II 253). That the table in my study exists in this hypothetical sense thus means that it should be perceived by me or some other finite spirit, if I or he be in my study.—There exist, on the other hand, many clear utterances by Berkeley showing that *"percipi"* in the phrase *"esse est percipi"* does not refer to possible, but only to

[5] Cf. A. A. Luce, *Berkeley's Immaterialism*, p. 61.
[6] Also other utterances can be adduced as evidences for this hypothetical interpretation of existence. Cf. *Pr.* § 58.

The Esse est percipi-Principle

actual perceiving. When Hylas, in the third dialogue, grants that "the existence of a sensible thing consists in being perceivable, but not in being actually perceived", Philonous blames him with the words: "And what is perceivable but an idea? And can an idea exist without being actually perceived?" (II 234). In *Pr.* § 78 Berkeley says that ideas "exist only in a *mind* perceiving them; and this is true not only of the ideas we are acquainted with at present, but likewise of all possible ideas whatsoever". The existence of a possible idea thus seems to mean that it is actually perceived by a mind. When I am out of my study, the table in the study is, according to Berkeley, always actually perceived, at least by God. If it exists, it is actually perceived. The counterfactual that I should perceive it, if I were in my study, may be true, but is irrelevant to the question of the existence of the table.

But how should then Berkeley's utterance in § 3 be explained? I think that the interpretation of the existence of an unseen thing in terms of possibility of perception is a residue from Berkeley's earlier way of thinking. In *PC* we are faced with this doctrine. There it is connected with Berkeley's opinion that bodies are powers in active substances. In the entry 293a we read: "Bodies taken for Powers do exist when not perceiv'd, but this existence is not actual. When I say a power exists no more is meant than that if in the light I open my eyes and look that way, I shall see it . . . etc." In entries 98 and 185a Berkeley again maintains the existence of a tree in the park or of colours in the dark in the sense that we should see the tree and the colours if we walked in the park or if light illuminated the colours. Later Berkeley abandoned this interesting idea. It has to be observed that at this time Berkeley had not yet laid down the argument for the existence of God, an argument which plays an important rôle in his published writings. One premiss of this argument is that the existence of material things presupposes their actual perception. This premiss obviously contradicts the earlier idea that the existence of bodies or colours means that they can be perceived.

3. The interpretation of *"est"* in the phrase *"esse est percipi"* presents a rather difficult problem. Here it seems to me quite certain that Berkeley, without being aware of it, takes the term in two different senses, a stronger and a weaker.

A. A usual expression in Berkeley's writings reads that the *esse* of the ideas "consists" in their *percipi*. Thus Philonous asks at the beginning of the first dialogue: "Does the reality of sensible things consist in being perceived? or, is it something distinct from their being perceived?" (II 175; cf. II 42 *et passim*). This expression seems to be plausibly interpreted, if we say that the property to exist and the property to be perceived are one and the same property. *Esse est percipi* then states the identity of *esse* and *percipi*. In contradiction to the common opinion that the term "to exist" designates one property and the term "to be perceived" another property, the new principle states that both terms designate the same property, viz. a relation to the perceiving mind.

In different contexts it may even seem as if the *esse est percipi* were introduced as a definition of the term *"esse"*, either as a declaration of the sense in which Berkeley wants to use this term, or as a statement what sense the term has in common speech. Thus Berkeley says in PC that he does not "take away existence. I only declare the meaning of the Word so far as I can comprehend it" (entry 593). In the entry 604 he is persuaded that people would agree with him, if they "examine what they mean by the word existence" (cf. entry 408). The same opinion Berkeley stresses in *Pr.* when introducing his new principle: "I think an intuitive knowledge may be obtained of this, by any one that shall attend to what is meant by the term *exist* when applied to sensible things" (§ 3).

Many investigators into Berkeley's philosophy have proposed the interpretation of the *esse est percipi* as a definition, at least as one alternative.[7] Another possible interpretation of the *esse est percipi* is as an analytic statement the truth of which follows from the definition of the term

[7] Cf. I. Hedenius, *Sensationalism and Theology in Berkeley's Philosophy*, 1936, p. 45.

"*esse*". Both interpretations seem, however, to contradict the abovementioned fact that Berkeley tries to demonstrate his principle. Indeed his text contains several arguments in which the principle is deduced from different premisses. Such arguments would be out of place, if the *esse est percipi* were intended as a definition or an analytic statement the truth of which follows from the definition of the term "*esse*".

There is at any rate much stronger evidence for the interpretation of the principle as a synthetic proposition which states the identity of *esse* and *percipi*. But here again the vagueness of Berkeley's text makes it impossible to know exactly, whether the relation between *esse* and *percipi* aimed at by him is the relation of identity or a weaker one, e.g. of strict or formal equivalence. Following a methodological rule mentioned in the introduction to this paper I select the weakest formulation of Berkeley's principle in the sense discussed so far:

$$(x) \ (x \text{ exists} \equiv x \text{ is perceived}) \qquad (2)$$

(where the values of x are restricted to ideas).

It may be observed that the extended sensationalistic thesis in Berkeley's philosophy (our proposition (1)) follows logically from the *esse est percipi*, irrespective of the interpretation of the relation between *esse* and *percipi* as identity, strict equivalence, or formal equivalence. If the *esse est percipi* is to be interpreted as the formal equivalence (2), then it can be said to be a conjunction of the extended sensationalistic thesis (1) and the formal implication:

$$(x) \ (x \text{ exists} \supset x \text{ is perceived}) \qquad (3).$$

In many contexts Berkeley adduces the *esse est percipi* as an argument for the sensationalistic thesis. Thus in Pr. § 88, when denying the possibility of doubting the "things which I actually perceive by sense", he says: "it being a manifest contradiction, that any sensible object should be immediately perceived by sight or touch, and at the same time have no existence in nature, since the very existence of an unthinking being consists in *being perceived*". Again, in the following argumentation of the third dialogue the sensationalistic thesis is taken as a consequence of the *esse est percipi*. Here Philonous wants to show that the *esse est percipi* corresponds to the view of commonsense. "Ask the gardener", he says, "why he thinks yonder cherry-tree exists in the garden, and he shall tell you, because he sees and feels it. . . . Ask him, why he thinks an orange-tree not to be there, and he shall tell you, because he does not perceive it" (II 234). Both answers, Berkeley seems to mean, are quite intelligible, if the gardener tacitly presupposes as a premiss the *esse est percipi*-principle. They are instances of the two implications constituting the principle: *a is perceived* ⊃ *a exists* and *a is not perceived* ⊃ *a does not exist* (or *a exists* ⊃ *a is perceived*).

B. Berkeley seems, however, to take his principle also in a weaker sense which may be expressed by the formal implication:

$$(x) \ (x \text{ exists} \supset x \text{ is perceived}) \qquad (3)$$

(or, perhaps, by the corresponding strict implication). Both in *Pr.* and in *D.* the presentation of the *esse est percipi*-principle is followed by a long argumentation which is meant as a motivation of this principle. But it is quite obvious that, in case the argumentation proves anything, it must be the weaker proposition (3) and not the stronger (2). The main question here is, whether or not the ideas "can exist without being perceived", and this is what Berkeley denies.

Sometimes one gets the impression that Berkeley himself oscillates between the two senses of the *esse est percipi*. Let us consider the following argumentation in *D*. (II 230): "(*a*) ideas cannot exist without the mind; (*b*) their existence therefore consists in being perceived; (*c*) when therefore they are actually perceived, there can be no doubt of their existence". The argumentation consists of three propositions, here called *a*, *b*, and *c*. The second proposition is introduced as a consequence of the first, and the third as a consequence of the second. This second proposition *b*, which is the *esse est percipi*-principle, thus acts the part of the conclusion in one, and the part of a

The Esse est percipi-*Principle* 329

premiss in the other argumentation. "Therefore" in *b* shows that *b* is meant to express that *b* follows from *a*. Now if this is to be the case the *esse est percipi*-principle must here be taken in the weaker sense (3). In this sense, but not in the stronger sense (2), the principle indeed follows from the statement that ideas cannot exist without the mind [i.e. (x) (x exists ⊃ x is within the mind)], and from the presupposed premiss that to be within the mind means to be perceived by the mind. But here the *esse est percipi* also acts the part of premiss in another argumentation, an argumentation of the same kind as the abovementioned in *Pr.* § 88. As in this paragraph, the principle must here have the stronger sense (2), if the argumentation shall be conclusive. If the passage quoted is really meant as an argumentation, it illustrates how the sense of the *esse est percipi*-principle can suddenly change in Berkeley's text.—Also another interpretation is of course possible: It could be said that the *esse est percipi*-principle always has the stronger sense (2), and that the argumentation quoted is logically inconclusive. The former interpretation is, however, preferable. The alternative, viz. that Berkeley did not clearly distinguish between the different senses of the term "*est*", is less improbable than the alternative that he has committed the more obvious logical fault which otherwise his argumentation would be found to contain.

Let us, however, drop the question, whether the weaker proposition (3) or the stronger proposition (2) expresses what Berkeley called the *esse est percipi*-principle. The essential point is that the proposition (3) has a great importance in Berkeley's philosophy, and that this proposition already expresses his idealism. (3) is also the proposition which Berkeley strives to prove by different arguments. In the rest of this paper I want to discuss one of these arguments. It is the argument which according to Berkeley is sufficient to prove his idealism. Berkeley is willing to abandon his idealistic philosophy, if the argument can be refuted. (Cf. *Pr.* § 22, *D.* II 200.)

The argument in question refers to what Perry has called "the ego-centric predicament", and is intended to prove our proposition (3). It is alluded to in *PC*, entry 472, and elaborated in *Pr*. § 23 and the first dialogue (II 200). In *Pr*. Berkeley asks, whether we could imagine trees in a park, or books in a closet, and nobody present to perceive them. His answer is that this can easily be done by framing in our minds certain ideas of trees and books, and at the same time omitting to frame an idea of anyone who may perceive them. But also then we ourselves must perceive them or think of them all the time. Although nobody is imagined to perceive the ideas, they are nevertheless perceived. But to imagine or to perceive ideas as not perceived at all is a contradiction. In order to show that ideas exist without the mind or unperceived, "it is necessary that you conceive them existing unconceived or unthought of, which is a manifest repugnancy".—In a similar way the argument is presented in the first dialogue. Hylas declares: "what more easy than to conceive a tree or house existing by itself independent of, and unperceived by any mind whatsoever?" Philonous then presses him: "How say you, Hylas, can you see a thing which is at the same time unseen? . . . Is it not as great a contradiction to talk of *conceiving* a thing which is *unconceived*? . . . The tree or house therefore which you think of, is conceived by you" and thus "in the mind." Hylas then finds out his mistake, and declares: "As I was thinking of a tree in a solitary place, where no one was present to see it, methought that was to conceive a tree as existing unperceived or unthought of, not considering that I myself conceived it all the while."

Now, what is the logical structure of this argument, and which are its premisses? Different interpretations are possible. In the following I intend to discuss five different interpretations.[8]

I. In his famous paper on the ego-centric predicament[9] R. B. Perry, without mentioning any particular philoso-

[8] Other possible interpretations, e.g. the interpretation given by A. N. Prior in his short paper "Berkeley in logical form" (*Theoria* XXI, 1955), will not be discussed here.
[9] R. B. Perry, "The Ego-centric Predicament", *Journal of Philosophy*, VII, 1910.

The Esse est percipi-*Principle* 331

pher, points to the opinion of idealists that idealism can be proved by an inductive inference. The following seems to be his way of reasoning. Let us examine different cases in which an idea can be said to exist, e.g. a book in the closet, or a tree in a park etc. Then we shall find that all these cases, without exception, agree also in so far as the ideas in question are perceived (at least by the person who examines the cases). Now, by the method of agreement the conclusion is drawn from the examined cases—unjustly according to Perry—that all ideas are perceived. Or, to state it in a different way which better fits Berkeley's words: in order to show the falsehood of the statement that there exists an idea without being perceived, let us consider different ideas, e.g. a book in the closet, or a tree in the park, etc. When examining them we must still think of them; they are thus perceived. And this being the case in all examined cases, without exception, it is probable that there is no idea at all which exists unperceived.

It is, however, very unlikely, that Berkeley in the passages quoted should have this argumentation in mind. Admittedly, he there considers different cases in which an idea is supposed to exist unperceived, and he shows that the idea is yet perceived, at least by the mind, who supposes it. But his conclusion seems not to be an inductive one. The issue is not that probably no idea exists unconceived, but that it is logically absurd to suppose an idea which exists unperceived. The exemplification indeed has its part to play, but rather as an illustration *in concreto* than as an induction. To prove the statement that every idea which exists is perceived, Berkeley endeavours to show the absurdity of supposing that there exists an unperceived idea. And in order to show this he discusses some examples. He argues as follows: it is absurd to suppose that the idea of a book exists unperceived, or that the idea of a tree exists unperceived, or that any idea whatsoever should exist unperceived. This is, however, not an induction.

In the following interpretations (II—V) of Berkeley's argumentation I shall presuppose that this argumentation is a deductive inference, and that Berkeley intended to show the assumption of an idea, which exists unperceived, to be not only false, but logically absurd.

II. According to this second interpretation it is absurd to suppose that an idea should exist unperceived, since this supposition itself entails that the idea in question is perceived. The argumentation looks like a *reductio ad absurdum* of the type $(\sim p \supset p) \supset p$. A proposition p (in our case the proposition *no idea exists unperceived*) is proved by showing that the negation of p implies p. I say that the argumentation "looks like" a *reductio ad absurdum*, because it clearly is not a *reductio ad absurdum* in the strict sense, though it may, at the outset, seem to be one. The proposition which is shown to be absurd is, indeed, not the negation of the proposition to be proved, i.e. it is not the proposition

(a) there is an idea, x, which exists unperceived,

but the proposition

(b) I suppose (perceive) that there is an idea, x, which exists unperceived.

In other words: what is absurd is not the supposed proposition that an idea, x, exists unperceived, but the very supposition of it.

Now, Berkeley was persuaded that the proposition (b) is absurd, and that it follows from (b) that the supposed idea x is perceived; but did he believe that his argumentation is a *reductio ad absurdum* in the strict sense? It is possible. The interpretation II states that Berkeley's argumentation is meant as a *reductio ad absurdum*, and that Berkeley thus commits a logical fault: he confounds the proposition (a) with the proposition (b). (In order to give a psychological explanation of this confusion, one could refer to the fact that if somebody utters ."p" he expresses what he means, i.e. p, and usually also that he believes in or supposes p. This makes it easy to confound the supposition of p with p itself.)[10]

[10] A. N. Prior also assumes (l.c., p. 122), that Berkeley in his argumentation commits a logical fault: he confuses the proposition (i) "I suppose that there is an idea, x, which is unperceived,

The Esse est percipi-*Principle*

III. Another interpretation is that Berkeley did not confuse the propositions (a) and (b). He found the transition from (a) to (b) quite natural and consistent, because he tacitly presupposed a premiss which makes the transition reasonable, e.g. the premiss that (a) implies (b). In this case his argumentation runs as follows. In order to prove the proposition (p) that no idea exists unperceived, let us suppose its negation (=a) to be true. Now, if (a) is true, also (b) is true (according to the tacitly presupposed premiss). But if (b) is true, it follows that x, which was assumed to exist unperceived, is perceived, i.e. that p is true. Thus from the negation of p follows the truth of p, which is absurd. But is there any evidence for this interpretation of Berkeley's argument? It is quite obvious that Descartes' well-known argument that the proposition *I think* is indubitable, serves as a model for Berkeley's argumentation in the entry 472 of *PC*. Descartes' argument can be made conclusive by adding a tacitly presupposed premiss, a proposition quite analogous to the premiss mentioned above, viz. the implication: *I do not think* implies *I think that I do not think*.[11] It is natural to presuppose the implication between a proposition p and the proposition *I think (suppose) that p* in the part of Descartes' system, where he decides to doubt of all propositions, and not to suppose any proposition to be true, before he had clearly conceived the proposition in question to be indubitable. By his resolution not to accept any proposition without first examining and doubting it, Descartes eliminates all propositions which are not objects of reflection. In this situation, if a proposition p is true, also the proposition *I think that p* must be true. The premiss that p implies *I think that p* is under such circumstances intelligible in Descartes. Although Berkeley quite certainly had Descartes' argument in mind, when writing the entry 472,

---

and x is unperceived" with the proposition (ii) "there is an idea, x, which I suppose to be unperceived and which is unperceived". Only (ii), not (i) is, according to Prior, a contradiction; Berkeley, however, must show the proposition (i) to be impossible if he is to establish his idealism.

[11] Cf. my paper "Descartes' Zweifel und der Satz *Cogito, ergo sum*" in *Theoria* 1954.

there is no reason to suppose that he laid down a premiss of this kind. As we shall see in a moment, Berkeley means that (b) implies (a), but his text furnishes no evidence for the supposition that he should believe that (a) implies (b).

The interpretations II and III both maintain that Berkeley's argumentation is meant to be a *reductio ad absurdum*. In meaning this Berkeley, according to II, commits a logical fault, according to III his argumentation can be made conclusive by adding a tacitly implied premiss, the weak, but rather strange proposition: (*a*) *implies* (*b*), which otherwise does not play any part in Berkeley's philosophy. If we only had to choose between these two interpretations, the choice would be very difficult. The suggested supplementary premiss being rather far-fetched, I should recommend the interpretation II, in spite of the rule, proposed in the introduction, according to which an interpretation by introduction of tacitly presupposed premisses is preferable to the view that the argument is a logical mistake. Fortunately there exist other possible interpretations (IV and V). According to them Berkeley's argument is not meant to be a *reductio ad absurdum* in a strict sense.

IV. The interpretation IV starts from the following idea. Berkeley may have meant the proposition *an idea, x, is perceived* to be such that it is absurd to question its truth, because the proposition *I suppose, that the proposition in question is false* entails that the proposition is true. The proposition *an idea, x, is perceived* is in this sense indubitable. Its truth follows from the supposition that it is false. According to the interpretation IV Berkeley may have been of the opinion that the questioning of a proposition *p* is absurd, and *p* itself indubitable, if *p* is such that its truth follows from the questioning of *p* (i.e. from the proposition *I suppose that p is false*). Some evidence for this interpretation may, perhaps, be found in PC, entry 472, which probably is the first outcast of the argument elaborated in *Pr.* and *D.*, although there are obvious differences. Berkeley here wants to prove that existence is necessary to an idea. The passage ending with the con-

The Esse est percipi-*Principle*

densed sentence "you can at no time ask me whether they (the ideas) exist or no, but by reason of that very question they must necessarily exist", I understand in the following way. Berkeley first shows that it is necessary for the ideas to be perceived. Then he concludes, referring to the *esse est percipi*-principle which is presupposed here in the sense that the existence of the idea consists in being perceived, that existence is necessary to the idea (the idea "must necessarily exist"). But how does he show, that it is necessary for the idea to be perceived? The idea is—he means—necessarily perceived, because the questioning of its being perceived (or its existence), i.e. the proposition *I suppose (perceive) that the idea is not perceived (or does not exist)* implies the proposition that the idea is perceived, and thus exists. That the idea is perceived or exists is thus indubitable in the sense that the truth of the proposition *the idea is perceived* logically follows from the questioning of this proposition. Analogically, Berkeley's argumentation in *Pr.* and *D.* may be interpreted in this way: That the proposition *whichever idea exists as perceived* follows from the questioning of this proposition, i.e. from the proposition (b): *I suppose that an idea, x, exists unperceived*, proves, according to Berkeley, that the existing idea is necessarily perceived.

A salient point in this argumentation as well as in II and III is the supposition that the proposition *the idea is perceived* follows from the proposition *I suppose that the idea is perceived*. If the interpretation IV is correct, this logical relation (or, perhaps, the weaker one of implication) between these two propositions must have been supposed by Berkeley. Now, this supposition is by no means self-evident. We have then to explain, how he could lay down this premiss. It has to be kept in mind that Berkeley takes the term "perceiving" in a very wide sense: it comprises different kinds of apprehension. In this connection it is of special importance that according to Berkeley also a question about something, a supposition, or even a mere mention of something implies that this something is perceived. If I suppose that something, *x*, has such and such qualities, I have perceived *x*. If an idea *x* is mentioned, *x* is perceived, Berkeley holds forth in *PC*, entry 472. Starting from this opinion about the nature of a supposition, Berkeley can conclude that the proposition *I suppose that something, x, exists unperceived* implies that *x* is perceived, since to suppose something about *x* implies to perceive *x*.

To sum up: According to our interpretation IV of Berkeley's argument for his *esse est percipi*-principle Berkeley tacitly presupposes in it two premisses. The first (α) means that a proposition *p* must be considered as proved or necessarily true, if the truth of *p* follows from the questioning of *p*, i.e. from the proposition *I suppose that p is false*; the second (β) means that to suppose something about *x* implies to perceive *x*. The former supposition seems to play some part in *PC*, entry 472; the latter follows immediately from Berkeley's definition of "perceiving".

If this interpretation is correct, Berkeley's argument may be criticized by questioning one of these premisses or both. An objection to the first premiss is this: In the case of a proposition which can be doubted, the truth of this proposition does not generally follow from our doubt. This is true, but it is not at all self-evident that a proposition must be considered as proved or indubitable, if its truth follows from the doubt of it. If Berkeley really has presupposed this premiss, the question arises, how he could take it as something self-evident or certain. We have then come back to the question, whether its explanation yet has to be found in a confusion of this situation with the one in which the truth of a proposition *p* follows from the negation of *p*. As an objection to the second premiss (β) one may insist upon that the supposition of something, *x*, having such and such qualities does not imply that *x* is immediately perceived, but only that *x* is pointed to by a description. If Berkeley's presupposed premisses are uncertain or not evident, his argument, of course, loses its force.

But there is another much more obvious objection against the interpretation IV. In the quoted passages of *Pr.* and *D.* Berkeley does not express himself exactly in the

The Esse est percipi-*Principle* 337

way supposed in the interpretation IV. He does not say that it follows from the supposition that an idea exists unperceived, that the idea is perceived. What he says is that it is a "manifest repugnancy" to perceive something as existing unperceived. He seems to understand the proposition *I perceive something, x, as existing unperceived* as a statement that x is both perceived and not perceived. He considers the proposition in question as absurd as the proposition *I see a thing which at the same time is not seen*. And this proposition is absurd, because it implies that the thing is both seen and unseen.

V. An interpretation of Berkeley's argument which seems to do better justice to this point is the following. A tacitly implied premiss is this: a proposition p must be considered as certain or proved, if the supposition of its negation, i.e. the proposition *I suppose that p is false*, is a contradiction. Now, with regard to the proposition *no ideas exist unperceived* it holds true, Berkeley may have meant, that the supposition of its negation, i.e. the proposition *I suppose that some idea, x, exists unperceived*, is contradictory, because it implies that x is both perceived and not perceived. Thus, the proposition *no ideas exist unperceived* is proved.

The first premiss (α) of the interpretation IV is here substituted by a similar one (α_1): a proposition p is proved, if the proposition *I assume that p is false* is a contradiction. For this premiss there is, however, as far as I can see, no evidence in other passages of Berkeley's writings. It is not at all clear, why Berkeley supposes it here. The second premiss (β) of the interpretation IV is, of course, presupposed also in the interpretation V. But here also a third premiss (γ) is presupposed which is not at all self-evident, viz. that the proposition *I suppose that x is unperceived* implies that x is unperceived. This premiss must be presupposed, since the contradiction of the supposition of an unperceived idea consists, according to Berkeley, in the fact that this supposition implies that the idea is both perceived and unperceived.

Certainly Berkeley thought of the possibility of making erroneous assumptions to the effect that something is the case. In fact he lets Hylas first mistakenly assume that there exists an idea which is not perceived. Assumptions such as these do not have the infallibility which belongs to sense perceptions. They may be erroneous. Thus our premiss γ cannot be regarded as a consequence of the extended sensationalistic thesis. Since, however, in this context it is evidently a question of assuming *truly*, premiss γ can still be easily explained. If I assume *truly* that x is unperceived, then it follows of course that x is unperceived.

I have tried to give different interpretations of Berkeley's argument, and have in each case discussed the question, how his argumentation should be explained. The fifth interpretation which seems to me to be the most probable, as it most exactly follows Berkeley's words in *Pr.* and *D.*, states that the argument can be made consistent by adding three tacitly presupposed premisses. For some of these premisses some evidence can be found in Berkeley's text in other contexts. If they are presupposed, the statement becomes logically correct that the supposition of the existence of an unperceived idea is obviously repugnant.

It is reasonable to criticize Berkeley's argument by questioning these tacitly presupposed premisses. If they are dubious, the argument is not conclusive. But also a wholly different objection can be raised against it by examining its bearings on other theories in Berkeley's philosophy. Even if the argument can be made conclusive by supplementary premisses, it is impossible to overcome some difficulties or inconsistencies which the argument leads to in Berkeley's system. I shall conclude this essay by pointing at two difficulties of this kind which, as far as I can see, cannot be avoided by any reasonable explanation.

1. Berkeley's argument proves too little. What Berkeley wants to prove is that there can be no idea which is unperceived at any time. But from the proposition *I suppose (perceive) that an idea, x, exists unperceived* and from Berkeley's presupposed premisses it only follows that the idea is perceived at t_1, if the supposition is made at t_1, but not that the idea is perceived at any time. There is no contradiction in the supposition of an idea existing un-

perceived at all other times except the time, when the supposition is made. We must distinguish between two quite different situations: to perceive at a given time that an idea exists unperceived at that time, and to perceive at a given time that an idea exists unperceived at another time. If what happened yesterday (at t_1) is perceived now (at t_2), an idea which existed at t_1 is perceived at t_2; and this does not entail that the idea was perceived also at t_1. What the argument proves is thus not the whole thesis which is a cornerstone in Berkeley's philosophy.

2. Berkeley's argument proves too much. If it is conclusive, one of its consequences contradicts another well-known thesis in Berkeley's theory. The argument implies that an idea about which I suppose something is perceived *by me*. But according to Berkeley's own theory an idea must not necessarily be perceived by me; it can exist as perceived by other minds, at least by God. From the argument, as interpreted above, it follows that it is impossible for me to suppose that an idea, e.g. the table in my study when I am out, exists unperceived by me, because my assumption of its existence implies that the idea is perceived by me. Berkeley's thesis that I can assume the existence of an idea unperceived by me, if only it is perceived by another mind, presupposes on the other hand that the supposition of something about an idea is possible without the idea being perceived by the person, who makes the supposition; and this contradicts one of the premisses of Berkeley's argument.

It has been maintained[12] that from the beginning Berkeley probably was of the opinion that I can only assume the existence of the idea which is perceived by me; only later he adopted the theory that the idea must be perceived by some mind, not necessarily by me who suppose its existence. If this is correct, it may be assumed that Berkeley let the earlier elaborated argument be a part of his theory, not observing that it now, by the change of his point of view, had become incompatible with other elements of the theory.

[12] Cf. Dawes Hicks, *Berkeley*, 1932, p. 113; A. Johnston, *The Development of Berkeley's Philosophy*, 1923, p. 190 f.

THE ARGUMENT FROM ILLUSION AND BERKELEY'S IDEALISM
KONRAD MARC-WOGAU

The argument from illusion is used by Berkeley both in A *Treatise concerning the Principles of Human Knowledge* (=Pr.) and *Three Dialogues between Hylas and Philonous* (=D.). It occurs in at least two different versions, and seems to lead to different conclusions. Sometimes it is intended to prove Berkeley's idealistic thesis.

Let us begin with an analysis of a version of the argument, adduced by Philonous in the first dialogue, when he discusses different sensible qualities.

In regard to the qualities heat and cold, Berkeley takes up Locke's example. Philonous first lays down that a doctrine which leads us into an absurdity cannot be true, and that it is "an absurdity to think that one and the same thing should be at the same time both cold and warm" (*Works* edited by Luce and Jessop, II 178). Next, he adduces the wellknown fact that, if I put my two hands, the one warm and the other cold, into the same vessel of water of an intermediate temperature, the water will seem cold to the one hand and warm to the other. Now, if we suppose that the perceived qualities really are in the water, then the absurdity arises that the water is at the same time both cold and warm (II 178 f.).

Thus, some presupposed premisses, together with the perceived fact that the water seems cold to the one hand and warm to the other, lead into an absurdity. Which are these premisses? I think, they can be summed up by the following four propositions:

From *Theoria*, Vol. XXIV (1958). Reprinted by permission of the author.

Argument from Illusion 341

(1) One and the same thing cannot simultaneously have two incompatible qualities;
(2) the qualities *cold* and *warm* are incompatible;
(3) a perceived quality is real or exists, i.e. is really a quality of the thing perceived, and
(4) the water which seems cold to the one hand and warm to the other, is (identically) one and the same object.

These premisses together with the proposition describing the fact that the water is perceived as cold by one hand and warm by the other, leads to an absurdity. According to (3) and (4) it follows from the perceived fact that one and the same water is at the same time both cold and warm, and this, according to (1) and (2), is an absurdity.

This version of the argument Berkeley applies also to other sensible qualities, colour, extension, etc. in respect to which a relativity of our perceptions can easily be established. Now, it is clear that the mentioned absurdity does not follow from the relativity of our perception of sensible qualities if some of the premisses should be abandoned. If, e.g., the premiss (2) does not hold true, i.e. if cold and warm are compatible, like cold and sweet, there is no absurdity in assuming that one and the same thing has both characteristics at the same time. The premisses (1) and (2) seem to be generally accepted, and Berkeley presupposes them as self-evident. The premiss (2) is tacitly presupposed, the premiss (1) Philonous refers to in the passage quoted. The status of the propositions (3) and (4) is not equally clear. It is worth while to examine them.

The premiss (3) states, that all perceived qualities are real, really exist in the object perceived. Hylas explicitly lays this down at the beginning of the first dialogue. He says: "Whatever degree of heat we perceive by sense, we may be sure the same exists in the object that occasions it" (II 175) and again in respect to colour: "each visible object has that colour which we see in it" (II 183). Every sense-perception is a perception of something existing or real; that is the opinion from which Hylas starts. This opinion, sometimes called "naïve realism", has, strangely enough, often been ascribed to commonsense. Hylas is indeed considered to represent the commonsense view. But such expressions in common speech as "this thing is in fact red, but appears pink to me just now", show clearly, that commonsense distinguishes between real and apparent sensible qualities. Hylas, when starting the discussion, does not make this distinction. Not until he realizes the absurdity shown up by the argument from illusion, is he willing to abandon the premiss (3), and to introduce the distinction between real and apparent sensible qualities. He remarks about the red colours of the clouds: "I must own, Philonous, these colours are not really in the clouds as they seem to be at this distance. They are only apparent colours" (II 184). This distinction is the first attempt to escape the consequences from the argument from illusion. This is also the objection to the argument which is most easily found. The argument is deprived its nerve by the abandonment of the proposition (3) which is one of its premisses.

But is this solution of the difficulty possible for Berkeley's part? There are two points which have to be noticed here. (i) Berkeley can at most give another interpretation of the proposition (3), but he cannot abandon the thesis that what is perceived is real, as this thesis is one of the basic principles of his theory. And (ii) Berkeley, when referring to the argument from illusion—at least in some passages—, intends to show the subjectivity not only of some sensible qualities, but of all such qualities.

Before discussing these points, let us examine another variant of the argument from illusion. In *Pr.* Berkeley states about sensible qualities: "It is proved that sweetness is not really in the sapid thing, because the thing remaining unaltered the sweetness is changed into bitter, as in the case of a fever or otherwise vitiated palate" (§ 14, II 47). In the first dialogue Philonous points to the fact that the perceived colours change or disappear entirely, when a change takes place in my eye or when the distance to the thing perceived alters without any alteration in the

Argument from Illusion 343

thing itself (II 185 f.). When he concludes that the perceived colours do not inhere in external things, he bases his opinion on the following argumentation: "in case colours were real properties or affections inherent in the external bodies, they could admit of no alteration, without some change wrought in the very bodies themselves" (II 185). We can take this proposition:

(5) if a quality inheres in the object, the change of the quality involves the change of the object,

as a premiss of the argument.

The proposition (5) is introduced by Berkeley as something self-evident; it seems to be meant as an analytic statement the truth of which follows from the meaning of the inherence of a quality in an object. Only if the object changes, with a change of the quality ascribed to it, is it correct to say that the quality inheres in the object. Considered as a premiss, the proposition (5) replaces the premisses (1) and (2) of the first version of the argument. It replaces (2), as the change of a quality means the change of one quality to another which is incompatible with the first. The first version of the argument covered the cases in which two incompatible qualities were perceived simultaneously in the object by one or several observers. This version needed, therefore, the premiss (1) which stated that two incompatible qualities cannot really simultaneously inhere in the object. The second version of the argument, on the other hand, covers the cases in which a change of a quality, i.e. a succession of two incompatible qualities, is observed by one or several observers. Here the premiss (1) has no function. It is replaced by (5). The proposition (5) and the abovementioned premisses (3) and (4) together with the fact that sensible qualities which are perceived in an object change, whilst the object remains unchanged, lead to a contradiction. If (3) and (4) hold true, the object in this situation ought to, but really does not, change.

To avoid this contradiction one needs only to question one of the premisses. The easiest solution of the difficulty seems also here to be the abandonment of premiss (3), that *all* qualities perceived in the object really are in the object. Some of them at least must be apparent or subjective. This is also the solution to which Hylas resorts in the passage quoted above. But can Berkeley accept this solution? It is worth while to examine his own view in respect to the argument in question.

In § 15 of *Pr*. Berkeley correctly points out what can be inferred from the given premisses. In respect to the different versions of the argument from illusion, "which are thought manifestly to prove that colours and tastes exist only in the mind", he urges, that "it must be confessed this method of arguing does not so much prove that there is no extension or colour in the outward object, as that we do not know by sense which is the true extension and colour of the object" (II 47). He remarks further in the same paragraph that other arguments elaborated in preceding paragraphs show that all qualities are in the mind. The *esse-est-percipi*-principle, he says, cannot be proved by the argument from illusion alone. Thus, according to Berkeley's argumentation in § 15, the relativity of our perceptions does not legitimate the idealistic conclusion that all sensible qualities exist only in the mind. What we can infer is only that not all qualities exist in the object. But then, Berkeley seems to argue, the way is open for the sceptical opinion: we have no means of knowing which of the perceived qualities, if any, really inheres in the object. In § 87 this sceptical view is referred to in connection with the abovementioned second variant of the argument from illusion. "Things remaining the same our ideas vary, and which of them, or even whether any of them at all represent the true quality really existing in the thing, it is out of our reach to determine" (II 78). This sceptical consequence, objectionable according to Berkeley, may be avoided, he thinks, by the idealistic point of view, i.e. by taking all perceivable qualities to be in the mind. In so far, but only in so far, the argument from illusion can be said to be an evidence for idealism.

In *D*. the situation is not quite clear. There we find two lines of thought mixed up in a puzzling way. One of them (a) represents the method of arguing, rejected by Berkeley in § 15 of *Pr.*; the other (b) corresponds to Berkeley's view in this paragraph. (a) On the one hand the argument from illusion seems to be used by Philonous as an argument for the *esse-est-percipi*-principle. Having enumerated different examples of the relativity of colour-perception, Philonous sums up: "From all which, should it not seem to follow, that all colours are equally apparent, and that none of those which we perceive are really inherent in any outward object?" (II 185). A few pages later he asks: "Was it not admitted as a good argument, that neither heat nor cold was in the water, because it seemed warm to one hand and cold to the other?" (II 189). Thus, Berkeley here finds quite correct the way of reasoning which he condemned in *Pr*. He draws the universal conclusion that none of the perceived qualities is in the object, although only the conclusion that not all of them are in the object follows from the argument.

Was it a logical blunder or is Philonous' argumentation meant as an *argumentum ad hominem*? It is hardly possible and not very important to decide this. Of greater importance is the fact that this line of thought in *D*. is mixed up with another. (b) The argument from illusion leads Hylas, as we have seen, to distinguish between real and apparent qualities, or, in other words, to give up the premiss (3). But Philonous is not satisfied with this result. He presses Hylas: There are no internal differences between real and apparent qualities and thus there exists no possibility to know which of the perceived colours is real. Having referred to the second variant of the argument from illusion, Philonous asks: "And now tell me, whether you are still of opinion, that every body has its true, real colours inhering in it", and adds: "and if you think it has, I would fain know farther from you, what certain distance and position of the object, what peculiar texture and formation of the eye, what degree or kind of light is necessary for ascertaining that true colour, and distinguishing it from apparent ones" (II 186). He means to say that there is no possibility of distinguishing them. This impossibility gives rise to the sceptical view. The sceptical view, this terrible philosophical theory, must be avoided, and it can be avoided by supposing all qualities to be apparent. This is obviously the same argumentation as the before-mentioned in *Pr*. Berkeley stresses in *D*., that, perhaps, the strongest reason for the adoption of idealism is the sceptical consequence of the alternative view. If an external object is to be supposed, he says, "the objections from the change of colours in a pigeon's neck, or the appearances of a broken oar in the water" (i.e. the variants of the argument from illusion) "must be allowed to have weight" (II 258). The objection has weight, Philonous seems to mean, as far as it shows that on this supposition we are driven to a sceptical consequence which can be avoided only by the idealistic supposition that there are no external objects.

According to this way of arguing, stressed both in *Pr*. and in *D*., a solution of the absurdity pointed out in the argument from illusion consists in abandoning the premiss (3) by distinguishing between qualities which are real and qualities which are apparent or mind-dependent. The argument from illusion as such does not justify the idealistic thesis that all perceived qualities are mind-dependent. This conclusion is reached by additional considerations. From the standpoint of Berkeley's idealism there lies, however, a difficulty in this argumentation which makes the interpretation of Berkeley's utterances much more complicated. The difficulty is not discussed by Berkeley himself. In its examination we must take into consideration some implications of Berkeley's utterances, not clearly noticed or deliberated by himself.

The passage of the first dialogue, where Hylas distinguishes between real and apparent sensible qualities in order to solve the difficulty pointed out by the argument from illusion, leaves at the first glance the impression that this is, according to Berkeley, a correct solution of the difficulty. If the premiss (3) is abandoned, the absurdity of two incompatible perceived qualities both simultaneously inhering in the same object is solved. It is, however, clear that Berkeley cannot accept this solution of the difficulty. The premiss (3) is indeed one of the corner-stones of his philosophy. It is the sensationalistic premiss that our per-

Argument from Illusion

ceptions are indubitable, and that what we perceive by our senses is real. Berkeley admittedly distinguishes between two senses of the statement (3) that the perceived quality is real: (3_1) the quality is real in the sense that it is in (inheres in) an external object, and (3_2) the quality is real in the sense that it is perceived by, or is in, a mind, and he denies the reality of the sensible qualities in the first sense. While Hylas clearly abandons the premiss (3), and distinguishes between qualities which really inhere in the object and apparent qualities, which are not real in this sense, Berkeley is of the opinion that all qualities are real in the same sense, and that none of them inheres in an external object. He thus only gives another interpretation of the proposition (3); he understands it in the sense (3_2) instead of the sense (3_1). All ideas are real as far as they exist in the mind. If one wants to say that they inhere in an object, this might, according to Berkeley, be understood as a statement that they are included in the set of ideas or sensible qualities which constitute what we call an object.

We now can put the question: can the absurdity, pointed out by the argument from illusion, be avoided by interpreting the premiss (3) as (3_2)? This surely is not the case. The same absurdity follows also from the premisses (1), (2), [or (5)], (4) and (3_2), i.e. when the step is taken from Hylas' realistic point of view to the idealistic one of Philonous. If the same water is perceived by me as cold and as warm at the same time, and if both perceived qualities are real, a difficulty arises, even if the reality of the qualities means that they are ideas in my mind, both constituting the same thing. The interpretation of the reality of the qualities and of the thing as existence in a mind has no bearing upon the argument from illusion.

Now, a possibility to solve the difficulty without abandoning the premiss (3), whether interpreted as (3_1) or as (3_2), is to give up the premiss (4) that the object perceived in different perceptions is not identically the same object. It seems to me that this is the solution to which Berkeley actually resorts, though his line of thought is not quite clear in this respect. It must be observed that if the premiss (4) is abandoned, i.e. if it is supposed that the water perceived as cold and the water perceived as warm is not identically the same water, the absurdity pointed out by the argument from illusion disappears, no matter which interpretation is given to the proposition (3). It disappears in other words both on Hylas' original and on Philonous' standpoint. On the other hand the difficulties of defining the meaning of the expression "one and the same", which arise when the proposition (4) is abandoned are the same also on these different standpoints.

Let us ask what Berkeley means when he speaks about "one and the same thing". First it can be observed that Berkeley supposes that the individual mind always is "one and the same"; it is a substance and not a set of states which, perhaps, are like each other, but have no persisting unity. As we shall see in a moment, Berkeley criticizes what he calls "the abstracted notion of identity", but he nevertheless obviously supposes that the expression "one and the same", when applied to the mind, has exactly the sense of numerical identity which philosophers have usually attached to this expression. The notion of numerical identity is thus not unknown to Berkeley. It is presupposed also in connection with the argument from illusion. The words "one and the same" in the proposition (1) must be understood as "identically one and the same", for this proposition to be true or self-evident.

Thus, it seems to be quite sensible to ask, whether two persons, who are said to perceive one and the same thing, have, from Berkeley's point of view, two different ideas which are very similar, but two and not one idea. It is however impossible to find in Berkeley's text a clear answer to this question. Moreover, this lack of clarity seems to be due to a haziness of Berkeley's notion of the idea. On the one hand the relation to one particular perceiving mind, on the other hand only the relation to a mind in general seems, according to Berkeley, to be essential to an idea. There is some reason to suppose that Berkeley first supported the former doctrine, but gradually and without realizing all the consequences of this change, shifted his

Argument from Illusion

standpoint and adopted the latter point of view. If the relation to one particular mind (M_1) is essential to an idea (i), the assumption must obviously be wrong that the same idea (i) can be perceived also by another mind (M_2). The relation to M_1 being essential to the idea i, everything which lacks this relation to M_1 is not i. Thus, the idea i ceases to exist as soon as M_1 ceases to perceive it. Now, when two persons (M_1 and M_2) perceive the same table it is always possible that one of them shuts his eyes; his idea then ceases to exist, whilst the other's idea persists. What M_1 and M_2 perceive is thus not identically one and the same idea, but two ideas which are similar or exactly alike. This consequence does, of course, not follow if the relation to a mind in general and not to one particular mind is held to be essential to the idea.

At the end of the third dialogue the question is discussed, whether, from Berkeley's standpoint, two persons can see the same thing. If it is so, that we "by our senses perceive only the ideas existing in our minds", can then—Hylas asks—"the same idea which is in my mind . . . be in yours, or in any other mind?" "Does it not . . . follow from your principles, that no two can see the same thing?" Philonous answers that "it is certain . . . that different persons may perceive the same thing" provided the term "same thing" is not used in the sense of "an abstracted notion of identity", which philosophers pretend to have, but in the vulgar sense (II 247). And he continues:

"Let us suppose several men together, all endued with the same faculties, and consequently affected in like sort by their senses, and who had yet never known the use of language; they would without question agree in their perceptions. Though perhaps, when they came to the use of speech, some regarding the uniformness of what was perceived, might call it the *same* thing; others especially regarding the diversity of persons who perceived, might choose the denomination of different things. But who sees not that all the dispute is about a word; to wit, whether what is perceived by different persons, may yet have the term *same* applied to it?" (II 247 f.).

Berkeley thus seems to consider a mere question of terminology whether or not the perceptions of two persons, X and Y, of the table in my study ought to be called perceptions of the same thing. What X perceives may be exactly alike what Y perceives, but a difference nevertheless exists in so far as the table is in the one case perceived by X, in the other by Y. As an answer to Hylas' question, this is, however, quite unsatisfactory. The question put by Hylas, when he asks, whether X and Y perceive one idea or two similar ideas, has to be decided in order to explain what the statement means that X and Y "agree in their perceptions". Without such an explanation also the meaning of the term "idea" remains obscure. The term "idea" being a technical term proposed by Berkeley, the question may be considered a question of terminology, i.e. as the question how to use the terms "one idea" and "two similar ideas". By leaving this question of terminology undecided, Berkeley indeed leaves obscure also the sense of his term "idea". If one has to pay attention to the difference between X and Y, i.e. if the relation to the particular perceiving mind is essential to the idea, X's idea and Y's idea must be called two different ideas, but if the difference of the perceiving minds is not essential to the idea, X and Y may be said to have one and the same idea. These two alternatives represent not only two different terminologies, but also two different lines of thought.

In some passages Berkeley expresses himself as if he favoured the first line of thought. Thus he says in *Pr.* § 140: "blueness or heat by me perceived" has resemblance "to those ideas perceived by another" (II 105). On the other hand there are many utterances in favour of the opinion that not the relation to a particular mind but only the relation to a mind in general is essential to an idea. Two persons, perceiving the table in my study, perceive, according to this doctrine, one and the same idea, and not two similar ideas. If I cease to perceive the table, the table, i.e. the idea which I perceived, does not cease to exist. Berkeley set forth in *Pr.* § 48: "It does not . . . follow from the foregoing principles, that bodies are annihilated and created every moment, or exist not at all during the intervall between our perception of them". The table, when not perceived by me, exists, according to Berkeley, as perceived by another mind. Here the interpretation that one idea (or one bundle of ideas=the table) is perceived by different minds is, at the first glance at least, the most natural. Of course, also another interpretation may be given here. The statement that my idea is not annihilated when not longer perceived by me could be said to have the following metaphorical sense: when I cease to perceive the table, an idea, similar to my former idea while I perceived the table, now exists in another mind. Although this interpretation sounds rather far-fetched, it seems to follow from some theories in Berkeley that we must resort to an interpretation of this kind in order to avoid some obvious contradictions. If the idea perceived by M_1 is exactly alike to the idea perceived by M_2, then it is plausible, as pointed out by Berkeley, to speak of one idea perceived by them both. But in the case of the perceptions of M_1 and M_2 not being exactly alike, it is no longer plausible to say that one and the same idea is perceived by both. In this case we must say, that they have *two* similar ideas. Now, Berkeley means that the table in my study continues to exist, even when no finite mind is in my study; it exists as perceived by God. It is, however, clear that the table perceived by God cannot be exactly alike the table perceived by me or another finite mind, God's perception being of a different kind than mine (cf. II 240 f.). In this case it seems necessary to interpret the statement that the table continues to exist as perceived by God as meaning that an idea continues to exist which is similar, but not exactly alike my idea of the table. Berkeley sometimes uses the terms "ectype" and "archetype" in order to characterize the relation between my and God's idea of a thing. It is clear that the ectype and the archetype are not exactly alike. Thus, the statement that I and God see the same table cannot be understood as asserting that both perceive identically one and the same idea.

It follows from what has been said that, according to Berkeley, the use of the word "one and the same" as applied to ideas does not presuppose that the ideas are numerically identical, neither does it presuppose, that they are exactly alike. There is therefore nothing contradictory in the assertion that two ideas, which are not exactly alike, as the idea of cold water and the idea of warm water, are "the same" idea or "one and the same" water.

If in the proposition (4) the term "one and the same" is taken in this wider sense which allows us to say that the water perceived as cold by the one hand and as warm by the other is the same water, in spite of the supposition that both perceived qualities are real, the absurdity pointed out by the argument from illusion does not arise. The expression "the same water" means then two different bundles of ideas which can be called "the same thing" in the wider sense, because they have many important characteristics (e.g. position in space) in common. This modification of the premiss (4) gives a solution of the difficulty which, as far as I can see, is the only solution acceptable from Berkeley's point of view.

BERKELEY'S LIKENESS PRINCIPLE
PHILLIP D. CUMMINS

In both the *Principles of Human Knowledge* and the *Three Dialogues between Hylas and Philonous*, Berkeley presents the representationalist with a dilemma which expresses his fundamental objection to that theory. In the *Principles* (Section 8), he writes:

> But, say you, though the ideas themselves do not exist without the mind, yet there may be things like them, whereof they are copies or resemblances, which things exist without the mind in an unthinking substance. I answer, *an idea can be like nothing but an idea; a colour or figure can be like nothing but another colour or figure*. If we look but ever so little into our own thoughts, we shall find it impossible for us to conceive a likeness except only between our ideas. Again, I ask whether those supposed originals or external things, of which our ideas are the pictures or representations, be themselves perceivable or no? If they are, then they are ideas and we have gained our point; but if you say they are not, I appeal to anyone whether it be sense to assert a colour is like something which is invisible; hard or soft, like something which is intangible; and so of the rest.[1] [Italics mine]

From the *Journal of the History of Philosophy*, Vol. 4 (1966). Reprinted, with minor corrections, by permission of the author and the *Journal of the History of Philosophy*.

[1] See also Section 57 and, for passages from the *Three Dialogues*, Berkeley, *The Works of George Berkeley*, A. A. Luce and T. E. Jessop, eds. (Edinburgh: Nelson and Sons, 1949), II, 189-90 and 206. (Hereafter, the Luce-Jessop edition will be referred to as *Works*.) Compare, too, entry B378 of the *Philosophical Commentaries*, in *Works*, I, 45.

The strength of this argument is that if it is conclusive, it establishes the impossibility of representationalism, i.e. the view that ideas represent or make known imperceptible material objects. (Note the position under attack is that "there may be things" of which ideas are copies.) It is not merely a matter of exhibiting the skeptical consequences which beset the theory.

Berkeley attacks the very heart of representationalism. It is the claim that in addition to sensory objects[2] (ideas), there are unperceived and unperceivable entities which in some manner resemble sensible objects. Berkeley intends to show there can be no such resembling entities. He begins with a pair of alternatives: the entities represented by sensible objects are either perceived by some mind or not. If they are perceived, then the representationalist: (a) has retracted his original claim that they are unperceived and unperceivable; and (b) must acknowledge that the represented entities are ideas which cannot exist unperceived. What is perceived is an idea. If, on the other hand, the representationalist contends that the entities represented by sensory objects are unperceived, then he is holding that unperceived entities and (perceived) sensory objects correspond to one another. This claim, Berkeley suggests, is contradictory or meaningless. The alleged correspondence rests upon a supposed resemblance or likeness between a perceived object and an unperceived object, but there can be no resemblance between these two. The "only thing like an idea is an idea." If an unperceived object resembles a perceived object (an idea which must be perceived), then it is itself an idea and is perceived. The representationalist's claim is self-refuting. And, Berkeley maintains, if it is claimed that an idea can be like or resemble a non-idea, the term, "resemble," is without meaning. Berkeley's argument, then, is that on the first alternative, the representationalist abandons his theory or asserts a contradiction, while on the second, he speaks in a meaningless or contradictory fashion.

[2] I shall use sensory object and presented object as equivalent expressions.

It seems clear that a serious representationalist would accept the second alternative and try to avoid Berkeley's conclusion. Hence, the principle that the only thing like an idea is an idea (hereafter, the *Likeness Principle*), is the critical premise in the argument. Furthermore, since the argument against representationalism is crucial for Berkeley's rejection of material substances, the Likeness Principle is a fundamental element of his immaterialism.[3]

It might seem that even more fundamental to Berkeley's philosophy is the term "idea." He seems to argue as follows: All the things we perceive are ideas. Ideas cannot exist unperceived. The only thing like an idea is an idea. Therefore, anything we perceive or anything like what we perceive cannot exist unperceived.[4] The trouble with this line of reasoning is that the use of "idea" for what we perceive seems to be a question-begging characterization designed to secure what is not otherwise self-evident, namely, the claim that no perceived entities can occur unperceived. What I want to show is that the word "idea" need not occur in Berkeley's attack on material substance. First, I shall explicate the Likeness Principle as a shorthand for three claims, two of which are relatively non-controversial and virtually axiomatic for Berkeley. The other is controversial, but if true it justifies Berkeley's use of "idea."

[3] Colin Turbayne, in his introduction to the Library of Liberal Arts edition of the *Three Dialogues* (New York: Bobbs-Merrill, 1954), pp. xii–xviii, suggests that the argument against representationalism is the strongest weapon Berkeley has for attacking belief in material substances and indicates the importance of the Likeness Principle. Note, though, that the representationalist could retreat to the view that there are material substances, but that presented or sensory objects do not represent them. Hence, despite Turbayne's claim, to refute representationalism is not to refute the claim that there are material substances.

[4] For instance, in Sections 1–4 of the *Principles*, Berkeley asserts that the immediate objects of sensation are ideas, then concludes they cannot exist except in relation to minds. The mentalistic aura of "idea" seems to carry the argument. See, too, Jessop's "Editor's Introduction" to the *Principles*, in *Works*, II, 8–11, where he states that Berkeley takes it as axiomatic that all known non-minds cannot occur unperceived. The axiom seems to be one one could easily reject.

Then I shall note that the third claim is defended in Berkeley's *Three Dialogues*. Finally, I shall indicate that Berkeley's argument against representationalism is an extension of his main argument against material substance.

The Likeness Principle is a shorthand formulation of the following claims: A, all qualities which are determinates of the same determinable have the same ontological status; B, a necessary condition of resemblance between two entities is that they are or possess qualities which are determinates of the same determinable; C, none of the qualities we immediately perceive (hereafter termed "sensible qualities") can occur unperceived. The refutation of representationalism requires all three; the proof of the impossibility of material substance, as traditionally formulated, rests upon A and C.

Some terminological points. *Quality* is used in a quite common way for the shade of color of a ball, the figure or shape of a table, and so on. Next, the distinction between *determinates and determinables*. There are numerous shades of color. The shades are determinates of the determinable, color. The idea expressed by A is one accepted by anyone engaged in metaphysics or ontology. If a philosopher shows that the quality we call red is a universal (by analyzing an example) he does not need to offer any arguments for blue being a universal. Again, if one establishes that one shade of color is mind-dependent, the same holds for all other shades. Philosophers argue about the ontological status of colors and sounds, not about the status of specific shades and tones.

The thesis concerning resemblance, B, requires more discussion because several distinctions must be drawn. First, B states no more than a necessary condition of saying two things stand in the relation of resemblance. Berkeley's further criteria can safely be ignored. Second, Berkeley distinguishes between objects (complexes) and qualities (simples) in dealing with sensory objects. With regard to complexes, resemblance between two things requires that a constituent of one be a determinate of the same determinable as some constituent of the other. To illustrate, suppose one thing is a colored spot and a second is a tone. Considered in isolation, so that we are not concerned with their respective ranks or places in ranges of colors or sounds, since they have no specific phenomenal qualities which are determinates of the same determinable, they cannot resemble. With respect to simples, where resemblance cannot be based upon constituents, thesis B requires that two simples which resemble be determinates of the same determinable.[5] (Berkeley might say only complexes resemble. I do not deny it. I merely want to indicate how B would be formulated to cover the case of simples. Note, too, that B does not predetermine the issue of whether Berkeley's simple qualities are universal or particular.) In both the case of objects (complexes) and that of constituent qualities (simples), B states a minimum requirement for resemblance.

To support this explication textually, I note that though Berkeley sometimes uses "idea" in discussing resemblance, he also seems to have in mind shades of color, tones, and the like. A color patch (assume its constituents are a shade, a size, and a shape) cannot resemble what has no color, no size, and no shape. So in Section 8 we find phrases like, ". . . a colour or figure can be like nothing but another colour or figure," and ". . . I appeal to anyone whether it be sense to assert a colour is like something which is invisible; hard or soft, like something which is intangible . . ."[6] It is not being claimed that something mental cannot resemble something non-mental, where "mental" is left vague, as "the only thing like an idea is an idea" suggests. Rather, Berkeley's claim is a color cannot be like a non-color, a shape cannot be like a non-shape and a sound cannot be like a non-sound. In discussing representationalism, then, he merely applies a general thesis about resemblance to a particular case.

So far, we have considered two elements of the Likeness Principle which, taken in tandem, establish that for one thing to resemble another, it must have a quality which has the same ontological status as some quality of

[5] *Works*, I, 45, especially propositions 12–14.
[6] Cf. *Works*, II, 206.

the other. Applying this to representationalism, which is at least the claim that presented entities resemble other entities which are not perceivable, we see that a requirement of the theory (given A and B) is that presented entities and those they allegedly resemble have the same ontological status. This sets the stage for the third thesis, claim C, that what is presented cannot occur unperceived. Now if what is presented is thought to represent (resemble) something which is not perceived, a contradiction results. What is not presented, i.e. is unperceived, cannot occur unperceived, if it resembles what is presented, because two things which resemble have the same ontological status and presented things cannot occur unperceived. So the entities which are allegedly represented by sensory objects are both perceived and unperceived. There can be no such represented entities. If it is claimed that the represented entity can occur unperceived, then it has a different ontological status from the presented entity. But then none of its qualities can be determinates of the same determinable as any quality of the presented entity, so how can it resemble the presented entity and be represented by it? If A, B, and C hold, they effectively preclude the possibility of representationalism.

Thesis C has been formulated in two ways, once in terms of presented objects and once in terms of the qualities immediately perceived. The blur is unimportant because Berkeley holds that only various qualities (colors, odors, sounds, shapes, and the like) are presented or immediately perceived. (He holds there are entities which are objects of attention or consciousness and these consist of qualities, like the color red or blue, which can be identified without reference to future objects of awareness. Such things, he says, are immediately perceived.)[7] A patch of color or a sound is a simple quality or a collection of simple qualities.[8] The important thing to notice is that a shade of color or a shape, not "ideas" of the shade or shape,

[7] *Works*, II, 174–75, 183 and 203–4.
[8] *Works*, II, 41, 175 and 249. See H. M. Bracken, "Berkeley and Malebranche on Ideas," *The Modern Schoolman*, SLI (1963), 1–15.

are immediate objects of awareness.⁹ Presented shades of color and the rest are called "ideas" because of the (alleged) fact that they cannot occur except in relation to a mind which perceives them.¹⁰ In our explication of the Likeness Principle, thesis C states just this claim.

In the *Principles* Berkeley does not argue for thesis C; it is assumed throughout. But in the *Three Dialogues* he

⁹ This lesson, one of the foundations of their "realistic" interpretation of Berkeley, Luce and Jessop have tried to instill. See, for instance, Luce, *Berkeley's Immaterialism*, (London: Nelson and Sons, 1945), pp. 40–47. Compare R. H. Popkin, "The New Realism of Bishop Berkeley," in *George Berkeley*, eds. S. C. Pepper, K. Aschenbrenner, and B. Mates (Berkeley: University of California Press, 1957), pp. 1–10.

¹⁰ In both the *Principles*, Sections 38–39, and the *Three Dialogues*, Berkeley says that this is why he uses "idea" to refer to what is given perceptually. Compare *Works*, II, 56–57, 235–36 and 250–51. Richard Watson, in his "The Breakdown of Cartesian Metaphysics," *Journal of the History of Philosophy*, I (1963), 177–97, construes the Likeness Principle differently. He lists a set of Cartesian principles, then claims that Simon Foucher, a French sceptic, and, subsequently, Berkeley found the set inconsistent. The principles in question are: (a) Like knows like, or what knows or makes known another thing must have the same attribute as the other; (b) Minds (ideas) fall under different attributes from bodies; and (c) Minds (ideas) know (make known) bodies. Foucher's point was that the Cartesians were committed to (a) and (b), so could not maintain (c). Watson, then, implies that for Berkeley ideas and bodies fall under different attributes—ideas are mental or unextended, bodies are extended, so that one cannot resemble (and represent) the other. The interpretation is incorrect. In the first place, whereas Foucher was claiming that the Cartesians could not hold extended things are known, Berkeley was not merely arguing *ad hominem*. He was prepared to assert there are no unperceived extended substances. Second, for Berkeley a perceiver is directly aware of a color or a size or shape. (Actually, size is not perceived, but it makes no difference here.) Extension is a sensible quality. As such, according to Berkeley, it is an idea. Suppose we ask, following Watson's schema, under what attribute extension should be classed. The question really makes no sense. Extension (which differs in kind from thought) is directly known by the perceiving mind and is considered dependent upon the mind. It is, however, unlike mind. So Berkeley rejects (a). To put it differently, there is no contrast between extension and idea, but, rather, a contrast between extension and minds. See Richard Watson, *op. cit.*, 181–84 and 193–95, and Colin Turbayne, *op. cit.*, p. xv.

attempts to establish it. After they have mutually agreed that only sensible qualities or collections of them are immediately perceived, Philonous and Hylas pose the question upon which their disagreement turns: Doth the reality of sensible things consist in being perceived? or is it something distinct from their being perceived, and that bears no relation to the mind?[11] Hylas holds the reality of sensible things consists in their being able to occur unperceived and, subsequently, he is forced to deny the reality of sensible things.[12] Philonous tries to show that none of the determinate qualities we immediately perceive, be they primary or secondary, can occur unperceived.[13] To my knowledge at no point does the argument that a certain kind of quality must be perceived to exist turn on its being typed as an idea.[14] Which is to say, Berkeley systematically uses "idea" for sensible qualities only after he has shown that thesis C holds for them.

It is often held that Berkeley's immaterialism is parasitic upon (Lockian) representationalism, but a merit of my explication of Berkeley's Likeness Principle is that his

[11] *Works*, II, 175.

[12] Consider the following exchange, *Works*, II, 175: "PHILONOUS: I speak with regard to sensible things only: and of these I ask, whether by their real existence you mean a subsistence exterior to the mind, and distinct from their being perceived. HYLAS: I mean a real absolute being, distinct from, and without any relation to their being perceived. PHILONOUS: Heat, therefore, if it be allowed a real being, must exist without the mind. HYLAS: It must." Compare *Works*, II, 194 and 206–7.

[13] *Works*, II, 175–94. Note that the conclusion is always stated in terms of the inability of the quality in question to occur unperceived, apart from the mind or without the mind: pain (177, 179), tastes (180), odors (181), sounds (183), colors (187), extension (189–90), all primary qualities (191). The point is stated in summary on p. 194. After several attempts by Hylas to elude the conclusion, the point is considered settled (194–97). Subsequently, arguments against representationalism and material substances are developed. See G. Warnock, *Berkeley* (London: Penguin, 1953), pp. 150–51.

[14] It should be noted that Berkeley tries to identify heat, tastes and odors with pleasures and pains, which Hylas grants are mind-dependent sensations. But the identification is the key element in the argument.

arguments against representationalism and, as we shall see, unperceived material substances, are not dependent upon any theory of ideas. We perceive colors, sounds, odors, and various tactile qualities, not "ideas" of colors, sounds, and the rest. Berkeley claims a careful analysis of what actually is presented to consciousness will show colors and the rest can occur only in relation to a perceiving mind.[15] Given thesis C, thesis A precludes the occurrence of any determinate of color, shape, or sound unperceived. Notice that the occurrence of any such determinates unperceived by any given mind is not forbidden, only the possibility of their existing independently of all minds.

Descartes, Locke, Gassendi, and most, if not all, of the philosophers against whom Berkeley argued defined material substance as an extended, solid, unthinking entity.[16] Theses A and C together show that such an entity cannot exist. As defined, material substance is as self-contradictory as a square circle. We experience determinates of size, shape, and solidity, so determinates of these cannot occur except in relation to a perceiving mind. But material substance, which has determinates of these determinables, is not a thinking thing and can, by definition, occur unperceived. Material substance, as defined, has incompatible properties.[17]

[15] A disclaimer: I am not asserting that Berkeley succeeds in establishing C. The pain-heat identification argument, if sound, would establish C for the qualities in question, but the perceptual variations argument (e.g. the lukewarm water case) is at best grounds for a phenomenalistic analysis of, for example, "The same water seemed hot to my left hand, cold to my right." The conclusion Berkeley draws that sensible qualities cannot occur unperceived requires several additional assumptions. See my "Perceptual Relativity and Ideas in the Mind," *Philosophy and Phenomenological Research*, XXIV (1963), 202–14, Watson, *op. cit.*, 193–95, and E. B. Allaire, "Berkeley's Idealism," *Theoria*, XXIX (1963), 229–44 (reprinted in *Essays in Ontology*: [The Hague: Nijhoff, 1963], pp. 92–105).

[16] Descartes, of course, did not include solidity as a defining property, but held whatever is extended is solid. Hence, no vacuum.

[17] See Sections 7–9, 15, 17, 67, 73, and 78 in the *Principles*, in *Works*, II, 43–45, 47–48, 70, and 72–74. For similar passages in the *Three Dialogues*, see *Works*, II, 208–9 and 216–17.

In the second of the *Three Dialogues,* where Hylas wants to introduce material substance as an unperceived entity specifically different from minds, his problem is that if he offers any description of it, he will ascribe to material substance qualities which previously have been judged mind-dependent. If, on the other hand, he wants to make his claim that matter may exist meaningful, he must in some way define or characterize it. That lands him in trouble. No wonder he says in exasperation, "Oh Philonous! now you think you have entangled me; for if I say it (matter) exists in place, then you will infer that it exists in the mind, since it is agreed, that place or extension exists only in the mind."[18] He finally opts for saying he believes matter exists even though he can assign no positive meaning to the term. Philonous points out that no one can show the impossibility of matter if the word is given no definite sense but adds,

> Where there is not so much as the most inadequate or faint idea pretended to: I will not indeed thence conclude against the reality of any notion or existence of anything; but my inference shall be, that you mean nothing at all: that you employ words to no manner of purpose without any design or signification whatsoever. And I leave it to you to consider how mere jargon should be treated.[19]

Philonous challenges Hylas to specify a meaning of "material substance." If a meaning is given, he tries to show it involves determinables, determinates of which have been shown to be incapable of unperceived existence, so that material substances cannot in fact occur unperceived.[20]

The Likeness Principle has been analyzed as a combination of three theses, two of which (A and B) are relatively non-controversial. The third, that the determinate quali-

[18] *Works,* II, 222. Cf. the bottom of 260.
[19] *Works,* II, 223. Note the context, 222–26.
[20] I might add here that one sense of "abstract ideas" which Berkeley rejects is of unspecified or undetermined determinables. He claims that no such things exist. See *Works,* II, 28–30, 45–46 and 192–93. He thereby precludes the claim that though determinates cannot occur unperceived, determinables can.

ties we immediately perceive cannot occur unperceived, Berkeley's idealistic premise, is highly controversial. A and C together secure the impossibility of material substance, as defined within the classical tradition. The three theses combine to refute representationalism. By thus explicating the Likeness Principle, we have succeeded in showing that Berkeley's arguments do not depend upon his use of the term "idea." And thereby we can see the truth of Berkeley's claim that the issue between the materialists and him is not a verbal one.[21]

[21] Nor is it a matter of the linguistic analysis of "appears" and related words. See *Works*, II, 239–40 and especially 261–62.

THE PLACE OF GOD IN BERKELEY'S PHILOSOPHY

J. D. MABBOTT

Berkeley is commonly regarded as an idealist whose system is saved from subjectivism only by the advent of a God more violently *ex machina* than the God of any other philosopher. I hope to show that this accusation rests on a misunderstanding of his central theory, a misunderstanding which gives God a place both inconsistent with his main premisses and useless in his system. I hope also to display by quotation the real Berkeley, whose theory of God's place and nature is directly supported by argument and consistent with his premisses, and makes (with his account of self) a system which, if it is less than a completely coherent philosophy, is more than an episcopal assumption.

I shall first show how the usual conception of Berkeley's God arose. Locke had shown that our ideas of colour, taste and other secondary qualities depend on the percipient, but he held that primary qualities (shape, size, solidity, etc.) reside in the object just as we perceive them. Berkeley applied Locke's arguments about colour against shape and size, and showed that our ideas of the latter qualities were also relative to the percipient. Thus all my ideas depend on my perceiving them. This raises the obvious problem. "You ask me whether the books are in the study now, when no one is there to see them?"[1] "Upon

From *The Journal of Philosophical Studies* (now *Philosophy*), Vol. VI (1931). Reprinted by permission of the author and *Philosophy*. [All references are to the Oxford Edition of Berkeley's Works (Ed. Campbell Fraser, 4 vols., 1901) C. = *Commonplace Book*. P. = *Principles*. D. = *Dialogues*.]

[1] C. i. 15.

The Place of God in Berkeley's Philosophy

shutting my eyes all the furniture in the room is reduced to nothing, and barely upon opening them it is again created."[2] Berkeley first suggests two inadequate solutions. "Whenever they [the books] are mentioned or discours'd of they are imagin'd and thought on. Therefore you can at no time ask me whether they exist or no, but by reason of that very question they must necessarily exist."[3] Not only perception but imagination (or conception) also confers existence, and it is therefore impossible to conceive something existing unconceived. He also suggests that physical objects may have a hypothetical or potential existence, anticipating Mill's view that an object is a permanent possibility of sensation. "The question whether the earth moves or no amounts in reality to no more than this, to wit, whether we have reason to conclude, from what has been observed by astronomers, that if we were placed in such and such circumstances, and such or such a position, and distance both from the earth and sun, we should perceive the former to move among the choir of the planets."[4] Neither of these two solutions confer any real permanence or stability on the world of nature. "The trees are in the park, *i.e.* whether I will or no, whether I imagine anything about them or no. Let me but go thither and open my eyes by day, and I shall not avoid seeing them."[5] If *esse* is *percipi*, objects when perceived by no finite spirit must be kept in existence by God's perceiving them. "Seeing that they . . . have an existence distinct from being perceived by me, *there must be some other Mind wherein they exist.* As sure, therefore, as the sensible world really exists, so sure is there an infinite, omnipresent Spirit who contains and supports it."[6] This completes the orthodox account of Berkeley's view of the status of physical objects. The *esse* of ideas is *percipi*; the *esse* of spirit is *percipere*. "From what has been said it is evident that there is no other Substance than *Spirit,* or that which per-

[2] P. § 45, i. 281. [3] C. i. 15. Cf. P. § 23. D. I, i. 411.
[4] P. § 58, i. 290. [5] C. i. 65.
[6] D. II, i. 424; Berkeley's italics. Cf. P. § 46.

ceives."⁷ "The question between me and the Materialists is not whether things have a *real* existence out of the mind of this or that person, but whether they have an *absolute* existence, distinct from being perceived by God, and exterior to *all* minds."⁸ The *esse* of physical objects is therefore their being perceived by God. It is clear that this theory will save Berkeley from subjectivism, and it is to Divine perception that his editor, in defending him on the subjectivist charge, constantly makes appeal.⁹ Yet it is a solution of the problem which excludes much of his most valuable work and raises more difficulties than it solves.

The alternative theory can best be approached through Berkeley's account of power or activity. We usually speak as if conditions of physical objects were due to the activity of other physical objects. But, in reducing physical objects to ideas in the mind, Berkeley saw that this view of cause could not stand. If the *esse* of ideas is *percipi*, "it follows that there is nothing in them but what is perceived; but whoever shall attend to his ideas, whether of sense or of reflexion, will not perceive in them any power or activity."¹⁰ Therefore "the very being of an idea implies passivity or inertness in it."¹⁰ Sometimes, however, I know that I have created my own ideas. When I imagine a ship, I am aware of the image but also of the activity of my self. Here perception differs from imagination; if I perceive a ship, I have no such awareness of spiritual activity. "It is that passive recognition of my own ideas that denominates the mind perceiving—that being the very essence of perception or that wherein perception consists."¹¹ Since I am aware that I do not create my own ideas of perception, some other agent must produce them in me. "I find I can excite ideas in my mind at pleasure. . . . This making and unmaking of ideas doth very properly denominate the mind active. . . . But, whatever powers I may have over my own thoughts, I find the ideas actually perceived by Sense have not a like dependence on *my* will."¹²

⁷ P. § 7, i. 261.   ⁸ D. III, i. 452.
⁹ Cf. i. 50, *n.* 4, 258, *n.* 3, 259, *n.* 5, and *passim.*
¹⁰ P. § 25, i. 271.
¹¹ C. i. 83.   ¹² P. §§ 28, 29, i. 272–3.

The agent which produces them cannot be matter, for "Doth not *Matter*, in the common current acceptation of the word, signify an extended, solid, moveable, unthinking, inactive substance?"[13] This was indeed the account of matter current in Berkeley's day. Subsequent theories of atoms as centres of force, and the replacement of the Indestructibility of Matter by the Conservation of Energy as the basic principle of physics, left later scientists a way out of Berkeley's dilemma which was closed to his contemporaries. Against them his argument was conclusive. Since the agent affecting me when I perceive cannot be matter, and since spirit can be active, the cause must be spirit. "There is therefore some other Will or Spirit that produces them."[14] The nature of this Spirit can be deduced from its effects on me, from the character of my ideas of sense. Its power is clear from the fact that, however I try, I cannot perceive things otherwise than as I do. "The ideas of Sense are more strong, lively, and distinct than those of the Imagination; they have likewise a steadiness, order, and coherence, and are not excited at random, as those which are the effects of human wills often are, but in a regular train or series—the admirable connexion whereof sufficiently testifies the wisdom and benevolence of its Author."[15] It may be noted in passing that Berkeley uses no arguments from theology to support his belief in the existence of God, nor does he appeal to religious experience. He holds, indeed, that we have no immediate intuition of God.[16]

From the argument so far several difficulties in the usual account at once emerge. If mind is essentially active and perceiving essentially passive the *esse* of mind cannot be *percipere*. At the one place where in the *Commonplace Book* Berkeley says the *esse* of mind is *percipere* he has added later "or *velle, i.e. agere.*"[17] I am most myself not in perceiving but in willing or imagining. "This making or unmaking of ideas doth very properly denominate the

[13] D. II, i. 429.   [14] P. § 29, i. 273.   [15] P. § 30, i. 273.
[16] C. i. 51. Cf. P. § 148.   [17] C. i. 10.

mind active."[18] God is Spirit, and to suppose that He perceives would be to make Him the passive recipient of ideas impressed on Him by some more powerful agency. Volition and not perception is therefore our clue to the nature of God. "The Spirit—the active thing—that which is soul and God—is the Will alone."[19] "Substance of a spirit is that it acts," causes, wills, operates."[20] Nor can the *esse* of ideas be *percipi*. The *esse* of my own fancies is that they are imagined, created by me; of my sense-data that they are created in me by God. The *esse* of *God's* ideas (if we find any reason to believe in them, which we shall not) would be that they were imagined by Him, and even this is made difficult by Berkeley's view that imagination presupposes perception. "The having ideas is not the same thing with perception. A man may have ideas when he only imagines. But then this imagination presupposeth perception."[21]

So we are led to a new conception of God, and of His relation to the stable world which our senses reveal. Its stability will now be due to the regularity and orderliness of His activity, and not to His permanently perceiving it. "Nothing without corresponds to our primary ideas but powers. Hence a direct and brief demonstration of an active, powerful Being, distinct from us, on whom we depend."[22] The laws of nature are not modes of relation between God's ideas, but "set rules, or established methods, wherein the Mind we depend on excites in us the ideas of Sense."[23] We learn that certain of our ideas regularly accompany others. This concomitance is due to "the Goodness and Wisdom of that Governing Spirit whose Will constitutes the laws of nature."[24] The situation is like that created by a "good resolution." If I resolve to tidy up my papers regularly on Ember Days, what exists permanently is a disposition of my will. What exists only on Ember Days is the spatial pattern I call "tidy papers." So the trees in the park are permanently represented only by a "resolve" of the will of God such that as occasion

[18] P. § 28, i. 273.   [19] C. i. 41.   [20] C. i. 53.
[21] C. i. 28. Cf. i. 52.   [22] C. i. 60.
[23] P. § 30, i. 273.   [24] P. § 32, i. 274.

The Place of God in Berkeley's Philosophy 369

arises a spatial visual pattern (my idea of the trees) appears regularly in my mind. The physical world is thus really a complicated "good resolution" of God's. Two further illustrations may be adduced to show how a spatial datum may be regular and reliable, but not itself permanent. If I run my head into a brick wall, I see stars. The stars are not permanently there; they are the regular product of the meeting of my wayward steps with the permanent wall. So the table I perceive has no permanent shape or size; it is the regular product of the collision of my wayward activity with the permanent volition of God. Again, a magnetic field is force in itself invisible, but such that when iron filings are introduced into it they form regular, visible patterns. The application is obvious. We noticed above that one of Berkeley's inadequate solutions of his main problem was to allow the physical world a hypothetical or potential existence. This solution is now made possible for us by our having some reality from which the possibility is derived—the orderly volitional activity of God. "Bodies, etc., do exist even when not perceived—they being powers in the active being."[25]

This complete and coherent theory is much more entitled to be regarded as Berkeley's main position than that previously sketched. It alone is consistent with his distinction between perception and imagination, with his view that spirit is essentially active, and with his account of the relation between finite spirits and God. There seems, indeed, to be no need whatever in such a system for the realm of God's ideas. Yet Berkeley appears to have believed in them, as several references show, and as one of his special discussions may illustrate. One of the earliest queries in the *Commonplace Book* is, "Qu: Whether succession of ideas in the Divine Intellect?"[26] He later answers this query in the negative, and is then faced with the problem of the meaning of the Creation. He solves it by saying that, while God's ideas have existed from eter-

[25] C. i. 61.
[26] C. i. 58, accepting the view of Lorenz that p. 58 is Berkeley's earliest writing.

nity, Creation occurred when He made them perceptible to finite spirits. But if "they became perceptible in the same manner and order as is described in Genesis,"[27] a further difficulty appears. The creation of sun and moon could not have meant their becoming perceptible to man, who was created two days later. Berkeley ingeniously introduces the angels, "there being other intelligences before man was created."[28] Berkeley also gives reasons why we cannot dispense with God's ideas. God must be omniscient as well as omnipotent, for "to know everything knowable is certainly a perfection."[29] "There is in the Deity Understanding as well as Will. He is no blind agent, and in truth a blind agent is a contradiction."[30] In the Third Dialogue Hylas suggests that power alone is sufficient to account for our sense-data without God's having ideas. Philonous replies, "A thing which hath no ideas in itself cannot impart them to me."[31] This does not seem obvious, especially when he goes on to allow[32] that God, without having sense-data, can impart sense-data to me, and when we recall that all ideas are sense-data or are derived from them. "Ideas of Sense are the archetypes. Ideas of imagination, dreams, etc., are copies, images, of these."[33] I hope to show that, despite these definite expressions of opinion, Berkeley did not make the Divine Ideas an essential part of his system, and that there is good reason to doubt whether he believed in them at all.

There are many reasons why he should not believe in them. What is to be the relation between my ideas and God's? At this moment I have my idea of the table before me, and God has His. Surely this raises all the difficulties of a correspondence theory against which Berkeley fought so persistently. All that he says against Matter can be applied to attack this new correspondence. "Qu. Did ever any man see any other things besides his own ideas, that he should compare them to these, and make these like

[27] Letter to Percival, i. 353.
[28] C. i. 42. Cf. D. III, i. 472, 3.
[29] D. III, i. 459.   [30] C. i. 51.   [31] D. III, i. 457.
[32] D. III, i. 459.   [33] C. i. 52. Cf. i. 28.

unto them?"³⁴ "Well, say I, Do you apprehend or conceive what you say extension is like unto, or do you not? If the latter, how know you they are alike? How can you compare any things besides your own ideas?"³⁵ God's ideas are as useless as Matter in Locke's theory. "Ask a man, I mean a philosopher, why he supposes this vast structure, this compages of bodies? he shall be at a stand; he'll not have one word to say."³⁶ "But then, that they should suppose an innumerable multitude of created beings, which they acknowledge are not capable of producing any one effect in nature, and which therefore are made to no manner of purpose, since God might have done everything as well without them—this, I say, though we should allow it possible, must yet be a very unaccountable and extravagant supposition."³⁷ "How therefore can you suppose that an All-perfect Spirit, on whose Will all things have an absolute and immediate dependence, should need an instrument in His operations, or, not needing it, make use of it? Thus it seems to me you are obliged to own the use of a lifeless inactive instrument to be incompatible with the infinite perfection of God."³⁸ "The Will of an Omnipotent Spirit is no sooner exerted than executed, without the application of means."³⁹ In all these passages the objections are as valid against God's ideas—all ideas being inactive—as against Matter.

Again, if the reality our ideas represent is the world of God's ideas, Berkeley's principal claim for his theory must fall—his claim that it is a direct theory of perception. "We must with the mob place certainty in the senses."⁴⁰ "There are others who say the wall is not white, the fire is not hot, etc. We Irishmen cannot attain to these truths."⁴¹ "We see the house itself, the church itself; it being an idea and nothing more."⁴² What I perceive directly *is* the physical object, and all theories to the con-

---

³⁴ C. i. 61.   ³⁵ C. i. 82.   ³⁶ C. i. 16.
³⁷ P. § 53, i. 287. Cf. D. II, i. 427.   ³⁸ D. II, i. 432.
³⁹ *Ibid.*, 433.   ⁴⁰ C. i. 44. Cf. D. I, i. 383.
⁴¹ C. i. 91.
⁴² C. i. 9. Cf. D. III, i. 463, and especially i. 445. ". . . the real things are those very things I see and feel."

trary are agnostic. "The reverse of the Principle introduced Scepticism."[43] "Colour, figure, motion, extension, and the like, considered only as so many *sensations* in the mind, are perfectly known. . . . But, if they are looked on as notes or images referred to *things* or *archetypes existing without the mind*, then we are involved all in scepticism. We see only the appearances, and not the real qualities of things. . . . All this scepticism follows from our supposing a difference between *things* and *ideas*."[44] It follows no less inevitably from supposing a difference between our ideas and God's.

A further reason why Berkeley might well have dispensed with a belief in Divine Ideas is his reiterated assertion that ideas are inert and passive,[45] and the fact that God's ideas would have necessarily to be spatial.[46] " 'Tis nevertheless of great use to religion to take extension out of our idea of God, and put a power in its place. It seems dangerous to suppose extension, which is manifestly inert, in God."[47] It is equally dangerous to suppose any ideas (for all are inert) in God, who is pure activity. "I do not understand how our ideas, which are things altogether passive and inert, can be the essence, or any part (or like any part) of the essence or substance of God, who is an impassive, indivisible, pure, active being."[48]

It may be suggested that Berkeley can avoid the correspondence difficulty and the scepticism it involves by identifying our ideas with God's. On this view, when we perceive, God reveals His ideas to us. "There is an *omnipresent eternal Mind*, which Knows and comprehends all things, and exhibits them to our view in such a manner . . . as He Himself hath ordained."[49] This view is still open to the objection that things passive and inert can be no part of God, and to the further difficulty that all our sense-data are private, because of our varied view-points, as the "New Theory of Vision" exhaustively proved. An identification of our ideas with God's is also attributed by

[43] C. i. 83. [44] P. § 87, i. 305–6. Cf. D. I, i. 382, 418.
[45] E.g. i. 10, 13, 37, 41, 271, 429.
[46] This will be defended later. See *Note* at end.
[47] C. i. 82. [48] D. II, i. 426. [49] D. III, i. 447.

The Place of God in Berkeley's Philosophy 373

Berkeley to Malebranche as the view "that we see all things in God," and attacked accordingly. The dualism might also be avoided by holding that, in the act of perceiving, my mind is identified with God's—the theory used by T. H. Green in the case of conceptual relation. But Berkeley was much too vague about the implications of personality, and too stout a spiritual pluralist for moral reasons, to rob the finite self of any independence. If both these theories are rejected, the correspondence with its difficulties must stand.

For the reasons given above, it does not seem likely that Berkeley himself believed in the Divine Ideas, at least as a necessary part of his system. It is true that he frequently mentions them, but we shall now show that some of these expressions are suggestively guarded. In one place[50] he discusses the view that "Matter, though it be not perceived by us, is nevertheless perceived by God, to whom it is the occasion of exciting ideas in our minds." He remarks first that this theory gives up the absolute independence of matter, and is therefore "the only intelligible one that I can pick from what is said of unknown occasions," but he adds that "it seems too extravagant to deserve a confutation." Yet this extravaganza is identified by most critics with Berkeleianism. "The upshot of all is, that there are certain *unknown* Ideas in the mind of God." "Whether there are such ideas in the mind of God I shall not dispute."[51] "I shall not dispute"—not only here, but in other places also, this is the best he can say for those Divine Ideas which are supposed to be the keystone of his own theory. Philonous is prepared to "allow" Hylas that there may be certain things perceived by the mind of God, which are to Him the occasion of producing ideas in us.[52] Berkeley is consulted on this very point by Rev. Samuel Johnson, who aims here a more shrewd blow against the Bishop than his notorious namesake. In reply Berkeley says he "has no objection against calling the Ideas in the Mind of God archetypes of ours."[53] He is prepared to "allow"

---
[50] P. § 70–75, i. 296 ff.
[51] P. § 76, i. 300.   [52] D. II, i. 434.
[53] Letter to Johnson, quoted, ii. 19.

Divine Ideas because they do not offend against his central doctrine that nothing is independent of Mind. But the admission is not readily made, for they are really foreign to his system.

It remains to ask why he should have mentioned them at all. Three reasons can be found. He probably came to them first; the simple symmetry of the crude theory sketched at the beginning of this paper makes it an obvious first refuge for a sinking subjectivist. If, however, such a development took place, it must have preceded all his published works, for the *Commonplace Book* shows the mature theory complete. The only shred of evidence for this suggestion may perhaps be found in the alteration of *percipere* to *agere* as the *esse* of spirit.[54] Secondly, theological considerations about omniscience would suggest the addition of the Divine Ideas to his completed system. Thirdly, it is much less alarming and revolutionary to think of the trees in the park existing when nobody perceives them, because they, with all their friendly, familiar qualities, are perceived by God, than to think of them as represented in God's mind by powers or volitions quite unlike them in character. Here is the real reason for the appearance of God's ideas in the published works, and especially in the popular Dialogues. In the *Commonplace Book*, Berkeley is uncompromising. "Bodies *taken for powers* do exist when not perceived."[55] "*Nothing* without corresponds to our primary ideas but powers."[56] But he resolves "Not to mention the combinations of powers, but to say the things—*the effects themselves*—do really exist, even when not actually perceived, but still with relation to perception."[57] And why? " 'Tis prudent to correct men's mistake without altering their language. This makes truth glide into their souls insensibly."[58]

If it is said that Divine perception is after all a possible theory and is quite definitely asserted by Berkeley, a much more striking example of his way of "humouring" his audience "in their own way of talking"[59] can be adduced.

[54] C. i. 10, quoted above. [55] C. i. 82. [56] C. i. 60.
[57] C. i. 50. Italics in last three quotations mine.
[58] C. i. 71. [59] C. i. 92.

In the *New Theory of Vision* he writes throughout as if tangible sense-data were independent of the percipient. The *Commonplace Book* shows that he had already decided that all sense-data were mind-dependent, so that this is part of a policy of gradualness. Not until the *Principles* does he attack tangibilia also. There is no question of development. The *Commonplace Book* (1705-8) gives the material for his whole system (except the technical term "notion"—the need of which is noted[60]); and the *New Theory* (1709), the *Principles* (1710), and the *Dialogues* (1713) show differences which are merely strategic. The Divine perception of the physical world is no more part of the system than is the independent reality of tangibilia. Both appear in the published works to mitigate the jar which the undiluted theory would administer to the plain man's system. The only difference between the two cases is that the reality of tangibilia (which is the more bluntly stated of the two) is incompatible with the whole system, while the existence of Divine Ideas conflicts only with parts of it, so that he can continue to treat their existence as an independently possible theological tenet, as the doctrine of the Trinity might be, but with as little connection with his philosophy as it has. "N.B. To use utmost caution not to give the least handle of offence to the Church or Churchmen."[61]

Campbell Fraser raises one point of difficulty for our insistence on the irrelevance of God's Ideas. The theory that our sense-data form a "natural language" continually recurs in Berkeley's works, and his editor explains the conception by saying "Sense-ideas are the letters of the alphabet in that language of natural order which God employs for the expression of *His* Ideas to us."[62] If this is correct, the natural language requires the existence of God's Ideas; otherwise the words of the language would be meaningless or express nothing. There are certainly difficulties about Berkeley's language theory. In the *New Theory of Vision* the words of the language were visible

---

[60] i. 21, "improper . . . to make ourselves ideas, or thinking things ideas."
[61] C. i. 41. [62] i. 309, *n*. 2.

colours and shapes, and they stood for the real or tangible objects. But when tangibilia are overtly admitted to be mind-dependent a difficulty arises. If we say one type of sense-datum (visible) expresses another (tangible), we lose the distinction of status which we should expect to separate a language from what it means. If, on the other hand, we make the whole world of sense-data the language, and also eliminate God's Ideas as unknown and self-contradictory, what will the language express? Berkeley sometimes answers—the attributes of God. "The steady consistent methods of nature may not unfitly be styled the Language of its Author whereby he discovers his attributes to our view."[63] But in other places he says that sense-data stand for other sense-data; "the proper objects of sight"—light and colours—"do form a language wonderfully adapted to suggest and exhibit to us the distances, figures, situations, and various qualities of tangible objects . . . as words suggest the things signified by them."[64] Perhaps a *modus vivendi* might be arranged by distinguishing what words *express* from what they *evince*. If I say "There is the door," my words express a relation in space, but they evince anger. So God's words—our sense-data—express or suggest other sense-data, but evince His power and good will. Whatever our solution may be, there is never a suggestion in the whole of Berkeley's work that the "natural language" stands for God's ideas. This possibility is definitely rejected in the pamphlet *The Theory of Vision Vindicated and Explained*, which was published in 1732, and which is interesting also as giving one of the clearest statements of the view we have ventured to call "the real Berkeley." "The objects of sense . . . are called ideas. . . . From our ideas of sense, the inference of reason is good to power, cause, agent. But we may not infer that our ideas are like unto this Power, Cause, or Active Being. On the contrary, it seems evident that an idea can be only like another idea, and that in our ideas . . . there is nothing of power, causality, or agency included. . . . Whenever, therefore, the appellation of sensible *object* is used in a

[63] P. § 108, i. 317.   [64] Alciphron IV. 10, ii. 168.

The Place of God in Berkeley's Philosophy

determined, intelligible sense, it is not applied to signify this absolutely existing outward cause or power, but the ideas themselves produced thereby. Ideas which are observed to be connected together are vulgarly considered under the relation of cause and effect, whereas, in strict and philosophic truth, they are only related as sign to the thing signified."[65]

It may also be objected that we have left "Siris" out of account. The reasons are many. If we exclude "Siris," Berkeley's system shows no development except the use of the word "notion" to cover our knowledge of spirits and some dissatisfaction with his attack on Abstract Ideas. In the "Siris" we find a new world. Its Platonic mysticism, its toleration of forms and influences, its reverent agnosticism, its dependence on the *Timæus* and Proclus, are poles apart from the Berkeley of the other works. It is true that Divine Ideas are important in "Siris," but they are no more than those "Forms" of Plato which the misunderstandings of Albinus and his followers (popularized by the deceptive transliteration of the Greek word "idea") had transmuted into "Ideas in the Divine Mind." There is nothing Berkeleian about them. To attempt to unite the hints and gropings of "Siris" into some kind of dusky Christian Platonism, and then to regard the result as characteristic of Berkeley, would be like making the Catholic faith the central belief of Voltaire on the strength of his reputed death-bed conversion. Catholicism and Voltaire make as strange bed-fellows as "Siris" and Berkeley.

If it is said that God must have some theoretical activity —He cannot be a blind agent—our answer is that this may well be true, but that all Berkeley's main tenets preclude it. His mistake no doubt was to limit theoretical activity to the passive reception of sense-data and their imaginative reproduction, and thereby to make such experience impossible for God. But Berkeley without these limitations is not Berkeley, but Kant or (as in "Siris") Plato. If he had extended his so-called doctrine of notions from spirits to relations, as he did, and from relations to universals, as he

[65] *Op. cit.*, §§ 12, 13, ii. 386.

did not, he could have allowed God to have notions. "God knows or has ideas, but his ideas are not conveyed to him by sense as ours are."[66] But the first extension, to relations, is illegitimate, for relations are passive and notions are of the active. Such extensions would take us far beyond Berkeleianism, though they might take us nearer truth. They would recall too much the methods of last century's Hegelians, who, when they had to examine a philosopher, tended inevitably to "elicit" from him the Hegelian position or to "develop" him until it emerged.[67] Berkeley in the history of philosophy must always be the Berkeley of 1705 to 1713, and that means a Berkeley to whom God is essentially Will and not Thought.

Note.—There are certain considerations which suggest that God's ideas, if He has any, must be spatial. We might be tempted to hold that they are "unknown"[68] in character, but represented to us by spatial data, as are Kant's things-in-themselves. In illustration of this we might quote the army system in which disciplinary relationships are represented in most languages by spatial terms. Lance-corporals and bombardiers are "on the same level," and "above them" are corporals. If a savage had this organization described to him, he would naturally suppose that an army meant a large pyramidal pile of men with a Field-Marshal sitting "at the top" and a thick layer of oppressed privates "at the bottom." The growing use of graphs has familiarized most people with this idea of representing a function with two variables (non-spatial in character) by means of a line plotted with the aid of two spatial axes. Why should not God's ideas (themselves non-spatial, like the spiritual relationships which unite an army) be represented to us by spatial sense-data (as we say "transfer, degrade, sous-officier, High Command," etc.)?

The answer is that the two dimensions in an army are not interconvertible. You could explain to a savage move-

[66] D. III, i. 458.
[67] Cf. Caird on Kant, or Bosanquet on Plato.
[68] P. § 75, quoted, p. 25.

The Place of God in Berkeley's Philosophy

ments in each "dimension" taken separately; the ease with which a private could become a corporal compared with the difficulty of his becoming a general marks one "dimension," the simplicity of transferring from one company to another contrasted with the difficulty of the transfer to another regiment giving the other. But you could not combine the two in a single measure; the distance between a Sergeant in the Seaforths and a Private of the Buffs is strictly immeasurable. In a spatial field there is such a "diagonal" distance. If X is three miles north of O and P is four miles west of X, then P is five miles northwest of O, both direction and distance being fully determinable. Space is a continuum whose three dimensions have a common unit of measure, and—here is the crucial point—it is the only continuum of this kind; therefore if God's ideas are to have all the varieties of relation which our ideas manifest, they must have a character which we find exemplified only in space itself. Otherwise the derivative will be richer in relations than that from which it is derived. Thus our illustrations by means of army organization, etc., all break down, and it seems that the reality our spatial ideas represent must itself be spatial. Here also, perhaps, we may find a reason for rejecting Berkeley's theory of the physical world, placing power in God, in favour of the view that places power in spatial centres. But the main aim of this paper was to determine what Berkeley himself believed, and not to find difficulties in his system.

BERKELEY AND GOD
JONATHAN BENNETT

It is well known that Berkeley had two arguments for the existence of God. A while ago, in trying to discover what these arguments are and how they fit into Berkeley's scheme of things, I encountered certain problems which are hardly raised, let alone solved, in the standard commentaries. I think that I have now solved these problems, and in this paper I present my results.

THE CONTINUITY ARGUMENT

The argument which is immortalised in the limericks about the tree in the quad, and which I shall call the continuity argument, goes as follows:
  (a) No idea, and therefore no collection of ideas, can exist when not perceived by some spirit;
  (b) Objects are collections of ideas, and therefore cannot exist when not perceived by some spirit;
  (c) Objects do sometimes exist when not perceived by any human spirit;
therefore
  (d) There must be one or more non-human spirits which perceive objects when no human spirit perceives them.

The first premiss reflects Berkeley's penchant for speaking of ideas which people 'perceive' where one would prefer that he spoke of sensory states which people may be in. This is one aspect of that reification of ideas or sense-data

From *Philosophy*, Vol. XL (1965). Reprinted, with minor corrections, by permission of the author and *Philosophy*.

which ran through Locke, Berkeley and Hume, and which has, in my opinion, vitiated much of the epistemology of the present century; but it raises issues which go too deep to be explored now. The second premiss reflects Berkeley's failure to see that, even if what we say about objects is reducible to what we say about sensory states, the mode of reduction might be too complex for terms like 'collection' to be in place. That is, it reflects his having opted for his kind of idealism, rather than for phenomenalism. If Berkeley had not taken this option, he could not have used the continuity argument, for its second premiss would then not have been available to him; but that too lies deep in Berkeley's thought and forms no part of my present concern. Nor shall I consider the yawning gulf between the conclusion of the argument and the Christian monotheism which it is supposed to serve. This gulf, and the moves which Berkeley might make to bridge it, are matters of routine apologetics which have little philosophical interest. The questions which I do wish to answer are these:

(1) Why does Berkeley think that he is entitled to the argument's third premiss, which says that objects do exist when not perceived by any human spirit? The argument depends, through its second premiss, upon equating statements about the existence of objects not with statements about sensory states which *would* be had if certain conditions obtained, but with statements about the existence of sensory states the having of which is the perceiving of objects. From this, one would have thought, it follows very obviously that there could not be grounds for saying that any object exists at a time when no human perceives it.

(2) Why does Berkeley not use the continuity argument in his *Principles of Human Knowledge*? It will not do to say that he did not think of it until after that work was written, and that this is why it appears only in the *Three Dialogues*. If Berkeley had seen how bad the argument is, he would not have used it at all; failing to see that, he ought to have thought it deeply satisfactory. If, in addition, the continuity argument came to him as a new discovery after the writing of the *Principles*, he would

surely have highlighted it in the later work which was supposed to remedy the unfavourable reception of the earlier. Yet in the *Three Dialogues* the argument is presented just once, in a passage consisting of two short sentences. This remark may be found surprising, but I shall justify it.

THE PASSIVITY ARGUMENT

Berkeley's other argument for God's existence, which I shall call the passivity argument, goes as follows:
(a) My ideas of sense (i.e. those which I have when I perceive objective states of affairs) come into my mind without being caused to do so by any act of my will;
(b) The occurrence of any idea must be caused by the will of some being in whose mind the idea occurs;
therefore
(c) My ideas of sense are in the mind of, and caused by the will of, some being other than myself.
Underlying this argument is Berkeley's belief that brute-fact regularities are not truly causal, and that the only genuinely causal activity is the purposeful behaviour of sentient beings. The argument also involves a dubious assumption about the notion of an 'act of the will'. These flaws in the argument go to the heart of what I take to be some of Berkeley's most radical errors, but I shall discuss neither them nor the extent to which the passivity argument, even if valid, falls short of creating a presumption in favour of Christianity. The questions which I wish to answer are these:

(3) Why does Berkeley accept the second premiss of the argument? Granted his belief that causal activity is the prerogative of 'the will of a spirit', why does Berkeley think that every change in anyone's sensory state must have a cause?

(4) Does Berkeley see—and, if so, why does he not *say* —that the passivity argument gives to God a quite different scope from that given to him by the continuity argu-

Berkeley and God

ment? By the passivity argument, God perceives objects when we perceive them; by the continuity argument, God perceives objects when we do not. The two arguments are not in conflict on this point; indeed they are, on the face of it, agreeably complementary. Why does Berkeley not call attention to this striking feature of his theological arguments?

THE POINT OF THE QUESTIONS

I have waived a number of objections which depend upon Berkeley's not having seen further than he did into the nature of objectivity concepts, causal necessity, volition, sensory states, and so on. He was only Berkeley, not God; it takes time, and generations of stumbling, to get these deep and difficult matters right. But my question (1), about the existence of objects when they are perceived by no human, does not concern a deep error on Berkeley's part, but simply points to an obvious conflict between the continuity argument and one of Berkeley's most cherished views. We must therefore answer the question if we are to be able to trace the movement of thought in Berkeley's pages. To understand a philosopher we need not believe everything he says, but we must at least be able to see how he could have made the mistakes which he did make. My answers to questions (2) and (4) will, it is true, rob (1) of most of its interest; but it is nevertheless just worth asking, and there are exegetical lessons to be learned from answering it.

My question (3), about the assumption that every change of sensory state is caused, is in a slightly different case. It is arguable that Berkeley was one of those philosophers—we know there have been many—who assume without question that there are no absolutely brute facts. I found this answer to (3) unconvincing, even before I had an alternative to it; and there *is* an alternative. Berkeley may not have taken it as axiomatic that every change of sensory state must be caused: he does give a reason for accepting this premiss of the passivity argument, though so far no commentator seems to have noticed it. I have found it only once in Berkeley's writings, and it may be that Berkeley put no weight upon it, and was after all one of those for whom it is axiomatic that every 'Why?'-question has an answer. Nevertheless, as with (1), there is profit to be gained from taking question (3) as seriously as possible, if only because (1) and (3) are useful pegs on which to hang some exegetical material which is vital for the answering of (2) and (4).

Questions (2) and (4) raise general issues about what sort of thing Berkeley thought he was doing with his theological arguments and—more important—*what kind of scepticism it was that he was so anxious to disavow*. Unless these issues are resolved, we cannot have an intelligent and informed picture of what is happening in the *Principles* and the *Three Dialogues*. I doubt if anything of live philosophical importance depends upon the answers to (2) and (4); but other aspects of Berkeley do still have something to teach us, and we shall not profit from them if we do not see clearly the total endeavour of which they form a part.

There is another matter which concerns all four questions. Berkeley's thought has more hard, complex structure than is usually realised. In his pages there is a less elaborate apparatus of self-conscious pros and cons, explanations and caveats, definitions and distinctions, than we should expect to find in a twentieth-century writer of similar scope; but the complexity and intellectual sophistication are there all the same; and it seems to me bad and unhealthy that Berkeley should be kept alive, to be hurriedly scanned from time to time and made the subject of elementary books, without proper attention being paid to the detailed ways in which his thought moved. I make this protest on behalf not only of Berkeley but also of Locke and Hume, Spinoza and Leibniz. A recent writer, for example, has described Hume's section 'Of Scepticism with regard to the Senses' as ironical. No one could say this who had toiled through that section trying to find out

Berkeley and God

in detail what is going on in it; and if the section is not studied in detail, it should not be studied at all. No one would skim through a chapter by Moore, say, and then expect to be thanked for an impressionistic account of its main drift; and yet this kind of condescension is accorded to the immeasurably tougher, abler, more sophisticated and more genuinely complex thought of such philosophers as Berkeley.

AN ANSWER TO QUESTION (3)

The question is: Why does Berkeley, in the passivity argument, help himself to the assumption that there must be what he would call a 'cause' for any change in anyone's sensory state? In *Principles* §26 he says: 'We perceive a continual succession of ideas, some are anew excited, others are changed or disappear. There is therefore some cause of these ideas whereon they depend, and which produces and changes them.' This suggests that Berkeley just is a philosopher of that familiar kind who cannot entertain the possibility that an intelligible 'Why?' might have no answer. This broadly rationalist frame of mind is sympathetically described by Warnock in connection with his answer to my question (3): 'The true foundation of his view is, I believe, the conviction that to hold that events merely *occur*, without any purpose and volition behind them or anything analogous with purpose and volition, is to say something which is really quite *unintelligible* . . .' (*Berkeley*, p. 123).

In the passage I have cited, Berkeley is not deploying the passivity argument for God's existence, but merely arguing quite generally for the existence of spirits. He could as well have left causes out altogether, and used his stock argument that there must be spirits because it is 'repugnant' that ideas should exist unowned. Since Berkeley is not here centrally concerned with the special case of ideas in respect of which one is passive, we should not put too much weight on his seeming to take it for granted that every change in one's ideas must have some cause. In *Principles* §29, however, the case is different: 'Whatever power I may have over my own thoughts, I find the ideas actually perceived by sense have not a like dependence on my will. . . . There is therefore some other will or spirit that produces them. . . .' We are now in the region where there is a prima facie case for denying that the change in one's ideas has a cause, because one is not the cause of them oneself; and yet Berkeley apparently takes it for granted that there must be some cause. This looks like support for Warnock's diagnosis of him as, in a broad sense, a rationalist.

On the other hand, Berkeley does not read like a rationalist. In his account of those regularities which are usually taken to be causal, he is as blandly and confidently final as Hume, and one does not have the impression that this is only because he thinks that in disqualifying observed regularities from counting as causal he is making room for something else equally comprehensive. This is a matter of tone and of nuance, and unaided it will bear no weight at all; but it is confirmed in *Principles* §146: 'Those things which are called the works of nature, that is, the far greater part of the ideas or sensations perceived by us, are not produced by, or dependent on, the wills of men. There is therefore some other spirit that causes them, since it is repugnant that they should subsist by themselves.' Here, if English grammar counts for anything, Berkeley gives a *reason* for saying that a change in my ideas which I do not cause must be caused by some other spirit, namely that ideas cannot 'subsist by themselves'. Normally, when Berkeley says that ideas cannot subsist by themselves, he is making a point about the ownership of ideas: every idea must be someone's. But now, it seems, he is inferring from this that the occurrence of any idea must be caused. This is a non-sequitur, but there is a distinction to be made between a thesis which a philosopher defends by an invalid argument and one which he sees no need to support with arguments at all.

There is something to be learned from this particular

non-sequitur. I think that it turns upon an ambiguity in the word 'depend': I suggest, that is, that in the passage I have quoted Berkeley slides from 'not dependent on (= not caused by) my mind' to 'dependent on (= caused by) some other mind', through the general formula that necessarily every idea must depend on (= exist in, or be owned by) some mind.

It is certainly true that when Berkeley discusses the relation between ideas and minds in terms of 'depend' and its grammatical cognates, he does use these words both to talk about the ownership of ideas by minds and to talk about the causing of ideas by minds. Some generous collaborators in Cambridge have put me in possession of all Berkeley's uses of 'depend' and its cognates throughout the *Principles* and the *Three Dialogues*; and the facts are as follows. There is a muddled and unclassifiable use of 'dependent' in *Principles* §12; there are half a dozen places where 'depend' is used logically, i.e. where a theory is said to depend upon another theory, or a problem to depend upon a prejudice; and there are a dozen uses of 'depend' or its cognates in which the items whose dependence is spoken of are not ideas at all, e.g. where Berkeley says that we depend on God or that God is independent of everything. Of the remaining uses of 'depend', etc., all but four fall squarely into one or other of two classes:

The ownership uses. In *Principles* §§6, 89, 91, in the first dialogue, pp. 158,[1] 163-64, in the second dialogue, p. 176, and in the third dialogue, p. 223, Berkeley uses 'independent', 'dependent' (once) and 'independency' (once) to make a point about the ownership of ideas. In each of these passages, the question of whether an idea is independent of a given mind is the question of whether it exists unowned by, not had by, or as Berkeley would say 'not perceived by', the mind in question.

[1] Page-numbers are those in David M. Armstrong (ed.), *Berkeley's Philosophical Writings*. Those who do not have this may be helped to check my references by the information that in the Armstrong volume the first dialogue is on pp. 135-171, the second on pp. 171-189, and the third on pp. 189-225.

The causal uses. In *Principles* §§10, 26, 29, 33, 106, in the first dialogue, pp. 159, 160, in the second dialogue, p. 177, and in the third dialogue, p. 197, Berkeley uses 'depend' and four of its grammatical cognates to make a point about the *causes* of ideas. In these passages, an idea is dependent on a given mind if it is caused or 'excited' by that mind.

Berkeley has, then, two distinct jobs for the 'depend' family to do; and he too must agree that they *are* distinct, since he does not think that the only ideas which occur in my mind are ones which are caused by my mind. Since he nowhere comments on this double use of 'depend', one suspects that he has not noticed it; and this suspicion is immeasurably strengthened by *Principles* §56 where Berkeley criticises an inference which turns upon the very ambiguity which I have noted (the italics are mine): 'Men knowing they perceived several ideas whereof they were not themselves the authors, as not being excited from within nor *depending on* the operation of their wills, this made them maintain those ideas or objects of perception had an existence *independent of* and without the mind, without ever dreaming that a contradiction was involved in those words.' Here Berkeley says that a contradictory conclusion has been drawn from a true premiss, and thus he implies that the argument is invalid. Its invalidity clearly turns upon the fact that in the premiss 'not . . . depending on' means 'not caused by', while in the conclusion 'independent of' means 'not owned by'; *but Berkeley does not remark on this ambiguity*. Apparently he is so totally unaware of the ambiguity as a possible source of danger that he does not spot it even where it engenders a fallacy which he is actively engaged in pointing out.

It therefore seems clear that the passage I have quoted from *Principles* §146 should be interpreted in the way I have suggested, i.e. as an unrecognised exploitation of the ambiguity of 'dependent on'. At any rate, Berkeley does argue from 'All ideas are owned' to 'All ideas are caused', and the word 'dependent' is *there*. If it is not the source of the trouble, then the passage involves a non-sequitur which is about twice as bad as anything else in the book.

THE ANSWER TO QUESTION (1)

The question is: Why does Berkeley, in the continuity argument, allow himself the premiss that objects exist while not perceived by any human? A possible answer is that this is such a deep-rooted, normal human assumption that Berkeley could not help making it even though he could not, on his own philosophical principles, be entitled to make it. Thus Warnock: 'Berkeley . . . knows that any plain man would insist that the furniture in an unoccupied room actually does exist, not merely that it would exist if the room were occupied; and he himself thinks that it would be merely absurd to question this' (*Berkeley*, p. 115).

This strikes me as false. In many places, Berkeley calmly says that if we clear our minds we shall see that we have no grounds for believing in the existence of objects while they are unperceived. See for example *Principles* §4, and also the following from *Principles* §6: 'All those bodies which compose the mighty frame of the world have not any subsistence without a mind; their being (esse) is to be perceived; consequently so long as they are not actually perceived by me, or do not exist in my mind or that of any other created spirit, they must either have no existence at all, or else subsist in the mind of some eternal spirit.' These are not the words of someone who would add that since objects do exist when not perceived by created spirits therefore there must be an eternal spirit which perceives them. The suggestion is rather that unless we can find independent grounds for believing that there is an eternal spirit we are not entitled to say that objects exist while not perceived by any created spirit; and someone whose mind is working this way cannot base the continuity argument for God's existence on the premiss that it is just obvious that objects exist when not perceived by any created spirit.

Again, in *Principles* §§45–8, Berkeley discusses the charge 'that from the foregoing principles it follows [that] things are every moment annihilated and created anew. ... Upon shutting my eyes, all the furniture in the room is reduced to nothing, and barely upon opening them it is again created.' He does not reply that of course *that* would be absurd, but.... On the contrary, he says that the charge itself is absurd, and that, since anyone who brings it must admit that it is impossible 'either for his ideas or their archetypes to exist without being perceived ... it is unreasonable for him to stand up in defence of he knows not what, and pretend to charge on me as an absurdity the not assenting to those propositions which at bottom have no meaning' (§45). He proceeds to devote two sections to arguing that certain rival schools of philosophy are committed to the same conclusion, and only then does he remark mildly that after all he is not committed to the conclusion himself: 'Though we hold, indeed, the objects of sense to be nothing else but ideas which cannot exist unperceived, yet we may not hence conclude they have no existence except only while they are perceived by us, since there may be some other spirit that perceives them, though we do not. Wherever bodies are said to have no existence without the mind, I would not be understood to mean this or that particular mind, but all minds whatsoever. It does not therefore follow from the foregoing principles that bodies are annihilated and created every moment, or exist not at all during the intervals between our perception of them' (§48). The crucial expressions are 'we may not thence *conclude*', 'there *may* be some other spirit', 'it does not therefore *follow*'. These are not the words of someone who proposes to base the continuity argument on the absurdity of denying that objects have a continuous existence.

(Among all the commentators who credit Berkeley with a confident belief in the existence of objects when they are not perceived by humans, Dawes Hicks and Luce do at least see that *Principles* §§45–8 needs some explaining away. Warnock, on the other hand, says: 'It would, he says, be absurd to suggest that "things are every moment annihilated and created anew" ...' (*Berkeley*, p. 115). Warnock gives no reference for the clause he quotes, but we have seen that it comes from *Principles* §45, in which Berkeley resolutely, and mockingly, refuses to say that it is absurd!)

We find the solution to the puzzle in the third dialogue (p. 193), where Hylas asks: 'Supposing you were annihilated, cannot you conceive it possible that things perceivable by sense may still exist?' Philonous replies: 'I can; but then it must be in another mind. When I deny sensible things an existence out of the mind, I do not mean my mind in particular, but all minds. Now it is plain they have an existence exterior to my mind, since I find them by experience to be independent of it. There is therefore some other mind wherein they exist, during the intervals between the time of my perceiving them: as likewise they did before my birth, and would do after my supposed annihilation.' Here we have the ambiguity of 'depend' etc., which I noted earlier, but this time exploited in reverse. I find 'by experience' that some ideas are independent of (= not caused by) my mind, and I therefore conclude that they are independent of my mind (= owned by some mind other than mine), and thence that they can exist after my annihilation.

The passivity argument has the dubious premiss that *all ideas are caused by some mind*, while the continuity argument has the dubious premiss that *some ideas are not owned by my mind*. Now if we replace 'caused' by 'owned' in the former of these, the result is something which Berkeley is entitled to accept; and similarly if we replace 'owned' by 'caused' in the latter. Berkeley has, in effect, performed these substitutions by expressing each premiss in terms of 'dependent on' and interpreting this in the way most favourable to the purpose in hand. If this is not a correct account of this third-dialogue passage, what other explanation can be given for Berkeley's allowing himself to say that we 'find by experience' that some of our ideas are 'exterior' to our minds in a sense which is relevant to their continuity 'during the intervals between the time of our perceiving them'?

It may be thought that I have rested too much on one brief and rather casual presentation of the continuity argument; but I make no apology for this, since the passage I have quoted from the third dialogue is Berkeley's *only* presentation of the continuity argument. In my next two sections I shall show that this is so.

'REALITY' IN BERKELEY

When Berkeley talks about the 'reality' of things, and about 'scepticism' in that connection, he is not talking about continuity or about anything which is relevant to the continuity argument. In *Principles* §33 he says: 'The ideas imprinted on the senses by the author of nature are called *real things*. . . . The ideas of sense are allowed to have more reality in them, that is, to be more strong, orderly and coherent than the creatures of the mind . . . They are also less dependent on the spirit or thinking substance which perceives them, in that they are excited by the will of another and more powerful spirit. . . .' This is all in the region of the passivity argument: it concerns ideas which exist *although not caused by me*, and it has nothing to do with ideas which exist *when not perceived by me*.

In *Principles* §34 Berkeley faces squarely the accusation that his principles lead to scepticism about the reality of things: 'It will be objected that by the foregoing principles, all that is real and substantial in nature is banished out of the world. . . . All things that exist, exist only in the mind, that is, they are purely notional. What therefore . . . must we think of houses, rivers, mountains, trees, stones . . . ? Are all these but so many chimeras and illusions on the fancy? To all which . . . I answer that by the principles premised we are not deprived of any one thing in nature. Whatever we see, feel, hear, or any wise conceive or understand, remains as secure as ever, and is as real as ever. There is a *rerum natura*, and the distinction between realities and chimeras retains its full force. This is evident from sections 29, 30 and 33, where we have shown what is meant by *real things* in opposition to *chimeras*, or ideas of our own framing. . . .' Here again there is not a word about the existence of things while they are not perceived by me, or by any created spirit: the question of reality is explicitly referred back to the earlier discussion which, like the re-play of it in §36, is conducted solely in terms of one's passivity in respect of ideas which one does have. Throughout §§30–44, where Berkeley treats of reality, chimeras, scepticism, etc., he does not once discuss whether sensible things exist when they are not perceived by me or when they are not perceived by any finite creature. Throughout fifteen sections the discussion is entirely confined to ideas which one does have, and thus entirely excludes the question of continuity.

This latter question is, as we have seen, raised in §§45–8, where the issue is clearly stated in terms of what can be the case at a time when I have no ideas in my mind. Notice, though, that Berkeley explicitly treats this as a new question, over and above the issues about 'reality' which he has been discussing for some pages. After an exhaustive discussion of reality, etc., he starts §45 with the words: 'Fourthly, it will be objected that from the foregoing principles it follows, things are every moment annihilated and created anew . . .'. And in §48 he refers back to 'the objection proposed in Section 45', not to 'the objection we have been discussing for the past fifteen or so sections'.

When in *Principles* §§82–4 Berkeley defends himself against the charge that he has so emptied out the universe as to be in conflict with holy writ, he deals with this entirely in terms of the real/imaginary dichotomy, and the matters of passivity on which it depends. There is again nothing about objects existing when not perceived by created spirits.

Finally, in *Principles* §90 Berkeley talks about externality: 'The things perceived by sense may be termed external, with regard to their origin, in that they are not generated from within by the mind itself, but imprinted by a spirit distinct from that which perceives them. Sensible objects may likewise be said to be without the mind in another sense, namely when they exist in some other mind. Thus when I shut my eyes, the things I saw may still exist, but it must be in another mind.' Berkeley calls this *another* sense of 'external': so far from running the two together, he explicitly distinguishes them.

Notice also his conspicuous failure to base any argument on the second sense of 'external': he says only that the things I saw *may* still exist, but it must be in another mind. This uncombative remark fits in with Berkeley's other treatments of the question about whether any ideas or sensible things exist when I do not perceive them. I showed in my preceding section that, so far from insisting that it would be absurd to deny sensible things a continuous existence, Berkeley normally contents himself with saying mildly that he is not positively committed to any such denial. It begins to look as if, as well as distinguishing 'reality' from continuity, we must also say that Berkeley cares deeply about the former but that the latter is not for him a matter of urgency or anxiety or even much interest. If this is true, as I believe it is, the implications for Berkeley's theological arguments are obvious.

THE 'FALSE IMAGINARY GLARE' PASSAGE

To prove Berkeley's unconcern with the question of continuity, I need to cite all the passages in which he raises the question of things' existing when not perceived by humans and show that in none of them (apart from the two-sentence continuity argument in the third dialogue) does he show any inclination to insist on the continuity of sensible things or to argue from their continuity to the existence of God. I have in fact already dealt with all Berkeley's discussions of continuity in the *Principles* and *Dialogues*; but the second dialogue contains one passage which looks a little as though it were concerned with continuity and is indeed sometimes adduced as a source for the continuity argument. I shall try to show that this is a mistake.

The passage in question occurs on pp. 173–77. Here Philonous sings the praises of the universe, and asks: 'How should those principles be entertained that lead us to think all the visible beauty of the creation a false imaginary glare?'. (Berkeley is here leading into the question of whether his own principles lead to such a conclusion; he is not, as Warnock implies in his *Berkeley*, p. 118, railing against Locke.) Hylas, who has been converted to what he takes to be Berkeley's principles, meets this with the forlorn remark that 'My comfort is, you are as much a sceptic as I am'; to which Philonous replies that on the contrary *he* is not a sceptic, that scepticism does not follow from his principles and indeed is not true, and that God will come to the rescue. 'As sure . . . as the sensible world really exists, so sure is there an infinite, omnipresent Spirit who contains and supports it.' He also distinguishes his position from the pious declaration that God sees all: 'Is there no difference between saying *there is a God, therefore he perceives all things*: and saying *sensible things do really exist: and if they really exist they are necessarily perceived by an infinite mind: therefore there is an infinite mind, or God*. This furnishes you with a direct and immediate demonstration, from a most evident principle, of the being of a God.' This has been taken as an exposition of the continuity argument, but it is no such thing.

Firstly, there is as I have already pointed out a sharp separation in Berkeley between the question of whether things 'exist when not perceived by human minds' and the question of whether anything 'is real', 'really exists', 'is not imaginary', etc., these latter expressions being elucidated by Berkeley mainly in terms of the *causes* of ideas. In the passage under discussion there is not one word about the existence of things when they are not perceived by us. Philonous speaks of depriving the world 'of all reality', of reducing it to 'a false imaginary glare', of the 'real existence' of things, and of inferring God's existence from 'the bare existence of the sensible world'.

Berkeley makes Philonous say that Hylas's scepticism arises precisely from his misunderstanding of what it is for something to be real; and we have already noted Berkeley's insistence that, properly understood, the notion of 'a real thing' is the notion of something which exists *although not caused by me*, and is not the notion of something which exists *when not perceived by me*.

Secondly, consider how the passage develops. Hylas asks whether Philonous's position differs from 'a notion entertained by some eminent moderns, of seeing all things in God'. The discussion then becomes mired in Philonous's attempt to understand and to criticise Malebranche; until finally Philonous brushes Malebranche aside and pulls the discussion back to his own views with the abrupt words: 'Take here in brief my meaning . . .', whereupon he launches into a lucid presentation of the passivity argument!

Why have some commentators associated the 'false, imaginary glare' passage with the continuity argument, in the face of such clear indications that this is a mistake? Part of the trouble doubtless lies in the prejudgment that it is useless to look to Berkeley for any distinction which couldn't be drawn with a three-inch brush; but there are two sentences which, I suspect, have had a special responsibility for the misconstruction of the passage as a whole. Philonous says: 'To me it is evident, for the reasons you allow of, that sensible things cannot exist otherwise than in a mind or spirit. Whence I conclude, not that they have no real existence, but that seeing they depend not on my thought, and have an existence distinct from being perceived by me, there must be some other mind wherein they exist.' Since the first sentence is explicitly concerned with the ownership of ideas, it might be argued that the second sentence concerns ownership too, so that the two together do introduce the continuity argument.

Since this reading of the two sentences makes nonsense of the rest of the passage, I do not think that anyone could *easily* accept it unless he had already overlooked all Berkeley's distinctions between the two sorts of scepticism which go with the two arguments for God's existence. In fact, though, the interpretation in question is probably wrong, as can be seen if we inspect the beginning of the paragraph in which the two sentences occur. Philonous says that his opinions *would* lead to the sceptical conclusion that sensible things are not real *if* Hylas were right in taking 'the reality of sensible things' to consist in 'an absolute existence out of the minds of spirits'. He goes on: 'But I neither said nor thought the reality of sensible things was to be defined after that manner. To me it is evident, for the reasons you allow of, that sensible things cannot exist otherwise than in a mind or spirit. Whence I conclude . . . etc.' The argument is not that sensible things cannot exist out of all minds, but do sometimes exist out of human minds and must therefore sometimes exist in a non-human mind. It is that sensible things cannot exist out of all minds, but are undoubtedly real, and therefore 'real' must be defined in some other way than 'capable of existing out of all minds'. The point about the ownership of ideas comes in here solely in order to highlight Hylas's wrong analysis of 'real'.

I do not contend that the passage is flawless. On my interpretation, Philonous's 'Whence I conclude . . .' is too abrupt: there should at this point be a reference to the analysis of 'real' which Philonous does accept. But if we are to take the passage as giving the continuity argument, then—apart from the difficulties already mentioned—we must suppose that in Berkeley's first and almost his only presentation of that argument he fails to make the point that something may exist out of all human minds without existing out of all minds whatsoever. He makes this point clearly enough in his other, unargumentative discussions of continuity; but now that continuity is supposed to become really important to him we are invited to believe that he neglects to say the one thing which most needs saying.

If someone still insists that in this passage Berkeley is nevertheless also thinking of the continuity argument and conflating it with the passivity argument, I cannot prove him wrong. In an earlier section I listed all but four of Berkeley's uses of 'depend' and its cognates in speaking of the relationship between ideas and minds. Of the four exceptions, one was the passage in §56 in which Berkeley criticises an argument which turns upon the ambiguity of 'depend' without himself mentioning this ambiguity; one was the passage in *Principles* §146 where Berkeley himself exploits the ambiguity in order to move from 'every idea depends upon (= is owned by) a mind' to 'every idea depends upon (= is caused by) a mind'; and one was the passage in the third dialogue, p. 193, where Berkeley exploits the ambiguity in reverse, in his one clear presentation of the continuity argument, moving from 'some ideas do not depend upon (= are not caused by) my mind' to 'some ideas do not depend upon (= are not owned by) my mind'. The fourth use of 'depend' which was omitted from my list of straightforward cases is the one in the second-dialogue passage now under discussion, and it may be that this too should be treated as a mixed use of 'depend', in which it does two things at once. But at least let it be recognised that in this case the mixture is quite different from the other three: each of the latter is clearly and explicitly concerned both with the ownership and with the causation of ideas, and the ambiguity of 'depend' is there invoked in order to explain how Berkeley is (or, in the first case, how his opponents are) trying to bring the two things together. In the 'false imaginary glare' passage, however, the only explicit reference to ownership admits of a perfectly good explanation as relevant to the criticism of Hylas's definition of 'real': there is no *need* to say that 'depend' is used ambiguously here, except the need created by an antecedent prejudice in favour of taking this passage to express the continuity argument.

THE ANSWERS TO QUESTIONS (2) AND (4)

Berkeley addresses himself to (a) the accusation that on his principles the sensible world is robbed of its reality, and (b) the accusation that on his principles the sensible world flickers in and out of existence as one wakes and sleeps, opens and shuts one's eyes, and the like. He cares deeply about (a), and is at great pains to rebut it by an account of the correct meaning of 'real', an account which, since it defines 'real' only for ideas which one *does* have, has no bearing on the question of whether any ideas exist which one does not have. Not only is Berkeley manifestly anxious to rebut (a), but he also takes this to be the focus of the one argument which he strenuously advances for the existence of God.

His treatment of (b), apart from two sentences in the third dialogue, is uniformly relaxed and agnostic. He would as soon say that (b) is meaningless as say that (b) does not follow from his principles; he rests no weight on the claim that he is not committed to (b); and he most certainly does not—with the one tiny exception already noted—argue from the falsity of (b) to the existence of God. He does in fact have a reason for saying that, God or no God, (b) is meaningless. For he has an argument whose conclusion is that one cannot make sense of talk about an idea's existing while not in *one's own* mind. The argument is extremely bad, but Berkeley liked it well enough to use full-dress versions of it in both his major works—in *Principles* §23 and in the first dialogue, pp. 163–64—which is more than he did for the continuity argument.

My second and fourth questions, then, may be answered as follows. Berkeley makes so little of the continuity argument, and is so silent about its relationship to the passivity argument, because he does not seriously wish to employ the continuity argument at all. Not only is Berkeley uninterested in arguing from the continuity of objects to the existence of God; he is not even interested in arguing strenuously from the existence of God to the possible continuity of objects. Those who think otherwise—those who accept the limericks' account of Berkeley's thought on continuity—have not attended carefully enough to what he actually wrote.

BERKELEY AND THE TREE IN THE QUAD
E. J. FURLONG

Why did Berkeley believe that the tree continues to be when no one's about in the quad? Or, to quote from Mr Jonathan Bennett's stimulating and provocative article ('Berkeley and God', reprinted in this volume, pp. 380–99), 'Why does Berkeley, in the continuity argument [for God's existence], allow himself the premiss that objects exist while not perceived by any human?' Mr Bennett continues: 'A possible answer is that this is such a deep-rooted, normal human assumption that Berkeley could not help making it even though he could not, on his own philosophical principles, be entitled to make it. . . . This strikes me as false. In many places, Berkeley calmly says that if we clear our minds we shall see that we have no grounds for believing in the existence of objects while they are unperceived.' And Mr Bennett refers to *Principles* § 4 and § 6, quoting from the latter a passage which ends '. . . they must either have no existence at all, or else subsist in the mind of some eternal spirit'. 'These are not the words of someone', Mr Bennett comments, 'who would add that since objects do exist when not perceived by created spirits therefore there must be an eternal spirit which perceives them' (p. 389).

Mr Bennett also refers to *Principles* §§ 45–8 where Berkeley discusses at length the intermittency objection to his philosophy. We might well think that in these paragraphs Berkeley's procedure is as follows: first, he asks, has not his *esse est percipi* been proved to the hilt, no matter how strange its consequences? then (§§ 46–7) he argues

From *Philosophy*, Vol. XLI (1966). Reprinted, with minor corrections, by permission of the author and *Philosophy*.

ad hominem that other theories are certainly liable to the intermittency objection; but finally (§ 48), having played sufficiently with the objection, he acts on his note-books maxim to 'bring the killing blow at the last': rounding on his objector he declares that the objection does not in fact do any damage to the Berkeleian theory. 'For thô we hold indeed the objects of sense to be nothing else but ideas which cannot exist unperceiv'd: yet we may not hence conclude they have no existence except only while they are perceiv'd by us, since there may be some other spirit that perceives them, thô we do not. . . . It does not therefore follow from the foregoing principles, that bodies are annihilated and created every moment.' Mr Bennett, however, takes a different view of § 48. 'The crucial expressions', he writes, 'are "we may not hence *conclude*", "there *may* be some other spirit", "it does not therefore *follow*". These are not the words of someone who proposes to base the continuity argument on the absurdity of denying that objects have a continuous existence' (italics Mr Bennett's). In fact, 'Berkeley resolutely, and mockingly, refuses to say that it [intermittency] is absurd'.

Mr Bennett considers that we have to wait till the third of the *Three dialogues* for an *argument* by Berkeley that objects continue to be when unperceived by us. In the *Principles* Berkeley 'cares deeply about' the 'reality' of sensible things but their continuity is 'not for him a matter of urgency or anxiety or even much interest'. (p. 394)

Now Mr Bennett is certainly right in claiming that in the *Principles* Berkeley does not state his continuity argument for God's existence: he gives only what Mr Bennett calls his 'passivity argument'—the argument to God as the cause of the 'continual succession of ideas' (§ 26). We have to wait till the *Three dialogues* for a statement of the continuity argument. But is Mr Bennett correct in his view that Berkeley, when writing the *Principles*, did not care very much about the continuity of sensible things? 'There *may* be some other spirit'. Is the 'may' a casual, detached, for-all-I-care 'may?' or is it a suggestive 'may', a 'may' of understatement, of confidence—the quizzical 'may' of the man who knows the way out of the maze, 'You *may* get out if you try that path'?

Was Berkeley unconcerned about intermittency?

At this point one naturally enquires, do Berkeley's note-books throw any light on our query? Do they indicate whether he is likely to have used a casual 'may', as Mr Bennett argues, or a suggestive 'may', as others have thought? The note-books have numerous references to the topic. But before we consider them there is a general point that may be conveniently made here. Berkeley was certainly anxious to show in both his *Principles* and his *Three dialogues*, that his system took nothing from the reality of things—and he was rightly anxious, as the reactions of such plain men as Dr Johnson were to show. Now a plain man, offered a currant bun which he was assured by Berkeley was perfectly real, would be somewhat uneasy if he were also informed that on Berkeley's philosophy the bun had an intermittent existence. How can I digest it? How will it nourish me? he might well ask. It is *prima facie* hardly likely that Berkeley should be concerned about the reality of sensible things, but indifferent to their continuity. And we might note that one of his criteria for the real as opposed to the imaginary is constancy (*Principles* § 33). Constancy is not the same thing as continuity, but they are near allied.

To return now to the note-books evidence. Here is a list of the relevant entries:[1] 98, 185, 185a, 194, 293a, 408, 424a, 429, 429a, 472, 473, 477a, 801, 802. These entries refer directly to our topic; others bear on it indirectly. Berkeley's thought on the subject, as on many other subjects during that remarkable year of discovery when his note-books were written, shows a striking development, in-

[1] The references are to Dr Luce's diplomatic edition, *Berkeley's philosophical commentaries* (1944). I shall refer to it as P.C. I am obliged to Dr Luce and to Dr G. E. Davie for comments on a draft of this paper.

deed revolution—an instance of what Dr Luce has recently called 'the dialectic of immaterialism'. Let us look at typical landmarks in the journey.

> \+ On account of my doctrine the identity of finite substances must consist in something else than continued existence, or relation to determin'd time and place of beginning to exist. the existence of our thoughts (wch being combin'd make all substances) being frequently interrupted, & they having divers beginnings, & endings.
> (Entry 194)
>
> \+ Bodies taken for Powers do exist w^n not perceiv'd but this existence is not actual. w^n I say a power exists no more is meant than that if in y^e light I open my eyes & look that way I shall see it i.e. y^e body &c. (Entry 293a)
>
> M or rather why he [a Cartesian] supposes all y^s Matter, for bodies & their qualitys I do allow to exist independently of Our mind. (Entry 477a)
>
> P I differ from the Cartesians in that I make extension, Colour etc to exist really in Bodies & independent of Our Mind. All y^s carefully & lucidly to be set forth. (Entry 801)
>
> M.P Not to mention the Combinations of Powers but to say the things the effects themselves to really exist even w^n not actually perceiv'd but still with relation to perception. (Entry 802)

The import of these entries is not hard to see. Entry 194 shows Berkeley clearly committed to intermittency. Entry 293a allows a hypothetical, non-actual existence to bodies when not perceived. Their actual existence is still intermittent. But, it will be observed, both these entries have the marginal sign +, which means 'reject'.[2] And when we come to entry 477a we find that Berkeley is, by impli-

---

[2] See *P.C.*, pp. xxvf. and A. A. Luce, *The dialectic of immaterialism*, p. 24. Chapter IX of the latter book deals fully with intermittency in the note-books.

cation, distinguishing between 'Our mind' and—though he does not say so, but what else can it be? —God's mind. When he writes entry 801 he is allowing an actual existence even to colours 'independent of Our Mind'. And entry 802 is a direct repudiation of the hypothetical existence view stated in 293a.

It is plain then that at the end of his note-book thinking Berkeley was quite sure that the tree continues to be when no one's about in the quad. He had found a way, by distinguishing between our mind and some other mind, of having the best of both worlds—of 'siding with the Mob' and at the same time retaining *esse est percipi*. When he had written his 'intermittency entries' 194 and 293a it had looked as if *esse est percipi* and the commonsense belief in non-intermittency were incompatible. Now he has found, to his relief, that they are compatible. And he states this achievement as a point in his favour as compared with the Cartesians. This is not the claim of one who was unconcerned about intermittency. It follows that when Berkeley says in the *Principles* passage we were discussing, 'we may not hence conclude they have no existence except only while they are perceiv'd by us', he would have been quite prepared to substitute 'we must not hence conclude' for 'we may not hence conclude'; and when he writes 'since there may be some other spirit that perceives them thô we do not', his 'may' is not, as Mr Bennett asserts, a casual, indifferent 'may' but rather a suggestive 'may', Socratically ironic. Or possibly we should put the matter in a slightly different way. Berkeley, towards the end of his note-books, had found, as we saw, that to accept *esse est percipi* does not imply giving up commonsense. There is no inference from *esse est percipi* to intermittency. 'We *may* not hence conclude . . .' The 'may' was good enough for him. It ruled out the objectionable inference. He would indeed have been prepared to go further, and put 'must' for 'may', but, with his fine sense of logic and drama, he used the minimum term the context needed.

We have seen how Berkeley's thought on intermittency changed in his note-books to the position he was to publish in the *Principles*. But the change did not stop there. As we noted already, we have to wait till the *Three dialogues* for the continuity argument. We might chart the whole process of thinking in the following stages:

Note-book entries 194, 293a: intermittency allowed to be a consequence of *esse est percipi* (*c*. autumn 1707).
Note-book entries 801, 802 and *Principles* §48: intermittency denied to be a consequence of *esse est percipi* because God may perceive things when we do not; i.e. God exists (why? the passivity argument) and may perceive when we do not, therefore there is no clash between *esse est percipi* and commonsense (*c*. summer 1708–spring 1710).
Three dialogues (*Works*, ed. Luce and Jessop, vol. 2, pp. 230–1): intermittency is false, continuity is true, i.e. commonsense is to be accepted, therefore God exists (*c*. 1712–13).

We might put the process of thought this way. First, commonsense and *esse est percipi* are believed to clash; since *esse est percipi* is intuitively true, commonsense must go (*P.C.* 194, 293a: there is an echo of this assertion in *Principles* § 45). Then it is seen that commonsense can be rescued (*P.C.* 801, 802, *Principles* § 48). Finally it is claimed that commonsense can be used as a premiss. We have in turn the relations of exclusion, compatibility and entailment.

(It should, perhaps, be added that Berkeley's commonsense belief in the continuity of objects did not prevent him from offering, by implication, a highly-refined analysis of what this continuity consists in; *Works*, vol. 2, pp. 245–48. He does, indeed, claim that his account of sameness in this connexion does not 'deviate either from propriety of language or the truth of things'. He may be unduly hopeful here; still, what in fact does the plain man believe about the colour of the leaves on the tree in the quad when unobserved, or at 3 A.M.?)

What right had Berkeley to his belief in the continuity of objects?

What I have so far been mainly concerned to argue, as against Mr Bennett, is that when Berkeley wrote the *Principles* he did believe in, and care about, the continuity of objects. But there is also the question of logic: what right had Berkeley to his commonsense belief in continuity? Does he offer any argument to support his position? We might well think that he does not. But Mr Bennett points out that in the *Three dialogues* statement of the continuity argument Berkeley does give a reason for his belief in continuity. 'It is plain', says Philonous, 'they [sensible things] have an existence exterior to my mind, since I find them by experience to be independent of it. There is therefore some other mind wherein they exist, during the intervals between the times of my perceiving them.' Berkeley here infers from 'independent of my mind', i.e. not produced by me, to existing unperceived by me. (It is an argument from what Hume will call 'distinct' existence to 'continued' existence.) The argument is indeed very shaky, but an argument it is, and Mr Bennett has rendered a service in drawing attention to it and to the ambiguities in the verb 'depend' which Berkeley's reasoning at key-points exhibits. (Bennett, *op. cit.*, pp. 387, 391.)

Did Berkeley clearly distinguish in the Principles *and* Three dialogues *two arguments for the existence of God?*

Mr Bennett asks why, if continuity were important to Berkeley, he makes so little of the continuity argument for God's existence, devoting in all but two (or three) sentences to it. The 'false imaginary glare' passage in the second of the *Three dialogues*, Mr Bennett holds, includes a statement, not of the continuity argument, but of the passivity argument: Berkeley here, as elsewhere, is much more concerned with the reality of sensible things, explained by reference to their production, than with their continuity. Mr Bennett does allow, indeed, that 'if some-

Berkeley and the Tree in the Quad

one still insists that in this passage Berkeley is nevertheless also thinking of the continuity argument and conflating it with the passivity argument, I cannot prove him wrong'. Prompted by this concession, I think we might wonder whether Berkeley was aware explicitly of the continuity and passivity arguments as two separate proofs or whether he did not think of them as two complementary pieces of reasoning. The continuity argument, he might have thought, puts the stress on perceiving, the passivity argument on willing. And we know from the protracted debate in his second note-book how closely connected he held perceiving, or thinking, and willing, to be. The three-sentence statement of the continuity argument, where the stress is on perception, concludes that there is an omnipresent eternal Mind, which 'knows and comprehends all things and *exhibits them to our view* . . .' (italics mine). The conclusion is to both a knowing and an active or willing being—to a conserver as well as a creator. If I am right in suggesting that Berkeley did not think of the continuity argument as clearly different from the passivity argument this would explain why he does not draw special attention to the former.[3]

To sum up—the main points I have made are as follows:

1. Mr Bennett asserts that in the *Principles* Berkeley shows little concern for the continuity of sensible things, their non-intermittent existence. I have argued that his note-books show *per contra*, that while he began by accepting intermittency as an implication of *esse est percipi* he came to see—with relief—that the implication could be avoided: he could both hold on to the intuitive truth of *esse est percipi* and also accept the continuity of sensible things. This is the position he adopted in the *Principles*. In the *Three dialogues* he goes further, and uses the continuity of objects as a premiss from which to infer the existence of God.

[3] E. A. Sillem, chap. 6 in *George Berkeley and the proofs for the existence of God* (Longmans, 1957), goes so far as to treat the two arguments as if they were in fact one. (He notes also the argument in *Alciphron* IV, a blend of Berkeley's earlier thinking (in part) and the usual argument from, or to, design.)

2. I accept Mr Bennett's point that in the *Three dialogues* Berkeley gives an argument, though not a valid one, for the continuity of objects.

3. I have suggested that Berkeley saw the continuity and passivity arguments as two complementary portions of the one proof, rather than as two separate pieces of reasoning.

BERKELEY ON "ABSTRACT IDEAS"
MONROE C. BEARDSLEY

I

There are three propositions which I hope to demonstrate by the present argument. I contend (in Section II) that Berkeley's attack on abstract ideas is not made wholly compatible with his atomistic sensationalism; (in Section III) that Berkeley does not provide or employ a single definite criterion for determining the limit of abstraction; and (in Section IV) that the doctrine of abstract ideas furnishes no real support to Berkeley's argument against the existence of material substance independent of perception. By "the doctrine of abstract ideas" I mean "the theory that there are no abstract ideas". But what sort of an idea would be an "abstract idea"? It would be one which "we are told"[1] by its defenders is achieved by abstraction; therefore it is this process which we must first consider.

Abstraction begins with an experienced thing (that is, a collection of qualities or ideas), and the first step (i) of the process occurs when the mind makes one quality the object of special attention. If a particular thing T consists of qualities Q_1, Q_2, Q_3, we can, Berkeley holds, "distinguish" and "consider" only Q_1 and ignore the other qualities of T, though they are co-present with Q_1 in our experience.[2] But he denies that we can perform the second step (ii), that of "resolving" T "into its simple, constituent parts, and viewing each by itself, exclusive of the rest".[3]

From *Mind*, Vol. LII (1943). Reprinted by permission of the author and *Mind*.

[1] *Principles*, Introduction, section 7.
[2] *Ibid.*, Intro., sec. 16.   [3] *Ibid.*, Intro., sec. 7.

If Q_1 could be thus "singled" out[4] and "framed" by the mind in separation from the other qualities, it would be an abstract idea. But such an idea does not occur as an element in consciousness. It is to be noted that in the second step the abstract idea would be merely the original idea conceived in isolation; it would not be a *new* idea.

But we do not know precisely what the isolation must be in order that the idea may be truly abstract, and it is not easy to determine what Berkeley means by "exclusive of the rest". (*a*) If we understand these words literally, he *says* that the abstracted quality Q_1 cannot occur as an element in consciousness unless the qualities Q_2 and Q_3 also occur with it (for these are "the rest"). To give an example, if T has the qualities *square, red,* and *moving,* then this *square* cannot occur later in consciousness unless this *red* and this *moving* accompany it. But Berkeley obviously does not mean this, since he admits that we are capable of "variously compounding and dividing" our ideas, and this rule would prohibit the imagining of a centaur[5] or a "blue horse".[6] (*b*) We might interpret him to mean that Q_1 cannot occur later without being accompanied by any idea at all; yet this would be too trivial for his purpose. (*c*) The best interpretation I can suggest then is the following one. Berkeley seems to mean that whatever qualities (including Q_2 and Q_3) may be absent from a later thought of Q_1, we cannot think of Q_1 without at the same time thinking of such other ideas as will, with Q_1, constitute a complex idea of a particular thing. That is, if Q_1 is originally perceived as part of a thing (T), then it can only be conceived later as part of a thing. To say that there is no abstract idea of a particular *red* is to say that there is no idea of that *red* apart from a thing. We may then define in a preliminary way the abstract idea of Type A: it is a *particular* idea perceived as a quality of a thing and later (supposedly) conceived without any thing which it qualifies.

[4] *Commonplace Book* 141; ed. G. A. Johnston (London, 1930); hereafter cited as *CPB*.
[5] *Prin.*, Intro., sec. 10.   [6] *CPB* 766.

Berkeley on "Abstract Ideas"

The second type of abstract idea requires (iii) a third step, by which[7] abstract ideas of Type A are themselves compared with each other, so that from a given class of abstract ideas we frame "a most abstract idea" which is not merely abstract, but also general. That is, given Q_a (the abstract *red*) and Q_b, Q_c, other abstract ideas, *blue*, *green*, *yellow*, etc., the mind frames an "abstract general idea", *colour*, which is not any particular colour, but is all and none of them. In this case there is a "twofold abstraction":[8] the particular colours are abstracted from particular objects, and then the general idea *colour* is abstracted from classes of the particular colours. It is to be noted that the abstract ideas of Type B would be *new* ideas created by the mind; in the third step the mind does not merely select what is common to all particular colours, but forms an idea of *colour* that is not one of the simple ideas perceived as part of a given coloured object. In the case of T, *colour* is not a "constituent" idea (like *red* or *square*) that could be "considered" and later segregated; it could never be abstracted from things save by comparison of an idea abstracted from a thing with other abstract ideas. Therefore the formation of abstract general ideas of Type B would depend on and presuppose the prior formation of abstract ideas of Type A.

The abstract idea of Type B is still a simple idea, a quality; that of Type C is a complex idea of a "being", such as *man* or *humanity*. In this case "several co-existent qualities" of each thing[9] are abstracted (as in Type A), then each complex of qualities is compared with others (as in Type B), and another idea is formed which is in effect a complex of ideas of Type B, and like them is a *new* abstract general idea. Now it is, I think, fairly obvious that Berkeley's attack on abstract ideas is specifically directed against abstract *general* ideas (of Types B and C); at them Berkeley delivered his "killing blow".[10] For (*a*) they are the ones which are "contradictory"[11] and "inconsistent" (Locke's term), and (*b*) Berkeley regarded his theory of

[7] *Prin.*, Intro., sec. 8.   [8] *Ibid.*, sec. 99.
[9] *Prin.*, Intro., sec. 9.   [10] CPB 699.   [11] CPB 566.

signs as supplying all that was required of these abstract general ideas, namely, a theory of the manner in which particular ideas can become general. But he saw that ideas of Types B and C are formed upon the prior step (ii), which yields ideas of Type A; and when he came to examine the ideas of Type A he rejected them as well. He rejected them, not because our ability to frame ideas of Type A implies our ability to frame ideas of Types B and C (that is clearly not the case), but because the purpose to which he decided to put his critique of abstraction seemed to require that he reject the first type as well. At an earlier stage of thought[12] Berkeley had noted that "'Tis one thing to abstract one concrete idea from another of a different kind, & another thing to abstract an idea from all particulars of the same kind", thus recognising the distinction between Type A and Types B and C. But in the *Principles* both are condemned.

Berkeley sometimes writes, in giving illustrations of abstract ideas, as though he meant that there are certain *abstract* ideas that cannot be abstracted from other *abstract* ideas, as when he says that the mind cannot "frame to itself by abstraction the idea of colour exclusive of extension".[13] But he is, of course, always referring to a particular *colour* (Q_1) and a particular *extension* (Q_2) in a particular thing, and saying that neither of these can become ideas of Type A. It is not that we cannot think of colour without thinking of extension, but that we cannot think of a particular *colour* without thinking of some particular *extension*. The doctrine of abstract ideas can then be expressed in this precise form: there are certain classes of ideas such that no member of one class can be thought of at a given time unless at least one member of the other class is thought of at the same time. To say that shape cannot be abstracted from colour is to say that if idea x is a member of C_s (the class of all particular shapes) and x occurs as an element of consciousness, then there will be some idea y such that y is a member of C_c (the class of all

---

[12] CPB 499.   [13] *Prin.*, Intro., sec. 7.

particular colours) and *y* accompanies *x*. The phrase "element of consciousness" is meant to include in its denotation thoughts of all sorts (images, concepts, ideas). For Berkeley would not merely hold that *x* could not be an image without *y*; he would say what he says of extension: "I do not find that I can perceive, imagine, or anywise frame in my mind such an abstract idea".[14]

II

With the above preliminaries we can approach the first question: that concerning the relation of the doctrine of abstract ideas to the general framework of Berkeley's epistemology. From this point on, when I speak of "abstract ideas" I shall be referring only to ideas of Type A. Those ideas become abstract when they are separated from things. But when we examine Berkeley's conception of what constitutes a thing, it becomes something of a problem to decide why these ideas should not be separable from things. Berkeley's view of perception does not seem to permit, much less necessitate, his doctrine of abstract ideas.

The difficulty may be stated thus. Berkeley's definition of the word "thing"—exclusive of spirits, which come under the most general range of "thing"[15]—is given in the first section of the *Principles* (Part I). My senses, he says, furnish me in their separate ways with various ideas, "and as several of these are observed to accompany each other, they come to be marked by one name, and so to be reputed as one *thing*".[16] A "sensible thing" is a "collection" or "congeries"[17] of ideas "blended or combined together".[18] When the ideas first appear to the mind they

[14] *Theory of Vision*, sec. 123.
[15] See *Prin.*, sec. 89, and *CPB* 653.   [16] *Prin.*, sec. 1.
[17] *Three Dialogues between Hylas and Philonous*, III; in the Selections ed. by Mary W. Calkins, Scribner's Modern Student's Library (N.Y. 1929), p. 324.
[18] *Prin.*, sec. 3.

come through various senses, by various channels; they are distinct and *several*, for they are observed severally to go together, and they may be "apprehended by divers senses, or by the same sense at different times, or in different circumstances".[19] Then they are "united into one thing by the mind".[20] It is the mind which gives them a substantial unity, and a name, and the mind is led to do this, not by any intrinsic relation among the ideas, but by extrinsic spatial and temporal relations; men, says Berkeley, select those collections of ideas which are "observed, however, to have some connexion in nature, either with respect to coexistence or succession; all which they refer to one name, and consider as one thing".[21]

If this is a true account of the manner in which Q_1, Q_2, and Q_3 came to constitute T, then we may ask with some surprise why the mind cannot abstract Q_1. Why can there not be abstract ideas of Type A? If things are *"arbitrarily* put together by the mind",[22] they should perhaps be arbitrarily separable by the same mind; if the ideas originally entered the mind as separated and discrete, it is strange that the mind should so tightly have bound them together that they can never occur again in the mind as separated and discrete. There are two explanations of this phenomenon which might be urged on Berkeley's behalf. (1) It might be said that there is an intrinsic and necessary connection between ideas as they are perceived and that the mind is to some extent guided by insight into this connection, in learning about objects. Then certain sorts of abstraction would be impossible. But Berkeley holds that we cannot discover any necessary connection between our ideas;[23] their only connections are adventitious and external. We know, and need only know, relations of "co-existence and succession" in order to form things.[24] As for *a priori* principles—such as one asserting a necessary connection between colour and extension—

---

[19] *Three Dialogues*, III, p. 319.
[20] *Ibid.*, III, p. 320; see also p. 324.   [21] *Ibid.*, III, p. 319.
[22] *Prin.*, sec. 12.   [23] *Ibid.*, sec. 31; see also CPB 896.
[24] See CPB 752.

these principles (since they would have to be expressed in abstract terms) would be particularly abhorrent to Berkeley's basic position. (2) It is true that in the case of some of the rejected abstract ideas Berkeley could say that these cannot be *abstract* ideas because they are not ideas at all. This is true of abstract general ideas like *colour* and *humanity*, as I have explained above. What is not perceived as one of the distinct qualities of T naturally cannot later be abstracted from T and conceived as a separate quality. In this way Berkeley can account for our inability to abstract *some* ideas, and if he were to apply this account to all ideas that cannot be abstracted, he would be adopting Hume's clearly-stated maxim, "all ideas which are different are separable". But it appears that, though Berkeley wavers on this point, he does not ultimately intend to maintain this general principle; and in certain crucial cases he does not apply it.

As an example we may take motion. Berkeley sometimes speaks as though a particular *motion* is an idea we acquire through sight, but an idea that is not abstractable from particular *extensions* and *shapes*.[25] Now Berkeley also says that every *motion* includes relation,[26] and relations are not ideas at all.[27] But whether a *motion* be "not one idea",[28] or "on 2d thoughts" a "simple idea",[29] Berkeley never definitely suggests that its unabstractability is a consequence of its not being an idea at all. But this is not the case with extension. First we must note Berkeley's statement that "the mind, 'tis true, can consider one thing without another; but then, considered asunder, they make not 2 ideas. Both together can make but one, as for instance colour & visible extension."[30] This seems to mean that in perception we cannot even *distinguish* or *discriminate* two ideas, *extension* and *colour*, as particular elements of a plane figure. Here Berkeley verges close upon Hume's position. For though we may, he holds, distinguish

---

[25] See *CPB* 877, 449, and also *Free-Thinking in Mathematics*, sec. 20.
[26] *Prin.*, sec. 112.   [27] *Ibid.*, sec. 89.   [28] *CPB* 188.
[29] *CPB* 448.   [30] *CPB* 330.

between two kinds of visible extension, the mathematical and the common,[31] the former may be defined as simply the co-existence of point-perceptions;[32] and the latter,[33] is not a visual idea at all, Berkeley says in some places, for there is no "idea intromitted immediately and properly by sight save only light and colours".[34] Thus, in a particular object T, the shape *square* is, on this hypothesis, not an idea at all: "in a strict sense, I see nothing but light and colours".[35] Now if this is Berkeley's position, then it would explain why colours and shapes, for example, cannot be abstracted: because they are the same idea. But Berkeley does not consistently adopt this standpoint; it is more in accord with the general position of the first part of the *Principles* when we find him referring to the *extension, colour,* and *motion* as "simple, constituent parts" of a particular object,[36] or when we find him speaking of "a certain colour, taste, smell, figure and consistence having been observed to go together",[37] which could not occur if they were not discriminable ideas. Finally, we may observe that if two particular ideas are unabstractable because they are identical, then neither can be "considered" in itself, and Berkeley's explanation of the manner in which we come to make words and thoughts general presupposes our ability to consider the particular ideas which Berkeley holds to be unabstractable. For these reasons I submit (*a*) that in both the *Principles* and the *Dialogues* Berkeley regards the particular unabstractable ideas as *genuine* ideas, and (*b*) that he offers no explanation of the impossibility of abstraction in these cases.

[31] *CPB* 396.
[32] *CPB* 295, 437, passages worth careful comparison with Hume's treatment of space and time. Berkeley adds that extension may also be defined as "length without breadth", which in some places he calls an "abstract" idea (*CPB* 263, 485, 385), and in other places no idea at all (*CPB* 384). In this last passage Berkeley significantly suggests that "It seems to consist in meer proportion—meer reference of the mind".
[33] *CPB* 459.   [34] *Theory of Vision*, sec. 130.   [35] *Ibid.*
[36] *Prin.*, Intro., sec. 7.   [37] *Ibid.*, sec. 1.

III

I have presented reasons for asserting that Berkeley's doctrine of abstract ideas derives no justification from his theory of perception and is even in contradiction with it. But even if we were to grant that he is right in holding that there are some ideas which are not abstractable, we would still have to enquire how we may know *which* ones are not abstractable. The obvious reply to this is an appeal (which Berkeley often makes) to immediate experience; but since his whole purpose (that of removing ancient prejudices about abstract ideas) presupposes that the common run of philosophers have misinterpreted their own experience, this appeal does not suffice.[38] Berkeley must provide a principle by which abstractable ideas are distinguished from non-abstractable ones, and by which the difference between them is made clear. We may put the question in other words: if qualities cannot be conceived apart from things, how do we know which collections of ideas may be things? What defines the limit of abstraction?

To this question Berkeley has an answer, but it is not a univocal one. "I do not deny it [the mind] may abstract in a certain sense", says Euphranor,[39] "inasmuch as those things that can really exist, or be really perceived asunder, may be conceived asunder, or abstracted one from the other." One interpretation to which this passage lends itself is, I submit, the following. A person may abstract those, and only those, ideas which experience indicates to be separable in fact, or to belong to classes of ideas which are separable in fact. If I have perceived at least one particular *shape* without any sort of *motion* at all, then I may

---

[38] Berkeley tacitly admits this, for example, when in writing to Samuel Johnson about the abstract idea of existence, he remarks, "I cannot find I have any such idea, and this is my reason against it . . ." (24 March, 1730; given in Works, ed. A. C. Fraser, Oxford, 1901; II, 20); see also *CPB* 615.
[39] *Alciphron*, VII, 5; Works, II, 328.

later conceive any particular *shape* without conceiving of any *motion* in it. Conversely, if every particular *motion* I have perceived has been accompanied by some *shape* (that of the thing moved), then I cannot abstractly conceive any particular *motion* without conceiving along with it some *shape*. This interpretation I shall call Principle A, defining it as follows: The ideas of Class C_1 are abstractable (in the sense of Type A) from the ideas of Class C_2 if and only if (i) there is an idea x such that x is a member of C_1, and x was perceived at time t, and (ii) there is no y such that y is a member of C_2, and y was perceived at time t, conjoined with x. To illustrate this Principle: it would imply that motions are not abstractable from shapes, but shapes are abstractable from motions; that colours and shapes are not abstractable from each other; and that, if I have perceived, for example, an electric light bulb apart from a socket, then I may conceive any electric light bulb apart from its socket. So far, Principle A seems to suit Berkeley's purpose and to represent his meaning faithfully.

But if it is closely examined, difficulties appear. "I can", says Berkeley,[40] consider the hand, the eye, the nose, each by itself abstracted or separated from the rest of the body"; and he evidently expects us to be able to perform the same feat. Similarly, he says that he is able to conceive a human head without a body, a human trunk without limbs, and a rose's smell without a rose, though he has not, he implies, perceived the members of these pairs separately. For, he reports, "I may, indeed, divide in my thoughts, or conceive apart from each other, those things which perhaps I never perceived by sense so divided".[41] Therefore Principle A is really too narrow for Berkeley's purpose; it limits abstraction too much and leaves too little freedom for the imagination. Moreover, Principle A involves a relativity for which there is no room in Berkeley's system. It must be stated in terms of every individual person's own experience, which bounds his ability to conceive abstractly; and as far as Berkeley's own experi-

[40] *Prin.*, Intro., sec. 10.   [41] *Ibid.*, sec. 5.

ence goes he can therefore never be certain (as he appears to be) that Locke and Hylas have never experienced any colour without extension or any motion without a thing that moves.

Therefore Principle A is not enough for Berkeley; and indeed there is another interpretation of the *Alciphron* passage which seems to represent Berkeley's intention more truly. The limit of abstraction, according to this principle, depends not on what actually has occurred in experience, but on what may *possibly* occur. That is, abstraction "extends only to the conceiving separately such objects as it is possible may really exist or be actually perceived asunder".[42] This principle is, of course, wider than Principle A, for it permits us to abstract what has not been perceived in separation but might be perceived in separation (such as the human nose or the human eye). We then may define Principle B as follows: The ideas of Class C_1 are abstractable from the ideas of Class C_2 if and only if it is *not impossible* that the following is true: (i) there is an idea x such that x is a member of C_1, and x is perceived at time t, and (ii) there is no y such that y is a member of C_2, and y is perceived at time t, conjoined with x.

The trouble with Principle B is that it does not help us to decide just what ideas are abstractable, and what not. For how are we to know which combinations of ideas (objects) are possible or impossible? Experience, Berkeley admits, reveals no such absolute necessities. The only way we know (if indeed we do know) that colours and shapes cannot *possibly* ever be perceived or exist in separation is by consulting our own minds and asking whether we can conceive them to be perceived or to exist separately. But if we decide whether they can be conceived abstractly by determining whether they can exist separately, and then decide whether they can exist separately by determining whether we can conceive them to exist separately, and then decide whether we can conceive them to exist separately by determining whether we can conceive them sepa-

[42] *Prin.*, Intro., sec. 5; see also Intro., sec. 10.

rately, then our decision in any particular case is thoroughly circular.[43] The only escape from this circularity would be to say that they cannot be conceived separately because they have not in fact existed in separation; but this makes Principle B equivalent to Principle A. And in the absence of this conversion of Principle B into Principle A, Principle B really is not an informative principle at all. But Principle A seems to be both doubtful and too narrow for Berkeley's argument.

IV

At various points in his refutation of realism Berkeley insists (*a*) that the prevalence of this erroneous belief among philosophers has chiefly been due to their uncritical assumption that we possess abstract (and abstract general) ideas, and (*b*) that the untenability of the belief is clearly exposed when we realise that we do not possess abstract ideas. There is no doubt that Berkeley regarded his doctrine of abstract ideas (as well as his doctrine of abstract general ideas, which I shall not discuss) as an essential ground of his immaterialism. So insistent is he on this point that we should expect the connection between his idealism and his doctrine of abstract ideas to be quite plain. There are, however, fatal obscurities in this connection, and the more seriously one considers them the more significance one discovers in Hume's position in the first and second parts of the *Treatise*, Book I.

The provoking situation we encounter in trying to trace this connection is that Berkeley turns out (even at the early stage of development represented in the *CPB*) to be employing the word "abstract" as a synonym for "nonexistent" and "unworthy"; and when he caps an argument for idealism with a poke at abstraction, we readily discover, in some instances, that abstraction has nothing to do with the case. For example, he declares that the object

---

[43] This circularity is perhaps even more evident in that passage from the *Alciphron*, VII, 6, omitted from the 3rd ed. (1752); see *Works*, II, 325 n.

T cannot exist apart from the sensation of it, for the reason that T cannot be abstracted from the sensation of it. But his statement[44] that "the object and the sensation are the same thing and cannot therefore be abstracted from each other" seems to mean only that T cannot be abstracted from Q_1, Q_2, and Q_3, since it is by definition just the combination of them. But since T is just its combined qualities (which are ideas), then T cannot even be *distinguished* from them (by step i), let alone *abstracted* from them (by step ii), so it is difficult to see how Berkeley's doctrine that there are ideas which are distinguishable but not abstractable (that is, which may be "considered" but not "separated") is relevant to the present case. Moreover, it may be a fact that "when we do our utmost to conceive the existence of external bodies, we are all the while only contemplating our own ideas",[45] but if we cannot do more than this, the important question arises: how did we come to think we could?

We seem to be opening a more fundamental vein of Berkeley's argument when we examine his statement that, "as it is impossible for me to see or feel anything without an actual sensation of that thing, so is it impossible for me to conceive in my thoughts any sensible thing or object distinct from the sensation or perception of it".[46] This assumes a shape different from that of the argument just considered, and at first seems clearly to turn on the doctrine of abstract ideas. We believe (a) that we can conceive a given object T as existing apart from the perception of it by someone; we make this mistake because we think on superficial examination (b) that we can have an idea of T existing without having any idea that T is being perceived. But the fact is (c) that we have never perceived T without perceiving it, and this fact (c), by Principle A, makes proposition (b) false. Our belief (a) is therefore ungrounded, and it follows from a denial of (a) that T cannot exist apart from our perception of it.

Now it is clear that the crucial point of this argument is the demonstration that the idea *T existing* cannot be

---

[44] *Prin.*, sec. 5.   [45] *Ibid.*, sec. 23.
[46] *Prin.*, sec. 5; see also *Three Dialogues*, I, pp. 261–262.

abstracted from the idea T *being perceived*.[47] When we look about for Berkeley's demonstration, we discover that he very often says quite explicitly (1) that the reason is, that "the existence of an idea consists in being perceived";[48] that, in short, the ideas are the same.[49] To be precise, we must heed his warning: "But it must be well noted that existence is vulgarly restrain'd to actual perception, & that I use the word existence in a larger sense than ordinary".[50] We can then express this view by the proposition that "T existing" is precisely identical in meaning to "T being thought of" in the widest sense (T_{ex} is T_{th}): "This I am sure", remarks Berkeley, "I have no idea of Existence, or annext to the word Existence".[51] That is, there is no unique idea of existence apart from perception: "'Tis on the discovering of the nature & meaning & import of Existence that I chiefly insist".[52] According to this argument, then, "esse est percipi" is analytic; I have no *abstract* idea of T_{ex} for the same reason that I have no abstract idea of *colour:* it is not an idea at all.

Now this is a perfectly good argument, if it *is* Berkeley's argument. What is noteworthy about it is that it owes nothing to the doctrine of abstract ideas. T_{ex} is so far from being an abstract idea apart from T_{th} that it is the same idea; not only can it not be abstracted (by step ii) from T_{th}, but, being identical with T_{th}, it could not (by step i) even be "singled out" from T_{th}—indeed, it could not even be "distinguish'd therefrom", as Berkeley admits.[53] If Berkeley's argument here is valid, then there could indeed be no "nicer strain of abstraction than to distinguish the existence of sensible objects from their being perceived, so as to conceive them existing unper-

---

[47] Since the idea T_1 *being perceived* includes reference to a self, which is a *notion*, the idea is perhaps more accurately called a notion. This would make no significant difference as far as the argument is concerned, I believe, since Berkeley holds also that we have no "abstract notion" of the powers and acts of the self apart from the self or apart from the self's ideas (*Prin.*, sec. 143).
[48] *Ibid.*, sec. 2.   [49] See *ibid.*, sec. 3; *CPB* 404.
[50] *CPB* 472; see also 471.   [51] *CPB* 681; see also 680, 557.
[52] *CPB* 493.   [53] *CPB* 655.

ceived".⁵⁴ Indeed one "might as easily divide a thing from itself", for that is precisely what one would be doing. But if the conclusion is that "to exist is to be perceived" is analytic, and for that reason true, it also follows that no one would even distinguish existence from perception, and therefore that no one could have been misled by the belief in abstract ideas to think that it is possible to conceive T_{ex} in abstraction from T_{th}.

As a matter of fact, Berkeley does not confine himself to the argument that "esse est percipi" is analytic; he also (2) holds to the position that it is synthetic. And this is quite incompatible with the other position, for in this case T_{ex} *is* an idea, distinct from T_{th}, but inseparable from it.⁵⁵ This argument does depend upon the doctrine of abstract ideas, as a statement of its steps discloses: (*a*) When T is perceived it is accompanied by the idea (T_{th}) that T is being thought of by someone; (*b*) no T has ever been perceived without being accompanied by such an idea; by (*c*) Principle A it follows that (*d*) T cannot later be conceived without T_{th}; therefore (*e*) T_{ex} (since it includes T) cannot be conceived without T_{th}, and hence (*f*) T cannot exist apart from being thought of.

We seem, then, to have discovered the point at which Berkeley applies his doctrine of abstract ideas to the refutation of realism. Step (*f*) of the above succinct version of his argument depends upon considering T_{ex} as an idea distinguishable, but not abstractable, from T_{th}. And yet it seems clear that Berkeley himself has provided his own answer to this argument. For we may ask whether steps (*d*) and (*e*) are in fact correct; "surely there is nothing easier than for me to imagine trees, for instance, in a park, or books existing in a closet, and nobody by to perceive them". To this Berkeley assents,⁵⁶ but he considers it irrelevant. It is no objection to his argument, he declares, to say that I can frame the idea of things existing "at the same time omitting to frame the idea of any one that may perceive them". This is only, he says, a case where "the mind, taking no notice of itself, is deluded to think it can

⁵⁴ *Prin.*, sec. 5. ⁵⁵ See *ibid.*, sec. 6. ⁵⁶ *Prin.*, sec. 23.

and does conceive bodies existing unthought of, or without the mind, though at the same time they are apprehended by, or exist in, itself". But (and this is the crucial question with respect to steps (d) and (e)) is not this possibility (which Berkeley here admits) that T_{ex} may occur in the absence of T_{th} (*i.e.*, that we may frame T_{ex} and omit to frame T_{th}) precisely what the doctrine of abstract ideas (as we have defined it in Section I above) denies? In the case of colour and shape, Berkeley strives to prove just this: that we cannot think of a colour without thinking of some shape. If we apply this to the present case, his argument must be that we cannot think of any particular thing without thinking that it is being thought of by someone. And yet in order to explain how philosophers have been tricked into realism by their belief in abstract ideas, Berkeley must (as in the passage above) contradict his general principle by saying that we *can* think of a particular thing without thinking that it is being thought of.

There is one more instance of Berkeley's use of the doctrine of abstraction which requires notice here. At one time he regarded the inseparability of the primary from the secondary qualities as "the great argument"[57] against materialism. According to this view the erroneous belief that extension and motion can be abstract ideas apart from colours has been chiefly responsible for the error of realism;[58] and when it is realised that we cannot conceive extension apart from colour, it will be understood that extension cannot exist apart from colour; and since the latter is admittedly subjective, so also must the former be.[59] In view of all the preceding discussion this does not call for much comment. For if the proposition (a) that I have no abstract idea of extension apart from colour is offered as ground for the proposition (b) that extension cannot exist apart from colour, this inference can only be effected by Principle B, as discussed in Section III. But Principle B cannot be applied without either begging the

---

[57] *CPB* 297.   [58] *CPB* 380.
[59] *Prin.*, sec. 10; see also *Three Dialogues*, I, p. 253.

question, or being converted into Principle A; and Principle A will not permit the inference of proposition (*b*), but only of the proposition (*c*) that I have never in fact experienced extension apart from colour. This is not to say that Berkeley's discussion of the relation between primary and secondary qualities amounts to no more than this; it is only to say that, as far as the doctrine of abstract ideas is concerned, the following conclusions seem to be warranted: (1) the doctrine appears to furnish less actual support to Berkeley's system than Berkeley supposes, and (2) it suffers from certain inner difficulties which cannot be removed without changing it in such a way that it furnishes no support at all.

G. J. WARNOCK'S *BERKELEY*
J. F. THOMSON

It is one of the chief merits of Mr. Warnock's book (and they are, I think, considerable) that he is concerned with making clear what Berkeley meant by *esse est percipi* and why he wished to hold this view. This is not an easy matter to be clear about, although it is often made to seem one. Mr. Warnock recognises, as few writers have, that there is a great complexity about Berkeley's use of his key-terms—*idea, in the mind, perceived*—and some of the best discussions in the book are those in which he separates off from each other various senses that Berkeley gives to *idea*. He claims, however, to be able to isolate a central use of *idea*, and an associated use of *in the mind*, and thus to be able to put forward in moderately clear terms one thesis which is wrapped up in *esse est percipi*. Then, in the light of this interpretation, he considers Berkeley's claim that when he denies the existence of material substance, or rather, the absolute existence of material substance, he is not taking away anything that plain men would miss, and rejects it. This work of clarification and interpretation takes up the middle part of the book (roughly half).

Mr. Warnock's interpretation of Berkeley's central use of *idea* is as follows. An idea is an immediate object of perception, and this is what is described in a statement of immediate perception. Such a statement is one in which a speaker, while saying how things seem to him, takes nothing for granted about how they actually are; such statements are ideally of the form: 'It seems to me as if I

From *Mind*, Vol. LXV (1956). Reprinted, with the addition of one footnote, by permission of the author and *Mind*.

were seeing (hearing, touching, etc.) a so-and-so'. Warnock now suggests that *esse est percipi* can be paraphrased as follows. "Every material thing is a 'collection of ideas'. Any statement about any material thing is really (can be analysed into) an indefinitely large set of statements about what it seems, or in suitable conditions would seem, as if the speaker and other people *and God* were hearing, seeing, feeling, tasting, smelling—that is, into an indefinitely large set of statements describing the ideas of which any material object is a collection. It is clear then that nothing is 'without the mind'; for any such statement about a material object is analysed into a set of statements, each of which mentions some 'spirit' (human or divine) *by whom* the ideas that constitute the collection are actually had" (pp. 179–180). Warnock denies, however, that statements about material things can be analysed in this way. "The whole force (he says) of saying 'It seems as if . . .' is to allow for '. . . but not so really'. But this is fatal to Berkeley's case; the force of 'It seems as if . . .' cannot be conjured away. If the sentence 'It seems to me and to God, and it would seem to anyone else, as if there were an orange on the sideboard' *means the same as* 'There is an orange on the sideboard', then to assert the first of these and deny the second would be *self-contradictory*. But in fact [sic] this is not the case. . . . However many people give 'their own impressions', it *makes sense* to say that they are all mistaken; and hence to say 'There is an orange on the sideboard' *cannot* mean the same as saying that everyone had or has, will have or would have, the impression that there is." Accordingly, Warnock concludes that "the common suspicion that Berkeley is somehow neglecting the distinction between what *seems* and what *is* turns out to be justified . . . he provides us with *a* version of this distinction, in the form of a distinction between 'consistent seeming' and *mere* irregular 'incoherent seeming'. But this distinction is *not enough*."

I should like to suggest, tentatively, the following criticisms.

Warnock assumes, without discussion, that it is not self-contradictory to say that it seems to God as if something were so, which is not so. I do not want to suggest that this obviously is self-contradictory, or that it would be profitable to discuss, as an isolated point, whether it is or not. But there is some reason to think that Berkeley would have regarded the question as important, and relevant to his claim not to have upset the distinction between reality and chimeras. And if a Berkeleian just said flatly that it was self-contradictory, I do not see what Warnock could say in reply. It is certainly not enough to say that the force of 'it seems as if' is always to allow for 'but not so', for this is in a way no argument but just a repetition of what has to be defended. It might be admitted that this is usually the force of 'it seems as if', but nevertheless held that in this case (admittedly a uniquely special one) the phrase loses some of its ordinary force. Alternatively, someone might concede the point about 'it seems as if', but conclude from this that it was a mistake to elucidate God's having ideas in terms of it *seeming* to him as if.

I think that Warnock's interpretation of *esse est percipi* underestimates the importance of God in Berkeley's philosophy, and this may be due to the fact that he does not properly see what role God is required to play. At one point, anyway, he seems to misunderstand how Berkeley thought he was able to prove God's existence. He writes (p. 125) "He was sure that he could prove that *'esse'* is *'percipi'*, and hence that we must either admit the existence of the universe in the mind of God, or deny the existence of everything *not actually perceived by human beings*. The second alternative clearly is not acceptable; and so, he believed, the first must be accepted" (my italics). I believe that this seriously misrepresents Berkeley's line of thought. To him it was self-evident that all our ideas have causes. Of some of our ideas we are ourselves the cause. But each of us may decide, by simple trial, that he is not the cause of all his ideas. Roughly; not all my ideas obey my will, so not all are produced by me. We must conclude then that there is 'some other will or spirit' that produces them, and this is God. The difference between the two accounts is important. It is not a premiss of the argument at all that material things exist when they are not actually perceived by a human being. It is not that Berkeley rebels against the idea that things cease to exist when people turn their backs, and invokes God as an all-seeing eye to avoid concluding this. The argument is rather meant to show that even the things that I am actually perceiving now must be in a mind other than my own. "[It is] plain that ideas or things by me perceived . . . exist independently of my mind, since I know myself not to be their author. . . . They must therefore exist in some other mind, whose will it is they should be exhibited to me" (*Three Dialogues*, p. 214, in the Luce-Jessop edition).[1]

The God whose existence Berkeley thought he could prove is not then just a ubiquitous observer. And it is because of this, and because Berkeley holds that our ideas of sense exist independently of our own minds, that he claims that the distinction between reality and illusion retains its full force.

If the question is, how do we in fact distinguish between reality and appearance, between what seems so because it is so and what merely seems so and is not so; then Berkeley's answer, in so far as he has one, seems to be much the same as Hume's, *i.e.* in terms of consistency and coherence. (If this is not entirely satisfactory, that is partly the fault of the question; if one is to answer such a *general* question in general terms, one can do little except to gesture vaguely with such phrases as 'the way the appearances hang together'.) But it is not clear that this answer to this question commits Berkeley to the view that when we say

[1] It now seems more plausible to me that Berkeley has two arguments for the existence of God. One, the argument Warnock had in mind, seems to appear clearly on p. 245 of the *Dialogue*. The second, the 'causal' argument, is that mentioned here.

It is worth pointing out that the causal argument is formally fallacious. Given that every one of my ideas of sense that is not caused by me is caused by some powerful spirit, it does not follow, as Berkeley wished to say, that some one powerful spirit causes all those ideas of sense. The way is thus left open for a kind of animism (one spirit for each physical object) and for views intermediate between this and theism.

that something about a matter of fact is so, we *mean* only that certain ideas have been had and others will or could be had. Mr. Warnock says that Berkeley identifies reality with consistent seeming. But it seems possible that Berkeley wished to identify reality with seemings caused by God; these seemings are consistent just because they are caused in this way. If I know that there is an orange on the sideboard, then doubtless I know this because certain ideas, suitably consistent with each other, have been had. But what I know is something about God. And on this view, to say that God has such-and-such an idea would be to say something about reality.

If it were suggested that our ideas of sense have no causes, that it just happens that we have them in the order that we do; then Berkeley would, I think, have regarded this as quite *abolishing* the distinction between what seems and what is.

It is also worth asking whether, even if we waive God, Mr. Warnock's grounds for rejecting *esse est percipi* are correct. It is difficult to discuss this, because, although his case is that a certain statement is not self-contradictory, he does not make it really clear just what statement it is that he is thinking of. Thus he says that the sentence 'It seems to me and to God, and it would seem to everyone else, as if there were an orange on the sideboard' does not mean the same as 'There is an orange on the sideboard', because it is not self-contradictory to say the first of these and deny the second; but he goes on to say, as if this were the same thing, that it is not self-contradictory to say 'It seems to me and to God and to absolutely everyone as if there were an orange on the sideboard, but really there is no orange there', and of course this is something quite different. Then later he says that however many people give their impressions, it makes sense to say that they are all mistaken; and this is something different again. And in the interesting discussion on pages 182–186, it seems that Berkeley is being taken to task for thinking that the evidence that one would ordinarily take as conclusive for such a statement as 'There is an orange on the sideboard' entails that statement. This is just not the position that Mr. Warnock started off to discuss.

A reasonably strong statement of what seems, at first anyway, under discussion, is this: Given that it seems to me and to everyone as if P, and given further that whatever I or anyone may do, it will continue to seem to me and to him as if P, and given further that there is nothing that anyone could do that would make it seem to him as if not-P, does it follow that P? I certainly think that it would not be correct to answer *Yes* to this question, and this means that on this interpretation of it *esse est percipi* is not obviously true. But Mr. Warnock seems to imply that it would be correct to answer *No*, and this is questionable. For if it is correct to say that the one thing does not entail the other, it should be possible to explain in what circumstances it would be correct to assert the one thing and deny the second. But what circumstances could these be?

And for that matter, in what circumstances would it be correct to say: 'It seems to me and to everyone, in every way it could, as if there were an orange on the sideboard, but there isn't'?

I think it is worth mentioning this difficulty, because it seems to be connected with one of the Berkeley's motives (or reasons) for holding *esse est percipi*, one that is often disregarded. There is one argument that Berkeley gives for his view, an argument to which he himself attached the greatest importance, which Mr. Warnock does not (as far as I can see) notice at all. This is the argument developed in *Principles*, 22–23 and again on page 200 of the *Three Dialogues* (Luce-Jessop edition). Berkeley here says that though we may think that we can imagine material things existing unperceived, we fail to notice that when we imagine these things we are ourselves perceiving them. As an argument this will doubtless seem contemptible. Its interest lies, however, in the identifications that have to be made if it is to have the slightest plausibility.

The first identification that needs to be made is that between perceiving something and thinking of it. "But do not you yourself perceive or think of them all the while"?

This same identification occurs rather interestingly in the following item (472) from the *Philosophical Commentaries*. (I have revised the spelling.) "You ask me whether the books are in the study now when no-one is there to see them. I answer *Yes*. You ask me, are we not in the wrong [sc. on Berkeleian principles] for imagining things to exist when they are not actually perceived by the senses? I answer *No*. The existence of our ideas consists in being perceived, imagined, thought on; whenever they are imagined or thought on they do exist. Whenever they are mentioned or discoursed of they are imagined or thought on, therefore you can at no time ask me whether they exist or no, but by reason of that very question they must necessarily exist." The next item, 473, should also be quoted here. "But say you then a Chimera does exist. I answer, it does in one sense. That is, it is imagined. But it must be well noted that existence is vulgarly restrained to actual perception, and that I use the word Existence in a larger sense than ordinary."

This identification explains, what is otherwise difficult to understand, why Berkeley thought that the belief in the absolute existence of bodies, independently of any mind, was due to the belief in abstract ideas. "Hence as it is impossible for me to see or feel anything without an actual sensation of that thing, so it is impossible for me to conceive in my thoughts any sensible thing or object distinct from the sensation or perception of it" (*Principles*, 5). This means: just as you cannot see or touch an orange without having sensations of a certain kind, so you cannot think of an orange without having sensations of that kind.

Berkeley really did believe, I think, that the meaning of a word is an image or a set of images. To think of an orange, and to think how an orange looks and feels and tastes and smells, are the same thing; and to understand something by the word *orange* is the same thing again. But not only are thinking of a thing and imagining a thing identified; imagining on the one hand, and seeing and touching and tasting and hearing and smelling on the other, are regarded as essentially similar, as species of the same genus. They all consist in having ideas. The only difference between looking at an orange and thinking of one is that the ideas one has in the former case, ideas of sense, are 'more strong, lively, and distinct' than those one has in the former case, ideas of imagination. (And of course, ultimately, the difference as regards causation.) See *Principles*, 30. Now in *one* way there is no difference between imagining what it would be like if there were an orange in front of one and imagining oneself seeing an orange. This is the force of the argument in *Principles*, 22–23. When Berkeley tried to understand the notion of a material substance external to the mind, he thought he was being asked to do something comparable to imagining how an orange would look to him if it were not there. And he thought that people could only have failed to notice the impossibility of this because of the prevalence of the doctrine of abstract ideas. The only way you can attach sense to a material-thing-word is by having ideas, *i.e.* images. You have to imagine how a thing—an orange, say—looks, tastes, and so on. Now if you are asked to imagine how an orange looks, you need not call up the image of a large orange, nor of a small one. But this does not mean (Berkeley insists) that you can attach sense to the word without having *some* image. Of course, as Berkeley himself says, often we don't in fact have images when we hear words; but our understanding of those words nevertheless depends on our being able to have images of the appropriate kind.

This also explains Berkeley's attacks on language, his insistence that we lay aside the veil of words, and his frequent requests to his readers that they look into their own thoughts and see whether what he says isn't so. These requests are not just that the reader reflect a little, but suggestions that he perform a certain kind of *Gedankenexperiment*. Words mislead us because they distract our attention from what is important in clarifying our views, *i.e.* our imagery. If what you want to know what a sentence really means, how it is to be understood, consider simply what images it excites in you. This cannot be misleading, because what you will be considering is of the same kind and the same structure as reality itself. (Philosophy as the logical syntax of the divine sense-language.) When Berkeley asked himself what it really meant to say that a sensible thing—a book, say—existed somewhere, he simply imagined a book, *i.e.* imagined himself looking at a book. Then he described this as having such-and-such ideas; and he supposed it to be, in every important respect, the same thing as perceiving a book. Then, because he could not (he thought) imagine that a book was in a closet without imagining himself seeing or touching a book, he concluded that for the book to be in the closet (to exist there) and for it to be perceived, were the same thing. (If this account of how Berkeley came to think that *esse est percipi* is even partially correct, then we should not expect him to take very seriously the difficulty expressed by his critics in the question "What about the *esse* of things that are not actually being perceived?"; as indeed he does not.)

Now one part of the force of *esse est percipi* on this account of it can be stated in quite a reasonable way: Really to understand what is meant by saying "There is an orange on the sideboard" you have to imagine how it would look and feel to you if there were one there. (Thus Berkeley holds, quite consistently, that a man blind from birth *cannot* attach the same meaning to this sentence as we do.) But then, what sense can we attach, on his view, to the sentence "It seems to me and to everyone, in every way it could, as if there were an orange on the sideboard, but there isn't one there really"? I suggested above that it was difficult to see in what circumstances one could say this; and one might put the difficulty by saying that it is difficult to *imagine* a situation in which this sentence would be called for. For it seems that we are asked to imagine a situation in which, while it seems to us in every way it could as if there were an orange on the sideboard, it is nevertheless correct to say that there isn't. But what, in the imagined situation, is it to be that makes it correct to say that there isn't? If in this situation it is to be correct to say there isn't, mustn't the situation be one in which, in some way or other, it seems to us as if there isn't an orange there, and thus one in which it *doesn't* seem to us in *every* way as if there *is*? This objection, which is quite natural to want to make against what Mr. Warnock says, reflects exactly the force of *esse est percipi* on one interpretation of it.

A NOTE ON BERKELEY AS PRECURSOR OF MACH AND EINSTEIN

KARL POPPER

> I had only a very vague idea who Bishop Berkeley was, but was thankful to him for having defended us from an incontrovertible first premise.
>
> SAMUEL BUTLER

I

The purpose of this note is to give a list of those ideas of Berkeley's in the field of the philosophy of physics which have a strikingly new look. They are mainly ideas which were rediscovered and reintroduced into the discussion of modern physics by Ernst Mach and Heinrich Hertz, and by a number of philosophers and physicists, some of them influenced by Mach, such as Bertrand Russell, Philip Frank, Richard von Mises, Moritz Schlick,[1] Werner Heisenberg and others.

I may say at once that I do not agree with most of these positivistic views. I admire Berkeley without agreeing with

---

First published in The British Journal for the Philosophy of Science, 4, 1953. Reprinted as chapter 6 of the author's *Conjectures and Refutations*. Reprinted here from *Conjectures and Refutations*, 2nd ed. (revised) 1965, by permission of the author, Routledge and Kegan Paul Ltd, London, and Basic Books, Inc., New York.

[1] Schlick, under the influence of Wittgenstein, suggested an instrumentalist interpretation of universal laws which was practically equivalent to Berkeley's 'mathematical hypotheses'; see *Naturwissenschaften*, 19, 1931, pp. 151 and 156. For further references see footnote 23 to section iv of ch. 3 of *Conjectures and Refutations*.

him. But criticism of Berkeley is not the purpose of this note, and will be confined to some very brief and incomplete remarks in section v.[2]

Berkeley wrote only one work, De Motu, devoted exclusively to the philosophy of physical science; but there are passages in many of his other works in which similar ideas and supplementary ones are represented.[3]

The core of Berkeley's ideas on the philosophy of science is in his *criticism of Newton's dynamics*. (Newton's mathematics were criticized by Berkeley in *The Analyst* and its two sequels.) Berkeley was full of admiration for Newton, and no doubt realized that there could have been no worthier object for his criticism.

II

The following twenty-one theses are not always expressed in Berkeley's terminology; their order is not connected with the order in which they appear in Berkeley's writings, or in which they might be presented in a systematic treatment of Berkeley's thought.

For a motto, I open my list with a quotation from Berkeley (*DM*, 29).

(1) *'To utter a word and mean nothing by it is unworthy of a philosopher.'*

(2) The meaning of a word is the idea or the sense-quality with which it is associated (as its name). Thus the words 'absolute space' and 'absolute time' are without

---

[2] I have since developed these ideas more fully in ch. 3 of *Conjectures and Refutations*; especially section 4.

[3] Apart from *DM* (= *De Motu*, 1721) I shall quote *TV* (= *Essay towards a New Theory of Vision*, 1709); *Pr* (= *Treatise concerning the Principles of Human Knowledge*, 1710); *HP* (= *Three Dialogues between Hylas and Philonous*, 1713); *Alc* (= *Alciphron*, 1732); *An* (= *The Analyst*, 1734); and *S* (= *Siris*, 1744). As far as I know, there does not exist an English translation of *DM* which succeeds in making clear what Berkeley meant to say; and the Editor of the latest edition of the *Works* even goes out of his way to belittle the significance of this highly original and in many ways unique essay.

any empirical (or operational) meaning; Newton's doctrine of absolute space and absolute time must therefore be rejected as a physical theory. (Cf. *Pr*, 97, 99, 116; *DM*, 53, 55, 62; *An*, 50, Qu. 8; *S*, 271: 'Concerning absolute space, that phantom of the mechanical and geometrical philosophers, it may suffice to observe that it is neither perceived by our sense, nor proved by our reason . . .'; *DM*, 64: 'for . . . the purpose of the philosophers of mechanics . . . it suffices to replace their "absolute space" by a relative space determined by the heavens of the fixed stars. . . . Motion and rest defined by this relative space can be conveniently used instead of the absolutes. . . .')

(3) The same holds for the word 'absolute motion'. The principle that all motion is relative can be established by appealing to the meaning of 'motion', or to operationalist arguments. (Cf. *Pr* as above, 58, 112, 115 'to denominate a body "moved" it is requisite . . . that it changes its distance or situation with regard to some other body . . . '; *DM*, 63: 'No motion can be discerned or measured, except with the help of sensible things'; *DM*, 62: '. . . the motion of a stone in a sling or of water in a whirled bucket cannot be called truly circular motion . . . by those who define [motion] with the help of absolute space. . . .')

(4) The words 'gravity' and 'force' are misused in physics; to introduce force as the cause or 'principle' of motion (or of an acceleration) is to introduce 'an occult quality' (*DM*, 1–4, and especially 5, 10, 11, 17, 22, 28; *Alc*, vii, 9). More precisely, we should say 'an occult metaphysical substance'; for the term 'occult quality' is a misnomer, in so far as 'quality' should more properly be reserved for observable or observed qualities—qualities which are given to our senses, and which, of course, are never 'occult'. (*An*, 50, Qu. 9; and especially *DM*, 6: 'It is plain, then, that it is useless to assume that the principle of motion is gravity or force; for how could this principle be known any more clearly through [its identification with] what is commonly called an *occult quality*? That which is itself occult explains nothing; not to mention that an unknown acting

cause might more properly be called a [metaphysical] *substance* rather than a *quality*.')

(5) In view of these considerations Newton's theory cannot be accepted as an explanation which is truly *causal*, i.e. based on true natural causes. The view that gravity causally explains the motion of bodies (that of the planets, of free-falling bodies, etc.), or that Newton discovered that gravity or attraction is 'an essential quality' (*Pr*, 106), whose inherence in the essence or nature of bodies explains the laws of their motion, must be discarded (*S*, 234; see also *S*, 246, last sentence). *But it must be admitted that Newton's theory leads to the correct results* (*DM*, 39, 41). To understand this, 'it is of the greatest importance . . . to distinguish between *mathematical hypotheses* and the *natures* [*or essences*] *of things*[4] . . . If we observe this distinction, then all the famous theorems of mechanical philosophy which . . . make it possible to subject the world system [i.e. the solar system] to human calculations, may be preserved; and at the same time, the study of motion will be freed of a thousand pointless trivialities and subtleties, and from [meaningless] abstract ideas' (*DM*, 66).

(6) In physics (mechanical philosophy) there is no causal explanation (cf. *S*, 231), i.e. no explanation based upon the discovery of the hidden nature or essence of things (*Pr*, 25). '. . . real efficient causes of the motion . . . of bodies do not in any way belong to the field of mechanics or of experimental science. Nor can they throw any light on these . . .' (*DM*, 41).

(7) The reason is, simply, that physical things have no secret or hidden, 'true or real nature', no 'real essence', no 'internal qualities' (*Pr*, 101).

(8) There is nothing physical *behind* the physical bodies, no occult physical reality. *Everything is surface*, as it were; physical bodies are nothing but their qualities. *Their appearance is their reality* (*Pr*, 87, 88).

(9) The province of the scientist (of the 'mechanical philosopher') is the discovery, 'by experiment and reason-

---

[4] Concerning the equivalence of '*natures*' and '*essences*' see my *Open Society*, ch. 5, section vi.

ing' (S, 234), of *Laws of Nature*, that is to say, of the regularities and uniformities of natural phenomena.

(10) The Laws of Nature are, in fact, regularities or similarities or analogies (*Pr*, 105) in the perceived motions of physical bodies (S, 234) '. . . these we learn from experience' (*Pr*, 30); they are observed, or inferred from observations (*Pr*, 30, 62; S, 228, 264).

(11) 'Once the Laws of Nature have been formed, it becomes the task of the philosopher to show of each phenomenon that it is in conformity with these laws, that is, necessarily follows from these principles.' (*DM*, 37; cf. *Pr*, 107; and S, 231: 'their [i.e. the "mechanical philosophers'"] province being . . . to account for particular phenomena by reducing them under, and showing their conformity to, such general rules.')

(12) This process *may* be called, if we like, 'explanation' (even 'causal explanation'), so long as we distinguish it clearly from the truly causal (i.e. metaphysical) explanation based upon the true nature or essence of things. S, 231; *DM*, 37: 'A thing may be said to be mechanically explained if it is reduced to those most simple and universal principles' (i.e. 'the primary laws of motion which have been proved by experiments . . .' *DM*, 36) 'and proved, by accurate reasoning, to be in agreement and connection with them . . . This means to *explain* and solve the phenomena, and to assign them their *cause* . . .' This terminology is admissible (cf. *DM*, 71) but it must not mislead us. We must always clearly distinguish (cf. *DM*, 72) between an 'essentialist'[5] explanation with appeals to the nature of things and a 'descriptive' explanation which appeals to a Law of Nature, i.e. to the description of an observed regularity. Of these two kinds of explanation only the latter is admissible in physical science.

(13) From both of these we must now distinguish a third kind of 'explanation'—an explanation which appeals to *mathematical hypotheses*. A mathematical hypothesis

[5] The term 'essentialist' (and 'essentialism') is not Berkeley's but was introduced by me in *The Poverty of Historicism*, and in *The Open Society and Its Enemies*.

Berkeley as Precursor of Mach and Einstein

may be described as a procedure for calculating certain results. It is a mere formalism, a mathematical tool or instrument, comparable to a calculating machine. It is judged merely by its efficiency. It may not only be admissible, it may be useful and it may be admirable, yet it is *not science*: even if it produces the correct results, it is only a trick, 'a knack' (*An*, 50, Qu. 35). And, as opposed to the explanation by essences (which, in mechanics, are simply false) and to that by laws of nature (which, if the laws 'have been proved by experiment', are simply true), the question of the *truth* of a mathematical hypothesis does not arise—only that of its *usefulness as a calculating tool*.

(14) Now, those principles of the Newtonian theory which 'have been proved by experiment'—those of the laws of motion which simply describe the observable regularities of the motion of bodies—are true. But the part of the theory involving the concepts which have been criticized above—absolute space, absolute motion, force, attraction, gravity—is not true, since these are 'mathematical hypotheses'. As such, however, they should not be rejected, if they work well (as in the case of force, attraction, gravity). Absolute space and absolute motion have to be rejected because they do not work (they are to be replaced by the system of fixed stars, and motion relative to it). '"Force", "gravity", "attraction",[6] and words such as these are useful for purposes of reasoning and for computations of motions and of moving bodies; but they do not help us to understand the simple nature of motion itself, nor do they serve to designate so many distinct qualities. . . . As far as attraction is concerned it is clear that it was not introduced by Newton as a true physical quality but merely as a mathematical hypothesis' (*DM*, 17).[7]

(15) Properly understood, a mathematical hypothesis does not claim that anything exists in nature which cor-

---

[6] The italics in the Latin original function here as quotation marks.

[7] This was more or less Newton's own opinion; cp. Newton's letters to Bentley, 17th January, and especially 25th February 1692-3, and section 3 of ch. 3, above.

responds to it—neither to the words or terms with which it operates, nor to the functional dependencies which it appears to assert. It erects, as it were, a fictitious mathematical world behind that of appearance, but without the claim that this world exists. 'But what is said of forces residing in bodies, whether attracting or repelling, is to be regarded only as a mathematical hypothesis, and not as anything really existing in nature' (S, 234; cf. DM, 18, 39 and especially Alc, vii, 9, An, 50, Qu. 35). It claims only that from its assumptions the correct consequences can be drawn. But it can easily be misinterpreted as claiming more, as claiming to describe a real world behind the world of appearance. But no such world *could* be described; for the description would necessarily be meaningless.

(16) It can be seen from this that the same appearances *may* be successfully calculated from more than one mathematical hypothesis, and that two mathematical hypotheses which yield the same results concerning the calculated appearances may not only differ, but even contradict each other (especially if they are misinterpreted as describing a world of essences behind the world of appearances); nevertheless, there may be nothing to choose between them. 'The foremost of men proffer . . . many different doctrines, and even opposite doctrines, and yet their conclusions [i.e. their calculated results] attain the truth . . . Newton and Torricelli seem to disagree with one another, . . . but the thing is well enough explained by both. For all forces attributed to bodies are merely mathematical hypotheses . . . ; thus the same thing may be explained in different ways' (DM, 67).

(17) The analysis of Newton's theory thus yields the following results:

We must distinguish

(a) Observations of concrete, particular things.

(b) Laws of Nature, which are either observations of regularities, or which are proved ('*comprobatae*', DM, 36; this may perhaps mean here 'supported' or 'corroborated'; see DM, 31) by experiments, or discovered 'by a diligent observation of the phenomena' (*Pr*, 107).

(c) Mathematical hypotheses, which are not based on observation but whose consequences agree with the phenomena (or 'save the phenomena', as the Platonists said).

(d) Essentialist or metaphysical causal explanations, which have no place in physical science.

Of these four, (a) and (b) are based on observation, and can, from experience, be known to be true; (c) is not based on observation and has only an instrumental significance—thus more than one instrument may do the trick (cf. (16), above); and (d) is known to be false whenever it constructs a world of essences behind the world of appearances. Consequently (c) is also known to be false whenever it is interpreted in the sense of (d).

(18) These results clearly apply to cases other than Newtonian theory, for example to atomism (corpuscular theory). In so far as this theory attempts to explain the world of appearances by constructing an invisible world of 'inward essences' (*Pr*, 102) behind the world of appearances, it must be rejected. (Cf. *Pr*, 50; *An*, 50, *Qu.* 56; *S*, 232, 235.)

(19) The work of the scientist leads to something that may be called 'explanation', but it is hardly of great value for *understanding* the thing explained, since the attainable explanation is not one based upon an insight into the nature of things. But it is of practical importance. It enables us to make both *applications* and *predictions*. '. . . laws of nature or motions direct us how to act, and teach us what to expect' (*S*, 234; cf. *Pr*, 62). Prediction is based merely upon regular sequence (not upon causal sequence—at least not in the essentialist sense). A sudden darkness at noon may be a 'prognostic' indicator, a warning 'sign', a 'mark' of the coming downpour; nobody takes it as its cause. Now *all* observed regularities are of this nature even though 'prognostics' or 'signs' are usually mistaken for true causes (*TV*, 147; *Pr*, 44, 65, 108; *S*, 252-4; *Alc*, iv, 14, 15).

(20) A general practical result—which I propose to call 'Berkeley's razor'—of this analysis of physics allows us *a priori* to eliminate from physical science all essentialist explanations. If they have a mathematical and a predictive content they may be admitted *qua* mathematical hypotheses (while their essentialist interpretation is eliminated). If not, they may be ruled out altogether. This razor is sharper than Ockham's: *all* entities are ruled out except those which are perceived.

(21) The ultimate argument for these views, the reason why occult substances and qualities, physical forces, structures of corpuscles, absolute space, and absolute motion, etc. are eliminated, is this: we know that there are no entities such as these because we know that the words professedly designating them must be meaningless. *To have a meaning, a word must stand for an 'idea'*; that is to say, for a perception, or the memory of a perception; in Hume's terminology, for an impression or its reflection in our memory. (It may also stand for a 'notion', such as God; but the words belonging to physical science cannot stand for 'notions'.) Now the words here in question do not stand for ideas. 'Those who assert that active force, action, and the principle of motion are in reality inherent in the bodies, maintain a doctrine that is based upon no experience, and support it by obscure and general terms, and so do not themselves understand what they want to say' (*DM*, 31).

III

Everybody who reads this list of twenty-one theses must be struck by their modernity. They are surprisingly similar, especially in the criticism of Newton, to the philosophy of physics which Ernst Mach taught for many years in the conviction that it was new and revolutionary; in which he was followed by, for example, Joseph Petzold; and which had an immense influence on modern physics, especially on the Theory of Relativity. There is only one difference: Mach's 'principle of the economy of thought'

(*Denkoekonomie*) goes beyond what I have called 'Berkeley's razor', in so far as it allows us not only to discard certain 'metaphysical elements', but also to distinguish in some cases between various competing hypotheses (of the kind called by Berkeley 'mathematical') with respect to their *simplicity*. (Cf. (16) above.) There is also a striking similarity to Hertz's *Principles of Mechanics* (1894), in which he tried to eliminate the concept of 'force', and to Wittgenstein's *Tractatus*.

What is perhaps most striking is that Berkeley and Mach, both great admirers of Newton, criticize the ideas of absolute time, absolute space, and absolute motion, on very similar lines. Mach's criticism, exactly like Berkeley's, culminates in the suggestion that all arguments for Newton's absolute space (like Foucault's pendulum, the rotating bucket of water, the effect of centrifugal forces upon the shape of the earth) fail because these movements are relative to the system of the fixed stars.

To show the significance of this anticipation of Mach's criticism, I may cite two passages, one from Mach and one from Einstein. Mach wrote (in the 7th edition of the *Mechanics*, 1912, ch. ii, section 6, § 11) of the reception of his criticism of *absolute motion*, propounded in earlier editions of his *Mechanics*: 'Thirty years ago the view that the notion of "absolute motion" is meaningless, without any empirical content, and scientifically without use, was generally felt to be very strange. Today this view is upheld by many well-known investigators.' And Einstein said in his obituary notice for Mach ('Nachruf auf Mach', *Physikalische Zeitschr.*, 1916), referring to this view of Mach's: 'It is not improbable that Mach would have found the Theory of Relativity if, at a time when his mind was still young, the problem of the constancy of velocity of light had agitated the physicists.' This remark of Einstein's is no doubt more than generous.[8] Of the bright

[8] Mach survived Einstein's Special Theory of Relativity by more than eleven years, at least eight of which were very active years; but he remained strongly opposed to it; and though he alluded to it in the preface to the last (seventh) German edition (1912) of the *Mechanik* published during his lifetime, the allu-

light it throws upon Mach some reflection must fall upon Berkeley.[9]

IV

A few words may be said about the relation of Berkeley's philosophy of science to his metaphysics. It is very different indeed from Mach's.

While the positivist Mach was an enemy of all traditional, that is non-positivistic, metaphysics, and especially of all theology, Berkeley was a Christian theologian, and intensely interested in Christian apologetics. While Mach and Berkeley agreed that such words as 'absolute time', 'absolute space' and 'absolute motion' are meaningless and therefore to be eliminated from science, Mach surely would not have agreed with Berkeley on the reason why physics cannot treat of real causes. Berkeley believed in causes, even in 'true' or 'real' causes; but all true or real causes were to him 'efficient or final causes' (S, 231), and therefore *spiritual* and utterly beyond physics (cf. HP, ii). He also believed in true or real causal *explanation* (S, 231) or, as I may perhaps call it, in 'ultimate explanation'. This, for him, was God.

All appearances are truly caused by God, and explained through God's intervention. This for Berkeley is the simple reason why physics can only describe regularities, and why it cannot find true causes.

It would be a mistake, however, to think that the similarity between Berkeley and Mach is by these differences shown to be only superficial. On the contrary, Berkeley and Mach are both convinced that there is no physical world (of primary qualities, or of atoms; cf. Pr, 50; S, 232, 235) behind the world of physical appearances (Pr, 87, 88). Both believed in a form of the doctrine nowadays

---

sion was by way of compliment to the opponent of Einstein, Hugo Dingler: Einstein's name and that of the theory were not mentioned.

[9] This is not the place to discuss other predecessors of Mach, such as Leibniz.

called phenomenalism—the view that physical things are bundles, or complexes, or constructs of phenomenal *qualities*, of particular experienced colours, noises, etc.; Mach calls them 'complexes of elements'. The difference is that for Berkeley, these are directly caused by God. For Mach, they are just there. While Berkeley says that there can be nothing physical behind the physical phenomena, Mach suggests that there is nothing at all behind them.

V

The great historical importance of Berkeley lies, I believe, in his protest against essentialist explanations in science. Newton himself did not interpret his theory in an essentialist sense; he himself did not believe that he had discovered the fact that physical bodies, by their nature, are not only extended but endowed with a force of attraction (radiating from them, and proportional to the amount of matter in them). But soon after him the essentialist interpretation of his theory became the ruling one, and remained so till the days of Mach.

In our own day essentialism has been dethroned; a Berkeleian or Machian positivism or instrumentalism has, after all these years, become fashionable.

Yet there is clearly a third possibility—a 'third view' (as I call it).

Essentialism is, I believe, untenable. It implies the idea of an *ultimate* explanation, for an essentialist explanation is neither in need of, nor capable of, further explanation. (If it is in the nature of a body to attract others, then there is no need to ask for an explanation of this fact, and no possibility of finding such an explanation.) Yet we know, at least since Einstein, that explanation may be pushed, unexpectedly, further and further.

But although we must reject essentialism, this does not mean that we have to accept positivism; for we may accept the 'third view'.

I shall not here discuss the positivist dogma of meaning, since I have done so elsewhere. I shall make only six observations. (i) One can work with something like a world 'behind' the world of appearance without committing oneself to essentialism (especially if one assumes that we can never know whether there may not be a further world behind that world). To put it less vaguely, one can work with the idea of hierarchical levels of explanatory hypotheses. There are comparatively low level ones (somewhat like what Berkeley had in mind when he spoke of 'Laws of Nature'); higher ones such as Kepler's laws, still higher ones such as Newton's theory, and, next, Relativity. (ii) These theories are not mathematical hypotheses, that is, *nothing but* instruments for the prediction of appearances. Their function goes very much further; for (iii) there is no pure appearance or pure observation: what Berkeley had in mind when he spoke of these things was always the result of interpretation, and (iv) it had therefore a theoretical or hypothetical admixture. (v) New theories, moreover, may lead to re-interpretation of old appearances, and in this way change the world of appearances. (vi) The multiplicity of explanatory theories which Berkeley noted (see Section ii (16), above) is used, wherever possible, to construct, for any two competing theories, conditions in which they yield different observable results, so that we can make a crucial test to decide between them, winning in this way new experience.

A main point of this third view is that science aims at *true* theories, even though we can never be sure that any particular theory is true; and that science *may* progress (and know that it does so) by inventing theories which compared with earlier ones may be described as better approximations to what is true.

So we can now admit, without becoming essentialist, that in science we always try *to explain the known by the unknown*, the observed (and observable) by the unobserved (and, perhaps, unobservable). At the same time we can now admit, without becoming instrumentalist, what Berkeley said of the nature of hypotheses in the following passage (S, 228), which shows both the weakness of his analysis—its failure to realize the conjectural character of all science, including what he calls the 'laws of nature'—and also its strength, its admirable understanding of the logical structure of hypothetical explanation.

'It is one thing', Berkeley writes, 'to arrive at general laws of nature from a contemplation of the phenomena; and another to frame an hypothesis, and from thence deduce the phenomena. Those who suppose epicycles, and by them explain the motions and appearances of the planets, may not therefore be thought to have discovered principles true in fact and nature. And, albeit we may from the premises infer a conclusion, it will not follow that we can argue reciprocally, and from the conclusion infer the premises. For instance, supposing an elastic fluid, whose constituent minute particles are equidistant from each other, and of equal densities and diameters, and recede one from another with a centrifugal force which is inversely as the distance of the centres; and admitting that from such supposition it must follow that the density and elastic force of such fluid are in the inverse proportion of the space it occupies when compressed by any force; yet we cannot reciprocally infer that a fluid endowed with this property must therefore consist of such supposed equal particles.'

BIBLIOGRAPHY

LOCKE

For a more complete list of Locke's works, and writings on Locke, see the bibliographies in Aaron's *John Locke* and Yolton's *John Locke and the Way of Ideas*. If a student can locate, in some ancient edition, *Locke's Correspondence with the Bishop of Worcester (Stillingfleet)*, he will find it worth reading.

Unfortunately, there is no standard edition of Locke's writings.

Locke's Writings

An Essay Concerning Human Understanding, ed. A. C. Fraser, 2 vols., Dover Publications, Inc., New York, 1959.

An Essay Concerning Human Understanding, ed. John W. Yolton, 2 vols., J. M. Dent and Sons Ltd., London, 1961. (This is the best edition of the *Essay* in print.)

An Early Draft of Locke's Essay, Together with Excerpts from his Journals, eds. R. I. Aaron and J. Gibb, Oxford, 1936.

Good brief surveys of Locke's philosophy may be found in

F. Copleston, *A History of Philosophy*, Vol. V, London, 1959, Chapters IV–VII.

D. J. O'Connor, "Locke," in *A Critical History of Western Philosophy*, ed. D. J. O'Connor, New York, 1964.

Books on Locke

Aaron, R. I., *John Locke*, 2nd ed., Oxford, 1955.

Gibson, James, *Locke's Theory of Knowledge and Its Historical Relations*, Cambridge, 1931.
Hofstadter, A., *Locke and Scepticism*, New York, 1935.
Leibniz, G. W. von, *New Essays Concerning Human Understanding*, translated and edited by A. G. Langley, La Salle, 1949.
Mandelbaum, Maurice, *Philosophy, Science, and Sense Perception* (Ch. 1), Baltimore, 1964.
Morris, C. R., *Locke, Berkeley, Hume*, Oxford, 1931.
O'Connor, D. J., *John Locke*, Pelican Books, 1952.
Yolton, J. W., *John Locke and the Way of Ideas*, Oxford, 1956.

Articles

Allison, Henry E., "Locke on Personal Identity," *Journal of the History of Ideas*, 27 (1966), 41–58.
Ammerman, Robert, "Our Knowledge of Substance According to Locke," *Theoria*, 31 (1965), 1–8.
Broad, C. D., "John Locke," *The Hibbert Journal*, 31 (1933), 249–67. (Reprinted in *Ethics and the History of Philosophy*, London, 1952.)
———, "Locke's Doctrine of Substantial Identity and Diversity," *Theoria*, 17 (1951), 13–26.
Davis, John W., "The Molyneux Problem," *Journal of the History of Ideas*, 21 (1960), 392–408.
Odegard, Douglas, "Locke as an Empiricist," *Philosophy*, 40 (1965), 185–96.
Yolton, J. W., "Locke and the Seventeenth-Century Logic of Ideas," *Journal of the History of Ideas*, 16 (1955), 431–52.

LOCKE'S POLITICAL PHILOSOPHY

Locke's Writings

Two Treatises of Civil Government, ed. Peter Laslett, Mentor Books, 1965.
The Second Treatise of Civil Government and A Letter

Concerning Toleration, ed. J. W. Gough, Basil Blackwell, 1948.

John Locke, Essays on the Law of Nature, edited with commentary by W. von Leyden, Oxford, 1954.

Two Tracts on Government, ed. Philip Abrams, Cambridge, 1966 (first English publication of Locke's earliest writings on politics).

Locke on Politics, Religion, and Education, ed. Maurice Cranston, Collier Books, 1965 (contains *The Second Treatise, A Letter Concerning Toleration, A Note on Happiness, The Sound Mind in the Sound Body, The Reasonableness of Christianity, The Conduct of the Understanding*).

Books on Locke

Gough, J. W., *John Locke's Political Philosophy, Eight Studies*, Oxford, 1950.

Lamprecht, S. P., *The Moral and Political Philosophy of John Locke* (Archives of Philosophy No. 11), New York, 1918.

Larkin, P., *Property in the 18th Century, with Special Reference to England and Locke*, Cork, 1930.

Macpherson, C. B., *The Political Theory of Possessive Individualism*, Oxford Paperbacks, 1964, Ch. v, "Locke: The Political Theory of Appropriation."

Strauss, Leo, *Natural Right and History*, Chicago, 1953, (pp. 202–51 on Locke).

Articles

Day, J. P., "Locke on Property," *The Philosophical Quarterly*, 16 (1966), 207–20.

Laslett, Peter, "The English Revolution and Locke's *Two Treatises of Government*," *Cambridge Historical Journal*, 12 (1956), 40–55.

von Leyden, W., "John Locke and Natural Law," *Philosophy*, 31 (1956), 23–35.

Simon, W. M., "John Locke, Philosophy and Political Theory," *American Political Science Review*, 45 (1951), 386–99.

Yolton, J. W., "Locke on the Law of Nature," *Philosophical Review*, 67 (1958), 477–98.

BERKELEY

The standard edition of Berkeley's writings is *The Works of George Berkeley, Bishop of Cloyne*, eds. A. A. Luce and T. E. Jessop, 9 vols., Nelson and Sons, Edinburgh, 1948–57.

A bibliography of writings by and on Berkeley up to 1962 is to be found in:

T. E. Jessop, *Bibliography of George Berkeley*, Oxford, 1934;

C. M. Turbayne and R. Ware, "A Bibliography of George Berkeley, 1933–62," *The Journal of Philosophy*, 60 (1963), 93–112. A revision, by T. E. Jessop, of his bibliography (brought up to date) is to be published shortly in The Hague by M. Nijhoff.

Selections from Berkeley's writings

Berkeley's Philosophical Writings, ed. David M. Armstrong, Collier Books, 1965 (contains the *Principles*, the *Three Dialogues*, the *New Theory of Vision*, the *De Motu*, the philosophical correspondence with Samuel Johnson, and selections from the *Commonplace Book*).

A New Theory of Vision and other writings, Everyman's Library No. 483 (contains the *Principles*, the *Three Dialogues*, the *New Theory of Vision*).

Three Dialogues between Hylas and Philonous, ed. Colin M. Turbayne, The Library of Liberal Arts, 1954.

The Principles of Human Knowledge, ed. Colin M. Turbayne, The Library of Liberal Arts, 1957.

Works on Vision, ed. Colin M. Turbayne, The Library of Liberal Arts, 1963 (contains the *New Theory of Vision*, *The Theory of Vision Vindicated*, with excerpts from *Alciphron* and the *Principles*).

The Principles of Human Knowledge with other writings, ed. G. J. Warnock, Fontana Library, 1962 (contains the

Principles, the *Three Dialogues*, and part of the correspondence with Samuel Johnson).

Good brief surveys of Berkeley's philosophy may be found in:

F. Copleston, A *History of Philosophy*, Vol. V, London, 1959, Chapters XI–XIII.

J. F. Thomson, "Berkeley," in A *Critical History of Western Philosophy*, ed. by D. J. O'Connor, New York, 1964.

Books on Berkeley

Abbott, T. K., *Sight and Touch*, London, 1864.
Armstrong, D. M., *Berkeley's Theory of Vision*, Melbourne, 1961.
Hedenius, I., *Sensationalism and Theology in Berkeley's Philosophy*, Uppsala, 1936.
Hicks, G. Dawes, *Berkeley*, London, 1932.
Johnston, G. A., *The Development of Berkeley's Philosophy*, London, 1923.
———, *Berkeley's Commonplace Book*, London, 1930.
Luce, A. A., *Berkeley and Malebranche*, Oxford, 1934.
———, *Berkeley's Philosophical Commentaries*, London, 1944.
———, *Berkeley's Immaterialism*, London, 1945.
———, *The Dialectic of Immaterialism*, London, 1963.
Morris, C. R., *Locke, Berkeley, Hume*, Oxford, 1931.
Sillem, E. A., *George Berkeley and the Proofs for the Existence of God*, London and New York, 1957.
Warnock, G. J., *Berkeley*, Pelican Books, 1953.

Collections of articles

"George Berkeley; Lectures on the Bi-Centenary of his Death," *University of California publications in Philosophy*, vol. 29.
Steinkraus, Warren E., *New Studies in Berkeley's Philosophy*, New York, 1966.

Articles

Bracken, H. M., "Berkeley's Realisms," *Philosophical Quarterly*, 8 (1958), 41–53.
Broad, C. D., "Berkeley's Argument about Material Substance," *Proceedings of the British Academy*, 28 (1942), 119–38.
Cummins, P., "Perceptual Relativity and Ideas in the Mind," *Philosophical and Phenomenological Research*, 24 (1963), 202–14.
Davis, John W., "Berkeley's Doctrine of the Notion," *Review of Metaphysics*, 12 (1959), 378–89.
———, "The Molyneux Problem," *Journal of the History of Ideas*, 21 (1960), 392–408.
Grey, Denis, "Berkeley on Other Selves: a Study in Fugue," *Philosophical Quarterly*, 4 (1954), 28–44.
———, "The Solipsism of Bishop Berkeley," *Philosophical Quarterly*, 2 (1952), 338–49.
Prior, A. N., "Berkeley in Logical Form," *Theoria*, 21 (1955), 117–22.
Suchting, W. A., "Berkeley's Criticism of Newton on Space and Motion," *Isis*, 58 (1967), Summer issue.
Turbayne, Colin M., "Berkeley's Two Concepts of Mind," *Philosophical and Phenomenological Research*, 20 (1959–60), 85–92. (There is a reply by Grave, S. A., "A Note on Berkeley's Conception of the Mind," *Philosophy and Phenomenological Research*, 22 [1961–62], 574–76. Turbayne rejoins in "Berkeley's Two Concepts of Mind," Part II, *Philosophy and Phenomenological Research*, 22 [1961–62] 577–80.)

INDEX

Abstract Ideas, 8, 9–11, 311–12, 377, 409–25, 432
Abstraction. *See* Abstract Ideas
Albinus, 377
Alexander, S., 76, 103, 128, 130
Allaire, E. B., 361n
Angels, 370
Archetypes. *See* Ideas
Armstrong, D. M., 313n
Atomism, 443
Awareness, 42–44
Ayer, A. J., 103, 104

Baeumker, C., 126n
Barnes, W. H. F., 7
Belief, 278, 282–83
Bell, P., 87
Bennett, J., 11, 12, 13
Berkeley, G., 8–13 *passim*, 128, 130, 139, 150, 255–449 *passim*
   conflation of doctrine of property instantiation and distinction between appearance and reality, 86–87, 91–95, 96, 99–103
   conflation of veil-of-perception doctrine and primary-secondary quality distinction, 118–24
   ideas, 17
   Jackson's withdrawal of one criticism, 127n

personal identity, 161–62, 173
primary and secondary qualities, 54–56, 71–72, 78–85, 107–10
resemblance of ideas, 151–53
Borderline cases, 173–74
   See also Vagueness
Bosanquet, B., 378n
Bourne, H. R. Fox, 206n
Boyle, R., 34, 52, 55–58, 66, 70, 126n
Bracken, H. M., 358n
Bradley, F. H., 72, 127n, 163
Brain, 289
Broad, C. D., 13, 58, 76, 103, 129, 136
Browne, P., 287n
Browning, R., 167
Butler, S., 159, 436

Caird, E., 132–33n, 378n
Calvinism, 214
   and the poor, 204
Cambridge Platonists, 15, 16, 26
Capitalist, 235–39, 241–44, 248–51
Cartesians, 16, 29, 32, 55, 56, 291, 318, 359n, 403, 404
Categorial and explanatory, 50–52
Causality, Berkeley's theory, 11–12, 82, 83, 281, 299n,

Causality (*cont'd*)
  382, 383–84, 385–88, 439, 440, 443, 446
Charles I, 211
Christianity and the poor, 208–11
Clark, G. N., 205n
Collectivism, 227–28, 231, 238
Color, 256, 257, 260
  abstraction, 411, 412–13, 415–16, 419, 424–25
  apparent and real, 342–43, 345
  existence unperceived, 269–70, 302–3, 344, 345
  extension, 9–10, 416, 419, 424–25
  resembles only color, 357
  See also Primary and Secondary qualities; Secondary qualities
Community, 187–88
Conscious, 158–59, 165
Consent, 192–93, 197, 223–24, 226
Consideration, 46–47
Constitutionalism, 228–29
Contract, 223
Copleston, F. C., 103
Cox, R. H., 231n
Cummins, P. D., 13

D'Avenant, W., 205n
Davie, G. E., 402n
Day, J. P., 244n
Democritus, 55, 73
Descartes, R., 58, 75, 255, 311, 333, 361, 361n
Dingler, H., 445–46n
Dreams, 259, 260, 279–80

Ego-centric predicament, 330–31
Egoism, 182–84

Einstein, A., 445, 445n, 447
Empiricism, 25–29, 34, 40–41
Equality, 194–95, 197
Erdmann, J. E., 126n
Essentialism, 440, 443, 447–48
Existence, 311, 321–23, 326, 417n, 422
Explanatory and categorial, 50–52
Extension, 257, 292, 344, 359n, 412–13, 415–16, 416n, 424–25
  See also Primary qualities; Primary and secondary qualities

Flew, A. G. N., 170n, 172n
Force, 438–39, 440–41, 444, 445
Foucher, S., 359
Frank, P., 436
Fraser, A. C., 74, 103, 128–29, 130, 134–35, 146, 150, 375
Freedom, 193–94, 197, 220–21
Furlong, E. J., 13
Furniss, E. S., 205n

Galileo, G., 75
Gassendi, P., 361
Gibson, J. J., 75, 128, 130, 144n
God, 8, 180–82, 287, 295, 319, 364–408 *passim*
  causality, 11–12, 366–69, 382–99, 406–8, 427–30, 446–47
  ideas of, 303n, 304–6, 323–24, 351, 369–79
  unobserved objects, 12, 268, 289, 292, 294, 297–98, 304–6, 325, 339, 351,

Index 459

God (cont'd)
    365–66, 380–82, 387–89, 400–8, 428–29
Gough, J. W., 202, 211n, 226, 231n
Grave, S. A., 13
Gravity, 438–39, 441, 447
Green, T. H., 373

Hacking, I., 87
Hallucinations, 259, 260, 279–80
Hamilton, W., 126n, 128, 133n, 134–35, 139n, 147n
Heat, 256, 257, 340–41, 347–48, 360n, 361n
Hedenius, I., 326n
Hegelians, 132, 378
Heisenberg, W., 436
Hertz, H., 436, 445
Hicks, G. Dawes, 103, 339n, 390
Hill, C., 204n
Hobbes, T., 15, 187, 202, 217, 219
Hobbists, 16
Hooker, R., 182
Human nature, 217–21
Hume, D., 33, 384, 415
  appearance and reality, 429
  causality, 33, 286
  ideas, 17, 40, 381, 444
  mind, 4, 276, 310
  Representative Perception, 128, 139
  space and time, 416n
  unperceived objects, 406
Huxley, T. H., 103
Huygenius, 34

Idealism, 381, 420
Ideas, 2–5, 8, 257
  archetypes, 79, 301–2, 304–6, 351, 369–78
  attention, 18, 19, 42
  attribute or character, 19
  causation, 11–12
  concepts, 18
  consideration, 18, 19, 42
  dependence, 387–88
  Locke and Berkeley on qualities and ideas, 79–80, 127–28
  Locke and Berkeley on types of ideas, 94
  manner of receiving, 146–47
  meaning, 2–3, 437, 444
  mind, 4, 19–25, 274–75, 287–88, 292–93, 296–313
  numerical identity, 348–52
  origin, 25–29, 43–52, 67–68
  perception, 266, 321–25, 334–37, 338–39, 426–27
  physiological account, 27, 41–44
  resemble ideas only, 151–53, 353–63
  sensory states, 96, 380
  simple, 3–4
  See also Abstract Ideas; God; Imagination; Perception; Sensations; Sense-data
Imagination, 270–71, 275, 299n, 320, 323, 330, 365, 366–68, 431–34
Immortality, 312n
Impenetrability, 56
Inconsistency and inconstancy, 131–32, 154
  real meaning, 133
Individualism, 213, 220, 226–30, 231, 238
Individuals
  particulars, 62
  perishing states, 63

Instrumentalism, 436n, 443, 447–48
Introspection, 43, 49

Jackson, R., 7, 78–85
James I, 211
James II, 252
James, W., 156, 276
Jessop, T. E., 355n, 359n
Johnson, S., D.D., 302, 309, 311, 312, 312n, 323, 373, 417n
Johnson, S., LL.D., 402
Johnston, G. A., 76, 83n, 339n

Kant, I., 30, 51, 131, 132–33n, 276, 284, 290, 293, 377, 378
Kendall, W., 187–89, 201, 231n
Kepler, J., 448
King, G., 204, 205n, 226n
King, W., 287n
Knowledge, 277–79, 289
  existences, 32–34
  general propositions, 29–32
  mathematics, 30–32
  natural law, 180–82
  nominal essence or natural kind, 34–37
"Knowledge by acquaintance," 277, 279, 319n

Labor, 213, 233–36, 244
Laboring class, 203–11, 212, 225, 233–39, 248–49
Lamprecht, S., 183n
Language, 375–77, 433–34
Laski, H., 200
Laslett, P., 218n, 247n
Law, 191, 194
Laws of Nature, 368, 439–40, 442–43, 448

Leibniz, G. W., 89, 257, 384, 446n
Locke, J., 1–7 *passim*, 14–254 *passim*, 384, 395
  abstract ideas, 411, 419
  existence, 311
  heat, 340
  ideas, 381
  material thing, 361, 371
  primary and secondary qualities, 364
  representative theory, 289, 301, 360
  substratum, 274, 307
Lorenz, T., 369n
Luce, A. A., 13, 103, 296–97, 303n, 324n, 359n, 390, 402n, 403

Mabbot, J. D., 13
Mach, E., 436, 444–47
Macpherson, C. B., 7, 185n, 232–54
McTaggart, J. M. E., 257
Majority rule, 188, 190, 194, 195, 197, 201, 226
Malebranche, N., 147n, 291, 304, 358n, 373, 396
Man. See Person
Marc-Wogau, K., 13
Marx, K., 249
Marxism, 195
Materialism, 291, 292
Material thing, 371, 373
  definition, 255–57, 361–63, 367
  unperceived, 270, 273
Matter. See Material thing; Substance
Meaning
  ideas, 2–3, 437–38, 444
  Locke's rejection of conventionalist account, 6–7

Index   461

Meaning (cont'd)
  Locke's rejection of extensional account, 4–6
Memory, 158–64, 277, 278, 320, 323
Mental images. See Imagination
Mill, J. S., 365
Mind, 257, 285, 286–87, 292, 306–13, 359n, 373
  causality, 11, 367–68
  substance, 274–76, 348
  See also Person; Personal identity; Soul
Mises, R. Von, 436
Modes, 292, 307–8, 312
  mixed, 47
Monarch, 248, 252–53
Money, 185–86, 215–16, 222–28, 233–36, 242
Monson, C. H., 7
Moore, G. E., 385
Morris, C. R., 102
Mosaic creation, 305–6, 324
Motion, 415, 416, 417–18, 438, 441, 444, 445

Naive Realism, 129, 152–53, 342
Natural law, 180–82, 184, 188, 189, 228, 233, 240
New Deal, 197
Newton, I., 29, 34, 52, 322, 437–48 passim
Newtonians, 29, 255
Nominal essence, 34–37
Notion, 285n, 323, 375, 377–78, 422n, 444
Numerical identity, 300–2, 348, 349–52

O'Connor, D. J., 101, 102
Odor, 269, 270

Ontological argument, 273

Pain, 323–24, 360n, 361n
Pantheism, 292
Passion, 285n
Paul, G. A., 231n
Perception, 258–61, 266–67, 289, 323–25
  awareness, 42
  infallibility of, 318–20
  property instantiation, 140–46
  qualities and ideas, 127–28
  See also God; Ideas; Naive Realism; Representative theory of perception
Percival, J., 305n
Perry, R. B., 329, 330–31
Person, 166–74
  See also Mind; Personal identity; Soul
Personal identity, 155–78
  borderline cases and vagueness, 173–76
  disembodiment, 166–67
  memory of past actions, 157–64
  responsibility, 168–69, 171–72
  unity of substance, 157
Petyt, W., 205
Petzold, J., 444
Phenomenalism, 12, 268–70, 306, 325, 365, 381, 446–47
Plato, 128, 377
Platonism, 377
Popkin, R. H., 359n
Popper, K. R., 13
Positivism. See Instrumentalism
Power, 57, 65
  See also Causality, Berkeley's theory

Price, H. H., 41, 43, 121, 122
Prichard, H. A., 265
Primary qualities, 55, 60, 62
   confused with ideas by Berkeley, 74, 95
   confused with powers by Gibson, 75
   determinate and indeterminate, 64
   determinate and variable, 65
   ideas of, 69
   Locke's account, 117
   macroscopic and microscopic, 66
   perishing states, 61
   powers, 59–60
Primary and secondary qualities, 13, 54–77, 364
   abstraction, 424–25
   Bennett's distinction, 111–17
   Berkeley's interpretation defended, 78–85
   Berkeley's misinterpretation, 71, 72
   current distinction, 76, 77
   distinction confused with other distinctions, 86
   Locke's distinction, 78, 104
   misinterpretations, 74–77
   "phenol" argument, 105–9
   Reid's criticism, 73, 74
Pringle-Pattison, A. S., 1, 2, 3, 5, 6
Prior, A. N., 330n, 332n
Proclus, 377
Property, 184–86, 201, 212–16, 222–28, 231–54
Property instantiation
   cause of ideas, 92
   knowledge by perception, 140–46
   Locke's view, 145
   substance, 87–89

Quinton, A. M., 170n, 172n

Randall, J. H., 103
Rationality, 210, 214–17, 218–21, 222–23, 231, 240
Real essence, 121–22
Reid, T., 133n, 147n
   ideas resemble ideas only, 152
   Locke's representative theory of perception, 128
   misinterpreted by Jackson, 127n
   misinterprets Locke, 71–75, 78
   personal identity, 165–66
   qualities and ideas, 54, 55, 56
Relations, 27, 29, 323, 377–78
Relativity, Theory of, 444, 445, 448
Remembering. *See* Memory
Representative theory of perception, 13, 353–63
   concept employment, 91
   Locke's version, 137–39, 289
   mixed theory, 130, 134–36
   scepticism, 90, 139, 370–72
Revolution, 207–8, 237, 247
Rights, 182–98 *passim*, 212–16, 227–30, 234, 244–50
Rousseau, J. J., 245
Russell, B., 103, 436
Ryan, A., 7
Ryle, G., 7, 169n

St. Paul's, 267
Scepticism, 392–99
Schlick, M., 436
Scholastics, 56
Science, 15, 51–52, 436–49 *passim*

Index

Secondary qualities
  Berkeley's criticism, 80–81, 291
  Locke's account, 65–66, 81
  Sensation, 17, 42, 258–65, 266, 272–73
  See also Ideas; Perception
Sense-data, 262, 264, 273, 287, 319n, 370, 372, 375–76
Sensible qualities, 256, 341–47
Shape, 417–18, 419
Sight, 8–9, 270, 271–73
Sillen, E. A., 407n
Simple ideas. See Ideas
Simplicity, 445
Smith, N. Kemp, 75
Solidity, 361n
  origin of idea, 45
Soul, 169–71
  See also Mind; Person; Personal identity
Sound, 268–71
Space, 45, 292, 378–79, 437–38, 441, 445
Spinoza, B., 292, 384
Spinozism, 292
Spirit. See Mind; Person; Personal identity; Soul
Stephen, L., 103, 200
Stillingfleet, E., 145
Stocks, J. L., 14n
Stout, G. F., 141–42, 276
Strauss, L., 180–87, 216n
Substance
  bearer of qualities and cause of ideas, 99–104, 122–23
  critique of Locke, 13, 98–99, 274–76
  Locke's doctrine, 96–97
  mental, 157, 274–76, 306–13
  properties, 89–90

Substratum. See Substance
Suggestion, 46
Swift, J., 295n
Sydenham, T., 34, 52

Tawney, R. H., 200, 201n, 204
Telepathy, 257, 259
Temperature. See Heat
Theology, 14, 16, 37–39
Thinking, 310–11, 431–33
Time, 310–11, 437–38
Toland, J., 15
Torricelli, E., 442
Touch, 271–73, 375
Turbayne, C. M., 308n, 355n, 359n

Unwin, G., 205n

Vagueness, 174–76
  See also Borderline cases
Vaughan, C. E., 189–91, 200, 231n
Voltaire, F. M. A. de, 377

Waissmann, F., 175n
Warnock, G. J., 99, 102, 103, 360n, 385, 386, 387, 390–91, 395, 426–35
Watson, R., 359n, 361n
Webb, T. E., 146–47n, 151
White, P. J., 49n
Whitehead, A. N., 76
Will, 11, 281, 367–69, 370, 371, 382, 385–86, 407
Williams, B. A. O., 158
Wilson, J. Cook, 126–27n, 137n, 141n, 151n
Wittgenstein, L., 436n, 445
Woodhouse, A. S. P., 226n

Yolton, J. W., 2